Dear Joe,

As a fellow Marquette graduate I hope you enjoy reading about the big tomes. Those were the days!

Best wishes,
John Turnpah

April 2009

WHEN SWING WAS THE THING
PERSONALITY PROFILES OF THE BIG BAND ERA

JOHN R. TUMPAK

WHEN SWING WAS THE THING
PERSONALITY PROFILES OF THE BIG BAND ERA

MARQUETTE
UNIVERSITY
PRESS

LIBRARY OF CONGRESS CATALOGING-IN-PUBLICATION DATA

Tumpak, John R., 1940-
  When swing was the thing : personality profiles of the big band era / John R. Tumpak.
    p. cm.
  Includes index.
  ISBN-13: 978-0-87462-024-5 (hardcover : alk. paper)
  ISBN-10: 0-87462-024-4 (hardcover : alk. paper)
  1. Musicians—Biography. 2. Musicians—History--20th century. 3. Big band music—Biography. I. Title.
  ML385.T87 2008
  781.65'4—dc22

                                                            2008041410

© 2008 Marquette University Press
Milwaukee, Wisconsin 53201-3141
All rights reserved.
www.marquette.edu/mupress/

FOUNDED 1916

MARQUETTE UNIVERSITY PRESS
MILWAUKEE

The Association of Jesuit University Presses

CONTENTS

PART THREE: THE VOCALISTS

PHOTOS FOR PART 3

PART FOUR: THE ARRANGERS

PHOTOS FOR PART 4

PART FIVE: THE CONTRIBUTORS

PHOTOS FOR PART 5

ACKNOWLEDGEMENTS

This book is a compilation of articles that originally appeared in four jazz publications. Special thanks must be extended to Myrna Daniels, publisher of *L.A. Jazz Scene*, with whom I have collaborated since 1995. We have a long and warm working relationship that has been most satisfying both personally and professionally. Appreciation also goes to publishers Patti Johnson and Michael Fitzmaurice of *Dancing USA*, Gene Joslin of *Joslin's Jazz Journal*, and Leslie Johnson of *The Mississippi Rag*. They have all been a delight to work with and I appreciate their introducing my articles in their publications.

Several jazz publications have reprinted many of my articles and I thank them. They are *Bandstand*, *Big Band Buddies*, *Big Bands International*, *Big Band World*, *International Musician*, *Jersey Jazz*, *Miller Notes*, *Moonlight Serenader*, and *Riverwalk Jazz*. Others include *The Bandstand*, *The BBC Big Band Club*, *The Herds*, and *The Voice*. Newspapers take in the *Eastern Group Publications*, *L.A.Watts Times*, *Los Angeles Sentinel*, and the *Pasadena/San Gabriel Valley Journal*.

I found the mediums of radio and television to be an outstanding source of information. Chuck Cecil's *Swingin' Years*, Don Kennedy's *Big Band Jump*, and David Miller's *Swingin' Down The Lane* are long running radio shows that feature live interviews with big band personalities along with historical comment. Also of considerable value were the many interviews with big band personalities that are available for listening online on Arnold Dean's *A One-Night Stand with the Big Bands* and Fred Hall's *Swing Thing*. NPR's *Jazz Profiles* series and its executive producer Tim Owens plus the BBC's excellent jazz documentaries were of great help as well. The many PBS fund raisers that featured the big bands on television included live interviews with Era luminaries and pointed me in the right direction to generate ideas and pursue research resources.

The Glenn Miller community was a source I could always depend on to answer any question related to the Era. Special thanks go to Alan Cass, Wilda Martin, Ed Polic, Tom Sheils, Paul Tanner, Zeke Zarchy, and the staff of the Glenn Miller Birthplace Society. Ed especially could always be counted on to quickly provide the most detailed information. Also, the late big band authority George T. Simon, who wrote the definitive book on Glenn Miller, was of exceptional help. George provided me a prodigious amount of information on the big band days along with guidance and encouragement. Most important, he became a good friend. It was a friendship I will always cherish.

Historical societies and public libraries associated with the hometowns of several of my subjects were also cooperative. They are far too many to individually site. The Institute of Jazz studies located at Rutgers University and the Smithsonian American History Museum graciously opened their archives to me. Los Angeles is a treasure trove of big band related material. I took many trips to the UCLA and University of Southern California music libraries and The Library of the Academy of Motion Picture Arts and Sciences. It was helpful to see vintage films featuring the big bands I wrote about and there is no better place to obtain them than the vast collection at Eddie Brandt's Saturday Matinee in North Hollywood, CA.

Personal collections were a valued source of information that is unavailable to the general public. The collections I gained access to were provided by several sources: the subjects themselves; the subject's families; musicians who performed in the Era; and private big band collectors. These individuals included Steven Beasley, Milt Bernhart, Nancy Cannon, Peggy Clark,

Rosalind Cron, Mark Gordon, Horace Heidt Jr., Roc Hillman, Henry Holloway, Joan Fila, Pat Knapp, Marilyn Leonard, Al Leopold, Gary Letts, Dolores O'Neill, Barbara Knowles Pinches, Rosetta Reitz, Lionel Sesma, Tom Sheils, Garry Stevens, and Skip Van Osten.

When I decided to take a crack at a book I was somewhat apprehensive about the entire publishing process. It was a milieu I was totally unfamiliar with, but help soon surfaced. Both author Peter Levinson and *International Musician* assistant editor Martin Walls patiently answered all my questions and willingly guided me through the process. They provided sound counsel and direction; their help was invaluable and will always be prized.

Individual thank-yous for valued contributions must be extended to Tony Agostinelli, Rob Bamberger, David Bernhart, Joe Butler, Don Castaldi, Lou Dumont, Dan Del Fiorentino, Stephen Fratallone, Don Gill, Mark Gordon, Don Graham, Curt Grosjean, Richard Grudens, Steven Harris, Charles Hazzard, Neal Hefti, Nancy Hoffman, Phil Holman, Bob Holmes, Perry Huntoon, Jerome Joseph, Al Julian, Wayne Knight, Annie Kuebler, Jack Lebo, Gene Lees, Rudolph Mangual, Mark Masters, Bobby Matos, Robert Melvin, Ken Moore, Arthur Newman, Chuck Niles, Ted Ono, Bruce Polin, Ken Poston, Harry Prime, Al Raymond, Terrence Ripmaster, Don Roberts, Wayne Roberts, Rob Ronzello, Bobby Sanabria, Duncan Schiedt, Cynthia Sesso, Bill Soule, Blair Whittington, and Alan Williams. I am grateful for your help.

Those personally interviewed for this book were Van Alexander, Steven Beasley, Ernani Bernardi, Milt Bernhart, Les Brown Jr., Stumpy Brown, Gloria Burke, Bobby Byrne, Tutti Camarata, Pete Candoli, Vince Carbone, Chuck Cecil, Bob Chiaco, Buddy Childers, Peggy Clark, Bob Comden, Frank Comstock, Jack Costanzo, Rosalind Cron, Tom Cullen, Bill Curtis, Helen Oakley Dance, Stanley Dance, Arnold Dean, Art DePew, Tony Dicks, Jan Eberle, Bob Eberly Jr., Joan Fila, Charles Filkins, Harry Fleitman, Jack Gordon, Fred Hall, Jake Hanna, Susie Hansen, Horace Heidt Jr., Roc Hillman, Henry Holloway, Jack Hotchkiss, Bonnie Janofsky, Herb Jeffries, Henry Jerome, Dick Johnson, Jack Jones, Paula Kelly Jr, Don Kennedy, Audree Kenton, Dick King, Donna King, Marilyn King, Pat Knapp, Don Krammer, Warren Lafferty, John LaPorta, Marilyn Leonard, Al Leopold, Gary Letts, Niles Lishness, Mundell Lowe, James T. Maher, Raymond Malone, Artie Malvin, Johnny Mandel, Peter Marshall, Bobby Matos, Billy May, E. R. McDonald, Chris McGee, Marian McPartland, David Miller, Jawn McKinley, Neville, Gene Norman, Dolores O'Neill, Ann Patterson, Dave Pell, Barbara Knowles Pinches, Ed Polic, Gene Puerling, David Raksin, Rosetta Reitz, Uan Rasey, Alvino Rey, Jose Rizo, Wayne Roberts, Pete Rugolo, Max Salazar, Lionel Sesma, Nick Sevano, Artie Shaw, Tom Sheils, George T. Simon, Sam Spear, Jo Stafford, Kay Starr, Garry Stevens, Butch Stone, Tom Talbert, Paul Tanner, Martha Tilton, Alan Timpson, Orrin Tucker, Dick Waco, Bea Wain, Kay Weber, Margaret Whiting, Alan Williams, Gerald Wilson, Bernie Woods, Edna Leonard Woods, and Zeke Zarchy.

Finally, no book covering the details of the life's of as many individuals as this does can be without imperfections. I owe a debt of gratitude to all who have helped me in my unswerving quest for accuracy. I close with the most important acknowledgement of all, to my beloved wife Ann for her constant support and patient review of my work.

INTRODUCTION

The Big Band Era that ran from 1935 through 1946 was a unique period in our nation's popular cultural history. It was a time when powerful fifteen-piece dance bands dominated American entertainment. Those big bands packed the nation's ballrooms, played at the posh hotels, dominated the radio airwaves, and routinely appeared in the movies. The swing music they played revived the recording industry, generating an enormous increase in annual record sales beginning in the mid 1930s. Moreover, the juke box business exploded and came into its own during the Era. From the perspective of public profile, all the top tier big bandleaders were among the most important celebrities of the day.

Through *DownBeat* and *Metronome* magazines teenagers were able to closely follow the goings-on of the several hundred active big bands. Young fans could name the musicians in all the top bands with the same ease that they could cite the starting lineups of all sixteen major league baseball teams. They formed fan clubs, waited patiently for the most obscure sideman's autograph after a performance, and developed their own hip jargon. In large cities truant officers were kept busy apprehending students who skipped school to attend daytime performances at downtown theaters. Their lives centered on the big bands that transformed American culture.

The Big Band Era was long over when I started to develop an interest in its music during the 1950s as a high school student in my hometown of Milwaukee. My attraction to the genre was initially sparked when I saw *The Glenn Miller Story* at the Fox Bay Theater in Whitefish Bay, a Milwaukee suburb. That experience led to an exploration of the dynamic big band sound of fellow Milwaukeean Woody Herman who at the time was leading his driving 1950s Third Herd. It didn't end there. After I graduated from Marquette University in Milwaukee in 1963 I moved to Los Angeles and continued to follow big band music during the 60s and 70s. Then came my discovery of Chuck Cecil.

Sometime around 1980 I started to listen regularly to big band radio personality Chuck Cecil who was broadcasting his weekly *Swingin' Years* program on Los Angeles radio station KGIL. I was fascinated by his Big Band Countdown that played the top ten hits and dispensed historical information of a specific Swing Era week and his Hall of Fame interviews with famous big band personalities. Cecil's show raised my interest in the big bands to an academic level and I soon started to read all the historical material on the Era that I could locate. I found that the more I read the more I became interested in the personal history of those who participated in the Era, i.e., when and where were they born, their formative years and paths to success, all-inclusive career histories, and post retirement activities.

It all came together in the early 1990s when I read *Tommy & Jimmy: The Dorsey Years* by Herb Sanford and became intrigued by the life of Jimmy Dorsey's popular vocalist Bob Eberly from Hoosick Falls, NY. I called the Hoosick Township Historical Society and was sent a thick package of information about Eberly by Edith Beaumont, a most pleasant lady who was the Society's museum director. As I poured through the stack of articles and documents she mailed me I became captivated by the details of Eberly's life. That was when I made the decision to write the personal backgrounds and character studies of those who shaped the Big Band Era.

The next step was to settle on a methodology for my pursuit. Since much had already been documented on many of the famous big band personages, I decided to choose primarily for my subjects successful individuals on whom little had been written. I felt that would fill a need and contribute information that might prove useful to future researchers. My objective was actually scholarly in nature.

For the big band enthusiast a distinct benefit of living in Los Angeles is having personal access to a considerable pool of persons who worked in the big bands during the Era and retired in Southern California. For my first subject I chose the then eighty-four-year-old former Jimmy Dorsey and Kay Kyser guitarist Roc Hillman who lived about ten minutes from my home in the San Fernando Valley. On the Sunday after Thanksgiving 1994 I had a delightful time chatting with Roc at his house and going through his scrapbook that included an article he wrote on New York Yankee legends Babe Ruth and Lou Gherig while a cub reporter for the *Denver Post*. It was evident Roc appreciated my visit and enjoyed talking about his colorful career. We bonded and to this day as boxing fans we regularly discuss major fights. My methodology was validated.

Since 1994 I spent many hours talking to my subjects and their families, relatives, and friends. I conducted these myriad personal interviews either by telephone or at the individual's residence. My home visits ranged from the lesser-known to the famous such as Artie Shaw, who was most gracious when I interviewed him at his gated house on Martin Luther King Day 2003. During my conversations I was treated courteously and my interest in my subject's stories was repeatedly met with a positive reaction. Numerous friendships were formed that are still in place today.

My quest for information on my subjects did not end with personal interviews. I was fortunate to obtain access to a number of individual personal collections and archives from major organizations such as the Smithsonian Institution and the Institute of Jazz Studies housed at Rutgers University. I also developed a personal association with Chuck Cecil and found the taped interviews that he provided me access to invaluable. As a complement to my research activities, actual visits to many of the great big band ballrooms across the country ranging from the Glen Island Casino in New Rochelle, NY, to the Hollywood Palladium were helpful in capturing a sense of, and feel for, the period of time I was writing about. Regardless of the source I approached, I was extended cooperation and treated with a spirit of goodwill.

What resulted are in-depth personality profiles that for the most part cover under-recognized bandleaders, musicians, vocalists, and arrangers who were active during the Big Band Era. Non-musical contributors are included along with major events in the careers of Benny Goodman and Glenn Miller. Putting this book together was an absolute pleasure and labor of love. When I started I never visualized the number of fascinating people I would meet, the voluminous amount of research I would have the privilege to examine, and the many big band events I would attend. I invite you to enjoy this nostalgic return to the Big Band Era, the time when Swing was the Thing.

PART ONE

THE BANDLEADERS

VAN ALEXANDER
FROM HARLEM TO HOLLYWOOD

In the mid 1930s, frequenting the Savoy Ballroom in Harlem to observe swing bands was not the conventional first step for career progression to big bandleader on to Emmy nominated arranger and composer in movies and television. However, in the case of Van Alexander, frequenting the Savoy indeed turned out to be the proper path to take to launch an eight-decade, multi-faceted career in music.

Van Alexander was born in Manhattan in 1915. His father owned a pharmacy at 131st Street and Amsterdam Avenue; his mother was an accomplished classical pianist who played on NBC in the early days of radio. She introduced him to the piano when he was six years old, but faced stiff competition for practice time from neighborhood stickball games in Manhattan's Washington Heights district. Baseball was his true love.

An outstanding student, Alexander graduated from George Washington High School in 1933 and matriculated at Columbia University to study music. By this time, his real interest in musicianship was not playing the piano, but arranging and orchestrating songs, his area of concentration at Columbia.

Soon after he completed high school, Alexander regularly took the A train to the Savoy, primarily to hear the sophisticated arrangements of the great black bands that included Don Redman, Erskine Hawkins, Lucky Millinder, and Chick Webb. Going to the Savoy as often as he did, he eventually developed a nodding acquaintance with Chick Webb that was to lead to his first big break in 1936.

Alexander relates the incident: "One night I approached Chick and told him I had a couple of arrangements at home that I thought might fit his orchestra. He said to bring them to his rehearsal next Friday night. I was bluffing. I had no arrangements but went straight home and did two, Fats Waller's "Keepin' Out of Mischief Now" and the Dixieland classic, "That's a Plenty." I went to the rehearsal on Friday that started at 2:00 am. Edgar Sampson went first with his arrangements. I came next. Chick liked my work and took a $10 advance from Charlie Buchanan, the Savoy manager, to pay me for them. It was my first sale and I was on cloud nine. That's how I got started as a professional in the business."

Alexander soon joined Webb as a fulltime arranger. His primary duty was to do the early recording arrangements for Webb's new vocalist, Ella Fitzgerald, who joined the band shortly before he did. They worked well together at the start and went on to become lifelong friends.

Then came 1938 and Alexander's second major break. Webb's band was playing at Levaggi's restaurant in Boston where they were on the air four times a week. Webb was performing on the restaurant's second floor, the Ink Spots downstairs on the first. Alexander has vivid memories of how the song came about: "I was writing three arrangements a week for Chick at my home in Manhattan and took the train to Boston every week to deliver them personally to him. One week at Levaggi's, Ella suggested I do something with the old nursery rhyme, A-Tisket, A-Tasket. I didn't get around to it for several weeks when she said, 'If you don't do something, I'll give it to

Edgar Sampson to work on.' That got me going. I took the train home and sat up all night and worked out the format and added a few novelty lyrics. Ella liked my arrangement and changed just a few of the words. The rest, as they say, is history. It went on to become the number one song in the country for ten straight weeks, and in 1986 Chick, Ella, and I were elected to the Grammy Hall of Fame for "A-Tisket, A-Tasket."

"A-Tisket, A-Tasket" was Alexander's entry into the big band business. On the basis of writing this song, he was approached by Eli Oberstein, head of RCA Victor records, who already had Bunny Berigan, Les Brown, and Larry Clinton in his stable of bands. Alexander immediately formed his own band and signed with Oberstein to record on the RCA Bluebird label for $100 a week against all royalties. Van Alexander was now a bandleader.

"I formed my band in late 1938," Alexander said. "Soon after, I had my first radio broadcast on the *Fitch Bandwagon Show*. We mostly played the Roseland Ballroom to get airtime on remote broadcasts, plus Lowe's State Theater and the Paramount. Cy Shribman booked us into Boston and the New England states. We appeared in Atlantic City a lot and went as far west as Chicago. Sometimes we traveled by car, mostly by bus. The band concentrated on ensemble sounds and had some very good musicians, Irv Cottler, Butch Stone, who also sang novelty tunes, Si Zentner, and a truly fine pianist, Ray Barr, who went on to arrange and conduct for Patti Page, Martha Raye, and Frankie Lane. I gave Shelly Manne his start when he was only sixteen years old."

By late 1943 it was difficult to find good musicians and with wartime gas rationing, almost impossible to travel. In 1944, after a five year run, Alexander decided to break up the band and concentrate on the lucrative writing of stock arrangements and teaching orchestration. His first ever music student was a then fourteen-year-old Johnny Mandel, who remains Alexander's close friend to this day.

Alexander's third, and arguably biggest break, came in 1945, although it did not appear to be a stroke of fortune at the time: "The Capitol Theater in Manhattan, which was an MGM theater, had been only showing movies and decided to bring back big band performances. My manager, Joe Glaser, put together a show with Bob Crosby and me that had a good four week run. When the Capitol engagement was over Crosby suggested I come to California with him to put together a band and do all the arrangements. In the back of my mind California was the place I wanted to be to break into writing for the entertainment industry. My wife and I talked it over and decided to go to Los Angeles with him. After nine weeks on the West Coast Crosby and I had a major disagreement and broke up. I was left high and dry with no work. At the time it was a traumatic experience, but it turned out to be a blessing in disguise."

Alexander's fortuitous blessing came about in the form of the top rated *Jack Benny Show*. He heard that Benny's popular Irish tenor, Dennis Day, was interested in finding a new arranger for his songs on the show. Alexander won the competition and spent a full season working with Day on Benny's radio show, firmly establishing himself in show business.

After a successful stint as a freelance arranger in Hollywood, in 1954 Alexander landed a spot arranging and conducting for Mickey Rooney's *Hey Mulligan* television show. The two quickly developed an instant rapport that led to an association that resulted in Alexander's composing and conducting Rooney's next five films. After Rooney's show came to a close in 1955, he next hooked up with the *Guy Mitchell Show* as its musical director.

By now, it was the early 1960s and Alexander was fully ensconced in the television industry working with Screen Gems doing arrangements for various segments of their *Bewitched*, *Dennis the Menace*, *Donna Reed*, *Hazel*, and *I Dream of Jeannie* shows. He also scored several movies, including two Joan Crawford films, *I Saw What You Did* and *Straight Jacket*, and *Safe at Home*, starring New York Yankee sluggers Mickey Mantle and Roger Maris.

Notwithstanding this frenetic level of activity, Alexander continued a longtime personal and professional friendship with baritone Gordon MacRae as his musical director playing the top clubs around the world and recording thirteen MacRae albums. In addition, he found time to produce three of his own record albums. His favorite of the three was his 1962 *Savoy Stomp*, a recreation of the themes of twelve different bands that played at the Savoy with eleven members of his original band participating in the recording session. *Savoy Stomp* holds great sentimental value for anyone who remembers the swinging Savoy days of the 1930s.

In 1965, Alexander embarked on the final leg of his professional career: "I got a call from the producer of *The Dean Martin Show* asking me if I would be interested in becoming the show's head arranger. I said 'yes' on the spot. My good friend Les Brown had the orchestra. The Vietnam War was on and Les frequently traveled with Bob Hope to entertain our troops. As a result, I also got to conduct for many of Dean's shows while Les was gone. My assignment with Dean Martin, who was a truly wonderful person, led to a lot of other television work. I wound up composing and conducting for *The Dom DeLuise Show*, several NBC specials, many with Gene Kelly, plus *The Wacky World of Jonathan Winters*. I guess the industry liked my work since I was nominated for three Emmys between 1970 and 1973."

When *The Dean Martin Show* came to an end in 1974, Alexander paused for breath to evaluate his station in life. After considerable deliberation, he decided go into semi-retirement and spend more time with his family and make an earnest attempt to lower his golf handicap. After thirty-eight nonstop years in music, he felt the time had come to smell the roses.

Since then, he has remained active doing occasional freelancing only if the project appeals to him and does not involve all-night deadlines, and stays connected to the music business with active participation in the American Society of Music Arrangers and Composers, of which he was past president, and the Big Band Academy of America, who in 1997 presented him their coveted Golden Bandstand Award. That same year he was also honored for a Lifetime of Achievement in Jazz by the Los Angeles Jazz Society, and in 1996 he received the Pacific Pioneer Broadcasters' prestigious Diamond Circle Award.

The new millennium has also been kind to Alexander in recognition. In 2002 he received the ASCAP Foundation's "Lifetime Achievement Award" for outstanding accomplishment in film and television music. A year later he arranged a twelve minute medley of songs with lyrics associated with Benny Goodman for Michael Feinstein's Carnegie Hall debut and was asked to take a bow before the standing-room-only audience. Alexander and Feinstein remain good friends and continue to collaborate on music projects.

Reflecting on his career during an interview at his high rise condominium on Wilshire Boulevard in the Westwood neighborhood of Los Angeles, Alexander said: "I feel I've done it all, from the Big Band Era to the modern era, with several hit records, twenty three feature films, and numerous television shows to my credit. I had my ups and downs, but that's part of life. Believe me; I'm definitely grateful for what the music business has done for me. I wouldn't change a thing if I could."

BENNY GOODMAN
LAUNCHES THE BIG BAND ERA

It is human nature to associate the start of a major historical episode with a specific event. For example, we think of the Great Depression beginning with the October 24, 1929, stock market crash and World War II beginning with the December 7, 1941, bombing of Pearl Harbor. For swing music enthusiasts, the start of the Big Band Era is thought to have begun with the famed August 21, 1935, opening of Benny Goodman at the Palomar Ballroom in Los Angeles. Before we examine the event that kicked off the Big Band Era, a few words about how Benny Goodman came to play his role in big band history are in order.

Benjamin David Goodman was born on May 30, 1909, in Chicago, Illinois. He was one of twelve children whose parents immigrated to the United States from Russia in the 1880s. Goodman was raised in poverty in a Chicago ghetto. His father, David Goodman, was a responsible, hard-working tailor who was barely able to make a sufficient living to meagerly support his family. He wanted the best for his children, and in his view music was the way out of the ghetto.

David Goodman seized the initiative. He enrolled ten-year-old Benny and his older brothers Harry and Freddy in the Kehlah Jacob Synagogue for music lessons for twenty-five cents a week. Instruments were given to the Goodman brothers in order of their physical size. Harry, the biggest, was given a tuba. Freddy, next in size, a trumpet. Finally, Benny, the smallest, was given a clarinet. Hence, fate launched Benny Goodman on the path to fame and fortune.

After a year of lessons, the synagogue band dissolved due to lack of financial support. Goodman then continued his formal training by joining the Hull House band. The Hull House was a settlement house founded by social reformers Jane Addams and Ellen Gates Star in 1889. At the same time, he also took clarinet lessons from Franz Schoepp, a well know classical clarinet teacher who played with the Chicago Symphony. His association with Schoepp nurtured a lifelong interest in classical music that culminated with a series of classical music concerts in the late 1960s.

By now it was the early 1920s and Chicago was a hotbed of jazz evolving what came to be known as the Chicago Style. Louis Armstrong, Bix Beiderbecke, Eddie Condon, Bud Freeman, King Oliver, Jess Stacy, and the great blues singer Bessie Smith were but a few who were part of the scene. Such was the milieu in which Goodman honed his craft.

Fellow Chicagoan Ben Pollack was six years Goodman's senior. He was a successful drummer having played in the early 1920s in the New Orleans Rhythm Kings, the top white jazz band of the day. Pollack moved to Los Angeles in 1924 and formed his own hot dance band in 1925 to play at the Venice Ballroom. He asked Goodman to join the band and in August 1925 sixteen year old Benny Goodman took a train to Los Angeles leaving Chicago for good. Upon arrival he struck up a strong friendship with Pollack's arranger, a young trombone player named Glenn Miller.

The story of Ben Pollack is indeed sad. He had an uncanny ability to recognize talent, being instrumental in developing the careers of Goodman, Miller, Harry James, and Jack Teagarden among others. Despite employing top musicians and obtaining good bookings, he never seemed to be able to put it all together and break the barrier to become a premier, big name band. Depressed over failing health and lack of recognition of his musical contributions, he hanged himself in Palm Springs, CA, in 1971.

Goodman stayed with Pollack gaining valuable experience until he left in 1929 after a dispute over band policy while the band was playing at the Fox Bushwick in Brooklyn. He spent the next several years making good money freelancing, primarily in Broadway pit orchestras and radio studio bands. Then in 1933 Goodman met John Hammond, who was to have a profound influence on his career.

John Hammond was born in 1910 into a socially prominent New York family that had ties to the Vanderbilt family. He was groomed for the professional world but dropped out of Yale after his sophomore year to pursue a career in the world of jazz. Hammond soon became a successful jazz critic and promoter and significantly contributed to the careers of Goodman, Count Basie, and Billie Holiday. Goodman married Hammond's sister Alice in 1942. They remained happily married until Alice's death in 1978.

In 1934, with assistance and encouragement from Hammond, Goodman put together his own orchestra. A key element of Goodman's band were the progressively swinging and rhythmic arrangements of Fletcher Henderson, the great black pianist, bandleader, and arranger. By the end of 1934 Goodman was able to secure a contract with NBC to appear on their new Saturday evening *Let's Dance* radio show.

The National Biscuit Company, with the intention of promoting their new Ritz party crackers, sponsored the *Let's Dance* show that ran from December 1934 through May 1935. The show's three hour format consisted of three bands alternating one half hour each. The sweet band was led by NBC Studio violinist Kel Murray. The Latin band spot was filled by Xavier Cougat. Goodman auditioned for the hot band job at the NBC Studios in Radio City. A ballot was conducted among those in attendance and Goodman won by just one vote over his competition.

Let's Dance deserves a respected place in big band lore as the show definitely paved the way for Goodman's seminal performance at the Palomar Ballroom. Due to the difference in time zones, the late-night broadcasts from New York were heard during prime time on the West Coast creating an interest in and demand for hot bands. The show served to not only sell Ritz crackers, but swing music as well.

Unable to manufacture and distribute their new Ritz crackers due to an employee strike, National Biscuit closed down the popular *Let's Dance* show after 26 broadcasts on May 25, 1935. Immediately after the show closed MCA's Willard Alexander booked the Goodman band on a nationwide tour that at best achieved spotty success. Goodman's reception at Elitch Gardens in Denver was such a disaster that he considered giving up the tour to return to New York.

It took an hour long telephone conversation from Alexander in New York to convince Goodman to continue the tour. Goodman next headed on to the West Coast and played to a surprisingly enthusiastic, packed ballroom at Sweet's Ballroom in Oakland, CA, arriving in Los Angeles in August of 1935.

The Palomar was Los Angeles's premier ballroom throughout the 1930s. Originally known as the Rainbow Gardens, it was located on Vermont Avenue between 2nd and 3rd Streets, west of downtown at the start of the city's mid-Wilshire area. Remote broadcasts emanated from the huge ballroom nightly with a dinner-dance special on Sunday evenings.

On October 2, 1939, the Palomar burnt to the ground from a fire caused by faulty stage wiring. The fire struck so swiftly that Charlie Barnet, who was appearing at the time, lost all his arrangements, and the musicians all their instruments. The Palomar was superseded as Los Angeles's prime dance venue by the Hollywood Palladium located on Sunset Boulevard in the heart of Hollywood. It opened on October 29, 1940, featuring Tommy Dorsey with Frank Sinatra, Connie Haines, Jo Stafford, and the Pied Pipers.

When Goodman and his band arrived at the Palomar the evening of August 21, 1935, they were surprised to see a crowd extending all the way around the block waiting to get in the ballroom. Still sensitive to his poor reception on his cross country tour, Goodman cautiously started out playing standard pop tunes. The response was lukewarm prompting Goodman to go for broke and risk going down in flames playing his kind of music.

According to most accounts, Goodman called out for one of his killer-dillers, "King Porter Stomp." The audience immediately mobbed the bandstand screaming for hotter numbers. Each night the crowds continued to grow breaking all attendance records. Goodman had his contract extended. Movie stars competed for publicity by making an appearance. The Big Band Era was officially born.

The Palomar event was not Goodman's only contribution to musical history. In 1938 his became the first jazz band to play a concert in Carnegie Hall and in 1962 he was chosen by the State Department to become the first bandleader to tour the Soviet Union since the 1920s. Active until the end, Goodman died of heart failure in 1986 shortly after completing a public television show highlighting his career.

To be sure, Goodman's was not the first hot band of the 1930s. There were the great black bands of Duke Ellington, Jimmy Lunceford, Benny Moten, and Chick Webb. The short lived Dorsey Brothers Orchestra, the Casa Loma Orchestra, and Goodman's old boss Ben Pollack also played the new swing music. However, the band that had the good fortune to be in the right place at the right time and break through to capture the public's imagination and inaugurate the Big Band Era was that of Benny Goodman, The King of Swing.

BENNY GOODMAN IS
MOBBED AT THE PARAMOUNT

If presented with the hypothetical Trivial Pursuit question "Who preceded Michael Jackson, the Beatles, Elvis Presley and Frank Sinatra as the first musical artist to cause fan pandemonium at a concert?" what would your answer be?

Surprisingly, the correct answer that stems not from the Rock Era, but the Big Band Era, is Benny Goodman. That's right, Benny Goodman, the bespectacled, reserved, jazz clarinetist from Chicago's Jewish ghetto. In fact, it was on March 3, 1937, that the opening of Goodman's historic engagement at the Paramount Theater in Times Square caused the sold out predominantly teenage audience to go wild and dance in the aisles.

A series of events that combined to cause the bedlam at the Paramount began in August of 1935 when Goodman launched the Big Band Era at the Palomar Ballroom in Los Angeles. This appearance made him our first pop-culture hero and the world's most famous bandleader.

After his sensationally successful Palomar stint ended in October 1935, Goodman headed home to Chicago for a six-month appearance starting in November at the Urban Room of the Congress Hotel, returning to the Palomar in Los Angeles for a two-month engagement in the summer of 1936. While at the Palomar he topped his previous success at the ballroom, made his first movie, *The Big Broadcast of 1937*, and began broadcasting on the popular CBS *Camel Caravan* radio show.

September found Goodman playing at the Steel Pier in Atlantic City, NJ. It was at the Steel Pier where Goodman discovered a powerful trumpeter by the name of Harry Finkelman playing in the house band lead by Alex Bartha. He hired Finkelman, better known as Ziggy Elman, on the spot. The band then moved on to New York, opening on October 1, 1936, for a long term run at the Madhattan Room of the Hotel Pennsylvania on Seventh Avenue across from Pennsylvania Station.

It is important to note that over the year and a half between his seminal 1935 appearance at the Palomar and through February of 1937 at the Madhattan Room, Goodman's appearances were attended by adults and college students only. He did not perform before teenage audiences whose only opportunity to listen to Goodman was on the radio or records, thereby creating a pent-up demand to see The King of Swing in person. This demand would soon explode at the Paramount Theater in Manhattan

MCA's Willard Alexander booked Goodman into the Paramount Theater at 43rd Street and Broadway for a two week engagement starting March 3, 1937. It was to be a demanding schedule, with the band continuing to play evenings at the Madhattan Room after five daily theater shows.

The Paramount Theater revolutionized the movie business when, over the Christmas holidays of 1935, manager Bob Weitman introduced a policy of alternating a well known band with a feature film. The first band to play the new format was the Casa Loma. Weitman also installed a rising orchestra bandstand that ascended from the basement like an elevator, coming to rest in the orchestra pit in front of the stage. One of the more dramatic experiences of the Big Band Era was to attend the Paramount and hear a band's theme song grow louder and louder while the bandstand rose with the musicians slowly coming in to view.

By the time the band arrived at the Paramount at 7:00 a.m. to rehearse before the opening show, there were several hundred youngsters lined up on Broadway from 43rd to 44th Streets, and around 44th Street to Eighth Avenue. It is purported that they were boisterously dancing, shouting and lighting fires to keep warm.

When the featured film, *Maid of Salem* staring Claudette Colbert, came to an end it was time for Goodman's first set. As the bandstand started to rise, Goodman gave the count for the band's opening theme "Lets Dance." As they came into view, they were met with a thunderous applause combined with shouting and whistling.

The equivalent of an electrical shock occurred when the band swung into its first selection, the killer-diller "Bugle Call Rag." The audience immediately cheered, screamed, crowded the bandstand, and started jitterbugging in the aisles. History was officially made as the first mass hysteria at a musical event took place.

Twenty-one thousand young fans from throughout New York saw the first day's five shows buying a record nine hundred dollars' worth of nickel candy bars. This uninhibited emotional outburst continued throughout the engagement that was extended for a third week with the kids actually starting to climb on stage to jitterbug. The band's stay would have been longer if they had not had other commitments.

Historically, there are two aspects of Goodman's Paramount engagement that have received little recognition. First, black patronage at Goodman's performances increased five hundred percent, shooting from a normal three percent to fifteen percent of the audience. This acceptance of Goodman's music by the black community helped pave the way for white bands to appear in Harlem. In fact, by the late 1930s Charlie Barnett broke opening-day records at the Apollo Theater and at a Christmas Eve appearance Glen Miller shattered the Savoy Ballroom attendance record set by none other than Guy Lombardo.

Second, the Paramount marked the official entry of teenagers into the paying customer ranks at big band events. Starting with Paul Whiteman's 1920 engagement at the Palais Royal in New

York City that many say marked the beginning of the jazz age, dance band performances were attended by adults only at night clubs. Starting in the early 1930s, the paying customer base expanded to include college students at locations such as the Glen Island Casino in New Rochelle, NY. Goodman ushered in a whole new box office era as young adults became an important source of revenue at live big band appearances.

Every era has its historical milestones, and certainly a major milestone of the Big Band Era was Benny Goodman's 1937 Paramount engagement that set the stage for a new standard of permissible audience involvement at musical events. Bobby-soxers in the 1940s swooning over Frank Sinatra, rock and rollers in the 1950s screaming at Elvis Presley, teenyboppers in the 1960s mobbing the Beatles, and today's MTV generation have Goodman to thank for making frenzied fan participation over their favorite musical artists an acceptable form of expression in our American society. Young popular music followers owe a debt of gratitude to Benny Goodman, a true musical pioneer.

BENNY GOODMAN MAKES BIG BAND
HISTORY AT CARNEGIE HALL

Since 1900 there have been only twelve major league baseball players who have won the coveted Triple Crown by leading their league in batting average, home runs, and runs batted in. The last to achieve this rare feat was the Boston Red Sox's Carl Yastremski in 1967. In the realm of music, there was but one Triple Crown winner during the Big Band Era, the King of Swing, Benny Goodman.

Clarinetist Benny Goodman had the good fortune to be the main participant in all three of the major historic events of the Era. First, he is acknowledged to have launched the Era in 1935 with his famous Palomar Ballroom engagement in Los Angeles. Second, he caused the first teenage mob scene at a music concert in 1937 while playing at the Paramount Theater in Times Square. And he officially won the Swing Era Triple Crown on January 16, 1938, when his became the first big band to play a jazz concert at hallowed Carnegie Hall, the sacrosanct home of high culture in mid-town Manhattan.

Benny Goodman's Carnegie Hall concert was not long in the making. It came about very quickly. In December 1937 Wynn Nathanson of the Tom Fizdale agency called impresario Sol Hurok's press chief Gerald Goode to suggest a Benny Goodman concert for Carnegie Hall. Nathanson had sound reason to promote a Goodman concert as the Fizdale agency had the *Camel Caravan* radio show account on which Goodman was regularly appearing. It would be great publicity for both Goodman and the show. Moreover, Nathanson had a sound product to sell to Hurok. Goodman had the most popular big band in the country that was grossing a then phenomenal $50,000 a week. In comparison, the 1938 World Champion New York Yankees paid Lou Gehrig $39,000 to play first base for the entire season.

Visiting with Goode when he took Nathanson's call was music critic Irving Kolodin who strongly recommended Hurok go through with the proposed concert. Goode immediately passed the information on to Hurok who then went to see Goodman perform at the popular Madhattan Room of the Hotel Pennsylvania. The legendary showman was so overwhelmed by seeing Goodman musically drive a well-dressed night club crowd to a frenzy that he immediately booked Carnegie Hall for Sunday, January 16, 1938, the night after Goodman completed his three-month engagement at the Madhattan Room. The event was billed as the *First Swing Concert in the History of Carnegie Hall.*

Goodman quickly went about the task of planning the program. In addition to a mix of standard, familiar songs, he incorporated a historical Twenty Years of Jazz segment at Kolodin's suggestion that included tributes to the Original Dixieland Jazz Band, Bix Beiderbecke, Ted Lewis, Louis Armstrong, and Duke Ellington. He also decided to feature a jam session with musicians from both the Count Basie and Duke Ellington bands along with his own soloists. There was also a spot reserved in the first and second halves of the program for both the Goodman trio that included Goodman, pianist Teddy Wilson, and drummer Gene Krupa, as well as the Goodman quartet with Lionel Hampton added to the trio.

Sunday, January 16, 1938, was a bitter cold night in Manhattan, but not cold enough to prevent a standing-room-only crowd estimated at three thousand from attending the performance. It was far larger than the normal turnout for the New York Philharmonic. Tickets for the concert sold out as soon as it was announced, quickly achieving the lofty status of a major event. In fact, Goodman himself was forced to deal with scalpers to obtain tickets for his family who decided to come from Chicago at the eleventh hour.

Goodman and the band were nervous and apprehensive when they took the stage at 8:45 p.m. Even though they received a thunderous three minute round of applause, they appeared tentative as they played their opening number, "Don't Be That Way." The band suddenly loosened up thanks to a powerful drum break by Krupa, with hair and body dramatically flailing in all directions, that drew wild cheers from the audience. The band was now in a groove, and the concert in full swing.

The Carnegie Hall concert version of "Don't Be That Way" was a slower rendition of the same song Edgar Sampson wrote at a more upbeat tempo for the Chick Webb Orchestra in 1934. Another Sampson song, the ever popular "Stompin' at the Savoy" that was a big hit for Goodman in 1936, was also on the program played by the Goodman quartet.

From the viewpoint of pure, fiercely intense swing music, Jimmy Mundy's arrangement of "Swingtime in the Rockies" with fancy Krupa drumming and a powerful Ziggy Elman trumpet solo was the highlight as exhibited by frenetic audience response. Mundy's hot arrangements spawned the Swing Era term "killer-diller" that designated up-tempo flag wavers that always pleased the audience.

Goodman truly felt that the concert in part was a tribute to the genre of swing music, generously sharing the Carnegie Hall stage with members of two other great big bands. For the Duke Ellington tribute, Johnny Hodges, Cootie Williams, and Harry Carney, all from the Ellington Orchestra, participated in the beautiful Ellington composition "Blue Reverie." The Duke himself was invited but deferred performing in anticipation of his own headline appearance at the Hall, a feat he repeated on many an occasion. Most likely at the suggestion of jazz enthusiast John Hammond, Goodman included Count Basie and four members of his band along with Hodges and Carney in a jam session version of "Honeysuckle Rose." The jam session provided excellent exposure for the then rapidly rising Basie.

There were two vocal numbers on the program, both sung by pert Goodman vocalist Martha Tilton who was attired in a charming pink party dress. She received tremendous ovations for her vocal work on the traditional Scottish song "Loch Lomond" and the Andrew Sisters's hit "Bei Mir Bist Du Schoen," a song with new lyrics from the 1933 Yiddish musical *I Would If I Could*. After Helen Ward left Goodman in early 1937, Goodman tried several vocalists before he settled on Tilton in mid-year. She stayed with the band for two years recording twenty-six charted hits.

The final song on the program was Louis Prima's composition "Sing, Sing, Sing." Krupa started out on the tom-tom and was followed by breathtaking individual solos culminating in pianist

Jess Stacy's almost hymn-like piece that according to Goodman stole the show. At the close of "Sing, Sing, Sing" the audience burst into applause for nearly five minutes and Goodman satisfied them with Sampson's "When Dreams Come True" and Horace Henderson's (Fletcher's younger brother) "Big John Special" for encores.

Fortunately, Albert Marx, Helen Ward's husband, made arrangements to have the concert recorded from a single overhead microphone connected to a nearby recording studio where acetate recordings were cut. A copy was given to Goodman and soon forgotten until it was uncovered twelve years later in a closet in his New York apartment by his sister-in-law, Rachel Speiden. The newly discovered acetate recording was transferred to tape and in November 1950 released as *Benny Goodman Live At Carnegie Hall.* It has become one of the top-selling jazz albums of all time.

The concert was widely acclaimed by critics as a smashing success and quickly became of significant importance to both Goodman and the music world. It brought tremendous publicity to Goodman and both added to and strengthened his base of already unswerving loyal fans. As for the not-yet-fully-accepted idiom of jazz, it served to legitimatize swing music by placing it in the category of an art form and providing the necessary prestige to gain acceptance in the public mainstream. Carnegie Hall was also never the same. Before the year was out, the venerable hall saw a performance by Ethel Waters, a sixty-fifth birthday celebration for W.C. Handy, and John Hammond's *Spirituals to Swing* concert.

There were many great bandleaders during the Big Band Era, but few had the historical impact of Benny Goodman who is credited for kicking off the Era in 1935, causing the first teenage riot at a live musical performance in 1937, and introducing jazz to staid Carnegie Hall in 1938. Congratulations to Benny Goodman for winning the Big Band Triple Crown!

HORACE HEIDT
FIVE DECADES OF TOP SHOW BANDS

The great show orchestras with their talented performers that played at the finest hotels during the 30s and 40s were an important part of the Big Band Era. Many Era enthusiasts still maintain that the premier show bandleader was Horace Heidt, who started out in 1923 leading a five-piece band and progressed from playing the vaudeville circuit to develop a smooth dance and show band that entertained at prestigious venues, dominated the airwaves, and generated over fifty hit records from 1937 to 1945. Although he was not an exceptional musician, Heidt possessed an uncanny ability to discover and develop new talent along with a gift for creating commercial appeal. Horace Heidt was one of the most popular entertainers in America during the Swing Era and continued on as a force in radio and television until he fully retired in 1964 to devote his efforts to managing his myriad business interests. Here is the story of his colorful and hard-earned rise to success.

Alameda, CA, is an architecturally historic community located on an island in San Francisco Bay next to Oakland. Here Horace Heidt was born on May 21, 1901. His father, John William Heidt, owned Pacific Metal Works, a business that imported and manufactured raw metals. His mother, Mary Elizabeth Heidt, was a kindergarten teacher who was orphaned in Nova Scotia and found her way to California. Heidt's parents were void of musical talent, but his mother insisted that that he take piano lessons when he was nine years old. Although his chief interest was sports, particularly boxing, he begrudgingly practiced under his mother's watchfulness and made his public debut at fourteen playing Liszt's "Second Hungarian Rhapsody." Then in 1917 he was sent by his father to Indiana to attend the Culver Military Academy, an outstanding college preparatory school for young men.

Heidt blossomed at the Academy. He developed leadership and organizational skills as captain of the Company D infantry unit and won the school's best all around athlete medal participating in baseball, boxing, football, swimming, and track. His athletic prowess was such that in his senior year he received an offer from the Chicago White Sox after striking out sixteen players in one game. His interest in music and entertainment was also sparked at the Academy when he developed a friendship with fellow student Red Nichols, who played in the Culver Jazz Band. After graduation, Heidt decided to eschew a professional sports career and returned home to continue his education at the University of California at Berkeley.

While competing at Berkeley in baseball, football, swimming, and track Heidt experienced an accident that would dramatically impact his future. As a star offensive lineman on the fabled Cal Wonder Teams he fractured his back in a 1921 football game against California's traditional rival, Stanford. After six painful surgeries and several months in a plaster cast his athletic career was over. To compound matters, the operations depleted his family's savings and he could not afford to go back to college. Horace Heidt was forced to give up his goal of becoming a football coach. Instead, he decided to become an orchestra leader.

After recovering from the fracture that could have permanently confined Heidt to a wheelchair he went to work at a Standard Oil service station in Alameda and started to organize his first group that he called the Californians. The five-piece band opened with a one-night engagement at the Claremont Hotel in Berkeley in 1923. Each band member received $10 with Heidt taking $5 from their combined pay to advertise by having fliers printed and personally distributing them around Berkeley and Oakland each Saturday. His promotional efforts paid off with the band securing a regular three-nights-a-week engagement at the posh establishment for the next two years. Heidt also started volunteer work as a Sunday school teacher and vocalist in the choir at First Methodist Church in Alameda.

When the Claremont was sold in 1925 Heidt and his band were let go. Without any musical prospects, he disbanded and sold real estate until 1926 when he convinced the manager of the new Athens Club in Oakland to hire his reformed band. From there he appeared on the local *Shell Ship of Joy* morning radio show. Notwithstanding a severe stuttering problem, Heidt was a success on the air and, with the show's producer Hugh Barrett Dobbs's help, landed what proved to be a most fortuitous booking at the American Theater in Oakland that was soon sold to the Fox West Coast Theater chain. Fox took over Heidt's contract and immediately booked him at the Campus Theater in Berkeley in1928.

The Campus Theater engagement was so successful that Heidt was moved up the theatrical ladder into Oakland's Grand Lake Theater, where he did record-breaking business as a show band for a whole year. The Grand Lake Theater appearance allowed Heidt to hone his craft. He changed shows each week trying out everything from variety acts to grand opera to unsuccessfully singing in costume on stage. Fox next put Heidt in the Warfield Theater in San Francisco as the house band where they accompanied Al Jolson for a week, gained invaluable exposure, and caught the eye of brother and sister vaudeville impresarios Franchon and Marco.

Sometime in 1929 Heidt joined Fanchon and Marco's vaudeville troupe as a traveling unit working their circuit. He now had a twelve-piece band that could play a bizarre assortment of unconventional musical instruments in addition to singing and dancing and dispensing its own diversified vaudeville entertainment. It was also around this time that Heidt featured the ultimate novelty act, Lobo, a trained purebred German shepherd that played the "The Bells of Saint Mary's" on a set of musical bells. The canine was exceptionally obedient on stage but was prone to aggressive behavior when his act was over. Lobo's popularity was such that when he died he was mentioned in the obituary section of *Variety*.

In 1930 Heidt's travels took him to the Palace Theater in New York where he became a sensation during a record breaking sixteen week performance. That success led to a three-month tour of Europe that included several weeks at a casino in Monte Carlo and the plum assignment of playing the year's biggest charity ball at the Paris Opera House. Next came what was expected to be a triumphant return to the Palace Theater. However, Heidt laid a king-sized egg and was cancelled after just a week. Several years later he attributed his New York debacle to the fact that the band developed a "champagne taste" and became complacent during its European tour. The organization excessively partied and did not sufficiently rehearse or develop fresh material to maintain its appeal and musical proficiency.

After the fiasco in the Big Apple a chastened Horace Heidt broke up his band and in late 1931 returned home to San Francisco to regroup. Spurred on by his beloved mother's encouragement, Heidt formed a new show band in 1932 that became the pit band at the Golden Gate Theater in San Francisco for the next two plus years accompanying vaudeville acts and entertaining on stage. It was at this point that Heidt started to develop quality musical talent, hiring electric guitarist Alvino Rey and a female vocal group, the King Sisters. Then in 1934 he again went east on what turned out to be an unsuccessful appearance for RKO at the Center Theater in New York. With no immediate bookings in sight Horace Heidt's future looked bleak. However, little did he know that fame and fortune was about to arrive thanks to a lucky misunderstanding based on similar sounding surnames.

The opulent Drake Hotel still sits in the heart of Chicago's Gold Coast overlooking Lake Michigan. During the Big Band Era an engagement at the Drake meant that you were positioned in the upper echelon of the big bands. In 1935 Heidt opened for a lengthy stay at the Drake when hotel official Benny Marshall hired him thinking he engaged popular black bandleader Les Hite, who became famous in the early 1930s as the house band at Frank Sebastian's Cotton Club located near the MGM studios in Culver City, CA. Louis Armstrong and Lionel Hampton were frequently featured performers with the Hite band at Sebastian's.

Marshall certainly had no regrets. Heidt was an instant smash hit and soon had his own network radio show, *Horace Heidt for Alemite*, which was beamed across the country. While on the air for automotive equipment manufacturer Alemite the company requested he change his band's name from the Californians to the Brigadiers for marketing purposes. Heidt was also on the air twice a week on powerful Chicago radio station WGN that covered the entire Midwest and a good portion of the East. Horace Heidt finally made it; he was now a household name.

Radio was not unfamiliar to Horace Heidt. In 1932 while playing at the Drake for the first time he accidentally dropped his microphone from the bandstand to the floor. Without losing a step Heidt jumped down to pick up the mike and spontaneously started to interview people on the dance floor. This led to the *Answers by Dancers* show that soon became widely imitated. At the Biltmore Hotel in New York in 1935 Heidt interviewed couples who were celebrating their anniversaries or about to be married. Games were also played and those who could not answer questions were made to walk the plank. The show was called *Anniversary Night with Horace Heidt*.

In addition to providing Heidt his first big radio break, the Drake gig gave him the opportunity to develop the Triple Tonguing Trumpeters and the High Trombone that became his signature music style. Having learned a lesson from his undisciplined days in Europe in 1931, Heidt diligently rehearsed the orchestra and built a dance-oriented library to create a solid sweet band that was the rage of the hotel circuit. Chicago served him well.

With his popularity in full swing and stuttering problem long in the past, Heidt moved up a step in prestige in 1937 to start a long-term engagement at the Biltmore Hotel in Manhattan. A year later, while still at the Biltmore, he permanently changed the band's name to the Musical Knights when his Alemite radio show came to a close. Big band authority George T. Simon reviewed a band performance at the Biltmore in the September 1937 issue of *Metronome*. He commented on the band's high level of showmanship and esprit de corps and cited Heidt for his bandleading and emceeing talents plus his inimitable ability to affably mix with the patrons. The positive esprit de corps was no doubt the result of Heidt's ongoing effort to nurture a family environment within the band.

Nineteen thirty-seven was also the year that Heidt, with great success, started recording for Brunswick. Two years later he moved over to Columbia. From 1937 into 1945 Heidt had fifty-two hit records, twenty-nine of which made the top ten. Three of those top ten hits made it to number one. Joel Whitburn's *Pop Memories 1890-1954* lists Heidt at fifty-fourth among the top one hundred selling artists during the 1890-1954 pre-rock period. Although it was not a huge hit, thanks to his considerable reputation he was chosen to record "Dawn of A New Day," the official song of the 1939 New York World's Fair. Heidt's phenomenal recording popularity dispelled any lingering doubt that his was just a show band.

During this halcyon eight-year run Heidt's band included several superb musicians. The pianist was the popular Frankie Carle, who wowed the audience by playing piano with his hands behind his back. He also arranged and fronted the band. When Carle left to form his own band in 1944 he was replaced by Jess Stacy. In the brass section there were trumpeters Bobby Hackett and Shorty Sherock and trombonist Warren Covington. Clarinetist Irving Fazola, drummer Frank Carlson, and saxophonist and arranger Frank DeVol also played in the band. After Glenn Miller disbanded in September 1942 Bill Finegan came over to arrange, along with Tex Beneke who stayed for a short time before he joined the Navy.

All the top big bands had quality vocalists, and Horace Heidt's was no exception. Larry Cotton sang most of the bands hit records. A fine tenor and crooner who was frequently lauded by George T. Simon, Cotton came to the band from Jimmy Grier's Orchestra. Ronnie Kemper, of Dick Jurgens fame, also recorded several hits. The King Sisters harmonized until they left the band in 1938 along with the skilled Alvino Rey who soon formed his own orchestra that featured the four sisters. They were followed by Donna and Her Don Juans that included Gordon Mac-Rae from 1941 to 1942. The appealing Donna was Donna Wood, sister of Gloria Wood, who sang for Kay Kyser. The multi-talented harpist Lysbeth Hughes also performed as a vocalist. Both she and Larry Cotton sang on Heidt biggest hit, "Ti-Pi-Pin," that was number one for six weeks in 1938.

The superbly rehearsed Heidt band still maintained a show element. Fred Lowery, billed as The Blind Whistler, came aboard in early 1939. He had special numbers crafted for him by Heidt to showcase the unique whistling talent he developed at The Texas School for the Blind. His roommate was Art Carney, who joined the band not long after he graduated from high school in Mount Vernon, NY, in 1937. They were a fun loving, practical joking pair who during their wild days put Heidt through his paces. They once staged a mugging of the blind Lowery by Carney at the corner of 42nd Street and Fifth Avenue in Manhattan during the rush hour and were so realistic that they were arrested by the police. Heidt was called by the authorities to bail them out of jail. Carney performed impressions of famous people, served as the show's announcer, and occasionally sang with Donna and Her Don Juans. His impersonation of Franklin Delano Roosevelt was enjoyed by FDR himself. Art Carney left the band in early 1941 after he embarrassingly flubbed his lines while inebriated on a *Pot o' Gold* radio program. In spite of his ignominious departure, Carney and Heidt remained lifelong friends. After Carney won an Oscar for his role in the film *Harry and Tonto*, Heidt took him out to dinner at Chasen's in Beverly Hills to celebrate.

Horace Heidt had an uncanny ability to develop popular radio shows, and the most successful of all was *Pot o' Gold*. According to Heidt, he was playing at the Gibson Hotel in Cincinnati in 1938 when a newsboy suggested he give money away on a radio show. He liked the idea and collaborated with two college fraternity brothers in Cincinnati to develop the first radio giveaway program. The format was amazingly simple. $1,000 was given to people who answered the phone when called after being randomly selected from telephone directories from around the country. *Pot o' Gold* debuted on NBC with Tums sponsorship in September 1939 and swept the country, causing movie theater attendance to plummet. Millions stayed home tuned to their radio every Tuesday evening between 8:30 and 9:00 p.m. in hope of being the lucky selectee. The catch phrase "Hold it Horace, stop the music." shouted by host Ben Grauer became a national sensation. However, after a few years the show was forced off the air by the Federal Communication Commission who determined that it was in effect a lottery. The ever-creative Heidt followed *Pot o' Gold* with *Treasure Chest*, a program where quiz winners reached into a golden treasure chest for valuable gifts.

It was inevitable that the *Pot o' Gold* radio show would spawn a movie of the same name, and indeed it did. The film *Pot o' Gold* essentially transplanted the radio show to the screen. It was produced by James Roosevelt, FDR's son, and starred James Stewart, Paulette Goddard, and the entire Heidt organization. Filming began in Hollywood in the fall of 1940; it was released in early1941. Although widely panned at the time, when viewed today it exudes an innocent charm along with providing the historical value of seeing Heidt and his orchestra performing at their Swing Era peak.

After extensively touring in 1942 Heidt spent a good portion of the balance of World War II in Southern California where he played at army camps and performed at bond rallies. He also did war-related radio work, appearing on Armed Forces Radio Service programs and the Coca-Cola *Victory Parade of Spotlight Bands*. In addition, Heidt developed a new radio show, *Welcome Home*, in which he interviewed returning servicemen to help them get work. Hundreds of soldiers obtained jobs through the program. The entrepreneurial Heidt also purchased the Trianon Ballroom on Firestone Boulevard in South Gate, CA, where he booked both his own band and other big name bands. The Trianon was a profitable investment until he sold it in the late1950s. Musically, George T. Simon gave Heidt's band a glowing review in the September 1943 issue of *Metronome* stating that it was the best and most musical band he ever had. Then riding the wave of success he worked so hard to achieve, Horace Heidt stunned the nation in mid 1945 by unexpectedly taking a two year self-imposed break from the world of entertainment because of a dispute with his booking agency, MCA.

Both Heidt and Benny Goodman were the most vocal among the many bandleaders dissatisfied with what they thought were lackadaisical booking efforts by MCA. Rather than work under their corporate control, Heidt turned his band over to Shorty Sherock after an unsuccessful legal battle to break free with two years remaining on his contract. As long as he did not perform as a musician or bandleader he had no legal obligation to MCA. In actuality, Heidt's decision was based not only on his desire to escape from MCA, but also to devote his efforts to organize and manage his rapidly growing business investments.

During his two-year Southern California-based hiatus Heidt bought property that included San Fernando Valley acreage, a Beverly Hills restaurant, the Lone Palm Hotel in Palm Springs, and the Biltmore Hotel in Las Vegas. There were also nonbusiness activities. Dedicated to the cause of community service, he founded the Horace Heidt School for Stammering to assist people afflicted with stuttering. With his business empire and philanthropic endeavor in place, Heidt was poised to return to the music business when his MCA commitment ended in 1947.

Radio was still dominating home evening entertainment when Heidt flew to New York to sell legendary Philip Morris president Alfred E. Lyons on sponsoring a new show he created. Part of his sales pitch included providing his own sales force to merchandise the product in key markets. This was the same successful strategy he used when on the air for Alemite and Tums. Lyons, a marketing genius who invented the famous slogan "Call for Philip Morris" yelled out by four foot tall bellhop Johnny Roventini, bought Heidt's concept and *Horace Heidt's Youth Opportunity Program* was born. Horace Heidt was back in show business.

Youth Opportunity involved Heidt traveling with his band from town to town weekly to audition local talent and working with civic leaders and service organizations to promote the program. He would then select the best of the auditions to compete on the air with the winners continuing to contend until a national champion was chosen. The program debuted on December 7, 1947, in Fresno with accordionist Dick Contino the show's first winner. Johnny Carson, Al Hirt, Pete Fountain, and The Dukes of Dixieland were among those who competed on the show. Business-wise, Heidt's merchandising team did their job with distinction. Philip Morris stock doubled soon after the show debuted. But there was still one final entertainment medium for Horace Heidt to conquer—television.

In October 1950 *Youth Opportunity* moved over to CBS television on primetime through September 1951. Three years later, after enduring a grueling schedule of nonstop one-nighters, Heidt started a local Los Angeles TV show called *Family Night with Horace Heidt* sponsored by Pontiac that in January 1955 went national for a year on NBC as *The Swift Show Wagon with Horace Heidt*. Patterned after *Youth Opportunity*, it was a variety show telecast from a different city each week and featured local talent. With TV still a novelty, each show was a major local event and the live broadcast a sellout. A dedicated golfer, Heidt faithfully took a lesson from the local golf pro in every city the show took place. Horace Heidt conquered television, but there was still one final involvement in radio in the early 50s.

The United States Government asked Heidt to build *The American Way* variety show in 1953 with the intention of taking it on an international friendship tour. He launched the show entertaining troops in Korea then went on to travel the world and take it to radio with Lucky Strike sponsorship. The production was also a popular nightclub attraction, playing to a sellout engagement at the Café Rouge of the Hotel Statler in Manhattan in 1954. A popular feature of the show was comedian Johnny Standley, who performed "It's in the Book," the number one hit record he recorded with Heidt that first charted in October 1952. Then in December 1955, after *The Swift Show Wagon* went off the air, Heidt decided to wind down his entertainment activities and focus his efforts on the development of his Horace Heidt Estates in Sherman Oaks, CA.

The genesis of the Horace Heidt Estates was the *Pot o' Gold* movie. Heidt bought a ten acre grapefruit orchard in Sherman Oaks to build facilities to house his organization while filming took place. During World War II he made the property his home and called it the Heidt Ranch. The Ranch also served as quarters to the Heidt Company during the downtime between their myriad tours. Then in 1956 Heidt opened the Horace Heidt Estates 180 unit apartment complex on the Ranch property. It includes waterfalls, swimming pools, an 18-hole golf course, and the Aloha Room where big band concerts and community events take place. There are both Palm Springs and Hawaiian sections, each architecturally unique. Numerous entertainment luminaries have lived in the Estates. Noted actors and comedians included Ed Begley, Pat Buttram, Robert Cummings, Barbara Hale, Dick Van Patten, Johnny Standley, and film noir siren Audrey Totter. The big band community was represented by Gus Bivona, Mahlon Clark, Henry Cuesta, Helen Forrest, Marilyn King, Jack Leonard, Barbara McNair, and Roberta Sherwood.

From 1956 on Heidt performed only at select special events. He culminated his storybook career in 1964 with a television reunion appropriately titled *Family Night with Horace Heidt*. The show's highlight was the Triple Tonguing Trumpets of Pete Candoli, Al Hirt, and Red Nichols playing a red-hot version of "Hot Lips." Following a comfortable twenty-two-year retirement, Heidt suffered a heart attack in June 1986 and underwent a quadruple bypass. After a long bout with pneumonia Horace Heidt died in Los Angeles on December 1, 1986, one of the wealthiest and most influential of all the big band leaders.

Horace Heidt may be gone, but his legacy lives on thanks to the efforts of his son, the gregarious Horace Heidt Jr., an accomplished vocalist and musician who conducts his own big band, the Musical Knights. Heidt's band has achieved significant success having appeared with the many shows he produced at the top hotels around the country, including the Drake in Chicago. The Knights also made two national tours for Columbia Artists that sold out at each stop and played at the 1985 inaugural ball for President Ronald Reagan. Their first tour in 1984 featured Johnny Desmond, Helen Forrest, and The Modernaires with Paula Kelly, Jr. In 1990 Henry Cuesta, Arthur Duncan, John Gary, and Martha Tilton were spotlighted.

There was also a long involvement with the Los Angeles Raiders professional football team. In late 1937 Horace Heidt helped the late Del Courtney secure a lucrative engagement with network radio exposure at the Radisson Hotel in Minneapolis. Courtney never forgot the favor. An associate of Raider owner Al Davis, he was instrumental in assisting Horace Heidt Jr. to secure the coveted job of conducting the Los Angeles Raiders Band at all home games during the team's entire thirteen-year stay in Los Angeles that ran from 1982 to 1994. Today, Heidt Jr., is as active as ever with his band, engaging in annual Southern California show tours at community civic auditoriums and hosting monthly big band programs at the Estates's Aloha Room. Since 2002 he has hit the air with his own weekly radio show, *America Swings*.

A Stanford and law school graduate, Horace Heidt Jr. is also carrying on the Heidt family business tradition. He manages the Estates that has a big band museum devoted to his father's career and in 2006 opened the forty-five-unit Haleakala Luxury Apartments next to the Estates that is now part of the total Heidt complex. But there is one unfinished item of business remaining on his agenda. Horace Heidt Jr.'s biggest dream is to create a national big band museum that features all the famous bands, provides scholarships, and gives live big band performances. It is a goal he is personally committed to and continues to actively pursue.

Horace Heidt Sr. was a complex, multifaceted individual whose career in entertainment could be assessed in many ways. First, he was an overwhelming show business success as documented by his fifty-two hit records and numerous radio and TV shows. Heidt was the feature subject of a movie and traveled the world with his show band braking attendance records wherever he appeared. He was a master discoverer of talent as well. Famous entertainers such as Art Carney, Frank DeVol, the King Sisters, Gordon MacRae, and Alvino Rey owe their start in show business to Heidt.

As a bandleader Heidt was not unlike Glenn Miller. Both were hard-driving perfectionists who painstakingly demanded the best from their band, but were fiercely loyal to their musical family and paid them well. He started out with a show band and developed it into a superior dance band during the Big Band Era. Radio transcriptions and air checks clearly reveal that from the late 40s until he retired Heidt had a solid swing band that played with a jazz tinge and could hold its own against any of its contemporaries.

There was also Horace Heidt the businessman. He had an uncanny sense for commerce combined with a true entrepreneur's ability to make decisions and act on them. Heidt did not let opportunity pass him by. It is remarkable that he was able to lead and manage a full show band with all its many challenges and simultaneously oversee his business empire, which was considerable and complex.

Probably Horace Heidt's most interesting behavioral characteristic was his exceptional creativity. He constantly reinvented himself and created a multitude of new shows for over thirty years. They were entertaining formats that always pleased his public and brought them unadulterated pleasure. His creative ability to manufacture wholesome enjoyment for his fans coupled with a genuine sense of community service is just possibly Horace Heidt's greatest achievement.

JOHN KIRBY
THE FORGOTTEN LEGEND

During the Big Band Era, bandleaders frequently led small groups that were comprised of musicians from their own bands. Bob Crosby's Bobcats, Tommy Dorsey's Clambake Seven, Woody Herman's Woodchoppers, Benny Goodman's many combinations, and Artie Shaw's Grammercy Five were among the better known bands-within-a-band. However, the most popular of all the Era small groups had no connection with a specific big band. That ensemble was the John Kirby Sextet that quickly became endeared to swing enthusiasts as the Biggest Little Band in the Land.

There is some mystery surrounding Kirby's birthplace. Jazz books and articles universally state that John Kirby was born in Baltimore and raised in local foster homes. However, in his 1993 book *The John Kirby Story*, Alan Williams states that John Kirk was born in Winchester, VA, on December 31, 1908, and raised there by Baptist minister Reverend Washington Johnson, a prominent member of the local African American community, in a home that still stands at 442 North Kent Street. It was in the Johnson home, where constantly surrounded by music, Kirk learned to play piano and was exposed to spirituals and hymns sung by the Reverend.

John Kirk got off to an early start as a musician. He began to take music lessons in 1917 at the Fredrick Douglass Elementary School in Winchester from Principal Powell Gibson soon after he was given a trombone by Reverend Johnson. Kirk quickly demonstrated prodigy-level talent on the instrument and continued to take formal training until 1923. The inquiring young Kirk also explored all genres of music and developed a particularly intense interest in and knowledge of classical music and the great classical composers, especially Bach. This plunge into classical music served him well when he formed his own chamber jazz group in New York in 1937.

According to Williams, Kirk moved to Baltimore in 1926 and stayed with Georgian Jackson, a lady who hosted African American jazz musicians that passed through town. While in Baltimore he took up the tuba, then a common instrument in jazz bands, and put his Winchester past behind him when he officially changed his name to John Kirby. Kirby's formative years in Virginia have been documented in the *Winchester Star* newspaper.

At this point all sources converge and agree that around 1928 John Kirby went to New York and spent the balance of the decade playing with Bill Brown and his Brownies at the Star Theater on 42nd Street, with pianist Charlie Skeets at the Bedford Ballroom in Brooklyn, and with John C. Smith's Society Band at Harlem's Alhambra Ballroom. His prowess on the tuba brought him in contact with Wellman Braud who was playing tuba and string bass with Duke Ellington at the Cotton Club. They developed a close friendship with Braud teaching Kirby how to play the string bass that was starting to replace the tuba in jazz bands. Little did Kirby realize that their association which resulted in his learning how to play a third musical instrument would dramatically change the course of his musical career.

John Kirby was gifted with a unique ability to form friendships with fellow musicians. Thanks to his relationship with Fletcher Henderson band members Jimmy Harrison and Coleman

Hawkins, he became a member of Henderson's band in 1930 and began to transition from tuba to string bass. Kirby left Henderson in 1934 and spent a year with Chick Webb, returning to Henderson in 1935. A year later he joined Lucky Millinder's Mills Blue Rhythm Band and met fellow band members clarinetist Buster Bailey, pianist Billy Kyle, and drummer O'Neil Spencer. All would soon become mainstays of his Sextet. Musically, he blossomed with Henderson and Webb, establishing a reputation for outstanding technique and a new, bouncy, lighter sound on the string bass. Come 1937, armed with professional know-how and myriad contacts, John Kirby was ready to make his mark at a club on New York's storied Swing Street with his own group.

In the mid-1930s the block between Fifth and Sixth Avenues on 52nd Street became known as Swing Street. Packed with jazz clubs situated in the cellars of old brownstone houses, 52nd Street was recognized as the unofficial capital of jazz well into the 1940s. One of the first establishments on Swing Street was the Onyx Club, run by Joe Helbock who also conducted the May 1936 Swing Music Concert to benefit the local chapter of the American Federation of Musicians at New York's Imperial Theater. It was the concert that brought Artie Shaw to public attention with his performance of his own composition "Interlude in B Flat" with a string quartet. Right from its start as a speakeasy during Prohibition, Helbock's concern evolved as a hangout for jazz musicians and a spot to jam. It was at the Onyx Club where in 1933 illustrious record producer John Hammond first met Benny Goodman.

In February 1937 the Stuff Smith Sextet was playing at the Onyx when Smith suddenly left his engagement for an invitation to go to Hollywood to try out for the movies. Helbock replaced him with a septet that debuted on May 15, 1937. It included Kirby, guitarist Teddy Bunn, drummer and scat singer Leo Watson, saxophonist Pete Brown, trumpeter Frankie Newton, pianist Don Frye, and clarinetist Buster Bailey. Kirby soon became the front man of the group and started to reshape it to create his own sextet to play the kind of music he envisioned. That same year he was also involved in a historic recording session with a then unknown vocalist named Maxine Sullivan.

An accounting of the career of John Kirby would not be complete without mention of his professional and personal involvement with Sullivan, who was born Marietta Williams in Homestead, PA, on May 13, 1911. She came from a strong musical background that included an aunt who sang contralto and an uncle who played drums in a local band in which Earl Hines played piano. Her first public appearance took place in 1918 when she sang "I'm Forever Blowing Bubbles" at the Carnegie Library in Homestead. In 1936, after singing with a local group called the Red Hot Peppers, Sullivan landed a job singing in Pittsburgh at an after-hours club called the Benjamin Harrison Literary Club for $14 a week plus tips. It turned out to be a fortuitous gig as she was discovered there in early 1937 by Ina Ray Hutton's pianist Gladys Mosier who told her to see her if she ever got to New York.

In June 1937 Sullivan did indeed get to New York and met with instant success that exceeded her wildest expectations. As soon as she arrived by train from Pittsburgh she immediately went to see Mosier who introduced her to pianist Claude Thornhill. He astutely sensed her talent and suggested she change her name to Maxine Sullivan and took her to myriad clubs all the way from 155th Street down to Swing Street to audition. It was at the Onyx Club where Joe Helbock's silent partner, guitarist Carl Kress, hired her as an intermission act. Thornhill next produced Sullivan's first record, "Stop! You're Breaking My Heart" on June 14, 1937. Then came her seminal August 6, 1937, recording date with Thornhill in which she sang a swing version of the Scottish folk song "Loch Lomond." "Loch Lomond" became a huge hit, propelling the four-feet, ten-inch tall Sullivan to national fame. John Kirby played bass in the seven-piece recording session group. He and Sullivan soon started seeing each other and married in 1938.

Maxine Sullivan made a significant contribution to the success of the John Kirby Sextet. She recorded with the Sextet in 1940 and at times sang with them at the Onyx Club with an understated air of self-confidence while standing erect with a slight tilt to her head and what appeared to be a mischievous smile. Kirby and Sullivan also achieved prominence on radio. Starting in 1940 they were featured on the Sunday afternoon CBS radio program *Flow Gently, Sweet Rhythm* for more than a year. The two were the first ever African American hosts of a national network radio series. Her place in John Kirby annals is secure.

By 1938 John Kirby was well ensconced at the Onyx Club with a sextet he formed that was ideal for the kind of music he wanted to play. It contained the same instrumentation as the original 1937 Onyx septet less the guitar. Classically trained clarinetist Buster Bailey remained from the original group. Light touch pianist Billy Kyle, subtly rhythmic percussionist O'Neil Spencer, and technically flawless trumpeter Charlie Shavers came over from Lucky Millinder's Mills Blue Ribbon Band which Kirby had left in early 1937 to go to the Onyx Club. Distinctive toned alto saxophonist Russell Procope joined after returning from playing in London and Paris. This was the group that remained intact through most of 1941 and gained renown as the John Kirby Sextet.

Kirby's success was both phenomenal and many-sided. Magnificently attired in white tie and tails, the Sextet quickly became the most popular group on Swing Street with a run at the Onyx Club that lasted all together around two and a half years. In late 1939 it went on the road and was a smash hit at the elegant Pump Room of Chicago's Ambassador East Hotel, establishing the Sextet as a darling of the carriage trade at stylish entertainment salons. Kirby's group went on to break ground as the first African American band to play at the Waldorf-Astoria Hotel, appeared at Boston's Copley Terrace, and made several return trips to the Pump Room in Chicago among its many well-received posh engagements. Debonair movie star Tyrone Power always made it a point to see the group whenever it played at the Café Society Uptown in Manhattan.

The Sextet was also active making records and appearing on radio shows and in short film features. It made its recording debut in a session that produced its biggest hit, "Undecided," on October 28, 1938. During the group's history it recorded for several major record labels and contributed to the war effort making V-Disc recordings in 1943. Its records sold well and are still regularly played on big band radio shows today. The Sextet appeared on two popular NBC radio programs, the comedy show *Duffy's Tavern* and the *Chamber Music Society of Lower Basin Street*, an avant-garde jazz show that played excellent swing music. Radio activity also included appearances on the Armed Forces Radio Service's *One-Night Stand* and *Jubilee* shows in 1944 and 1945. Additionally, it made two film Soundies in 1942. The John Kirby Sextet's success was definitely multi-faceted.

Resplendent attire notwithstanding, the considerable popularity of the John Kirby Sextet derived from its music. The group played a new kind of jazz, a unique, lightly swinging, breezy yet highly orchestrated style that was both sophisticated and easy to listen to. The music always flowed smoothly as the Sextet cohesively played a repertoire that included standards, original compositions, and light classics. It was a fresh and innovative style of chamber jazz that the public readily embraced.

The primary architect of the John Kirby sound was the brilliant twenty-year-old Charlie Shavers who did most of the band's composing and arranging. As opposed to the head arrangements that were common on 52nd Street, Shavers's scores were intricate and demanding to play. Shavers proved himself early on when he arranged the Sextet's smash hit, "Undecided." Both he and the talented arranger and songwriter Lou Singer adapted the classic works of Beethoven, Chopin, Donizetti, Dvorak, Grieg, Mendelssohn, Schubert, and Tchaikovsky to swing for the Sextet. Shavers's work with Kirby was most impressive considering his youth and experience.

There was also the matter of professional recognition. It should be noted that Kirby had the respect of his fellow musicians and the jazz community. During the peak of his career he recorded with both the Benny Goodman and Lionel Hampton small groups and the great Billie Holiday. In 1942 Kirby appeared at Carnegie Hall with guitarist Eddie Condon, saxophonist Bud Freeman, clarinetist Pee Wee Russell, and trumpeter Max Kaminsky in a program that also featured a Fats Waller organ and piano concert. His stature was such that in May 1942 *Music and Rhythm* magazine ran an article in which Kirby discussed his ten favorite bass players. He listed Artie Bernstein as number one.

John Kirby's incredible run first showed signs of slowing down in mid-1941. Drummer Spencer, who kept time with tasteful brush work and provided soulful blues-tinged vocals, started to exhibit erratic behavior. He left the band to return for a short time in 1942 before he sadly passed away from tuberculosis on July 24, 1944. He was only thirty four years of age. When Spencer left for the first time in 1941, he was replaced by Specs Powell who had been playing with jazz violinist Eddie South's group. After Spencer's final departure from the Sextet, Bill Beason, who had the unenviable task of replacing Chick Webb after he died of spinal tuberculosis in 1939, stepped in. It was the group's first personnel change in three years within a cohesive unit whose members were all personally close to each other and enjoyed playing together.

Next came the inevitable impact of World War II on the careers of jazz musicians and the fortunes of the groups they performed with. John Kirby's Sextet was no exception to wartime demands. In late 1942 Billy Kyle left to join the navy soon followed by Russell Procope who served in the army. Kyle was replaced by Clyde Hart and Procope by George Johnson, both of whom had recently played in Frankie Newton's Café Society Orchestra. The loss of half his Sextet within a few months had a dramatic impact on Kirby's spirits and drive.

Turnover in the band was not the only problem confronting Kirby. The early 1940s were also a time of personal tumult for him on two fronts. First, there were health issues as around that time he was diagnosed with diabetes. Second, he and Maxine Sullivan divorced in 1941 and went their separate ways.

Kirby and Sullivan had begun to drift apart as they became famous and developed their own careers with Sullivan extensively touring across the country and spending time in Hollywood filming two movies, *Going Places* (1938) and *St. Louis Blues* (1939). After they divorced, Sullivan had two long runs singing in Manhattan at Le Ruban Bleu and the Village Vanguard. In 1957 she retired to her home in the East Bronx to raise her daughter Paula, who was born in 1945, and became active in school affairs as president of the PS 136 Parent-Teachers Association. Her professional hiatus proved of value as Paula went on to become a registered nurse who worked in cardiac surgery and radiology, as well as an accomplished photographer. Sullivan made a comeback in 1966 and remained active singing in the United States, Europe, and Japan until her passing in 1987. She departed having achieved significant recognition, garnering a nomination for a Tony Award for her performance in the 1979 Broadway musical *My Old Friends*, and three Grammy nominations in the 1980s.

Another major personnel change occurred in 1944 when the genial Charlie Shavers left to join Raymond Scott's CBS house orchestra. He was briefly replaced by Dizzy Gillespie, the first of many who occupied the trumpet chair for the remainder of the Sextet's existence. The floodgates were now open; there would be many more changes among the Sextet's musicians over the next two years. Among those who passed through the band, albeit briefly, were Denzel Best, Hank

Jones, Cliff Leeman, Hot Lips Page, Bud Powell, and Ben Webster. It is to Kirby's credit that he was able to maintain stability and the band's sound and style given the constant state of flux.

By now it was apparent that the John Kirby Sextet was in the throes of its final stages. It played at the Aquarium on Broadway in 1944 and went to Los Angeles in early 1945 to appear at Joe Morris's Plantation Club at 108th Street and Central Avenue in Watts. Late that year through early 1946 the Sextet accompanied Sarah Vaughn at the Copacabana in Manhattan in what was its last prestigious booking. On the recording front, it recorded four sides with Vaughn on January 9, 1946. The group's last recording session took place on September 3, 1946, in New York. The only original member of the Sextet that participated that day was Buster Bailey, who held a note on the clarinet for forty-six seconds on the Sextet's 1942 recording of "St. Louis Blues." It was in effect the end of the Biggest Little Band in the Land.

In 1947 Kirby ventured to Hollywood to appear in the film *Sepia Cinderella*. He soon returned to New York where he spent the remainder of the 1940s trying to revive his Sextet along with exacerbating his diabetic condition with the excessive consumption of scotch and sweets. Finally, Kirby's indefatigable efforts to resuscitate his band paid off when he arranged for the Sextet to play at a concert at Carnegie Hall on the evening of December 22, 1950. With the exception of Sid Catlett who replaced the late O'Neil Spencer on drums, the entire original 1938 group was there performing with Kirby. Musically they were in top form and garnered a good review in *DownBeat*. Commercially, they were a failure. Despite considerable publicity generated by the Carnegie Hall PR staff, it was an embarrassingly empty house. The end was now official. The public no longer had any interest in the John Kirby Sextet.

After his ill-fated Carnegie Hall concert, Kirby worked in lesser New York clubs and in late 1951 played an unsuccessful engagement with a group he formed in Milwaukee at the Capitol Lounge in Chicago, the city in which just a dozen years earlier he was the toast of the town at the Pump Room. Still continuing to ignore his physical condition, he decided to move to Los Angeles. Kirby drove to the West Coast in his Cadillac with Charlie Shavers and settled in an apartment on Harvard Boulevard in Hollywood. He landed a few local gigs thanks to the largess of his good friend Benny Carter and Shavers. But the books closed on John Kirby on June 14, 1952, when he suddenly died from complications of diabetes with no financial assets and in virtual obscurity in his sparsely furnished apartment. Benny Carter arranged and paid for Kirby's funeral.

John Kirby's sad final years should not obscure the contributions he made to contemporary listening pleasure, the development of jazz, the enrichment of jazz musicians, and our popular culture. First, his Sextet's sound and style is still popular today. Wayne Roberts is a New York bassist who has studied at the New England Conservatory of Music and Julliard. He is comfortable in both the worlds of jazz and classical music. In 1998 he formed the Onyx Club Sextet that features primarily the music of the John Kirby Sextet along with selected jazz classics. Its December 1998 debut was at a Monday evening engagement at the Firebird Café in Manhattan that lasted six months. Since then the Sextet has been in demand playing at clubs, concerts, and jazz festivals in the United States and Europe. Its popularity documents that the music of John Kirby has not died but is definitely alive and well.

Creatively, the music produced by the John Kirby Sextet was innovative and influential. By playing lyrical arrangements with soft tones it can be argued that the group was a precursor of cool jazz. The sextet also anticipated bebop with several arrangements that utilized cyclic chord progression. Billy Kyle's composition "From A Flat to C" is a good example. Moreover, much of Charlie Shavers's writing had experiments in phrasing that could be associated with bebop. Bop legends Thelonius Monk and Charlie Parker quoted a number of Kyle and Shavers compositions while Bud Powell admired Kyle's piano work.

There are a host of contemporary jazz musicians that have been enriched by the music of John Kirby. One is Dave Pell, a respected tenor saxophonist, Big Band Era sideman, record producer, and leader of his own popular octet since 1953. An admirer of the Kirby sound, he recorded a John Kirby Sextet tribute album in 1961 titled *I Remember John Kirby*. It featured Benny Carter and was well received with both good record sales and critical acclaim. Pell also discussed Kirby as a panelist at the Los Angeles Jazz Institute's May 2004 symposium *Springsville: Celebrating the Birth of Cool and Beyond*, documenting Kirby's underappreciated contribution to the genre of cool jazz. Five decades after his passing, Kirby remains highly regarded by the jazz community.

Finally, there is the matter of personal accomplishment. Enigmatic pop artist Andy Warhol once said every person will be world-famous for fifteen minutes. John Kirby had far more than fifteen minutes of fame. He had an eight-year run achieving national recognition as one of the most popular jazz artists of his day. His Sextet played a cheerful style of music that put people in high spirits at the best jazz and night clubs across the country and on radio. In the process he became part of our American popular culture and jazz history. That's a legacy most of us would be proud of achieving.

KAY KYSER

BANDLEADER, MOVIE STAR, RADIO AND
TV HEADLINER, AND HUMANITARIAN

Here is a question for all Big Band Era mavens. Who is the popular bandleader that had forty-five top-ten hit records between 1936 and 1948, starred in seven films and guest appeared in two others, hosted one of America's most popular radio shows for eleven consecutive years, and spent the last thirty-five years of his richly productive life pursuing humanitarian causes?

The answer is Kay Kyser, who, blessed with enormous creative theatrical talent and indefatigable energy, achieved the pinnacle of success as an entertainer, and then suddenly left the limelight to retire and devote his life to civic and religious causes. Unfortunately, with his abrupt, permanent, and reclusive departure from the entertainment world, Kyser quickly faded from public memory. Therefore, a retrospective of his multi-faceted career is categorically in order.

James Kern Kyser was born to a professional family on June 18, 1906, in Rocky Mount, NC. His mother, Emily Royster Howell, was a descendent of naval hero John Paul Jones and the first registered woman pharmacist in the state. His nearly blind father, who was of Dutch ancestry and changed the spelling of the family name from Kyzer to Kyser, also practiced pharmacy.

The pattern for Kyser's dynamic career was set at Rocky Mount High School when he engaged in myriad extra-curricular activities. Two are of note. First, he organized and coached his own club football team comprised of players too small to make the varsity. Second, he launched his theatrical career participating in minstrel shows conducted by his school's fraternity, Tau Nu Tau. In addition to activities he forged, Kyser still found time to play on the school basketball team, perform as head cheerleader, earn a letter in debating, serve as editor of the school yearbook, and graduate with honors as class president.

Kyser matriculated at the University of North Carolina in 1923, where there was already a strong family presence. His uncle Vernon Howell founded the University's School of Pharmacy in 1897. Howell Hall, constructed in 1925 and named after uncle Vernon, housed the School of Pharmacy for many years.

The family's professorial legacy at the University continued long after Kyser graduated. His cousin Vermont Royster, Pulitzer Prize winning editor of the *Wall Street Journal*, taught at the School of Journalism as a William Rand Kenan Jr professor of journalism and public affairs for nine years after he retired from the Dow Jones & Co., the *Journal's* publisher, in 1971.

Kyser was just as active at the University as he was at Rocky Mount High. He joined the Sigma Nu fraternity and once again became head cheerleader and founded the Cheerios, an organized cheering section of 250 students that practiced and rehearsed choreographed cheers for Saturday afternoon football games.

Enamored with the stage, Kyser put together theatrical performances and soon became known as the Flo Ziegfeld of the campus. It was while he was orchestrating campus shows that he developed a strong friendship with Charlotte's Hal Kemp, who originally aspired to become a symphony conductor and went on to become a highly successful bandleader and favorite of British royalty. Kemp tragically died in an automobile crash in Madera, CA, in 1940 while driving from Los Angeles where he had finished playing at the Cocoanut Grove to a scheduled engagement at the Mark Hopkins Hotel in San Francisco. Kyser was each production's impresario, Kemp the maestro presiding over his campus band, the Carolina Club Orchestra.

Kemp graduated before Kyser and encouraged him to follow in his footsteps and form his own band. Hesitant at first because he could not play an instrument or read a note of music, Kyser finally capitulated to Kemp's urging and formed a six-piece band in the fall of 1926 that included fellow student Sully Mason, who was to remain a fixture with the organization until 1945 when he left to form his own band. A short time later, George Duning left his studies at the Cincinnati Conservatory of Music to join the band. He worked with Kyser as an arranger for over twenty years.

After taking a short hiatus from the University to build and promote his band, Kyser returned to Chapel Hill, graduating in 1928, and officially started his career as a professional bandleader. He paid his dues driving with his band in a $30 Ford playing southern colleges and venues such as the Bamboo Gardens in Cleveland, OH, and the Willows in Oakmont, PA, where in 1931 he hired Merwyn Bogue, a solid trumpet player recommended by his old friend Hal Kemp. Bogue would soon go on to become better known to the nation as Ish Kabibble. Dressed in colorful suits and wearing his hair in bangs, he performed novelty numbers that became a highly popular feature of the band for the balance of its existence.

With eight grueling years of traveling the country behind him, Kyser finally established a national reputation in 1934. That was the year he developed his trademark, singing song titles while he was playing at the Miramar Hotel in Santa Monica, CA. The stratagem involved a vocalist singing the title at the start of each number, then after a few bars of melody Kyser would introduce the vocalist. It was an original and distinctive concept that immediately gained public notice.

Then his big break came while he was still at the Miramar. In September of 1934 Hal Kemp had finished a long engagement at the famous Blackhawk restaurant in Chicago and recommended Kyser to replace him. Kyser jumped at the chance to play the prestigious venue with daily broadcasts on powerful Radio Station WGN. He immediately gave notice to the Miramar and headed east to Chicago where he became an instant hit and stayed on at the Blackhawk for a nineteen-week engagement.

Two important personnel developments also took place at the Blackhawk. First, Kyser hired a new girl singer, Ginny Simms, who was to become a star for her duration with the band that ended in 1941 when she struck out on her own successful career. Second, with guidance from comedian and trombone player Jerry Colonna who was in Chicago playing with Gus Arnheim's band, Merwyn Bogue perfected his Ish Kabibble comedy act he originally created a year earlier when the band was performing at the Bal Tabarin restaurant and dance spot on Columbus Avenue in San Francisco. Kay Kyser was finally on his way.

In 1935 a little known incident took place that highlighted Kyser's rapidly growing popularity. Although Benny Goodman is credited for launching the Big Band Era with his historic Palomar Ballroom engagement in Los Angeles in August 1935 he was a complete box office failure as he worked his way west to the Palomar from New York on a national tour. Goodman hit rock bottom and actually considered quitting when his engagement at Denver's Elitch Garden, where he was overwhelmingly outdrawn by a rival band playing at nearby Lakeside Park, was canceled. That band was Kay Kyser's.

Vocalist Harry Babbitt traveled from his home town of St. Louis to Chicago to join the band in early 1937. He went on to record several hit records and to form an extremely popular duo with Ginny Simms. Babbitt stayed with Kyser until he went into the service in 1944 rejoining Kyser after the war. His replacement was Michael Dowd, who became famous not as a vocalist, but as television personality Mike Douglas. The nucleus of the organization was now set in place, and unbeknownst to even Kyser himself he was about to experience an unexpected firestorm of popularity that was to propel him to the top of the entertainment world.

Kyser returned to his old haunt, the Blackhawk in Chicago, in the fall of 1937. It was there that he developed, some say with assistance from MCA's Lew Wasserman, his famous audience participation show *Kay Kyser's Kollege of Musical Knowledge* that featured Kyser attired in full academic cap and gown. The show was quickly picked up by WGN and with Kyser's homespun humor combined with the unique quiz show format it became an instant hit throughout the Midwest.

George Washington Hill was then the president of the American Tobacco Company who was also blessed with uncanny promotional instincts. He traveled to Chicago to see the *Kollege of Musical Knowledge* show in person. Hill was so impressed that he signed Kyser on the spot for a national weekly radio program on NBC sponsored by Lucky Strike cigarettes. The *Kollege of Musical Knowledge* debuted in 1938 and swept the nation as the year's top new program, lasting eleven consecutive years under varying sponsorship until it went off the air in1949. Kay Kyser was now a household name and his hauntingly beautiful theme song "Thinking of You" one of the most recognized melodies in America.

With his exposure from his highly popular radio show and number one novelty hit record "Three Little Fishes" dominating the charts, it was inevitable Hollywood would beckon, and beckon it did. In 1939 Kyser made *That's Right—You're Wrong*, the first of seven feature films. It was a resounding box office success.

His next two films involved elements of cinema history. *You'll Find Out*, released in 1940, marked the only time that Boris Karloff, Peter Lorre, and Bela Lugosi appeared in a movie together. *Playmates*, released in 1941, was John Barrymore's last film appearance. Both were smash hits.

Two films with wartime musical comedy themes were next, with *My Favorite Spy* in 1942 and *Around the World* in 1943, completing Kyser's contract with RKO. Kyser made his final two films in 1944, *Swing Fever* for MGM and *Carolina Blues* for Columbia Pictures. Seven feature films in five years along with appearances in *Stage Door Canteen* and *Thousands Cheer* add up to quite a productive and successful movie career.

With *Kay Kyser's Kollege of Musical Knowledge* perennially among the top radio shows in the country, a string of hit records, successful motion pictures, and prestigious bookings for public appearances, Kyser had the highest grossing band in the land with the possible exception of Glenn Miller. His huge financial success provided him the flexibility to hire the best musicians.

Commented Big Band Era guitarist Roc Hillman, who co-wrote Kyser's instrumental hit "Pushin' Sand": "I was playing with Jimmy Dorsey in 1940 when I was given an offer by Kyser. Jimmy said take it, I could never match Kyser. That was around the time Kay moved from a novelty band to a truly fine musical unit that could really swing with the best of them."

Then came World War II. With the possible exception of Bob Hope, no celebrity did more to entertain servicemen during the war than Kyser. Not only did he donate his professional time, he also donated his personal financial resources. When war was declared, he vowed to play no commercial dates for the duration of the conflict except for previously booked engagements, paying all expenses out of his own pocket.

It is estimated that Kyser played at over five hundred military installations throughout the world. He was also instrumental in founding the fabled Hollywood Canteen with Bette Davis and is credited with emceeing star-studded tours that sold $400 million worth of war bonds. Near the end of the war he toured the Pacific Theater with Ish Kabbible and was formally requested to have an audience with Douglas MacArthur so the five star general could personally thank them both for their contributions under battle conditions.

According to famous big band disc jockey Chuck Cecil, Kyser also did his part on the home front: "Kay Kyser seemed to have more wartime hits than any other bandleader. "The White Cliffs of Dover" was the unofficial theme song for that troubled time before the war, and hits like "He Wears a Pair of Silver Wings" and "Praise the Lord and Pass the Ammunition" did much to shore up morale here in the states during the conflict."

In 1944 Kyser took time out from his frenetic wartime efforts to elope to Las Vegas to marry Georgia Carroll, a John Robert Powers model from Dallas who appeared on the covers of nine *Redbook* magazines. Carroll was under contract with Warner Brothers when they became involved while doing USO shows. Kyser developed her as a vocalist and she went on to serve a short stint as the band's girl singer and appeared in *Carolina Blues* before she retired from the entertainment world to raise their family that included three daughters.

What was it like working for Kay Kyser during the bands heyday? In a 1978 interview with Cecil, Harry Babbitt said: "Kay Kyser was a perfect gentleman. It was a real pleasure to be associated with him. We stayed in the best hotels and were provided the best in transportation. He in turn insisted that we conduct ourselves like ladies and gentlemen at all times. Kay was sincere, hardworking, and just a class individual."

Jack Martin, soprano saxophone player and vocalist on Kyser's 1942 mega hit, "Strip Polka," talked about the tremendous loyalty that the band members had for Kyser during an interview with Cecil at Disneyland in the early 1970s: "Kay gave us all the royal treatment above and beyond what could be expected of any bandleader. During the war he continued paying my salary to my family. The guys would do anything for him."

Kyser remained active in the entertainment world after World War II, continuing to make public appearances and recording three million sellers in "Ole Buttermilk Sky," "On a Slow Boat to China," and the novelty hit "Woody Woodpecker Song." He took the *Kollege of Musical Knowledge* to television in late 1949 then on Christmas day 1950 he stunned the nation when he gave up his television show and permanently retired back to North Carolina, where he lived in the same house in Chapel Hill that was built in 1814 at 504 East Franklin Street, until he passed away on July 23, 1985. Kyser spent those thirty-five years vigilantly avoiding all public contact, maintaining total personal privacy.

Why did Kyser unexpectedly leave the entertainment world never to return? The answer is twofold. In addition to feeling he contributed all he possibly could to entertaining mankind over a quarter century of whirlwind, non-stop performing, he truly wished to devote the balance of his mortality to giving back to his country that gave so much to him in fame and fortune.

The seeds of Kyser's humanitarian philosophy were sown while entertaining troops at military installations and hospitals during World War II, an experience he termed the most gratifying time of his life. Immediately after the war he launched his beneficent career spearheading a galaxy of Hollywood stars for fundraising campaigns to add a new wing to St. John's Hospital in Santa Monica, CA, and upgrade the delivery of health care in his native North Carolina through the North Carolina Good Health Plan he created and developed.

One of his first post-retirement projects was to bring public television to North Carolina. Notwithstanding his commitment to such civic affairs, Kyser's main focus in retirement was his dedication to and work for the Christian Science Church. A deeply religious person, he served as a practitioner, an official lecturer, designated spokesman, and spent five years in the 1970s heading the church's film and broadcasting division at its world headquarters in Boston. Kyser was honored for his contributions to the Christian Science Church in 1983 when he was appointed honorary president for a one-year term.

Kyser never lost touch with the University of North Carolina throughout his career as an entertainer and humanitarian, taking great pride in his involvement with his beloved alma mater. The University, in turn, appreciated Kyser's efforts. In a 1981 interview with Kyser on the North Carolina public television network that Kyser was instrumental in founding, then University president William C. Friday said: "We are delighted that Kay chose to settle in Chapel Hill when he retired, and it was an honor to bestow on him the University's Distinguished Service Award in recognition of his outstanding service to the University through the years."

With all he accomplished as an entertainer and humanitarian, how would Kyser himself like to be remembered? Roc Hillman speculated on the matter: "I knew Kay well. In my opinion, he would rather be thought of as a caring and considerate human being with a great sense of humor than a big name celebrity. That's the Kay Kyser I remember."

BILLY MAY
EIGHT DECADES IN SWING

Here is a quick quiz on the Big Band Era. What famous self-taught arranger, bandleader, and trumpet player significantly contributed to the careers of Charlie Barnet, Glenn Miller, Frank Sinatra, and Bozo the Clown? The answer is the multi-talented Billy May, who died of a heart attack on January 22, 2004. He was a true giant of the swing genre whose body of work is so broad and vast that it is impossible to completely catalog.

William Edward May was born of German, English, and Scotch-Irish heritage in Pittsburgh on November 10, 1916, the oldest of three children of a totally non-musical family. He grew up in Pittsburgh's Lawrenceville area and in 1935 graduated from Schenley High School where he studied the tuba and dabbled with the bassoon, string base, trombone, and trumpet. While he was in high school he became intrigued with the interplay of the musical instruments within a band and started to teach himself arranging.

May's first professional job was with his high school friend, Gene Olsen and the Polish Aristocrats. They played Friday nights at a Polish Catholic Church with May doubling with the tuba on polkas and trombone on American numbers. He was less than satisfied with the band's banjo player as told during a telephone interview: "Gene had a banjo player named Bucky who was great for polkas. But when we played American tunes he did a terrible job on the guitar just making noise that didn't fit at all. I said to Gene one day, why don't you let Bucky go and get a banjo player who can play American numbers too. Gene said I have to keep Bucky because he knows the priest."

Next came a series of Pittsburgh area jobs with Lee Rivers, Al Howard, Etzi Covato, and Baron Elliott, who had a sweet band patterned after Guy Lombardo. May played trombone and doubled on trumpet on jazz numbers and show tunes with Elliott. Lee Rivers had four saxophones providing May with an opportunity to arrange in the Benny Goodman-Fletcher Henderson style for the first time. He also had some interesting experiences working with Rivers: "We used to play Sunday concerts at a park over in Carnegie from 8:00 pm until a fight broke out, usually around one in the morning. We'd immediately play the "Star Spangled Banner" and go home. That was my classical training."

By now it was 1938 and Charlie Barnet's band came to play in Pittsburgh. May told about his big break on a 1974 interview on Chuck Cecil's *Swingin' Years* radio show: "Charlie hit Pittsburgh with a great, wild-swinging band. I went to see him with my manuscript paper in hand and asked him if I could write an arrangement. He told me to give it a try, so I stayed up all night and wrote one. He rehearsed it the next day, and that was the start of a lifelong friendship."

May played trumpet and arranged for Barnet starting in March 1939, when he formally joined the band. He wrote Barnet's two biggest hits, the distinctively wah-wah sounding "Cherokee" that served as an inspiration for Charlie Parker's be-bop classic "Ko-Ko," and "Pompton Turnpike," featuring the call and response of Barnet's soprano saxophone and May's trumpet. On Cecil's show he talked about recording "Cherokee" at a session that served as a perfect example of how May developed a legendary reputation for working fast and developing charts under pressure at the eleventh hour: "It was July 17, 1939. We were working up in Westchester County and had a Sunday afternoon recording date at 3:30 at the old Victor studios at 24th and Park Avenue. I had written the beginning of "Cherokee," but I remembered Sunday morning that I didn't have an out chorus, the ensemble chorus, so I wrote it out in the car without a copyist while we were driving to the studio and passed it out to the band when we got to Victor."

Did May enjoy his association with Barnet? "Charlie was a free spirit and had a band that emulated Duke Ellington. In fact, we played the Apollo Theater a lot. It was a loose band with a lot of room to improvise and express yourself. I never had as much fun playing for anyone and at the same time had an opportunity to develop my arranging skills. I used to turn out three or four arrangements a week for Charlie."

In the fall of 1940, May was presented an offer he couldn't refuse, a then impressive $150 a week to join Glenn Miller's band. It was double what he making with Barnet. He recalled his first day at work for Miller in a 1993 interview on Don Kennedy's nationally syndicated *Big Band Jump* radio show: "The day Roosevelt was elected in 1940 I joined Glenn Miller. The reason I remember that was because everybody was wondering if FDR was going to be re-elected, so nobody came to hear the band and Glenn was mad because business was bad."

May talked about his role in Miller's band in an article in the January-February 1993 issue of Kennedy's *Big Band Jump Newsletter*: "I came into the band as one of the section trumpet players, but Glenn gave me a couple of solos to play, and he liked them so well he put me over on the ad-lib chair. John Best and I did most of the ad-lib work. I did quite a bit of arranging for Miller, but nothing that was important because he had two really great arrangers, Jerry Gray and Bill Finegan. They turned out most of the Glenn Miller-style stuff."

It should not go unrecognized that May did make a significant arranging contribution for Miller by writing the hauntingly romantic introduction to "Serenade in Blue." One of Miller's biggest hits, it was featured in the film *Orchestra Wives* and was on the charts for eighteen consecutive weeks in 1942: "Bill Finegan brought the arrangement in but Glenn was undecided about how it was going to be used in the picture. Then at the last minute the music director decided they should have an orchestra introduction. He asked me, Finegan, Gray, and George Williams, who was also working with the band at the time, to write an introduction. So all four of us brought in an introduction and Glenn tried mine first and he never tried the other ones. I just used part of the tune and adapted around it."

May remained with Miller until Miller broke up the band in September of 1942 to voluntarily join the Army as a Captain. He talked about his leaving Miller on Cecil's radio show: "I left Glenn with a respectful handshake. That's the last time I saw him. But John Best saw Glenn in England shortly before his ill-fated plane trip. He told John that he hoped that both John and I would be in his organization after the war. He wanted me as an arranger and John as a trumpet player."

Through the years May has maintained his association with Miller alumni both professionally and socially. On Saturday night, April 17, 1954, May was the conductor and musical director for *The Original Reunion of the Glenn Miller Band*. The concert was performed by all ex-Miller musicians and was held before a capacity audience at the cavernous Shrine Auditorium in Los Angeles, longtime home of the annual Academy Awards ceremony. It was both a nostalgic and festive occasion for the Miller gang, many of whom had not seen each other since their days in the band.

May's last formal involvement with Miller alumni as a musician occurred when he participated in Glenn Miller reunion tours of Australia in 1984, 1985, and 1986. Including May, eight former members of the original Miller band played in the touring reunion big bands.

On a personal level, May had a warm relationship with Tex Beneke. He was at both Beneke's August 14, 1985, Glenn Miller alumni get-together at Beneke's home in Costa Mesa, CA, and the May 30, 2000, memorial service for Beneke at the Musicians' Association building in Santa Ana, CA. A close friend of Willie Schwartz, May acted as emcee at his 1990 funeral. He regularly kept in touch with fellow Southern Californians John Best, Paul Tanner, Zeke Zarchy, and Tom Sheils, Miller's business manager, who was instrumental in securing the booking for the band's historic 1939 breakthrough engagement at the Glen Island Casino.

In summing up his experience with Miller, May said: "I was paid well and certainly enjoyed working with Glenn. His band was much more structured than Barnet's but the gig gave me an opportunity to learn the band business from a master businessman and observe a very good arranger, which Glenn was. I had a great time working with Finegan and Gray on the songs in *Sun Valley Serenade* and *Orchestra Wives*. In fact I even composed two songs for *Orchestra Wives* that Glenn liked but were left on the cutting room floor."

After the Miller breakup, May spent an enjoyable stay in New York as a staff trumpet player for NBC on *The Chamber Society of Lower Basin Street* radio show before he moved to Los Angeles in the spring of 1943 to do freelance arranging. Then came 1944, the year Billy May firmly established himself in Hollywood working in radio and the recording industry.

May did work for Ozzie Nelson in 1943 and went on to play trumpet in Nelson's band that played Red Skelton's radio show in 1944. When Skelton went into the service, *The Adventures of Ozzie and Harriet* replaced his show. May became bandleader and arranger for Nelson's show during its entire radio history from 1944 until 1954 when it went on television. While he was working with Nelson, May began his celebrated career in the record business.

Paul Weston was the musical director of the fledgling Capitol Records label in 1944 when he started calling on May to ghost write for him. This was the start of a twenty-year association with Capitol in which he arranged for many of their incredible stable of vocalists, including Nat "King" Cole, Peggy Lee, Ella Mae Morse, the Pied Pipers, Frank Sinatra, and Margaret Whiting. It was the beginning of a multi-faceted involvement with Capitol that would eventually propel May back into the big bands. First came an involvement with Bozo the Clown.

Over the years, May developed a professional and social relationship with both Alvino Rey and the all the King Sisters. Donna King's husband, Jim Conklin, was an executive at Capitol Records in 1946 when he introduced May to Alan Livingston. Together May and Livingston produced nearly one hundred children's albums over a nearly ten-year period featuring Bozo the Clown, Disney cartoon characters, and Warner Brothers Looney Tunes characters with the voice of Mel Blanc. They also wrote "I Taut I Taw a Puddy Tat" that became a number one hit in England. May's body of work for children at Capitol also included *Little Johnny Strikeout*, a 1949 album he did with Joe DiMaggio. Many a current retirement-age adult grew up listening to Capitol's children albums with background music arranged by Billy May.

In 1950 the mambo was starting to sweep the country-fueled in part by the big three of Machito, Tito Puente, and Tito Rodriguez playing with their powerful Latin big bands at the famed Palladium in Manhattan. In an attempt to profit from this new dance craze, Capitol had May lead the band and arrange mambo-style for the Chuy Reyes *Midnight at the Mocambo* album in which he emulated the famous Perez Prado grunts. The success of the album led to May arranging and recording under the name of the Rico Mambo Orchestra an Arthur Murray dance album titled *Arthur Murray's Favorites: Mambos*. It was while working on these albums that May developed his signature sliding saxophone sound.

May talked about his inspiration for the distinctive sliding saxes on Cecil's show: "It was noth-ing new. Johnny Hodges and Willie Smith both did a sliding sax thing as soloists with Duke El-lington and Jimmy Lunceford. All I did was take that idea and do it with the whole sax section."

Excited by the distinctive sliding saxes sound, Capitol Records executives encouraged May to start his own big band. On September 24, 1951, Capitol released the Billy May band's first three records, the classic "All of Me," his theme song "Lean Baby," a light swinging song with a spiritual touch, and "Fat Man Mambo," a perfect example of May's renown musical sense of humor. All three were well received, and the band established itself placing tenth in *DownBeat's* Best Band category for 1951.

May capitalized on the public's growing interest in his fresh new sound. On February 22, 1952, he took his band on what we would be close to two years on the road, opening at the Rainbow Gardens in Pomona, CA. He discussed his experiences with his road band on Kennedy's radio show: "The band did good business everywhere we played, but after about three months I found out I didn't miss the road. We wound up playing the same joints I played at with Barnet and Miller fifteen years earlier plus I didn't have the temperament to cater to birthday requests and schmooze with the patrons. I preferred to arrange and live permanently in California."

Although May's band moved up to fifth in the 1952 *DownBeat* poll and was still a top draw, he made his final appearance with it during an October-November 1953 engagement at the Hol-lywood Palladium. He wanted out of the band business and in early 1954 sold the band to Ray Anthony and returned to arranging at Capitol.

A personal highlight of May's post-bandleading days was making a 1957 tribute album to Jimmy Lunceford, whom he truly admired: "It was one of the happiest moments in my career. I went to work and copied the original songs. We used as many of the old Lunceford guys as we could. We got Willie Smith and Joe Thomas to come out from Kansas City. Dan Grissom was around still singing and Trummy Young came over from Hawaii. It was a labor of love because I loved that Lunceford band."

During the 1950s May made several of his own albums at Capitol, wining a Grammy for Best Arrangement for *Big Fat Brass* in 1958. He would be nominated for a total of seven Grammys over the years. However, May would return to public recognition working with Frank Sinatra, with whom he had a longtime association: "I knew Frank from 1939 when I was playing with Barnet at the Hotel Lincoln. A lot of the musicians lived around the corner of 45th and Eighth Avenue in New York. There were a couple of big apartment hotels west of there and all the guys used to hang out at a couple of bars around the hotels. I first met Frank in one of those bars when he was just a boy singer with Harry James. Then I got to know him through the years. Near the end of 1944 Axel Stordahl needed an arrangement in a hurry for Frank for the *Your Hit Parade* radio show. I did Cole Porter's "Don't Fence Me In" and Frank liked it. When Sinatra went over to Capitol in 1954 he worked with Nelson Riddle. They did a lot of successful albums, but in 1957 he decided he wanted a change and gave me a call."

It was indeed a most fortuitous call. Sinatra and May would collaborate on three of Sinatra's most popular albums, his 1958 *Come Fly With Me*, 1958 *Come Dance With Me*, and 1961 *Come Swing With Me*. The jauntily swinging *Come Fly With Me* was Sinatra's first number one ranked album of the 50s, the hard driving *Come Dance With Me* was on the charts for 141 consecutive weeks, and the bouncy *Come Swing With Me* won May his second Grammy. This time it was for Best Vocal Background. May and Sinatra enjoyed working together during their time at Capi-tol.

May's contribution to Sinatra's career was not solely musical in scope. The popularity of these three albums contributed to the development of the image of Sinatra as a swinging hipster and leader of the Rat Pack. Frank Sinatra's place in American popular culture is in part the product of Billy May's creative arrangements.

In 1963 May took a year's hiatus from the music business when he suffered a near fatal heart attack brought about by years of heavy drinking and smoking two to three packs of cigarettes a day. He immediately eschewed both habits and through the years remained fully recovered in the best of health. While recuperating, he spent some time on his hobby of building model railroad trains and remained a lifetime member of the National Model Railroad Association.

When May returned to work in 1964 he increased his activity in two mediums, movies and television. Prior to his heart attack, May did work on the *Naked City* TV series and three films, *Fuzzy Pink Nightgown*, *Sergeants 3*, and *Johnny Cool*. He also appeared in *Nightmare*, the 1956 film noir classic, acting as a bandleader in a dimly lit, noir-style nightclub.

After his physical comeback May scored for several noted TV shows including *Batman*, *Mod Squad*, *Emergency*, and *CHiPs*. *Tony Rome* and *Lady in Cement* (both staring Frank Sinatra), *Pennies from Heaven*, *Racing with the Moon*, *Cocoon*, **batteries not included*, and *Field of Dreams* were among the many films he was involved with.

May's last extended recording project was with the 1969-1973 Time-Life Recording Sessions: "Around 1968 there was a Capitol executive named F. M. Scott who went over to work for Time-Life when they were thinking about doing a re-creation of the Swing Era. He suggested to Dave Cavanaugh who did a similar project with Glen Gray at Capitol in the early 1960s to ask me if I wanted to do a couple of sample records dates. They liked the samples and I wound doing at least one recording session a week for the next three or four years. Depending on the scheduling a lot of times I'd get snowed down and Sam Nestico and the late Carl Brandt, a very talented arranger, would help me."

May painstakingly copied hundreds of big band hits that were played by a studio orchestra he conducted. The end result was fourteen volumes, each containing about thirty songs. To this day it is difficult to tell the difference between May's re-creations and the original hits.

After completing the Time-Life project, May was in the desirable position of taking on only work he found challenging and interesting. He continued doing studio work and conducted four concerts in England with the BBC Big Band between 1982 and 1990. Recording projects included arranging and conducting a fifty-five-piece orchestra for the *The Past* and Part II of Frank Sinatra's 1980 *Trilogy* album on Reprise, and Stan Freberg's *United States of America, Part II* album in 1996. It marked the forty-fourth year of an association with Freberg that began when they first worked together on comedy records at Capitol in 1952.

1998 proved to be a milestone year for Billy May: "Around 1998 John Williams retired from leading the Boston Pops. I did a lot of arranging for him with the Pops going back to the 70s. I did a chart a month and that's a lot of work. Then Sinatra died and he had been giving me a lot of work through the years. I figured those were good signs to pay attention to. I had just turned eighty-two and figured that's enough, its time to slow down."

Billy May went on to live comfortably in his home near the Pacific Ocean in picturesque San Juan Capistrano, CA. He took daily walks to the beach and received awards such as the American Society of Music Arrangers and Composers Golden Score Award and an appointment to the Big Band Academy of America's Golden Bandstand at their annual reunion held March 2001 at the Sportsman's Lodge in Studio City, CA. His phone constantly rang with calls from old friends and requests to appear at music-related events. It was a well-deserved regiment for a self-taught musician who starting as a trumpet player in the Big Band Era made major contributions over the last eight decades to American art and entertainment through his music's role in film, radio, records, and television.

RAY MCKINLEY
75 YEARS WITH THE BIG BANDS

Few have contributed as much to the Big Band Era as Ray McKinley has. With his subtle and musical drumming and his humorous vocals he was a driving force behind the success of the Dorsey Brothers, Jimmy Dorsey, and Will Bradley bands into the early 1940s. During World War II he played a major role as a drummer and small group leader in Glenn Miller's Army Air Force Band. After the war he led his own musically innovative band for five years and the Glenn Miller ghost band for nearly ten years. Overall, McKinley was professionally involved with big bands for eight decades, stretching from the very early1920s until near his death in 1995. His number of accomplishments and the length of career most certainly qualify him for a prominent place in big band history.

Two major stars of the Big Band Era who developed close ties to Glenn Miller were born and raised in Fort Worth, TX. Raymond Frederick McKinley was born in the then cattle industry capital of the Southwest on June 18, 1910. He was followed four years later by Gordon "Tex" Beneke born February 12, 1914. The two did not associate with each other as McKinley had left Fort Worth to tour with a big band shortly before Beneke matriculated to Paschal High School.

Ray McKinley came from an established Texas family. His great-grandfather, Colonel Abe Harris, selected the site on the Trinity River for the original fort that developed into the city of Fort Worth. His father, Raymond Harris McKinley, owned a Fort Worth newspaper and for nine years managed the rodeo at the annual Fort Worth Stock Show and Southwestern Exposition. He is also credited with staging the first ever indoor rodeo. A low-keyed man of many interests, McKinley's father was also a county clerk and secretary of the Fort Worth Texas League baseball team that employed eventual Hall of Fame star Rogers Honrnsby as its batboy.

Drumming came naturally to McKinley even though he came from a nonmusical family. Without any formal music lessons, at around six years of age he took to playing a tin snare drum and made his first public appearance performing a snare drum solo that his father arranged for at an Elks Club Circus at the North Fort Worth Coliseum in front of several thousand people. It was also at this time that his slightly farsighted mother, Flora Newell McKinley, regularly took him to the local vaudeville house where she always sat in the first row to accommodate her myopic condition. Young McKinley was mesmerized by watching a pit show drummer named Johnny Grimes play just a few feet in front of him. He instantly fell in love with the drums.

When he was twelve years old McKinley launched his professional career playing with a local five-piece band called the Jolly Jazz Band that featured a girl piano player. Over the next few years he played with virtually every significant band in Fort Worth and was behind the drums at a 1925 Charleston competition at Fort Worth's Texas Hotel that was won by an ambitious teenage dancer named Ginger Rogers. A highlight of his early Fort Worth days was playing at a club called the Meadowmere in James Maloney's highly regarded band out of the University of Texas called Jimmie's Joys as a substitute for the drummer who suffered an appendicitis attack the previous evening. The next day he was asked to travel to Kansas City with the Orchestra for an Okeh recording session. McKinley's father would not let him out of school to go with the band. It was the last time his father refused him permission to leave his classes and Fort Worth.

In 1926 the Duncan-Marin Serenaders came through Fort Worth looking for a drummer. To account for the hyphen, Marin was the booking agent while Duncan led the band and played saxophone and sang. This time with his father's blessings, McKinley eagerly joined the band and left both school and Fort Worth for good at age fifteen to travel with them to Chicago to play at the Moulin Rouge nightclub where he received an unexpected sixteenth birthday surprise from a Chicago gangster.

While McKinley was playing with the Serenaders at the Moulin Rouge the night of June 16 a gangland fight broke out when a patron was pistol whipped right in front of the bandstand. Bullets started flying and McKinley was struck in the leg by a .45 caliber slug. The gangsters generously paid all medical expenses and put him up at the posh Palmer House Hotel to recuperate. McKinley used that recuperation period wisely. With the aid of crutches he made the rounds of all the top clubs in Chicago, seeing Louis Armstrong at the Sunset Café and Ben Pollack's band that included Benny Goodman and Glenn Miller at the Hotel Southmoor. McKinley met the guys in the band and several months later sat in with Pollack in Chicago at the Blackhawk Restaurant and impressed the ever-observant Miller with his drumming. It was an impression that would pay dividends just a few years later.

Beginning in 1927 McKinley embarked on a three-year odyssey that eventually took him to the hub of the big band world, New York City. His journey started when he left the Duncan-Marin Seranaders in El Paso to join the Nashville-based Beasley Smith Orchestra. In 1929 he went on to Pittsburgh and spent an enjoyable year or so playing with another hyphenated organization, the Tracy-Brown Orchestra. Tracy was the bass player and leader and Brown played violin. It was a larger orchestra that was very popular in the Pittsburgh area and had quality musicians such as Matty Matlock. Then came 1930 and a major career step forward to Manhattan.

Thanks to recommendations from friends in the Pollack band, McKinley landed a job with Milt Shaw's Detroiters, one of two house bands alternating in half-hour sets at the Roseland Ballroom. During his two-year stay at the Roseland with Shaw he had the unique opportunity to play opposite both the Fletcher Henderson and Chick Webb bands. Observing Chick Webb and Henderson's superb percussionist Walter Johnson perform proved to be a valuable learning experience for McKinley. He often stated that he began to effectively play cymbals after listening to the under-recognized Johnson play the hi-hat. During his Roseland days McKinley also managed to squeeze in two trips to England on the S.S. Leviathan with David Bernie's band. David was Ben Bernie's younger brother. But bereft of opportunities to move ahead with the Great Depression in high gear, McKinley was delighted when he received an unexpected call in the spring of 1932 from Glenn Miller, who remembered him from the night he sat in at the Blackhawk in Chicago, about an opening with the Smith Ballew Orchestra.

Smith Ballew was a tall, handsome vocalist who resembled Gary Cooper. He had some success leading his own hotel-style band but was unable to break through to the higher echelon of big bands. But good fortune came his way in 1932 when MCA, his booking agency, landed him a May 27 through July 21 engagement at the prestigious Palais Royale nightclub in Valley Stream, Long Island. Ballew realized he needed a topflight band so he called on master organizer Glenn Miller to put it together. The first musician Miller contacted was Ray McKinley, whom fellow Texan Ballew knew from back in Fort Worth. McKinley talked about his time with Ballew during a 1974 interview on Chuck Cecil's *Swingin' Years* radio show: "Those were the Depression years and we were trying to keep body and soul together. We would play a hotel then break up and a couple of months later play another hotel. They were good hotels, but it was a constant series of engagements and then layoffs until we broke up for good early in 1934."

It was Billy Goodheart, an MCA executive and good friend of Smith Ballew, who provided work, albeit sporadic, for the Ballew organization. He booked the band into the Cosmopolitan Hotel in Denver staring January 9, 1934. While in Denver Glenn Miller picked up three new members for the Ballew band from the Vic Schilling band that was playing at the Broadhurst Hotel. The three were saxophonist Skeets Herfurt, trombonist Don Matteson, and guitarist Roc Hillman. He also acquired vocalist Kay Weber who was singing with the Donnelly-James Orchestra at the Brown Palace Hotel. Roc Hillman tells what happened next during a conversation at his home in Woodland Hills, CA: "After the Cosmopolitan Hotel engagement ended on Valentine's Day the band headed east to New York. When we got there our booking was cancelled and we disbanded. That's when Glenn started talking with Tommy Dorsey about starting a new band. All the guys liked Smith and I'm glad he landed on his feet. He eventually wound up in Hollywood and made quite a few movies."

The new band that Hillman referred to was the Dorsey Brothers Orchestra that included Ray McKinley, the four Denver acquisitions, and Glenn Miller, who played trombone, functioned as the band's chief arranger, and assisted with its organization. It is considered by many to be one of the best of the early swing bands, and with McKinley driving the ensemble it did indeed solidly swing. The band started off with a series of one-nighters through New England in the spring of 1934 and wound up at the Sands Point Bath Club on Long Island for the summer season. Then Harvard student and future Big Band Era historian George T. Simon saw the band at one of its first appearances that spring at Nuttings-on-the-Charles in Waltham, MA. He was overwhelmed by both the buoyant new jazz-oriented sound of the band and McKinley's drumming and occasional spontaneous singing in lieu of drum breaks. Unfortunately, there were storm clouds on the horizon.

Jimmy and Tommy Dorsey squabbled with each other from the time they were children growing up together in Lansford, PA. Their bickering never stopped. It continued even after they formed the Dorsey Brothers Orchestra, so much so that Glenn Miller, who was frequently caught in the middle of their heated disputes that usually centered on a song's tempo, left to help Ray Noble organize a new orchestra. It all came to a head on Memorial Day 1935 at the Glen Island Casino in New Rochelle, NY, when Tommy suddenly stomped off the bandstand and left the entire Dorsey Brothers Orchestra that included McKinley to Jimmy. The brothers essentially remained estranged until they reunited to film *The Fabulous Dorseys* in 1947.

The Dorsey brothers did have definite contrasting temperaments. In a 1983 interview on Fred Hall's *Swing Thing* radio show, McKinley discussed their personalities: "Jimmy was relaxed and the easiest to get along with. Tommy either liked a fellow or he didn't. If you could play he would put up with a lot and not give you a hard time. If he didn't like you or if you couldn't play you wouldn't be there and if you were he would make it very uncomfortable. Tommy was impatient, always in a hurry, and he would let you feel it and know it."

Ray McKinley's four year tenure with the Jimmy Dorsey Orchestra that lasted until mid-1939 involved nearly equal time on the East and West Coasts. Soon after the Memorial Day breakup Dorsey landed the musical director position for Bing Crosby's *Kraft Music Hall* radio program that broadcast from Hollywood. In late 1935 McKinley drove to California with Dorsey's boy singer, Bob Eberly, for whom he had the highest regard both personally and professionally. The show debuted on January 2, 1936, kicking off an eighteen-month stay in Southern California.

It was an exciting time, what with the radio show and recordings with Bing Crosby, Dixie Lee Crosby, Frances Langford, Ginger Rogers, and his idol, Louis Armstrong. The band also played the sound track music of three movies and performed locally at the Palomar Ballroom. As for himself, McKinley recorded four songs in Los Angeles on March 31, 1936, with a six-piece group he called Ray McKinley's Jazz Band. Released several months later, *Metronome* rated them the best Dixieland recordings for 1937. But, all good things must come to an end.

Although he was well known, thanks to the *Kraft Music Hall* show, Dorsey was anxious to get back to the thriving milieu of the Big Band Era. The band bid adieu to the *Kraft Music Hall* in July 1937 and headed east to New York, performing in a series of cross-country one-nighters. During the remainder of McKinley's stay with Dorsey the band worked primarily on the East Coast with occasional travel to the Midwest, primarily Chicago. There was also considerable recording activity.

Starting in New York on September 19, 1935, the Jimmy Dorsey Orchestra actively recorded on Decca. McKinley sang a few novelty songs over the next few years, one of which, "The Love Bug," was a top ten hit in 1937. He also introduced vocal comments while laying down the beat. A classic example was his vocal interjection in "John Silver" when he shouted out "Fifteen men on a dead man's chest." "Parade of the Milk Bottle Caps" exemplifies his drumming skill and was always a crowd pleaser at live performances.

What do fellow Dorsey band members have to say about Ray McKinley? Trombonist Bobby Byrne played with McKinley from 1935 to 1939. He talked about McKinley during a telephone conversation from his home in Irvine, CA: "Ray was a first-rate drummer with marvelous natural rhythmic quality. He drove the band with musical taste and gave it a distinct flavor with his vocals and good humor. Ray was also a fine human being. When I joined the band he voluntarily took me aside and showed me how to play jazz. I've always considered him a dear friend and remember the many good times we had together. Ray also got along extremely well with Jimmy and was very loyal to him. Everyone in the band liked and professionally respected him."

Legendary big band booker Willard Alexander was responsible for Ray McKinley's departure from the Jimmy Dorsey Orchestra. In June of 1939 the keenly foresighted Alexander suggested to McKinley and trombone player Wilbur Schwichtenberg that they start their own band. The good-looking Schwichtenberg was a highly respected trombonist within the music business but little known by the general public. He played with McKinley in Milt Shaw's band then went on to Red Nichols and Ray Noble before he settled into anonymity working as a staff musician at CBS. Glenn Miller once said that he thought Schwichtenberg was the best all-around big band trombone player considering both quality of tone and versatility.

Having known each other well in Milt Shaw's Detroiters as roommates at the Belvedere Hotel, McKinley and Schwichtenberg agreed to work with Alexander and form a band. However, one problem remained to be solved. It was accommodating available billing space on theater marquees. The creative Alexander suggested that Scwichtenberg change his name to Will Bradley and call their new ensemble Will Bradley and His Orchestra featuring Ray McKinley. It was in effect a partnership organization with the two functioning as co-leaders, running contrary to the basic principles of organizational management. Alexander felt it best to give Bradley bandleader credit because trombone playing bandleaders such as Tommy Dorsey, Glenn Miller, Russ Morgan, and Jack Teagarden were in vogue.

Willard Alexander immediately went to work and secured financial backing and a Columbia recording contract. The band commenced practice at the Nola Studios in Manhattan and made its debut with Carlotta Dale as vocalist in the fall of 1939 at the Roseland State Ballroom in Boston with the moody "Fatal Fascination" as its theme song. During its two-and-a-half-year history the well-balanced band played the top hotels, theaters, and ballrooms in the country; broadcast its own weekly radio show; featured a six-piece band-within-a-band called the Texas Hot Shots;

appeared at Harlem's Savoy Ballroom; and charted eight hit records, five of which made the top ten. Although not its biggest hit, the crisply swinging "Celery Stalks at Midnight" is one of its most unique and a big band cult favorite. It is the recording in which McKinley shouts in falsetto the vocal break "Celery stalks along the highway." However, the band's major recording success and fame came from the rollicking boogie-woogie blues.

The eight-to-the-bar boogie-woogie piano style was first brought to significant public attention at John Hammond's 1938 *From Spirituals to Swing* Carnegie Hall concert with the appearances of Albert Ammons, Meade Lux Lewis, and Pete Johnson. However, the genre had met with only modest commercial success when the Bradley band started to specialize in it in early 1940. Their leap into boogie-woogie came about in large part because of the solid left-handed skill of pianist Freddie Slack, who came over to the Bradley band when it started from Jimmy Dorsey's band at McKinley's urging. The end result was a string of boogie-woogie recordings that included two blockbuster hits, "Beat Me, Daddy, Eight to the Bar" and "Scrub Me, Mama, With a Boogie Beat." Both featured down-home vocals by McKinley and peaked at number two on the charts. "Beat Me, Daddy" was 1940's twenty fourth best selling record; "Scrub Me, Mama" was 1941's nineteenth best seller. The two songs defined the orchestra. Soon after "Scrub Me, Mama" hit the top ten, Glenn Miller told McKinley that the band had the boogie-woogie market cornered. Unfortunately, their dominance of the idiom was not strong enough to keep the band together.

Back to basic management theory which states that an organization run with divided authority will not survive. This proved to be the case with the Bradley-McKinley association. By late 1941 co-leaders Bradley and McKinley developed a strong and basically unsolvable difference of opinion as to the band's musical direction. Bradley wanted a sweeter band with a Benny Goodman type of sound that would more prominently feature his smooth trombone on romantic ballads. McKinley thought the band should pursue its boogie-woogie bread and butter that that would showcase his vocal work and showmanship. It all came to a head when they amicably parted ways after playing the annual military ball at West Virginia University on February 16, 1942.

The professionally responsible McKinley did not leave Bradley in the lurch. He persuaded Shelly Manne to leave the Raymond Scott Orchestra and replace him on drums and vocals. Bradley continued on until June 1942 when he lost five of his men to the draft. With no recording contract and facing the constant pressure of replacing personnel lost to military service he disbanded in St. Paul, MN, and returned to studio work in New York where he carved out a very comfortable living. Ray McKinley's was a different story. He wasted no time and started to organize his own band immediately after he and Bradley formally dissolved in Alexander's office at the William Morris Agency for whom Alexander was then working.

The new Ray McKinley and his Orchestra debuted in April 1942 at the Commodore Hotel in Manhattan. His theme song was "Stop, Look and Listen." George T. Simon reviewed the opening for *Metronome* and gave the band a more than respectable A minus rating. He cited it as a strong swing band with a solid rhythmic beat and powerhouse brass section thanks in large part to both the lead and jazz trumpet work of seventeen-year-old Dick Cathcart. Simon also positively commented on both the band's attractive vocalist Imogene Lynn and use of tuba player Joe Park as a fifth man in the rhythm section who provided richness in tone coloring that helped identify McKinley's style of music.

The late trumpeter Pete Candoli played with nearly twenty big bands from 1940 well into the 1950s; one of those bands was Ray McKinley's 1942 organization. Candoli commented on his experience with McKinley at his home in Studio City, CA: "That was a solid swing band. I remember playing a solo on an excellent flag-waver Perry Burgett composed and arranged called

"Jive Bomber." Ray was a fine bandleader and well liked by everyone in the band. He was really a very funny guy and a good singer. The band was always well rehearsed and had it not been for the war would have gone far."

During its eight-month existence Ray McKinley and his Orchestra played prestigious venues on both the East and West Coasts. It also had a Capitol recording contract and generated a hit record, "Big Boy," with a vocal by Imogene Lynn along with a jukebox favorite, "Hard Hearted Hannah," which featured a classic Ray McKinley vocal. While in Hollywood, the band made the movie *Hit Parade of 1943* that also featured Count Basie and Freddy Martin. The future looked promising for McKinley, but with World War II raging, the military draft inevitably made its presence felt.

In late 1942 McKinley's band was playing at the Golden Gate Theater in San Francisco, when, within a few days of each other, seven band members, including McKinley, received their Greetings from Uncle Sam. McKinley had earlier proposed to the Marine Corps that the band join the Corps as a unit at Camp Pendleton. They even went so far as to take physicals in Los Angeles, but the project never materialized so McKinley joined the Army as a private. However, little did he imagine that all would turn out for the best thanks to his old friend, Glenn Miller.

McKinley returned home to Fort Worth for a few weeks then entered the Army on February 8, 1943, in Dallas and was assigned to Camp Wolters in Mineral Wells, TX. His first order of business was to get in touch with Miller who, when they spoke via telephone on January 13, 1943, told McKinley that as soon as he joined the Army to contact him for the drum chair in his military band. Miller used his clout, and on February 23, 1943, Ray McKinley arrived in Atlantic City, NJ, where musician service personnel were gathering for basic training prior to joining Glenn Miller's great Army Air Force Band (AAFB).

The AAFB was one of the finest musical organizations ever assembled. It was a forty-piece band with 21 strings that included musicians Miller hand picked from the top big bands and symphony orchestras. The band played jazz and pop numbers with equal skill driven by Miller's best ever rhythm section of bassist Trigger Alpert, pianist Mel Powell, guitarist Carmen Mastren, and percussionist McKinley. Skilled arrangers Jerry Gray, Norman Leyden, Mel Powell, and Ralph Norman Wilkinson worked with the band to create imaginative charts. It was a versatile ensemble that could execute a diversity of musical assignments with sophisticated style.

During March of 1943 musicians assigned to the AAFB reported to the Army Air Force Technical Training Command at Yale University where the band was organized and headquartered until it went overseas in June 1944. Its official duty was to provide military music for all Post functions that included daily retreat parades and review formations, mess hall luncheons, and weekly dances. Publicly, the band played at war bond rallies, military hospitals, Air-WAC recruiting drives, and traveled to New York every week to do the popular Saturday *I Sustain the Wings* radio show at the Vanderbilt Theater. It also recorded both a transcribed fifteen-minute program called *Uncle Sam Presents* and V-Discs for distribution to servicemen located outside the United States.

On top of playing in the AAFB, Ray McKinley was assigned additional responsibilities. Starting around August 1943 he organized a separate dance band that primarily used his civilian band's arrangements written by Perry Burgett. His band took over the duty of playing at messes and occasional dances. It also did a radio show called *Wings for Tomorrow* that was broadcast on a six station New England network. The show, that featured McKinley's sixteen-piece band with vocals by Artie Malvin and The Crew Chiefs, was structured to recruit soldiers for the Army Air Force in the New England area and ran from October 1943 to January 1944. He also occasionally led the AAFB band when Glenn Miller was not available. However, it was not all official duties. McKinley had some interesting unofficial musical and personal experiences during his time at Yale.

Musically, McKinley thought it a good idea to jazz up the conventional and repetitive marching music the band played on the way to official ceremonies where they performed only standard military music. He felt that the "St. Louis Blues" structure was ideal for drum adaptation so he and Perry Burgett tailored a marching beat to the song and renamed it "St. Louis Blues March." Tex Beneke used that arrangement and turned it into a top ten hit in 1948 with the postwar Glenn Miller Orchestra.

Personally, wedding bells rang when McKinley married Chicagoan Gretchen Haveman on May 15, 1943, at a ceremony held in Yale's Dwight Chapel. Haveman was a ballet dancer who toured with the Vincenzo Celli Ballet Company and was the line-captain in charge of the women in the chorus of Mike Todd's first musical, *Bring on the Girls*. They had a daughter, Jawn, who graduated with honors from Syracuse University and has had a dual career as an accomplished actress and professional recreational therapist.

Glenn Miller patriotically gave up the most successful of all the big bands to entertain our troops overseas. His wish came true in June 1944 when the AAFB sailed to the United Kingdom aboard the Queen Elizabeth which was converted to a troop transport ship for wartime duty. Miller flew ahead of the band and left band leading duties to entertain the troops on board the ship to Technical Sergeant Ray McKinley for the full duration of the six-day transatlantic crossing.

The AAFB arrived in London on June 29, 1944. It was the start of a backbreaking fourteen month tour of duty in England and Europe. In his book *Next to a Letter from Home* Geoffrey Butcher states that the band played 956 separate engagements in the European Theater of Operations that included 505 radio shows and 353 personal appearances to a total audience of one and a quarter million. They averaged three performances a day, frequently flying to each location in whatever military aircraft was available.

In addition to playing drums in the band, McKinley once again assumed extra duties. He led The American Dance Band whose primary responsibility was playing on the thirty-minute *The Swing Shift* radio show that was broadcast to troops of the Allied Expeditionary Forces. The band broadcast over 100 radio shows from July 1944 through May 1945. It also made several recordings. The American Dance Band was essentially the AAFB without strings. McKinley also played drums in The Uptown Hall septet that had their own fifteen-minute radio show and was involved in added AAFB band leading activities.

As he did at Yale University, McKinley led the AAFB in England when Glenn Miller was not present. When the AAFB traveled to France three days after Glenn Miller disappeared over the English Channel on December 15, 1944, its leadership was reorganized. Jerry Gray became responsible for arranging and the radio shows; Ray McKinley was responsible for fronting the band and emceeing. The popular McKinley also provided an unassigned and invaluable service. With Miller gone, he served as the spiritual leader of the band and its focal point of communication with military authority during its seven months of performing in Europe from its base in Paris.

While stationed in Paris with the AAFB McKinley took musical advantage of the local scene and jammed at Parisian jazz clubs with French musicians. He was also involved in small group recordings, one of which was with the renowned gypsy guitarist Django Reinhart. McKinley admired Reinhart's skill in playing the guitar with only three fingers on one hand, but he was not overly enthusiastic about the recordings themselves.

On August 12, 1945, the AAFB returned to the United States at New York aboard the S.S. Santa Rosa. As troops boarded the ship in LeHavre, France, on August 4 McKinley and the American Dance band provided a concert. Upon arrival home band members were given a thirty day furlough during which time McKinley recorded with the Bud Freeman Orchestra. In September he and Jerry Gray were presented Bronze Stars for their dedicated efforts in leading the AAFB after the disappearance of Glenn Miller. McKinley was discharged from military duty on October 27 at Mitchel Field, Long Island. His last official activity with the AAFB occurred on November 13, 1945, when he led the band at the Annual Concert for the National Press Club's Dinner for the President at the Hotel Statler in Washington, D.C., with President Harry S. Truman and General Dwight D. Eisenhower in attendance.

After the war the late Glenn Miller's personal manager Don Haynes approached McKinley about the possibility of his leading a re-organized Glenn Miller Orchestra that would play the music Miller made famous, but McKinley decided instead to form his own civilian band allowing him the flexibility to play selections of his choice. McKinley's new band made its first appearance during February 1946 in New York at the Commodore Hotel. In April, George T. Simon gave the band a positive review in *Metronome*, citing the cutting-edge arrangements of Eddie Sauter and the musicianship of saxophonist Peanuts Hucko and guitarist Mundell Lowe. During its five-year history it played all the prestigious big band locations and appeared on myriad late night remote radio broadcasts. Billed as The Most Versatile Band in the Land, its ability to play both swing and sweet music effectively allowed it to establish itself as a favorite for college proms, playing over one hundred formal spring dances during its existence. McKinley himself maintained a high profile, appearing in the 1949 film *Make Believe Ballroom*.

Featuring adventurous arrangements by Eddie Sauter, who Glenn Miller always felt was tunefully ahead of his time, supplemented by saxophonist Dean Kincaide's more conventional charts, the Ray McKinley Orchestra quickly became an outstanding musical ensemble that swung with sophistication and gathered rave reviews from musicians and critics, especially the late Leonard Feather. Sauter's brilliant scores of "Borderline," "Hangover Square," and "Tumblebug" were progressively avant-garde. McKinley was at his humorous, vocal best on novelties such as "Arizay," "Hoodle, Addle," "In the Land of the Buffalo Nickel," and "Red Silk Stockings and Green Perfume." On his catchy theme song "Howdy Friends" that he developed with the AAFB in England, McKinley introduced the key soloists in the band in rhyming couplet.

Notwithstanding poor-quality recording and promotion by the Majestic label before it switched to RCA in late 1947, the McKinley band did achieve recording success. Between 1947 and 1949 it charted 8 hit records, the most successful of which was "You Came a Long Way From St. Louis." During the Chuck Cecil interview McKinley told how the song came about by beating a strike deadline the evening of December 31, 1947: "We were recording just before midnight while we were playing at the Paramount Theater because Petrillo's recording ban was going into effect on January 1. We didn't have a final song ready and then Artie Malvin turned up with this tune a guy had written called "You Came a Long Way From St. Louis." We just took the rhythm section and went in the next room and outlined it and came back just in time to record it. It turned out to be our biggest hit of all."

Musicians enjoyed playing in the band. Mundell Lowe talked about his three years with McKinley from his home in San Diego: "I met John Hammond in the army and we became good friends and spent a lot of time together. I got back home to Louisiana from military service in time for Christmas 1945. On Christmas day I got a call from John and Ray asking if I wanted to join the band. I said yes and left for New York. We rehearsed for a few weeks and went out on the road. It was a wonderful band. All went well and everyone quickly became good friends.

Eddie Sauter's arrangements featured me on the guitar a lot and that gave me good exposure. Ray served in Europe and I in the South Pacific, so we developed a father-son relationship. I created a name for myself with the band and stayed friends with Ray for life."

Don Kennedy summed up the postwar state of the big bands during a 2004 feature on Ray McKinley on his *Big Band Jump* radio show: "Jiminy Crickets" was one of McKinley's Eddie Sauter arrangements. It should have been intensely popular, but there was a factor working against it. It was the fact that the big bands were fading after the war." With the market for big bands rapidly declining and restless to tackle new projects, McKinley disbanded in 1951 and spent the next five years freelancing around the New York area from his home in Stamford, CT. It was a busy and exhilarating period filled with a diversity of activities that included forays into new avenues of entertainment.

The new medium of television took up much of McKinley's time during the first half of the 1950s. He appeared on local New York ABC and NBC television stations as a bandleader, vocalist, show host, weatherman, and made guest appearances on the musical TV variety show *Music at the Meadowbrook* that featured Frank Dailey. There were more New York stints as a radio disc jockey and with big bands at the Roseland Ballroom and the Paramount Theater. McKinley also performed in jazz bands in gigs in Chicago and Las Vegas and recorded on Decca, Dot, and Grand Award. Then in 1956 yet another Glenn Miller related opportunity came his way.

In 1946 Tex Beneke assumed the leadership of the newly formed Glenn Miller estate band, but by late 1950 Beneke and the estate developed a difference of opinion as to the band's musical direction. As a result, Beneke struck out on his own and the Miller estate band became inactive. Then with the huge popularity of the 1954 film *The Glenn Miller Story* and the success of Miller style bands led by Ray Anthony and Ralph Flanagan, Willard Alexander prodded the Miller estate to reactivate the dormant Glenn Miller band. Ray McKinley was the logical choice and this time he was eager and ready to assume control.

The new Glenn Miller Orchestra officially started performing on June 6, 1956, with a tour of six Midwestern states and Canada. During McKinley's nine and a half years with the Orchestra it met with great success. It recorded ten albums, eight on RCA Victor and two on Epic. All sold well. Under McKinley its popularity took it internationally to England, Europe, Japan, North Africa, and the Far East. In fact, the Orchestra has the notoriety of being the first postwar band to play behind the Iron Curtain in 1957 in Warsaw, Poland. However, travel in Eastern Europe was not without excitement. While going from a cancelled concert in Prague to Vienna the entire band was locked in a train car on a railroad siding for several hours without food or water.

There was also considerable television work. The Orchestra was a featured regular on two coast-to-coast musical variety shows, *Be Our Guest* in 1960 and *Glenn Miller Time* in 1961, along with individual guest appearances on the *Johnny Carson*, *Patti Page*, and *Ed Sullivan Shows*. There is excellent DVD footage of the *Glenn Miller Time* show with Johnny Desmond singing that is included in the CD/DVD set, *Glenn Miller, The Centennial Collection 100*. When not traveling overseas, the Orchestra was constantly on the road. The grueling physical demands of performing in a new city night after night and virtually living on the band bus eventually took its toll on McKinley. He led the Orchestra for the last time on January 5, 1966, at the Mark Twain Riverboat in New York, passing leadership of the Orchestra to clarinetist Buddy DeFranco.

After his departure from the Glenn Miller Orchestra, McKinley segued into a well-deserved semi-retirement. He relocated to Largo, FL, and until well into the 1980s appeared annually at the Disneyland Big Band Series in California with bands contracted by his good friend, trumpeter Art DePew, who still remembers McKinley's patience in mentoring young musicians in those bands. In 1971 he served as a consultant for Walt Disney World in Orlando and played there on several occasions through the mid 80s. His hobbies were golf, reading all genres of literature, and listening to the music of his favorite musician, Louis Armstrong. There was also business and personal travel. McKinley appeared in Australia twice, on a 1985 BBC television special in England with Peanuts Hucko and Zeke Zarchy, and was frequently a featured personality on big band cruises. Starting in the early 1980s, he and Gretchen regularly traveled between their homes in Florida and the Canadian Province of Ontario.

McKinley's longtime association with the legacy of Glenn Miller also kept him busy. For several years starting in 1973 he appeared in tours produced by Tom Sheils saluting Glenn Miller that also included Cab Calloway, Ray Eberle, and The Modernaires with Paula Kelly. McKinley also took great pride in his involvement with the National Museum of the United States Air Force located near Dayton, OH. He worked closely with then curator Royal Frey to establish a Glenn Miller AAFB exhibit at the Museum that opened in July 1976. In conjunction with the Museum, he played with the United States Air Force Airmen of Note at numerous Miller concerts and celebrated his eightieth birthday there in 1990 performing "Anvil Chorus" in a program that included Peanuts Hucko and Louise Tobin. A staunch supporter of Public Television, McKinley sang and played drums in the 1989 PBS special *The Glenn Miller Big Band Reunion*. His last public appearance occurred in December 1994 during an Airmen of Note tribute to Glenn Miller at Constitution Hall in Washington D.C. where he was honored for his work with the AAFB. The concert was held on the 50th anniversary of Miller's disappearance in a flight across the English Channel. McKinley passed away on May 7, 1995, eight days short of his fifty-second wedding anniversary. He preceded Gretchen by three years.

Ray McKinley is still fondly remembered by big band enthusiasts and the Glenn Miller community. He is also historically valued. In his biography of Buddy Rich titled *Traps, The Drum Wonder*, Mel Tormé lists McKinley as one of the great hi-hat cymbal experts of the 30s and 40s and states that Rich himself thought McKinley a superb musical drummer. In *Drummin' Men*, Burt Korall's fascinating tribute to the great drummers of the Swing Era, Korall discusses the careers of seven percussionists in depth. McKinley is one of those seven. All in all, Ray McKinley's greatest accomplishment just might be his career longevity. Starting at twelve years of age in 1922 he was professionally involved with big bands as a drummer, singer, and leader until he died just short of eighty five in 1995. Few have advanced the cause of big band music and impacted our American cultural history as Ray McKinley, a true drumming legend.

GLENN MILLER RALLIES ENGLAND
DURING WORLD WAR II

The name Glenn Miller is synonymous with the Big Band Era. Miller's band was far and away the most popular, generating blockbuster hits and securing the top bookings throughout the country. However, his contributions to the Era were not purely musical. He provided much-needed wartime relief to England shoring up morale during the later stages of World War II immediately before his death in a plane crash over the English Channel on December 15, 1944.

Before we talk about Miller's war efforts, a bit of history is in order. Alton Glenn Miller was born in 1904 in Clarinda, IA, the location of a museum in his honor. After brief moves to Missouri and Nebraska, his family settled in Fort Morgan, CO, where he graduated from high school and was honored as an all-state end on the football team. He went on to attend the University of Colorado, leaving in 1923 with trombone in hand to seek his musical fortune.

Miller eventually headed west to Los Angeles, receiving his first big break when he joined the Ben Pollack band there in 1925. Pollack's was one of the top bands of the 1920s and over the years launched the careers of such big band greats as Benny Goodman and Harry James.

After leaving Pollack in 1928, Miller settled in New York where he was in demand as an arranger, free-lance trombonist on recording sessions, and musician in Broadway pit orchestras. Although the money was good, he longed to start his own band which he did in 1937, failing miserably.

He reorganized in 1938 and sputtered along until the spring of 1939 when he hit the big time in popularity at Frank Dailey's Meadowbrook in Cedar Grove, NJ, followed by an equally successful summer engagement at the prestigious Glen Island Casino in New Rochelle, NY. The heavy coast-to-coast air time generated from remote radio broadcasts at both locations made him a household name.

The rest is musical history. big band standards such as "In the Mood" and "Chattanooga Choo Choo," two featured movies, his own radio show, and constantly sold-out venues made his the most popular big band in the world.

It all came to an end in September 1942, at the Central Theater in Passaic, NJ, when with true patriotic intent, Miller announced he was dissolving his phenomenally successful orchestra to join the Army as a captain. He spent 1943 at Yale University in New Haven, CT, organizing his famed Army Air Force Band, shipped out to England in June of 1944, and was promoted to major in August.

Glenn Miller's first bout with fate came soon after he arrived in England, and he luckily won. That summer Miller and his musicians were headquartered in a house at 25 Sloane Court in London in an area known as Buzz Bomb Alley. On Sunday, July 2, burdened with responsibility for the well being of the men he recruited, Miller moved the band to quarters 50 miles outside of London. The next day, July 3, a buzz-bomb hit directly in front of the building Miller evacuated the previous day killing twenty-five military personnel.

While in England the Army Air Force Band conducted a back-breaking schedule of daily radio broadcasts on the BBC and live concerts throughout the British Isles for troops stationed at military bases. It was at this time that Miller became a legend in England.

Tony Dicks grew up in Liverpool and lived through numerous blitzes. Around 1960 he moved to La Canada, CA, and was active in the British United Services Club as the organization's president.

"There is no doubt that Glenn Miller was the most popular American entertainer stationed in England during the war," Dicks said during a telephone interview. "In fact, he is more popular than ever in England today and probably more respected than in the United States."

Jack Gordon who lived in Yorkshire during the war was the longtime manager of the popular Ye Olde Kings Head Pub and Restaurant in Santa Monica, CA. Gordon succinctly sums up Miller's contributions: "To put it simply, Glenn Miller pulled England through 1944."

From a musical perspective, Miller's contributions in England were revolutionary.

Vince Carbone played tenor saxophone with the Army Air Force Band in England. He passed away in 1997 in Woodland Hills, CA, where he was serving as a personal manager to several celebrities including Frank Sinatra Jr. and working on a book on his experiences with the band.

"A major part of Miller's overseas success was that the Army Air Force Band was the first American style swing big band to be heard in England," Carbone commented shortly before his passing. "It was something new, and the country went wild over our BBC broadcasts."

Carbone went on to state that many band members developed lifelong friendships with fans they met while playing in England. He also said: "Final proof of Miller's impact is that there are more big bands playing Glen Miller style music in England today than in the United States."

Major Glenn Miller had his rematch with fate on December 15, 1944. This time he lost.

December 15 was an overcast, drizzly, near-freezing day, the day Miller took off from Bedford, England, in a single-engine plane to fly to Paris to make arrangements for his Army Air Force Band's first appearance on European soil. The plane went down somewhere over the English Channel. There are numerous theories as to what caused Miller's plane to crash, but none have yet to be substantiated.

Not only did Glen Miller lose his life on that cold day over the English Channel, but the Big Band Era lost its heart and soul and the citizens of England lost their guiding light of wartime spirit.

GLENN MILLER LAUNCHES HIS
BANDLEADING CAREER IN 1937

What do film animation pioneer Walt Disney, automobile manufacturer Henry Ford, candy bar magnate William Hershey, and bandleader Glenn Miller have in common? The correct answer is that all four were unsuccessful in their first business venture.

There is no doubt that the name most commonly associated with the romantic glamour of the Big Band Era is Glenn Miller. He dominated the record charts from 1939 to 1942 and became a still-revered household name in England by entertaining allied troops on British soil in 1944. However, few are aware that the first band Miller formed in 1937 ended in failure. In light of this entrepreneurial debacle, a discussion of his little-recognized 1937 band is in order.

By late 1936 the thirty-two-year-old Miller had acquired an impressive professional resume as an arranger and musician. His credentials included arranging and playing trombone for two years with Ben Pollack, playing in Broadway pit and radio studio orchestras, recording with Red

Nichol's Five Pennies and Benny Goodman's early bands, arranging for the Smith Ballew and Dorsey Brothers bands, and organizing British bandleader Ray Noble's orchestra that was a huge draw at the elegant Rainbow Room on the sixty-fifth and top floor of the Rockefeller Center's RCA Building. Miller had more than paid his dues and was ready to strike out on his own.

With the assistance of *Metronome* magazine editor and Swing Era authority George T. Simon, Miller went about the task of hiring and molding musicians for his first band, rehearsing at the Haven Studio located on 54th Street between Sixth and Seventh Avenues in Manhattan. Notwithstanding his reputation as a rigid perfectionist, Miller exhibited saint-like patience in working with the musicians he hired.

Miller's first recording date took place in March 1937 when he waxed six sides at a Decca recording session arranged by Rockwell-O'Keefe, the band's booking agent. Although well played and arranged, the cuts met with little commercial success and went unnoticed as they were conventional period-pieces, typical but not unique in style.

The band played its first live engagement on May 7, a one-nighter in the Terrace Room of the Hotel New Yorker, substituting for Gus Arnheim's band that had an aspiring young pianist from Los Angeles named Stan Kenton. Next came their first steady engagement, a two week stint at the Raymor Ballroom in Boston, an aging ballroom on Huntington Avenue with a loyal clientele.

By now it was June, and Miller had a second recording session, this time with Brunswick. Although he recorded more up-to-date material in a swing vein, one of the cuts sounded very much like that of Benny Goodman, his old friend whom he met when they were in the Ben Pollack band in Los Angeles in 1925. Record sales were negligible.

Also in June, Seymour Weiss, President of the Roosevelt Hotel in New Orleans, booked Miller into his famed Blue Room for a two week engagement beginning on the 17th. Miller proved so popular in the Crescent City that his stay was extended through the end of August for a ten week run, handily breaking the old Blue Room house record of five consecutive weeks for a band engagement. The 1937 Miller band had achieved what was to be its high point.

Although Miller was a resounding success in New Orleans, two events occurred there that did not bode well for the band's future. First, after all expenses were covered, Miller wound up with an operating loss for the entire engagement. Second, he hired a brilliant, rotund, hard-drinking clarinetist, Irving Prestopnik, better known as Irving Fazola, who had less than a sobering effect on his fellow band members.

Miller's band left New Orleans and went on to play at the Adolphus Hotel in Dallas and the Hotel Nicollet in Minneapolis. He did not replicate the degree of success he achieved at the Blue Room; both hotels failed to exercise their options to extend his stay. Most important, the band continued to operate at a loss with Miller pumping in his own money to meet expenses.

With little recent success and a mounting personal debt, Miller returned to the Raymor in Boston thanks to the largess of manager Hughie Galvin who liked Miller and was willing to take him back. However, he barely broke even and was unable to reduce his personal debt. Two more recording dates with Brunswick followed in November and December. Unfortunately, the recordings had no commercial success. It was the beginning of the end.

December 1937 was unkind to Miller both professionally and personally. His musical style demanded tight precision, and he was unable to achieve that precision due to constant personnel turnover in the band. Exacerbating the problem was heavy drinking by several of his musicians, one of whom demolished one of the two cars the band used for transportation.

It appeared Miller might get a break when he got a coast-to-coast radio hook up on Boston's NBC affiliate WBZ. Even that much-desired opportunity fizzled when the band failed to generate audience interest. The band's bookings also heavily conspired against any chance of success. They were playing grueling one-night stands traveling from town to town in the dead of winter through snow and on icy roads, with no future engagements scheduled that had any chance of bringing the band the level of recognition needed to break through to the big time.

Finally, Miller's personal financial situation was at low ebb, with having futilely sunk by some accounts close to $20,000 into the band. To put his losses in historical perspective, the world champion New York Yankees paid Joe DiMaggio $17,500 to play center field in 1937.

On a personal note, Miller's wife Helen had major surgery rendering her unable to have children. As is the case in most film biographies, there were many inaccuracies in the popular 1954 movie the *Glenn Miller Story*. However, the tender affection Glenn and Helen Miller showed each other as portrayed by Jimmy Stewart and June Allyson was totally accurate, they were a most devoted couple. Helen's surgery was a major blow to Miller and her recovery weighed heavily on him.

It all came to an end on New Year's Eve at the Valencia Ballroom in York, PA, when Miller made the decision to disband. They played their final date on January 2 at the Ritz Ballroom in Bridgeport, CT. So ended Glenn Miller's first attempt to lead a band.

Ever the tenacious competitor who could not accept defeat, Miller regrouped and started a new band in March 1938. With more reliable and sober sidemen that were younger and easier to manage, better bookings provided by Rockwell-O'Keefe, generous financing from legendary ballroom impresario Cy Shribman, and the final evolution of the of the famous Miller sound of a clarinet lead over four saxophones, Miller was on the road to success.

At a public event the former The Walt Disney Company CEO and Chairman of the Board Michael Eisner once said: "In business you cannot succeed without experiencing failure." Eisner's philosophy could not better be applied than to the career of Glenn Miller.

1939 - GLENN MILLER'S BREAKTHROUGH YEAR

Behavioral psychologists unanimously agree that perseverance, the ability to forge ahead in spite of adversity and difficulty, is one of the key traits necessary to succeed in any line of business. The most famous of all Big Band Era personalities, Glenn Miller, unswervingly persevered for over two years as a bandleader before he meteorically rose to fame and fortune in 1939. His arduous climb to success is a testimony to tenaciously carrying on in spite of what appeared to be insurmountable odds.

After nearly fifteen years in the music business as a trombone player, Broadway pit orchestra musician, arranger, and organizer of several successful bands, Glenn Miller started his own orchestra in January 1937. Unfortunately, he met with ill success. Saddled with hard-drinking and hard-to-control musicians, poor bookings, no truly refined and distinctive sound, and rapidly mounting financial losses, he disbanded in January 1938.

Miller spent February playing Raleigh cigarette radio commercials in his old friend Tommy Dorsey's band. Then in March, still convinced he had the ability to succeed, he made the monumental decision to try once again. With financial help from his wife Helen's parents, who took out a second mortgage on their home, Miller formed his second band and started rehearsals at the Haven Studio in Manhattan.

This time around Miller hired younger musicians whom he could teach to play his way. Two of his new musicians proved to be of particular importance. The first was Willie Schwartz, who was discovered by then *Metronome* big band writer George T. Simon while playing in the Julie Wintz band in Newark, NJ. Schwartz skillfully played the clarinet lead over four saxophones that was to give the Miller band its famous, unique sound.

Next came featured tenor saxophone player and occasional vocalist Gordon "Tex" Beneke, who was hired on the recommendation of Miller's old friend, Gene Krupa. Beneke would go on to achieve considerable fame as the band's major personality. After returning from World War II he remained enormously popular leading bands in the Miller style until he passed away in 2000.

Two important full time vocalists also joined the band in 1938. Ray Eberle, brother of Jimmy Dorsey's acclaimed vocalist Bob Eberly, came aboard early on. Soon after, Marion Hutton made the switch from the Vincent Lopez Band, with which she was singing at the Ritz-Carlton Hotel in Boston with her sister, Betty. She was only seventeen, so Glenn and Helen Miller assumed her legal guardianship.

Ray Eberle's entry into the Miller organization is an interesting story. In May, Jimmy Dorsey was playing at the Terrace Room of the Hotel New Yorker. One evening Miller was in the audience sitting next to Dorsey's manager chatting while Dorsey was on stage with Bob Eberly singing. Eberly's teenage brother Ray, who had never sung professionally before, was in New York visiting Bob. He walked by their table and Miller did an instant double take because he looked identical to his sibling. Dorsey's manager told Miller it was Bob's brother. Miller immediately sensed opportunity and asked Ray to come to a rehearsal the next day. He sang a few songs and Miller offered him a job at $35 a week. Eberle, who was still in high school, immediately called his father in upstate New York for his blessings.

Eberle stayed with Miller until mid-1942. In a 1970 interview with big band radio personality Chuck Cecil, he stated that he left the band during an engagement at the Hotel Sherman in Chicago because of a disagreement with Miller over compensation for his appearance in the film *Orchestra Wives*. Ray Eberle was a major contributor to the band's success recording eleven number one hits, the biggest of which was "Moonlight Cocktail" that was at the top of the charts for ten consecutive weeks in early 1942. He died from a sudden heart attack at his Douglasville, GA, home in 1979.

On April 16, the band opened at the Raymor Ballroom in Boston, a venue Miller frequently played with his first band in 1937. Then in mid-June, Miller secured a much desired, steady New York engagement at the Paradise Restaurant at 49th Street and Broadway. The Paradise was a magnet for visiting salesmen, and featured a six-piece novelty band called Freddie Fisher and his Schnickelfritzers. Although Miller was given second billing to the Schnickelfritzers, he at least received valuable exposure in New York and was featured on coast-to-coast radio broadcasts several times a week.

Come fall, Miller was once again experiencing both financial difficulties and slim prospects, but good fortune was to soon come his way. That fortune was to arrive in the personage of Cy Shribman. An outwardly jovial and physically substantial man, Schribman was one of the legendary personalities of the Big Band Era.

Boston-based Cy and his brother Charlie started out running ballrooms in New England in the 1920s. When they found a band they believed in, they would provide financing against a percentage of the band's profits. Tommy Dorsey, Woody Herman, and Artie Shaw were among the many bands that benefited from the Shribman's shrewd investment decisions.

Shribman liked Miller and provided work for him at college dates and the New England ballrooms the brothers owned, including Boston's Roseland-State Ballroom. However, to make it to the top Miller knew playing in New York was a must, so he returned to the Paradise Restaurant in December.

Miller's stint at the Paradise that ended in January proved to be a major turning point. In addition to very well-received air time at the reveling out-of-town salesman's Mecca, Miller squeezed in a Christmas dance at Iona Prep in New Rochelle, NY. The young booker of the band who obtained Miller's services through Charlie Shribman's New York representative was Tom Sheils, a recent Notre Dame graduate whose father was a New York State Supreme Court Justice. Sheils was so impressed with the band's performance that he immediately went to the management of the famed Glen Island Casino in New Rochelle to recommend Miller as the next summer season's featured band. He soon moved on to handle Miller's business affairs and after the war carved out a career as a highly successful personal manager in Hollywood. Things were starting to look up for Glenn Miller.

It was also around this time that Miller discovered a shy, reserved young arranger from Rumson, NJ, who was a close high school friend and neighbor of the late Nelson Riddle. His name was Bill Finegan, and he would go on to become a major contributor to Miller's book with his creative arrangements that included Miller's first up-tempo swing hit in 1939, "Little Brown Jug." In the 1950s he would team with Eddie Sauter to form the innovative Sauter-Finegan Orchestra.

Frequently good news comes in spades, and indeed it did for Glenn Miller in early 1939 when in February he was informed that the band had been booked into Frank Dailey's Meadowbrook for a March engagement. Then came the corker. While the band was rehearsing at the Haven Studio on Wednesday, March 1, Miller's thirty-fifth birthday, he was notified that he was selected to play the Glen Island Casino for the summer season. A summer at Glen Island was the single most prestigious big band booking in the country. All those one-night stands, radio broadcasts from the Paradise, and the indefatigable booking efforts of Cy Shribman finally paid off.

Few ballrooms represent the essence of the Big Band Era better than the Meadowbrook, located in Cedar Grove, NJ. With the announcers introducing each of several weekly radio broadcasts with "This program comes to you from Frank Dailey's Meadowbrook on the Newark-Pompton Turnpike, Route 23 at Cedar Grove, NJ," the ballroom was nationally known to all big band enthusiasts.

Miller opened on March 5 and was an immediate smash hit, so much so that Dailey extended his contract from four to seven weeks. While at the Meadowbrook, Miller met another person of fame in big band lore, George "Bullets" Durgom, a short, prematurely bald, superb dancer who was the nerve center of the Meadowbrook. His stamp of approval was necessary for any band to make it at the Meadowbrook, and he instantly became a Glenn Miller devotee. Durgom would go on to work for Miller as his band boy and eventually land in Hollywood as a top personal manager handling the likes of Jackie Gleason. He passed away in 1992.

It was all coming together quickly. In April, Miller had the first two of a phenomenal nineteen top ten 1939 hits, "Sunrise Serenade" and his haunting theme "Moonlight Serenade." They were the A and B sides of the same record. Of those nineteen hits, seven reached the number one position on the charts. The biggest hit of his career, "In The Mood," initially charted in October 1939. It was on the hit parade for thirty consecutive weeks with twelve of those weeks as number one. He was the year's top recording artist, hands down.

Next on the agenda was the Glen Island Casino, located on Long Island Sound. With a sweeping view of the Sound and boats bobbing on the water with their lights blinking at night, it was without a doubt the most romantic of the big band ballrooms. Of prime importance, with a slew of national radio broadcasts any band playing there was virtually guaranteed to become famous. The Casa Loma, Ozzie Nelson, the Dorsey Brothers, Charlie Barnet, and Larry Clinton with his vocalist Bea Wain all made their initial mark playing the summer season at the Casino,

Miller opened on May 17. George T. Simon attended the event squiring a then unknown and aspiring young vocalist named Dinah Shore. In his definitive biography of Miller, *Glenn Miller and His Orchestra*, Simon recalled that was the evening Miller chose to introduce his famous Something Old, Something New, Something Borrowed, Something Blue medley format.

Miller's engagement was a sensation. According to his pianist and close friend, Chummy MacGregor, the response of the Glen Island Casino waiters to a band was a key indicator of that band's acceptance. During a Chuck Cecil radio interview MacGregor said the service staff snapped their fingers while waiting on the clientele when the band was playing and attended rehearsals on their own time. They loved Miller's music.

What with recording sessions with RCA Victor and nightly shows at the Casino, the pace was intense, so much so that late in July Marion Hutton collapsed on the bandstand from exhaustion and had to be hospitalized for observation for over a week. Miller brought in a sixteen-year-old singer from Memphis, TN, named Kay Starr to substitute for her. Starr was to go on to a highly successful recording career of her own starting in the late 1940s.

Miller closed at the Casino on Wednesday, August 23, with the packed house throwing a party for the band, a first for the ballroom. Few big bands ever capitalized on a Glen Island Casino booking as did Glenn Miller.

After the Casino, Miller played a series of East Coast one-nighters, breaking attendance records wherever he appeared. He next moved on to the theater circuit with an appearance at the Paramount Theater in Times Square. His stint there was of such success that the Paramount management booked him in advance for 1940.

Miller had achieved outstanding commercial success. But on October 6 he also received the official professional respect of his peers when he played along with three other famous bands at venerable Carnegie Hall. According to George T. Simon, the band created even more of a sensation than its competition on that night that included Benny Goodman, Fred Waring, and Paul Whiteman.

It was back to the Meadowbrook in November where Miller hired Artie Shaw's arranger Jerry Gray who was without a job when Shaw suddenly broke up his band and sojourned to Mexico for a pause from the music business. Gray worked perfectly with Miller and wrote several of band's major hits. Two of the biggest were "Pennsylvania 6-5000" and his most famous composition, "A String of Pearls."

Miller closed the year signing a contract with Chesterfield cigarettes to appear three times a week on his own *Moonlight Serenade* radio show. He began the series on December 27, 1939, followed by a three-month engagement at the Cafe Rouge of the Hotel Pennsylvania in Manhattan that started on January 4, 1940. Glenn Miller was now the most famous bandleader in the world.

From a historical perspective, Miller's sudden and unexpected rise to fame in 1939 was equivalent to the pandemonium associated with Elvis Presley's breakthrough in 1956 and the Beatles invasion of the United States in 1964. Glenn Miller finally made it, once again proving that perseverance is indeed a very desirable trait to possess to successfully compete in the world of business.

ALVINO REY AND THE KING SISTERS
A BLOCKBUSTER COMBINATION

In American popular history, certain names will be forever associated. In comedy there is Abbot and Costello, in boxing Louis and Schmeling, in romance DiMaggio and Monroe, and in the world of big bands Alvino Rey and the King Sisters. Here is the story of how a pioneering electric guitarist and female vocal quartet became forever linked in public recognition during the Big Band Era.

In February 1907 William King Driggs arrived in the Mormon colony town of Sanford, CO, from Provo, UT. His middle name, the name he preferred to use, was in honor of Utah's United States Senator William H. King, who was engaged to Driggs's very attractive sister Ella. Sadly, Ella died just a few days before they were to be married. An all-around musician and baritone vocalist, he was hired to teach music at the local school and hoped to save enough to return to Provo and complete his education at Brigham Young University.

His first day in Sanford, Driggs met Pearl Mortensen at the town's general store. She was the last of twelve children of a respected local family. They married a year later after he obtained his degree from Brigham Young and produced eight children, two boys and six girls; all six girls would at one time or another sing as part of The King Sisters. In order of birth, the Driggs children were Karleton (1910), Maxine (1911), Luise (1913), Alyce (1915), Donna (1918), Yvonne (1920), Billy (1923), and Marilyn, an afterthought, born a decade later.

After teaching in numerous Mormon colony towns and writing and presenting his own operettas and plays, Driggs formed the Driggs Family of Entertainers in 1922. They performed for the first time at the Lyric Movie Theater in Sanataquin, UT. King Driggs played C-melody saxophone, sang deep bass solos, and directed the group on stage. Each child played a musical instrument. Some of the children danced, recited monologues, and sang together. Pearl, ever the perfect lady, played the cello sidesaddle and performed dramatic readings. The show was a smashing success, and word about the Driggs family act spread like wildfire through Mormon communities.

The Driggs contingent relocated to Los Angeles in 1923 and soon started performing throughout California, traveling packed together in a Graham Paige automobile that replaced their old, second-hand, windowless Dodge. After a brief stint touring through Colorado and Utah in the late 1920s, they returned to the Los Angeles area in 1929, settling in Glendale. They were unknowingly positioning themselves for what would be the breakthrough to fame for the Driggs sisters a year later.

By 1930 Maxine, Luise, and Alyce had become a popular vocal trio, singing at all Glendale High School events. Their inspiration was the three Boswell Sisters. With the Great Depression ravaging the country, they decided to help supplement the family income by singing professionally. The sisters arranged what was an unsuccessful try-out at Los Angeles radio station KFWB. However, thanks to the efforts of their cousin Golden Driggs, who lived in San Francisco, they landed an audition for an opening at San Francisco's KGO. At the time KGO was the main studio for NBC on the West Coast.

The try-out did not go well. They did not pass, but there was still hope. As a backup, Golden had lined up an audition at KLX across the Bay in Oakland. This time the girls were at their best and landed a $25-a-week job to do three fifteen-minute shows each week. The station also suggested they change their name from The Driggs Sisters to a catchier professional name. The King Sisters were officially born.

After a little over a year with KLX, the sisters were offered $50 a week by powerful 50,000-watt KSL in Salt Lake City, thanks in part to the efforts of their Aunt Golda who lived across the street from station president Earl J. Glade. It was an opportunity to be heard by a much larger audience. Then in 1932 they received a telegram from Horace Heidt offering them a two-week try-out for his orchestra that was playing at the Golden Gate Theater in San Francisco. They passed with flying colors, joined Heidt's organization, and would meet his soon to be hired tall, good-looking guitar player, Alvino Rey.

Alvino Rey was born Alvin McBurney on July 1, 1908, in Oakland, CA. He exhibited an early interest in electronics, earning a ham radio operators license when he was only eight years old. In 1921 the McBurneys moved from their Piedmont, CA, home to Cleveland where McBurney's father established a typewriter business. Soon after moving, young Alvin requested a saxophone for a Christmas present. Concerned that the saxophone's mouthpiece was unsanitary, his mother gave him a banjo instead. It was the start of a lifelong career in music.

By 1927 McBurney was playing banjo professionally in the Cleveland area with Ev Jones's band. His prowess on the instrument created a dilemma when he graduated from Lakewood High School in 1928 as told by Rey on Don Kennedy's *Big Band Jump* radio show in 1991: "I never expected to get into music. I was going to go to Stanford or MIT to study engineering and work in the electronics industry. But somehow I never got out of the music business."

Right after graduation McBurney opted to go to New York in lieu of college to replace banjoist Eddie Peabody in Phil Spitalny's band. Spitalny had a popular dance band that received good radio exposure playing at the Hotel Pennsylvania. In 1934 he went on to form and gain fame with his all-girl Hour of Charm Orchestra.

It was while he was in New York at the urging of his visiting father that McBurney changed his name to Alvino Rey. He also consorted with his idol guitarist Eddie Lang, formally studied with Joseph Schillinger, and branched out to master the Hawaiian and Spanish guitars. His interest in the Spanish guitar grew to the extent that he would study under Andres Segovia at three different classical guitar seminars in Europe.

Not long after the 1929 Stock Market Crash, Spitalny left the Pennsylvania and Rey headed back to San Francisco where he joined the KGO NBC Orchestra that was led by Meredith Wilson. Harold Perry, who would go on to fame as the Great Gildersleeve, was also starting his career in radio at the station. He became Rey's close friend and attended Donna King's wedding in 1942. Rey quickly developed a reputation as a showstopper on the guitar and caught the attention of Horace Heidt. Presented a lucrative offer he couldn't refuse, Rey joined Heidt's Orchestra a few weeks after the King Sisters came west from Salt Lake City.

Heidt and his stage band would remain based in San Francisco for around two and a half years, accompanying vaudeville acts and entertaining with his own band at the Golden Gate Theater. The ensemble included a trained German shepherd, a vocal glee club, the King Sisters, and Alvino Rey soloing on the guitar. Shortly after the shy Rey joined the band Heidt arranged a date for him with Luise King. After a four-year courtship, they married in May 1937 in New

York City. It was during this time that Donna and Yvonne kicked off their careers singing in a trio they formed at the Lake Merritt Hotel in Oakland.

In early 1935 the Alemite Corporation offered to sponsor Heidt on both a national radio show and as the featured band at the posh Drake Hotel on Chicago's Michigan Avenue Gold Coast. It was an opportunity to move east and step up in prestige. Heidt jumped at the chance.

While in Chicago, the King Sisters would experience a permanent change in their makeup. After a few months Maxine left to raise a family with her husband Lavarn Thomas, whom she met while singing on KSL in Salt Lake City. Donna, the next in-line, replaced her. In 2001 Donna talked about her experiences singing in Chicago: "We used to mix with the crowd during breaks. I remember as a teenager joking with the presidents of big corporations like Coca Cola, Ford, and the Pennsylvania Railroad. It was a lot of fun. They were all nice wholesome people who enjoyed their families and ours too."

Yvonne also joined the group in Chicago. There were now four King Sisters, forming the first all-girl four-part harmony vocal group of the Big Band Era. With occasional substitutions among the six sisters, they would remain a quartet for the balance of their history. Meanwhile, Alvino Rey continued to build on his reputation as a soloist and worked on the development of the amplification of the electric steel guitar with the Gibson Guitar Company by using built-in pickups on the strings.

Horace Heidt and his Brigadiers finally hit the big time when they opened at the Biltmore Hotel in Manhattan in the spring of 1937. Donna King commented on the band's transformation when they arrived in New York: "Horace developed a pretty good dance band by the time we got to the Biltmore. He still provided a variety of entertainment, but he also had some solid musicians like Frank DeVol. I remember that George T. Simon gave us a good review in *Metronome* that summer and we recorded several hit records with Horace while we were at the Biltmore."

According to Donna King, in 1938 a faux pas was the catalyst for Rey and the King Sisters to leave the Heidt organization. Alyce, a popular crowd favorite at the Biltmore, accidentally knocked over a microphone that nearly hit the head of the wife of a would-be sponsor who complained to the hotel management. The unintended incident led to Alyce soon leaving Heidt. The three remaining King Sisters and Alvino Rey eventually followed her. They all relocated in Los Angeles where they began to travel the road to big band fame.

Once they settled in Los Angeles their careers started to jell. The King Sisters signed a recording contract with RCA's Bluebird label at the recommendation of Spike Jones and appeared with Artie Shaw on his popular *Old Gold Show* during the summer of 1939. Alvino Rey worked as the musical director at Mutual Network's KHJ where he had his own fifteen minute sustaining show. He also started to develop his famous Singing Guitar. Rey talked about how he did it on Kennedy's 1991 radio show:"It was really simple. We used throat microphones and controls that went thru the strings and modulated the output of the guitar. We did that in 1939."

Rey also started putting his band together in 1939 with Frank DeVol as the chief arranger and the King Sisters as the organization's vocal group. Late that year the band made its debut at the Pasadena Civic Auditorium that was packed to capacity with screaming and frenetically dancing teenagers. They were a smash hit.

In April 1940 the band headed east in a five-car caravan to open at the Biltmore Hotel in New York, hoping to piggyback on the reputation Rey and the King Sisters built with Horace Heidt two years earlier. Romance was again in the air when Yvonne married pianist Edwin "Buddy" Cole who would soon join the band. Nine-year-old Marilyn performed with the group for the first time, superbly substituting for Yvonne while she was on her honeymoon in the Poconos. As Marilyn's sisters married and had children, she substituted for each of them throughout junior and senior high school. As a result, she sang all four parts in the vocal group. However, fate did not smile on the Biltmore engagement. After several weeks of dutifully playing subdued music at the sedate hotel, one evening Rey cut loose with the torrid, up-tempo "Tiger Rag." The shocked hotel manager gave the band its two-week notice on the spot.

Thanks to the efforts of MCA, the band was not out of work for long. They soon landed Rey an engagement that would last a year at the Rustic Cabin in Englewood Cliffs, NJ, the spot were a singing waiter named Frank Sinatra was discovered by Harry James. The cycle of East Coast romance was completed at the Rustic Cabin. It was there that Alyce met and later married shipping heir Syd de Azevedo and Donna met and later married Jim Conklin, who would go on to become a legendary recording executive as the first ever vice president of Capitol Records, and president of Columbia and Warner Brothers Records. He was also a founder and first national chairman of the Grammy Awards and head of the Voice of America during the Reagan administration.

The band and the King Sisters shared a large three-story house next to the Rustic Cabin that they fondly called the chateau. It was a veritable open house for all their friends that included Ozzie and Harriett Nelson. Rey would wake up the gang each morning by playing transcriptions of their Rustic Cabin radio show at a deafening 500-watts.

Alvino Rey and the King Sisters hit the big time in 1941. Donna tells how it all came about: "Dinah Shore was playing at the Paramount Theater on Times Square. She suddenly developed a bad case of laryngitis and we were asked to fill in for her at the last minute. The Paramount was filled to standing room only that night and the crowd went wild. Little did we know that we had become famous thanks to our radio shows from the Rustic Cabin. The audience cheered us so much that we couldn't leave the stage. It was like Benny Goodman's famous Paramount opening all over again."

The Paramount appearance kicked off over two years of Camelot for Rey and the King Sisters. They played the top locations across the country that had network radio hookups such as Frank Dailey's Meadowbrook in Cedar Grove, NJ, the Hollywood Palladium, and the historic Avalon Casino on Santa Catalina Island. There were also the movies. Rey and the King Sisters appeared in several films in the early 1940s, one of which, *Sing Your Worries Away*, is archived in the Library of Congress. The pedal steel guitar Rey played in the film is on display at the Museum of Making Music in Carlsbad, CA. However, the jewel of their accomplishments was their phenomenal recording success.

Both Rey and the King Sisters had their own recording contracts with Bluebird. Between early 1941 through late 1943, Rey had nine charted hits, four of which made the top ten. "Deep in the Heart of Texas," his all-time best seller, hit number one on the charts and ranked as the twenty second most popular song for 1942. Bill Schallen and Skeets Herfurt did the vocals.

The King Sisters sang on four of Rey's first nine hits, and Yvonne King sang solo on three. Two of those three deserve special mention. "I Said No" got as high as number two and was the 18th-most popular song of 1942. Her tantalizing "Nighty Night" became Rey's closing theme song and was immensely popular with GIs during World War II.

While fulfilling their Bluebird contract, The King Sisters themselves did quite well. They achieved thirteen charted hits between 1941 and 1945. Their very first record, "The Hut-Hut Song," cracked the top ten peaking at number seven. Their biggest hit was "It's Love-Love-Love," which was on the charts for eleven consecutive weeks in 1944. They were one of the first groups to record a vocal rendition of Glenn Miller's "In the Mood."

A hallmark of the Rey band was its superb arrangements that, in addition to DeVol, were crafted by the likes of Dean Kincaide, Billy May, and Nelson Riddle. May commented on his association with Rey from his home in San Juan Capistrano, CA, in 2001: "Alvino was a much schooled guitar player whose abilities were far above the work he did with Horace Heidt. What I remember was that it was such a pleasure working for him and the King Sisters because they were all so cooperative. We got along great and wound up seeing each other socially. He had a really good band with fine musicians like Nick Fatool and Ralph Muzillo, and the King Sisters were truly a quality vocal group with outstanding harmony and could really swing."

It all came to an end in April 1943 when Rey disbanded and joined the Navy. He had been playing at the Casa Mañana in Culver City when he made his decision to enlist. During a 2001 telephone conversation from his home in Sandy, UT, he talked about his wartime experiences: "Thanks to my technical background, I passed a very difficult electronics test. After basic training at the Great Lakes Naval Training Base, I wound up teaching electronics at the Navy Pier in Chicago for the rest of the war. I enjoyed the assignment."

After the war Rey formed a new band with a ten brass section that had the power to rival Stan Kenton and his ten brass Progressive Jazz Orchestra. He turned out three top ten hits between mid 1946 and early 1948 when with the Big Band Era winding down he decided to break up his nineteen-piece band, forming a new twelve-piece band with Marilyn King and the Blue Reys as the vocal group. In 1950 he downsized to a seven-piece bebop-oriented combo that once again incorporated Marilyn and the Blue Reys. They played the Lake Merritt Hotel in Oakland and did the weekly *Ford Show* live television show in San Francisco that won an Emmy. Their TV success led to an engagement with a new twelve-piece band that replaced Freddy Martin at San Francisco's Saint Francis Hotel. The band's lead saxophone player and romantic interest of Marilyn King was Paul Desmond of Dave Brubeck fame.

In the meantime, the King Sisters made their contribution to the war effort. They sang at Hollywood's Stage Door Canteen, Army camps, Air Force bases, on Navy destroyers, and made a pair of appearances on the Armed Forces Radio Service's *Command Performance* show that was broadcast to our troops overseas. The sisters also kept busy performing on popular radio shows including *The Adventures of Ozzie and Harriett, Gene Autrey's Melody Ranch, The Edgar Bergen-Charlie McCarthy Show,* and as a summer replacement with Phil Harris on *Kay Kyser's Kollege of Musical Knowledge.*

When the war ended, they collectively decided to take time off to raise their families and run the boutique and beauty salon they opened in the San Fernando Valley. The first hairdresser they hired at the beauty salon was a young redhead named Jheri Redding, who was instrumental in the founding of Redken Laboratories. On a personal postwar note, Alyce married actor Robert Clarke, Yvonne remarried television producer Bill Burch, and Marilyn married Kent Larson, Stan Kenton's lead trombone player. After Larson's death, she married Kenton's lead trumpeter, Dalton Smith.

The King Sisters decided to resume their career in 1954 when Alyce moved back to Los Angeles from New York after her husband Syd de Azevedo died from a sudden heart attack at thirty-seven. With Marilyn permanently replacing Donna who was living on the East Coast, they landed a NBC television show in Los Angeles that led to a successful engagement at the Copacabana in Manhattan in 1955, a spot on the Dean Martin and Jerry Lewis national farewell tour, and a five-day-a-week CBS network radio show with Jack Carson, all with Alvino Rey's orchestra. Next came a recording comeback thanks to Capitol Records.

Glenn Wallichs, one of the original founders of Capitol Records, signed the King Sisters to a Capitol recording contract in 1957. Their first album was titled *Aloha*, a collection of Hawaiian music. They followed it up with the critically acclaimed and highly popular *Imagination* in 1958. A Grammy nominee, the album catapulted them back into public recognition.

Imagination presented the King Sisters using a totally new musical approach. They sang in an innovative jazz vocal style with close harmony similar to the then popular male group, the Hi-Lo's. Their scat treatment of Woody Herman's instrumental "Four Brothers" clearly demonstrated their versatility and ability to sing jazz. Their next album after *Imagination* was the 1959 *Warm and Wonderful*, in which they were backed up by a vocal group led by Jimmy Joyce who sang the vocal on Alvino Rey's 1947 top ten hit, "Near You." Rey led the Capitol orchestra on all three albums.

The exposure generated by their Capitol recording success led to a new career for the King Sisters. They became a popular act singing at Las Vegas and Lake Tahoe hotels and appeared on major television shows such as Ed Sullivan's, Steve Allen's, and Johnny Carson's, with Alvino Rey as their musical director. This activity set the stage for their foray into the only entertainment medium they had not conquered—television.

In the early 1960s Yvonne King organized a benefit show at Brigham Young University that included the entire, ever-growing King family. ABC saw a tape of the show and decided to feature the King family on a 1964 *Hollywood Palace* television show. They were a huge success with ABC receiving over fifty thousand letters from viewers, and in January 1965 *The King Family* show debuted on the air. The wholesome family musical variety series with Alvino Rey's orchestra ran from 1965 into 1966 and for a part of 1969. What with reruns and several holiday specials, they were on television through 1976.

There was one sad note to the series. During a taping of a show in 1965 patriarch William King Driggs suffered a massive stroke. Fortunately, he lived just long enough to say farewell to each of his children before he passed away at seventy-nine.

Throughout the 70s and into the 80s Alvino Rey and the King Sisters appeared together or individually at big band concerts and tours, resort hotels, and Disneyland, that held an *Alvino Rey and the King Family Day* as did the Worlds Fair in New York, and on major television talk and variety shows. Rey was honored in 1978 when he was installed as a charter member of the Steel Guitar Hall of Fame in St. Louis. In 1985 the sisters performed at President Reagan's second inaugural ball.

Alvino Rey and the King Sisters were blessed with long and productive lives. Rey died on February 24, 2004, in Draper, UT. He was active to the end, practicing the guitar and swimming daily, and keeping up with his passion of gourmet cooking. He also played at special events and concerts, conducted occasional college seminars, and in 2002 performed at the annual Reunion of the Big Band Academy of America where he and the King Sisters were presented the Academy's Golden Bandstand Award. There is little out on his 1943 band because of the recording strike, so he was in the process of organizing material for new CDs from old remote broadcasts. Along with Artie Shaw and Orrin Tucker, Rey was the last of the surviving 1930s and 40s big band leaders at the time of his death.

As for the King Sisters, Alyce King passed away from chronic bronchial asthma in 1996 followed by Luise from cancer in 1997. Karleton and Billy died from cancer within a few months of each other in 1982. Although they occasionally performed with the King Family, they were primarily active in various business capacities.

After Jim Conklin died in 1998, Donna moved to Mesa, AZ, from where she traveled to visit her five children and twenty-three grandchildren until she passed away in 2007. Maxine is enjoying her retirement in Corona, CA, while the energetic Yvonne lives in Sacramento and volunteers with the production of her church's theatrical events. Then there is baby sister Marilyn who lives in Sherman Oaks, CA, near the original site of the King Sister's boutique and beauty salon.

Marilyn King has carved out her own distinguished solo career singing for several big bands, including Ray Anthony, Les Brown, Freddy Martin, and Billy May. In the spirit of keeping the memory of the big bands alive, she sang in the 1998 two-month *Harry James Tribute to the Music That Won World War II*. It played nationwide to packed audiences of all ages. Marilyn also appeared and sang in movies and television and played the lead role in *Hello Dolly* and *Guys and Dolls*. Armed with a classically trained voice, a comedic flair, and a theatrical background, she regularly sings at jazz spots around Los Angeles with top musicians. She covers a wide range of jazz, popular music, Broadway show tunes, and songs from her CDs, combined with witty commentary. She has her own following and is always well received by cabaret patrons. The tradition of the King Sisters is in good hands.

What is the legacy of Alvino Rey and The King Sisters? Certainly they were major stars of the Big Band Era that generated huge recording success with Rey leading the only Swing Era band that featured the electric guitar complimented by the King Sister's dynamic stage presence and attractive appearance. Most important, Rey and all six King Sisters have stood the test of time performing together as a close-knit family unit for over half a century in music, radio, television, and film. To quote from George Gershwin's standard "Nice Work if You Can Get It," "Who could ask for anything more?"

JAN SAVITT
FROM THE CLASSICS TO SWING

Most bandleaders of the Big Band Era apprenticed in the jazz and popular music idioms. However, there was a bandleader who received his musical training in the classics. That was the handsome five-foot-five-inch-tall Jan Savitt, who studied at the prestigious Curtis School of Music and played under Leopold Stokowski in the Philadelphia Orchestra. His was a remarkable and unique transition from the world of Bach and Stravinski to the packed ballrooms of the Big Band Era.

Jacob Savetnick was born in Shumsk, Russia. Although several dates have been listed for his birth ranging from 1907 to 1913, his father Joseph's Petition for Naturalization states that Jacob was born in 1908. This date seems the most likely considering when his major career events occurred. A year later, the Savetnick family immigrated to the United States, settling in an Eastern European-Russian Orthodox Jewish community in South Philadelphia.

Young Jacob's life in music began in 1913 when Joseph, who is purported to have played in Czar Nicholas II's Imperial Regiment Band, gave him a violin for a present. His mother Ida had visions of the youngest of her four sons becoming a successful musician. Young Jacob did not disappoint her. He immediately displayed a marked interest in and prowess on the instrument and embarked on a series of lessons with classically trained violinists.

Nineteen nineteen was a milestone year for the Savetnick family when Joseph legally changed their name to Savitt and moved them up the ladder to West Philadelphia where Jacob attended the Philadelphia High School for Boys at 48th and Walnut Streets. The institution became West Philadelphia High School in 1926. By the time he started high school he had logged extensive playing experience in the first violin section of the Civic Symphony Club Orchestra, coming to the attention of prominent musicians who encouraged him to pursue a solo career. Jacob Savitt was on his way on to what appeared to be a life in classical music, a life that would include intense academic study.

Mary Louise Curtis Bok, daughter of Cyrus Curtis who founded the Curtis publishing empire, had a great love of music. In 1924 she established The Curtis Institute of Music. One of the finest music conservatories in the world, it faces Rittenhouse Square in downtown Philadelphia and provides merit-based full tuition scholarships to all its students. Savitt applied for admission and received a full scholarship, joining the institution's first-ever class in the fall of 1924. He left Curtis in mid 1930 and officially received a bachelor's degree in violin and conducting in the school's second degree-granting ceremony held in 1935. The first ceremony was held a year earlier. A highlight of his stay at Curtis was the four years he spent from 1924 to 1928 studying under renowned classical violinist Carl Flesch that included a summer spent with Flesch in Germany in 1927.

Thanks to his fast-growing reputation in classical music circles, an opportunity that would ideally complement Savitt's academic training unexpectedly came his way from a renowned classical music orchestra. The Philadelphia Orchestra was founded in 1900. After steady growth under its first two conductors, Leopold Stokowski was appointed chief conductor in 1912. He quickly proceeded to mold the organization into one of the leading orchestras in the world. In early 1926 the Savitt family was aghast when Stokowski himself offered Jacob a position in the second violin section of the orchestra. He immediately accepted and became the orchestra's youngest member up to that point. It was the start of an eight-year career with the orchestra during which Savitt would move up to the second position in the second violins among eighteen musicians in that section. What with his associations with The Curtis Institute and Philadelphia Orchestra, Jacob Savitt was a respected classical musician.

Sometime in 1932 Jacob Savitt became known as Jan Savitt. That same year he was also introduced to the medium of radio when he formed the Savitt String Quartet that broadcast on 50,000-watt Philadelphia super station WCAU. His twice-weekly show became an instant hit, prompting a fan letter from actor Edward G. Robinson. Inspired by the music of Paul Whiteman, in the fall of 1933 the ever creative and restless Savitt expanded his activies by forming a thirty-five-piece symphonic jazz orchestra with David Raksin, who was then a student at the University of Pennsylvania, as his arranger. Raksin, who would go on to a distinguished career arranging and composing in Hollywood that included the haunting film noir theme "Laura," found him a delight to work with. The stage was set for Jan Savitt to tackle new opportunities.

Nineteen thirty-four marked a dramatic shift in Savitt's career path when he resigned from the Philadelphia Orchestra to accept a position as music director at WCAU, a CBS affiliate. His scheduled programs ranged from concert music, to light opera, to swing-oriented jazz. It was a demanding job that required broad musical knowledge. In the fall of 1934 his own *Savitt Serenade* show debuted on WCAU and he started playing outside engagements with the WCAU house band. His musical calling was taking a new turn.

Jan Savitt's reputation as a promising swing bandleader took true hold in 1935. That January his WCAU band filled in for Eddy Duchin's orchestra on Tuesday evenings at the Arcadia Restaurant, a top Philadelphia nightspot that opened a year earlier. New *Metronome* magazine staff writer George T. Simon gave Savitt positive coverage in their June issue. It was the first mention of his jazz accomplishments in a national publication. Savitt's pleasurable and fruitful association with the world of classical music was now in the past.

In early 1936 Savitt's band acquired the epithet Top Hatters from his new radio show of the same name and they started to make their public appearances attired in top hats and tails. It was also around this time that his alto saxophonist Jimmy Schultz composed the band's new theme song, the lively "Quaker City Jazz." The theme was an instant hit with both radio listeners and radio station program department management. Personnel wise, the band featured two historically under-recognized big band vocalists who had superb phrasing and intonation. There was George Tunnell, better known as Bon Bon. He was the first African-American to attain a permanent position as a singer with a white band. The female song stylist was the sultry Carlotta Dale, who knew Savitt since his early days at WCAU. Both were personal favorites of George T. Simon.

The Marine Ballroom of the Steel Pier in Atlantic City was one of the legendary ballrooms of the Big Band Era. In July 1936 Savitt's prestige in the swing community moved up a notch when he played the fabled venue. The cover of the Savitt *Futuristic Shuffle* CD shows the band in a standard publicity shot before a packed Marine Ballroom. The following summer he would appear twice at the Steel Pier's rival Million Dollar Pier.

Come the fall of 1936 Savitt caused quite a stir in the Philadelphia radio scene when he left WCAU to become music director at rival NBC affiliate KYW. He introduced his *Music for Moderns* show on KYW in early 1937 and cut his first recordings on the Variety label in New York. Saxophonist-arranger Johnny Warrington wrote a shuffle rhythm arrangement for the session, marking the birth of the Top Hatters's distinct shuffle rhythm sound. Later that year Savitt signed a contract with RCA Victor to record on their Bluebird label. The Top Hatters would switch to Decca a little over a year later.

Jan Savitt had a definite flair for publicity as documented by two 1937 promotions the Top Hatters participated in. On April 28 the entire band boarded a Douglas aircraft dressed in white ties and tails for their 10:45 p.m. broadcast on the NBC Red network. Carlotta Dale, who was hospitalized and receiving treatment for injuries she suffered in an automobile accident with Savitt while they were returning from an engagement at a suburban Philadelphia country club several months earlier, was electronically connected to the band and sang. While the plane circled Philadelphia at five thousand feet the first live radio broadcast from an airplane took place. The stunt generated huge exposure in the broadcasting trade press. Continuing with Savitt's penchant for aerial events, the Top Hatters participated in the promotional laying of a cornerstone ceremony at the new KYW building on Walnut Street on a windy September 14. They broadcast from a makeshift platform set on the steel beams of what would constitute the fourth floor. A recording of the program was placed in the building's cornerstone.

Nineteen thirty-eight found Savitt active in the recording studio and increasing his bookings which included college dance dates, another summer stint at the Million Dollar Pier in Atlantic City, and two tours of Cy Shribman's New England ballroom circuit. At the end of the year the Top Hatters played a smash hit engagement at the Arcadia Restaurant that was broadcast on NBC through KYW. It brought them to national attention. Their December 2nd program is available on CD and clearly demonstrates why the dynamic Top Hatters were the talk of all top big bands. Jan Savitt's salad days were about to begin.

When Savitt's KYW contract expired in January 1939 he decided not to renew it and abandoned assured security to strike out on his own. It proved to be a wise decision as he hit instant pay-dirt when Maria Kramer chose the Top Hatters to replace Artie Shaw at the Blue Room of the Hotel Lincoln in New York. It was at the Blue Room where Shaw erupted to national fame in 1938. With sudden swiftness Savitt achieved what all swing bandleaders strove for, a booking at a major New York hotel and all the national exposure through network radio broadcasts that went with it.

Maria Kramer was one of the colorful personalities of the Big Band Era. Born of French and Spanish descent to a Tucson ranching family with the maiden name of de Ramirez, she married New York building magnate Max Kramer after extensive travel overseas and the proprietorship of an exclusive salon at 47th Street and Fifth Avenue in Manhattan. During that period Kramer frequently appeared on lists of the world's ten best-dressed women. Max and Maria Kramer owned both the Hotel Lincoln and Hotel Edison in Manhattan and the Roosevelt Hotel in Washington, D.C., featuring big bands at each. The exotic looking Kramer allegedly mixed business with pleasure consorting with Harry James when in her 50s. Her hectic regimen did not affect her health. She died in a Manhattan nursing home at 103 in 1986.

Beginning in February, the Top Hatters spent much of 1939 at the Blue Room squeezing in an important November booking at the Paramount Theater. They returned to the Blue Room for the spring of 1940, a year in which they were on the road playing all the top spots and college functions in the East, Midwest, and South, including the Panther Room of the Hotel Sherman in Chicago. A young Steve Allen would frequently stop by the Panther Room to see the Top Hatters perform with Niles Lishness, his classmate and good friend from Chicago's Hyde Park High School whose name he used in later years as a character on his television shows. They particularly enjoyed listening to Georgie Auld play in the band's saxophone section.

The Hotel Lincoln engagement was important to Savitt both professionally and personally. In the spring of 1939 he met Barbara Stillwell, a strikingly attractive model, at the Blue Room. She was a Chicagoan who was visiting New York with her girl friend. They would marry on April 7, 1940, in Peekskill, NY, with Savitt's brother Bill and Maria Kramer as witnesses. Jan and Barbara had two daughters, Devi and Jo Ann, both of whom live in Southern California. Tragically, Barbara died in a home swimming pool accident in 1995.

Big band historian George T. Simon, who passed away in 2001, was an enormous Jan Savitt fan. In the May 1939 issue of *Metronome* he reviewed a Top Hatters Blue Room performance citing the band for playing solid dance music, having strong musical arrangements, and featuring two of the better singers in the business in Bon Bon and Carlotta Dale. Notwithstanding Simon's positive feature, Carlotta Dale left the band in late 1939 to join Will Bradley's new orchestra that featured Ray McKinley. Bon Bon would depart a year later to strike out on his own. He would return to the band for a short stay in late 1941.

The peak of Jan Savitt's recording popularity was in 1939 and 40. Among his eight charted hits were "720 in the Books" and "'Make Believe Island" that included a Bon Bon vocal. "Make Believe Island" cracked the top ten in August 1940. The instrumental "720" epitomized the music of the Big Band Era as much as "In the Mood" and is still played today at swing dance competitions. The popular "It's a Wonderful World" that featured Bon Bon replaced "Quaker City Jazz'" as the Top Hatters theme song. Although inexplicably not huge hits, "El Rancho Grande" and "Rose of the Rio Grand" showcased the Top Hatters's ability to powerfully swing with the best bands of the Era

Savitt's recordings covered a wide spectrum of music, reaching far beyond solid jazz. It is not surprising that with his classical background he popularized the classics with numerous swing arrangements of works such as Bach's "Fugue in G Minor" and Grieg's "In The Hall of the Mountain King." The talent was also there for scat vocals and Savitt used it effectively. Bon Bon was a naturally creative scat singer who was sophisticated in his use of the style as demonstrated in "Paper Picker" and "Volvistu Gaily Star." Intertwined in most of Savitt's diverse works was the hard-driving shuffle rhythm that gave his band its distinctive style.

Proper credit has not been given Savitt for the high quality of his band's musicianship. Johnny Austin played fiery trumpet with a power comparable to Ziggy Elman. Alto saxophonist Gabe Galinas was a favorite of Glenn Miller. Al Leopold could play any style of trombone. His opening solo on "Rose Of The Rio Grande" is a swing classic. Although their stays were relatively short, Georgie Auld, Gus Bivona, and Nick Fatool played in the Top Hatters. Savitt's chief arranger was the skilled Johnny Watson, a favorite of no less than Johnny Mandel and Billy May. Pianist Jack Pleis and baritone saxophonist George Siravo also contributed arrangements. Both would go on to successful careers in the recording industry, Pleis as an orchestra conductor with Coral and Decca, and Siravo as an arranger who worked with Tony Bennett, Rosemary Clooney, Doris Day, and Frank Sinatra at Columbia. Savitt also commissioned Jimmie Lunceford arrangers Eddie Durham and William Moore to write occasional charts.

An event of far reaching consequence for Jan Savitt took place in April 1941 when he changed booking agents, moving from Consolidated Radio Artists to MCA. Under MCA's management, he would regularly play grueling cross-country tours, albeit at leading venues like the Hotel Astor in Manhattan, throughout World War II. To complicate matters, despite initial promises MCA did not land Savitt steady radio work. There were however, several interesting developments during the war years.

Musically, Savitt incorporated a six-string section in 1942 that included him, three musicians from the Curtis Institute, and one from Julliard. The late jazz writer and historian Barry Ulanov commended Savitt in a June 1943 *Metronome* article for his intelligent integration of strings in a swing band in comparison to Tommy Dorsey's and Harry James's use of strings. Several vocalists also passed through the band during this period. They included Phil Brito, Alan De Witt, Eugenie Baird, Lorraine Benson, Betty Bonney, and a promising young movie star named Gloria De Haven.

Cinematically, Savitt appeared in two Universal film shorts. In October 1942 the sixteen minute short *Jan Savitt's Serenade in Swing* was released. Martha Tilton sang in the film and had an enjoyable experience working with Savitt. The band next starred in the fifteen minute *Swing High, Swing Sweet* with Ella Mae Morse and The Delta Rhythm Boys. Morse was then at the peak of her recording popularity with Capitol Records. They shot the film in August 1945. He also scored for the film *The Outlaw* that starred Jane Russell and was cited for his work by Barry Ulanov in *Metronome*.

Socially, Savitt developed a close friendship with Frank Sinatra. He was a frequent dinner guest at Sinatra's house, rubbing elbows with the elite of the entertainment world. That association resulted in Savitt accompanying Sinatra on a three-city tour (Boston, Pittsburgh, and Philadelphia) in December 1943 and for a three-week engagement at New York's Paramount Theater in November 1945. It was the last time Savitt would appear in the East. He was unfortunately unable to work with Sinatra at the Paramount in 1944 because of a contractual obligation with the Palace Hotel in San Francisco.

Patriotically, the Top Hatters were mainstays on the weekly Coca-Cola's *Victory Parade of Spotlight Bands* radio show. They were afforded the prestige of being the eighth band selected to participate in the series and between late 1941 and early 1946 made numerous broadcast appearances at defense plants and military installations across the country. The top big bands of the day appeared on the program, and the Top Hatters's shows were always among the most popular.

After World War II ended, Savitt returned to the familiar world of radio. Starting in January 1946 he scored the music and conducted a string quartet for the *Louella Parsons Show*, a fifteen minute Sunday night feature on ABC. His work on the *Louella Parsons Show* prompted a good *Metronome* review by Ulanov. That summer his band was chosen by Old Gold cigarettes to play on their new *Rhapsody in Rhythm* show from June 16 through September 15. It was a summer replacement for the comedy series *Meet Me At Parky's* and had a supporting cast of Connie Haines, The Golden Gate Quartet, and Skitch Henderson, who acknowledged Savitt as a first-class musician.

The movies also beckoned Savitt in 1946. He and the Top Hatters appeared in three B films, *Betty Co-Ed*, *High School Hero*, and *That's My Gal*. Live performances also continued throughout the year. Savitt was always tremendously popular with college students and by this time had appeared at over sixty college campuses with the Top Hatters. He added to that list in November when he played the homecoming dance at the University of Nevada at Reno.

It was business as usual in 1947 with the Top Hatters spending the year appearing on the West Coast. On a personal note, in December Savitt purchased a home in Toluca Lake around the corner from Bob Hope's home and permanently settled in the San Fernando Valley. It would be the home in which his beloved Barbara suffered her fatal 1995 accident. However, there was a ticking time bomb. Specifically, Savitt was plagued with acute hypertension that rendered him ineligible for World War II military service. With there being little medical knowledge of how to treat the condition at the time, Jan Savitt was about to enter into his final days.

According to George T. Simon in his book *The Big Bands*, Savitt incurred a tax debt when an associate misappropriated the band's tax reserve. To help satisfy the IRS obligation he scheduled a twenty-four performance tour of the Pacific Northwest that was to begin in Sacramento on

October 2, 1948. But all was not well health wise. His personal eye doctor counseled him about his severe high blood pressure and advised him to cancel the tour and rest.

Ignoring medical advice, Savitt decided to drive to Sacramento on October 2 rather than fly. He left Toluca Lake that Saturday morning in a station wagon filled with the band's arrangements with his arranger Lenny Corris at the wheel. On the drive north through the San Joaquin Valley Savitt appeared to fall asleep. When they got to Sacramento Corris could not awaken him so he drove to the Sacramento County Hospital where it was immediately diagnosed that Savitt was in a coma suffering from a cerebral hemorrhage. He died in the hospital on October 4 with Barbara at his bedside. Savitt was buried at Forest Lawn Memorial Park in Glendale, CA. The pallbearers included Frank Sinatra and Edward Dukoff, who was Maria Kramer's publicist when he introduced Savitt to Barbara at the Hotel Lincoln in 1939.

How should Jan Savitt be remembered? Certainly as a musical innovator and colorblind pioneer who incorporated the use of the shuffle rhythm, converted the classics to swing, hired the first African American to regularly sing with a white big band, and established himself as the only big bandleader who was actually a member of a world-class symphony orchestra.

There was also Jan Savitt the paradox. He was highly sophisticated yet had a child-like passion for amusement parks. He was equally comfortable navigating the disparate worlds of classical music and swing dance bands. He was constantly on the road but remained a devoted family man. He was uncommonly intelligent though somewhat naive in business matters. He was emotionally high-strung, nonetheless methodically unswerving in the pursuit of his career objectives.

But Jan Savitt just might be best remembered for a unique contribution to the human spirit. On stage Savitt was a positively enthusiastic, animated bandleader who had a genuinely enjoyable time effusively entertaining his audience. On recordings, his upbeat music is truly joyful to listen to. Just take notice of "It's a Wonderful World" for proof. Thanks in part to the pulsating shuffle rhythm, his was one of the happiest sounding bands of the Big Band Era. Anyone who had the good fortune to have seen Savitt perform or hear his songs today experiences pure, uncomplicated musical pleasure. Through past live appearances and the material available on myriad CDs, Jan Savitt made and still makes people feel good. Frankly, that's not a bad way to be remembered.

ARTIE SHAW'S
POSTWAR MUSICAL ODYSSEY

When most Big Band Era enthusiasts think about Artie Shaw they tend to reflect on his great prewar bands that spawned blockbuster hits such as "Begin the Beguine" and "Frenesi" along with his glittering association with Hollywood and the movies. Few, however, ponder his considerable postwar body of work that made unique contributions to big band jazz. Therefore, a look at Shaw's under-recognized, but highly productive and creatively varied, mid 1940s to mid 1950s period is justly in order.

On December 7, 1941, Shaw and his largest-ever band that included fifteen strings and musicians of the ilk of trumpeter Oran "Hot Lips" Page and drummer Dave Tough were playing at a theater in Providence when he heard on a radio broadcast during a break between sets that Pearl Harbor was attacked. Overwhelmed by the enormity of the world events that were rapidly unfolding, he immediately put the band on notice and after fulfilling contractual obligations enlisted in the Navy at 90 Church Street in New York City. Initially he served on a minesweeper but was given orders by then Under Secretary of the Navy James Forrestal to form a band to tour battle zones throughout the Pacific.

During 1943 Shaw's band, the Rangers, toured the entire Pacific Theater under battle conditions that included numerous bombing attacks (forcing the Rangers to hide in foxholes on Guadalcanal) and torpedo attacks at sea. It was a superb unit with sidemen such as John Best and Max Kaminsky on trumpet, Sam Donahue on tenor saxophone, the brilliant Conrad Gazzo on lead trumpet, and five-foot, one-hundred-pound Dave Tough, whom Shaw was able to miraculously maneuver around certain 4-F status to obtain his services. Sadly, recordings by this outstanding band have not been released. Near the end of the year his entire organization was declared victims of combat fatigue and ordered to return home to San Francisco from Brisbane, Australia. In early 1944 Shaw was honorably discharged from a Naval Hospital near Oakland. After being named by *Metronome* as its Musician of the Year for 1943 for his contributions to the war effort, Artie Shaw was back in civilian life.

By the fall of 1944 Shaw was ready to form a new band. With help from Freddy Goodman, Benny's brother, he found young musicians like guitarist Barney Kessel and pianist Dodo Marmarosa who were comfortable in the increasingly popular idiom of bebop. He also brought a fiery spark to the band with the infusion of the great trumpeter Roy "Little Jazz" Eldridge, who Gene Krupa called the most electrifying trumpet player he ever heard. Eldridge did some of his finest work with Shaw. There was also Ray Conniff on trombone and a pre-Woody Herman "Four Brothers" Herbie Steward on tenor saxophone.

Since the 1970s Artie Shaw lived in a home on a cul-de-sac in Newbury Park, forty-five miles west of downtown Los Angeles. In a pleasant 2003 interview in his living room that was filled with myriad CDs, books of all subjects, and an eclectic variety of paintings Shaw commented on the reclusively enigmatic Marmarosa who also played for a short time in his 1949 band: "Dodo was totally unpredictable. With the 1949 band one night he said if you call "Frenesi" again I'm leaving. I called it again. I had to because the audience demanded it. He got up and left and I never saw him again."

Shaw's 1944-45 band was his most jazz-oriented to date thanks to three great arrangers who wrote advanced charts that incorporated the latest in modern concepts. Ray Conniff came into his own as an arranger with the band. His "'S Wonderful" and "Lucky Number" stand out as examples of the fresh writing that would eventually bring him to the attention of Columbia Records where he gained instant fame in the mid 1950s with his first ever-vocal album titled 'S Wonderful.

Eddie Sauter was at the peak of his arranging prowess with the 1945 Shaw band as exemplified by his stunning treatments of "The Man I Love" and Gershwin's "Summertime" that featured a growl trumpet solo by Eldridge and Shaw's liquidly emotive clarinet passage. Sauter's composition of "The Maid with the Flaccid Air" is of unique interest. When asked by Chuck Cecil during a 1974 interview on his *Swingin' Years* radio show what his favorite recording was, Shaw answered: "When you set out to make a record you have in your mind that concept. But life is what it is and it doesn't always allow you to do exactly what you want. Sometimes you come closer than others. "The Maid with the Flaccid Air" came closer to what I had in mind than others which didn't."

Canadian-born Lavere "Buster" Harding's contribution to the development of big band jazz is not sufficiently recognized. He was at his best with Shaw penning two propulsively swinging numbers in "The Glider" and "The Hornet." They both reflect powerful contributions by the brass section. His "Little Jazz" was an ideal vehicle to showcase the power of Roy Eldridge's trumpet.

Not to be overlooked is the second edition of the Grammercy Five that evolved from the larger band. The band-within-a-band included Shaw, Eldridge, Kessel, Marmarosa, bassist Morris Rayman, and drummer Lou Fromm. Without the harpsichord that was part of the original 1940 Grammercy Five, the group played much more freely, stimulating Shaw to create dramatic clarinet solos. Their six recordings on RCA's Bluebird label capture the group's up-to-date sound that in the case of "The Gentle Grifter" and "Hop Skip and Jump" evoke thoughts of the genre of music that evolved from after hours jam sessions at Minton's Playhouse in Harlem in the early 1940s.

Notwithstanding a top ten hit with "Ac-Cent-Tchu-Ate the Positive" that included a vocal by the attractive and provocatively voiced Imogene Lynn, the superb 1945 band did not rack up huge record sales or consistently pack ballrooms and theaters to capacity during its year of touring. After leaving RCA in late 1945 and signing with Albert Marx's new independent Musicraft label Shaw disbanded and started to record with a studio orchestra he formed that incorporated a lush string section.

An artistic highlight of the year Shaw spent with Musicraft was his work with Mel Tormé and the Mel-Tones that included the hip "What Is This Thing Called Love?" that featured rhythmic scat singing early in the recording by the Mel-Tones shifting to Tormé's clearly phrased vocal at the end. Shaw commented on the state of Tormé's development as a vocalist at that time: "Mel was a good singer. I made him sing solo for the first time in his life but you could hardly hear him. We had to put him behind a lot of baffles because the band would leak into his microphone. He was very soft then, it was his Velvet Fog period."

It should be noted that Shaw and Tormé developed an association that extended far beyond their Musicraft recording sessions. In his biography *It Wasn't All Velvet*, Tormé spoke glowingly of Shaw both personally and professionally. They remained close friends until Tormé's passing in 1999.

An interesting part of Shaw's work with Musicraft was his unintended groundbreaking contribution of the use of overdubbing in the recording industry. Due to dental problems he was unable to play with his orchestra when they recorded "Love for Sale." To avoid squandering the recording session, the band went on to record without him and his separate solo was dubbed in later, a then unique commercial recording practice.

Shaw's stay at Musicraft was not without commercial and artistic success. First, he had two hit records, "I Got the Sun in the Morning" sung by Tormé and the Mel-Tones, and "My Heart Belongs to Daddy" sung by Kitty Kallen. Second, his *Artie Shaw Plays Cole Porter* album that included several songs by Tormé and the Mel-Tones received critical acclaim. But by 1947 the restless Shaw was ready to head in two dissimilar creative directions.

Developing a career as a writer appealed to Shaw as far back as 1933 when he purchased a farm in Pennsylvania's Bucks County to devote the year to learn the craft. In early 1947 he moved to Norwalk, CT, where he spent the next year and a half resuming his writing efforts. He also immersed himself in classical music: "I wanted to see what would happen if I stopped playing jazz for awhile. I played a lot of Finzi, Beethoven, Berezowsky, and Schumann. I had an accompanist named Virginia Passecantando. She was a Julliard student who could read a page at a time and worked with me on rehearsals. She would take the breakdown of the orchestra score and use that as a background."

The first half of 1949 marked the culmination of Shaw's foray into classical music. He played such works on several radio and television shows and performed with the New York Philharmonic Orchestra, the Denver and Rochester Symphony Orchestras, and the National Youth Symphony at Carnegie Hall. Shaw also entered a recording studio for the first time since 1946 when he recorded a now-hard-to-find classical album for Columbia titled *Artie Shaw: Modern Music For Clarinet*. Then in mid-year Shaw stunned the music world when he announced that he was ready to start a new band.

Although it never swept the country in mass popularity, bebop hit its peak in 1949. It was around that time that Charlie Barnet, Benny Goodman, Gene Krupa, and Woody Herman with his Second Herd fielded bop-oriented bands. This was the climate in which Shaw organized his new ensemble, which had a bop tilt by virtue of the musicians he hired. The superb saxophone section of altos Herbie Steward and Frank Socolow, tenors Al Cohn and Zoot Sims, and baritone Danny Bank all had strong bop associations as did trumpeter Don Fagerquist and Dodo Marmarosa, who as previously noted, walked out during a live performance to be replaced by Gil Barrios. Although not steeped in the bop idiom, guitarist Jimmy Raney and drummer Irv Kluger blended in and made important contributions.

As with all Shaw bands there were superbly crafted and musically varied arrangements. Johnny Mandel contributed two strong bop tunes, "Krazy Kat" and "Innuendo." The definitive bop arranger Tad Dameron wrote the smooth flowing "Fred's Delight" and "So Easy." Shaw conspired with Lennie Hayton to pen new arrangements of "Stardust" and "I Cover the Waterfront." Ray Conniff updated "'S Wonderful" and Gene Roland composed a bop-structured "Aesop's Foibles" while George Russell penned an exotic "Similau."

Discussions of Shaw's 1949 band frequently give short shrift to its exceptional work in the then increasingly popular realm of Afro-Cuban jazz that was brought to public attention by Machito, Dizzy Gillespie, and Stan Kenton. Shaw masterfully acquired the services of arranger John Bartee who, according to Latin jazz historian Max Salazar, worked closely with Mario Bauza to develop a big band sound for Machito's original Afro-Cubans. He did not lose his touch collaborating with Shaw, writing pulsating compositions of "Orinoco," "Afro-Cubana," and "Mucho de nada." They hold their own with any Latin jazz recordings of the day.

As for his clarinet playing, Shaw was in top form with the 1949 band. His soloing was exciting and up-to-date on the bop tunes and emotionally compelling on the standards such as "I Cover the Waterfront" and "Moonglow." Shaw's improvisations on "Innuendo" reflected all that was happening in the world of jazz at the time.

Many jazz critics rate Shaw's 1949 group with its bopish book as one of the best in the annals of big band jazz. Unfortunately, the public did not share those opinions. They wanted to hear Shaw's old hits, not cutting-edge music. In January 1950 he gave up this fine band that was going nowhere commercially and checked into Lenox Hill Hospital in Manhattan for gallstone surgery.

Upon recuperating from surgery Shaw elected to experiment: "I decided I would see what would happen. If the public disliked the best band I ever had what would they do if I went back and redid the 1938 band? So I did and they loved it. We played Bop City and the Apollo Theater in New York, and a lot of the other black theaters on the East Coast."

Next came what today Shaw calls his private joke band: "Then after a few months with the 1938 band I thought, what would happen if I gave them the worst band I ever had? So I hired a guy who was a viper who always wanted to manage my band to put together a band that would play stock arrangements. I sent my band boy Tommy Thompson around to publishers to get them. Our menu was the Top Ten *Billboard* chart numbers. Tunes like "Hoop-Dee-Doo" and "If I Knew You Were Comin' I'd've Baked a Cake," tunes that I would never look at. There were never problems with requests because whatever they requested I would say 'Don't worry; we're going to get there.' Musicians would look at me like what are you doing? I'd just point to the audience. When a theater owner told me I did the best business since Blue Barron came through, I knew it was time to quit."

After a short stint with his joke band Artie Shaw did indeed quit the music business in the summer of 1950. He retired to a dairy farm he purchased in Pine Plains, NY, where he wrote his critically acclaimed and gripping biography, *The Trouble With Cinderella*. It was the first of three books he would eventually have published. Over the next three years he ran the farm, made occasional sorties into Manhattan to appear on television game shows such as *What's My Line*, and sporadically recorded for Decca with a studio orchestra. There was also a May 1953 appearance before the House Un-American Activities Committee: "At the time I testified before HUAC I was also being harassed by the IRS. Later I found out that the two incidents were not unrelated."

In order to satisfy his IRS obligation, Shaw formed what was probably the greatest of his small jazz groups, the final edition of the Gramercy Five, in the fall of 1953. Its greatness was best testified to by Gary Giddins in his award winning book *Visions of Jazz* when referring to the group's recordings: "For these are among the finest performances by one of the eminent clarinetists of the century, and among the most enchanting small band recordings in jazz history, virtually unrivaled in defining the nexus between swing and bop."

The 1953-54 Gramercy Five debuted at the Embers on New York's East Side. It was made up of Shaw, pianist Hank Jones, guitarist Tal Farlow, bassist Tommy Porter, former George Shearing vibraphonist Joe Roland, and veteran Shaw percussionist Irv Kluger. They were all respected young musicians who were comfortable with swing, bop, and the emerging cool style of jazz. The book comprised old Shaw standards like "Star Dust" and "Summit Ridge Drive" along with new, never-before-recorded songs.

Shaw recorded his last Gramercy Five at his expense on several separate sessions. The first was in New York in March 1954 and included a blues-tinged "Sad Sack" borrowed from his 1945 Gramercy Five and the Latin rhythms of "Besame Mucho." The swinging "Pied Piper Theme" evolved from the music he composed and arranged for the fairy tale *The Pied Piper of Hamelin* for CBS Radio in 1946. Several of the songs hinted of the sound of George Shearing's quintet thanks to the mallets of Joe Roland.

By the time the concluding recording session took place in Hollywood in June, Joe Roland had left the group and Joe Puma replaced Tal Farlow on guitar. The quality of the music did not suffer. The sadly romantic "My Funny Valentine," bopish "Dancing on the Ceiling," haunting "Bewitched, Bothered and Bewildered," and difficult-to-play Shaw original "Lyric" stand out.

Shaw strove for and achieved creative improvisation with his last Gramercy Five. The musicians blended perfectly together and Shaw played with a light, ethereal tone. The group's output still stands up today as a milestone in chamber group jazz history.

After their Ember's date, Shaw's group played at the top jazz clubs around the country. They worked their way west and wound up performing at the Sahara Hotel in Las Vegas in June. After the engagement was completed, Shaw disbanded for the last time. He then went on a brief package tour of Australia and in the fall of 1954 put away his clarinet and never played it again. However, the books on Artie Shaw's personal involvement in the world of music were not yet fully closed.

In 1983, twenty-nine years after he played his clarinet for the last time, Artie Shaw was back in the big band business: "Somebody sent me a demo of Dick Johnson playing clarinet. I wrote back with some enthusiasm that he was the best I'd ever heard, thinking of him as a possible leader if I wanted someone to run a band, though I really didn't want to start one. But Willard Alexander, who was always on a crusade to bring back the big bands, finally persuaded me to put together a band. So I went out and got a lot of bookings and went to Boston and Dick Johnson and I got the band together. I stood in front of it for a few weeks to make sure they were doing what they should and now they're on their own."

The Artie Shaw Orchestra debuted on December 3, 1983, at the fabled Glen Island Casino in New Rochelle, NY. Over twenty years later the band still actively tours and performs all the great Shaw arrangements under the leadership of native Bostonian Dick Johnson who also plays the clarinet solos.

As his last major musical project before he passed away in December 2004, Shaw put together his well-received five CD box set titled *Artie Shaw Self Portrait* virtually single-handedly. The retrospective won 2003 Grammy nominations in two categories, Best Historical Album and Best Liner Notes. Shaw personally chose all ninety-five tracks starting with "Cream Puff," recorded for the old Brunswick label with strings on December 23, 1936, by Art Shaw and His Orchestra, through "Scuttlebutt" taken from his last Gramercy Five recordings in June of 1954. Selections from each of his bands are included giving the listener a comprehensive overview of Artie Shaw's entire band leading career. He also wrote the informative liner notes that discuss his thoughts and the songs. *Self Portrait* presents an insightful look at the musical development and unique personality of one of the great contributors to modern American music.

Artie Shaw's enormous musical accomplishments as a clarinet virtuoso with stunning technique and a musically innovative bandleader have been well documented. However, there is an aspect of his professional career that receives little attention. Johnny Mandel commented from his home in Malibu, CA, on Shaw's ability to develop talent: "Artie would get people as players who weren't the best in the country, but he would work with them and shape them to his sound. He would teach them how to play. Les Robinson and Buddy Rich are two good examples. He would bring them along so they wound up being the finest around. I think he was an ideal leader."

Johnny Mandel's observation fits in neatly with a comment Shaw made while conversing at his home: "I have a basic philosophy. I believe that while you are here you should try to make the world a little better place." Artie Shaw has done just that as a musician, bandleader, and maker of men.

MY MEMORIES OF ARTIE SHAW

Big Band Era icon Artie Shaw passed away at his home in Newbury Park, CA, on December 30, 2004. I had the honor of attending his memorial service held at the Chapel of the Oaks in Westlake Village, CA, on January 9, 2005. It was a well-organized and tastefully conducted service that drew close to one hundred friends and business associates who came in a driving rainstorm to pay their final respects to the jazz immortal. In fact, that day's torrent was the deluge that caused the deadly mudslides that devastated Southern California the next day.

Shaw's casket situated in the mortuary chapel was flanked by two displays. The first consisted of two photos of Shaw, one in his youth and one of recent vintage. In observing the picture of the handsome young Artie Shaw it is easy to understand how he served as a magnet to the most attractive movie stars of his time. In addition, there was on display both the National Endowment for the Arts (NEA) Jazz Master Award posthumously presented to him two days earlier on January 7 at the 32nd Annual International Association for Jazz Education (IAJE) Conference in Long Beach along with a letter from President Bush congratulating him on the award.

Celebrated comedian Red Buttons delivered the eulogy and brought respectful humor to the event while sharing memories of his 60-year friendship with Shaw. He told about meeting him for the first time: "Artie and I originally met during World War II. We were both in uniform. He was in the Navy and I was a bellhop at the Hotel Astor."

Buttons went on to say that Shaw could converse on virtually any topic imaginable. For instance, he mentioned that Shaw once went into an extended dissertation on the ideal composition of the substance used in mud wrestling matches. It was his opinion that eggs should be included to produce an optimal mixture.

Subsequent speakers went on to reveal several interesting facts about Shaw: he had and read over 10,000 books in his library including one of the first books ever written on computers; he changed the location of the myriad paintings in his home weekly; he learned to speak Armenian from a musician in one of his bands; and he mastered the Japanese national anthem in case he was captured performing with his band, the Rangers, in the Pacific Theater during World War II. He was cited by all for the broadness of his knowledge, consistent honesty, and dedication to the cause of racial equality.

Clarinetist Dick Johnson has led the reconstituted Artie Shaw Orchestra as Shaw's leader of choice since its debut in 1983. He also accepted the NEA Jazz Master Award at the IAJE Conference on behalf of Shaw. Johnson spoke and played an emotional rendition of "I'll Be Seeing You" on a Selmer clarinet he rented from a Long Beach music store. The memorial concluded with a 1939 recording of Lee Wiley accompanied by Fats Waller on the organ singing George Gershwin's classic "Someone to Watch Over Me." Wiley was one of Shaw's favorite vocalists.

While driving back to my home in the San Fernando Valley my thoughts drifted to a personal visit I recently had with Artie Shaw and how it came about. I was always an Artie Shaw enthusiast and wanted to do an article on him. In early 2002 I called my friend author Peter Levinson who gave me Shaw's address and phone number. He also cautioned me that I was on my own and there was no guarantee of a warm reception when I called.

I thought quite a bit about Levinson's advice. Rather than immediately contact Shaw, I thought it best to mail him a copy of every article I had published up to that point with a note stating that I hope he enjoys them. Over the next year or so I sent him each new article as it came out. Finally, by early January 2003 I felt that he was familiar enough with my work so that I could call him and ask for an appointment for an interview. It proved to be a successful strategy.

With great anticipation I placed a call to Artie Shaw at his home in Newbury Park. His long-time personal assistant Larry Rose answered and to my surprise gave the phone to the legendary clarinetist. I was delighted with Shaw's response. He was most pleasant and said that he would be happy to participate in an interview. He even suggested possible times to meet. After some discussion we settled on 3 p.m. on Martin Luther King Day 2003.

January 20, 2003, was a warm, sunny Southern California day. I drove west on the Ventura Freeway and after exiting navigated through a typical residential neighborhood to the cul-de-sac on which Shaw's house was located. It was directly across from another house, the two of which stood alone in the area before it was developed. I parked next to the gate and immediately set off a sound track of vicious dogs barking that served as a security measure. I would wager that the canine voice used was either that of a Doberman or Rottweiler.

Larry Rose came to the gate and escorted me to the home's living room where Shaw was resting on a long couch. The room was just as I imagined it would be, filled with stacks of CDs of numerous musical genres, books of all subjects, and paintings from many schools of art. Shaw pleasantly greeted me, shook hands, and asked me to sit down in a comfortable lounge chair next to the couch.

After briefly commenting on how much I admired and enjoyed his body of musical work I set my tape recorder and got down to business asking Shaw a series of questions I had prepared. During our entire one hour interview he was genuinely accommodating, providing considerable detail for each topic we discussed. His recall and acuteness of mind was amazing. As we progressed it quickly became apparent to me that I was in the presence of a remarkable individual.

During our interview a few unexpected topics popped up and Shaw articulated his feelings about them. I commented on how much I enjoyed his great 1938-39 Buddy Rich-driven swing band and that *King of the Clarinet*, the 3 CD set featuring the band's radio broadcasts from the Ritz Carlton Hotel in Boston and the Hotel Lincoln and Hotel Pennsylvania in Manhattan, is among the most frequently played of all my personal collection. He turned to his side and wistfully said: "It was a hell of a band. That band was no accident. It evolved under my tutelage from a bunch of guys who could hardly play to become a great musical organization." In spite of giving up the band in December of 1939 and exiling himself to Mexico it was evident that Shaw was proud of what he accomplished in molding the band along with his contributions as an arranger to achieve its phenomenal success

While discussing his 1946 work with Mel Tormé and the Mel-Tones, Shaw's legendary independence surfaced. He talked about his resolute approach to the business side of his career: "I was always in charge of whatever I did. I would never sign a contract that allowed anyone else to tell me what to do musically. Whatever project I did I was totally responsible." Artie Shaw did not answer to anyone when it came to his creative output.

Shaw also brought up his close friendship with Chick Webb who frequently came to his band's rehearsals. He also mentioned he had great admiration for Count Basie and thought he was a true genius. Shaw then went on to discuss the concept of genius at length and gave his definition of the word: "A guy for whom there is no explanation in his background for what he accomplished."

After the interview was over Shaw offered to review my article before it was published. I eagerly accepted his proposal and in early March mailed him a completed draft. A few weeks later I received my draft back in the mail with Shaw's comments that I incorporated into the final copy. The article, that covered his postwar musical activities, appeared in the September 2003 issue of *L.A. Jazz Scene* with a picture of Shaw that graced the cover page. I sent him several copies.

My professional relationship with Artie Shaw did not end with that article. In September 2003 I started an article on Johnny Mandel, who contributed outstanding arrangements to Shaw's 1949 bop-tinged band. When I called him for a quote Larry Rose once again answered and immediately connected me to Shaw who spent considerable time pleasantly discussing Mandel and providing me extensive material for a quote. There would be one more involvement with the jazz master.

In the fall of 2004 I started to gather information for an article on Dolores O'Neill who, in addition to singing for Bob Chester in 1939 and 1940, also sang for Shaw in 1937 and again in 1950. I called Shaw for a quote on her but this time was told by Larry Rose that it would be best for him to obtain the quote from Shaw for me. I called back a few days later and Rose read me an excellent quote by Shaw about his experiences with O'Neill. I had the ominous feeling that it was my final interaction with Artie Shaw. Indeed it was.

Myriad stories about the complex behavioral makeup of Artie Shaw abound. I can only speak about my personal experiences. In my business dealings with Shaw I found him to be highly professional, wryly humorous, cooperative, and patient with all my questions. Never once did I feel ill at ease. He made our dealings a very pleasant occurrence, occasions that I truly looked forward to. Moreover, his complex brilliance and deeply penetrating philosophical views of life itself were always manifesting themselves, adding an element of flair to our communications. I have nothing but fond memories of Artie Shaw.

ORRIN TUCKER
HE PLEASED THE PUBLIC

Here is a spot quiz for all students of the Big Band Era. What famous dance bandleader who wrote several of his own hits was active in community service in the Los Angeles area well into the 1990s? Here is a hint. When he was growing up, football immortal Red Grange delivered ice to his family's home in Wheaton, IL, circa 1920.

The answer is Orrin Tucker, born in Saint Louis on February 17, 1911. When he was three years old Tucker's family moved to Wheaton, a suburb of Chicago, where his father took a job with the Chicago, Aurora, and Elgin Railway. They settled in the upper apartment of a duplex on Illinois Street, just a few blocks from Wheaton High School.

Tucker recalls delivery visits from the fabled Galloping Ghost while growing up in Wheaton with fondness: "I clearly remember Red bringing seventy-five pound blocks of ice slung over his shoulder to our house when he worked for the local ice company while he was in high school and college at the University of Illinois. He was the only iceman around strong enough to do that, and he was just a teenager. Red was a great guy, not the least bit affected by his fame as a star athlete."

When he was at Wheaton High School, Tucker started to take saxophone lessons: "I became fascinated with the saxophone when I saw a picture in the Sears catalog. It seemed to have just the right amount of buttons to push. I saved money from my paper route and bought a shiny new sax from Sears on time payments. As soon as I learned how to play, I started my own band, mainly performing at local country clubs."

Tucker graduated from Wheaton High in 1929 as class vice-president and director of the Jazz Band, with thoughts of a career in medicine. His graduating class included Grote Reber, the celebrated radio astronomer who in 1937 developed the radio telescope that was instrumental in the study of black holes and other astronomic phenomena.

Lacking the financial capacity to go on to college, he spotted an announcement for one scholarship out of the entire state of Illinois for one year at Northwestern University's School of Speech. Aggressively taking the initiative, he personally visited the speech school's dean to sell himself and won the scholarship, hoping he could squeeze in a few pre-med courses.

When his scholarship expired Tucker enrolled in a pre-med curriculum at North Central College in Naperville, IL. In dire need of income to pay his tuition and expenses, Tucker approached Clarence Croft, owner of Naperville's popular Spanish Tea Room, and persuaded him to add dancing at his restaurant. Croft installed a dance floor and Tucker played with a nine-piece band that was a huge success, regularly drawing patrons from nearby Chicago.

Word about this new band spread fast. Chicago-based agents soon heard about Tucker and started to bombard him with lucrative job offers. In the last semester of his senior year he was finally presented an opportunity that was too good to pass up, playing the Mardi Gras in New Orleans. His all-student band voted to drop out of school and take the offer. There was one problem; they had no transportation: "I went to Chicago and found a seven-passenger Lincoln limousine for $100. Then I went to talk to the president of a Wheaton bank who loaned me the $100. All nine of us were on our way in the limousine and my two-seat Ford coupe."

After the one-month New Orleans engagement ended, the band again took a vote, this time unanimously deciding to try their luck on the dance circuit and not go back to school, ending Tucker's college career just short of graduation. He then hustled and landed a six-week job playing at a hotel in a small east Texas town for room, board, and a few dollars a week. Next came a month-long gig at the Southern Mansion, a restaurant in Kansas City, followed by two years on the road playing countless locations between Denver and Pittsburgh. The entire band was avid baseball fans, stopping to play ball whenever weather permitted.

It was at the William Penn Hotel in Pittsburgh in early 1936 where Tucker found himself in the right place at the right time. Eddie Duchin came by to hear the band and was so impressed that he called his close friend Bill Dewey, manager of the posh Edgewater Beach Hotel in Chicago, to recommend Tucker for the summer season. Tucker was a huge hit and received valuable radio exposure that served to vault him to the upper echelon of the big bands, playing all the prestigious venues.

The stage for Tucker's second big break was set in 1938 when he hired Evelyn Nelson, a short, pert vocalist originally from Orange, TX: "We were playing in Saint Louis when Louis Armstrong called me to recommend Evelyn whom he just saw singing in town. The first thing I did was change Evelyn's name to "Wee" Bonnie Baker. A name with two Bs back to back sounded much catchier. Then I wrote cute types of new songs for her to suit her unique voice and distinct personality."

That second break came in 1939 while the band was playing at the Cocoanut Grove in Los Angeles: "I was talking with Lana Turner and Jimmy Stewart during a break when I got a phone call from CBS President Bill Paley. He just bought Columbia Records and told me that he wanted me to be the first artist to record for him and that I could choose the songs."

Tucker chose wisely when he selected "Oh Johnny, Oh Johnny, Oh!," the old World War I hit song he ran across in a record store in Chicago. It became an instant blockbuster spending fourteen weeks as a national smash hit, and made Tucker and Bonnie Baker household names. It was so popular that Columbia devoted their entire Bridgeport, CT, production factory to printing an initial run of a million copies. Orrin Tucker had achieved stardom.

As a sidelight, George Liberace played violin in the band's string section. He frequently commented that playing for Tucker and being besieged for autographs as a sideman due to the popularity of "Oh Johnny" was a career highlight.

Over the next three years Tucker played the prime theaters, recorded six top ten hits, frequently appeared on the *Your Hit Parade* radio show, and in 1941 made a movie for Paramount. The film, *You're the One*, starred Tucker, Bonnie Baker, Edward Everett Horton, and Jerry Colonna. The plot involved agent Horton's attempt to book his client, "Wee" Bonnie Baker, into Tucker's band. After several comedic attempts, he finally succeeds.

Then came World War II. Armed with a college ROTC commission and a pilot's license, Tucker entered the Navy with officer's status as a lieutenant. He had just negotiated a lucrative twenty-four-week National Theater tour that he quickly had to cancel.

Tucker commented on his wartime activities: "I originally requested to be involved in training pilots, but I spent the entire war in Hawaii in charge of a logistical operation with a troop of 3,600 African-American soldiers. Our unit received several decorations. It turned out to be a truly rewarding experience."

After the war, Tucker returned with a band that played heavy swing arrangements with eight brass and five saxophones. His first two bookings were at the Waldorf Astoria and Mark Hopkins hotels, and were well received by both critics and patrons. However, hotel management did not agree. Both Waldorf and Hopkins managers told Tucker that if he would like to return he would have to change back to a commercial dance band. Ever the businessman, he rewrote his book to feature sweet music and went on to play the smartest dance spots until 1955: "In 1955 we did a weekly television program from the Hollywood Palladium. Over the years I acquired interests in the insurance, oil drilling, and radio broadcasting industries. After the TV series ended I decided to take a few years off to manage my investments."

By 1959 Tucker was ready to return to bandleading with his usual sweet hotel-band style, primarily playing in Hollywood, Lake Tahoe, and Las Vegas until 1975 when he appeared as the ballroom band with Martha Tilton as the vocalist in the made-for-TV movie *Queen of the Stardust Ballroom* starring Maureen Stapleton and Charles Durning. His involvement in the film generated a vision that led to the purchase of an abandoned skating rink on Sunset Boulevard in Hollywood. He converted it to a dance facility he aptly named the Stardust Ballroom.

In addition to band leading and playing the saxophone, Tucker was also a more-than-competent vocalist whom no less than big band authority George T. Simon rated as having a pleasant voice and pleasing vocal style. He put that skill to use one last time in 1980 when he recorded a political spoof called "Tucker for President."

Tucker told about it in a 1980 interview with noted big band radio personality Chuck Cecil: "The politicians make so many promises that on an impulse I decided that I would write a satire about what I would promise to do if the public were to elect me president. We put signs about all my mock promises on the bandstand, and it became the most requested number at the ballroom during that fall's presidential election."

Tucker successfully entertained dancers at the Stardust Ballroom for seven years and gave an annual summer concert at the venerable Ramona Bowl in Hemet, CA. Starting in the early 1980s he devoted his major efforts to volunteering visits to rehabilitation centers, hospitals, and nursing homes to give talks on the music publishing business during the Big Band Era. His presentations were in great demand and kept his schedule filled. Providing service to cheer the institutionalized and helping others was the prime focus of his activities through the 80s and 90s.

In reflecting on his sixty-plus-year career in music at a park near his South Pasadena, CA, home in 1999 Tucker commented on the philosophy that he feels served to make him a success: "I always thought that what the people want comes first. There were so many musicians that said regardless what the public wants I'll play the way I want to play. I've always tried to play the music people are fond of and play it the way they want to hear and the way it is easy to dance to. I made it a point to know what the public liked and did my best to please them."

CHICK WEBB DISCOVERS MARIO BAUZA

In the grand design of life, fate sometimes affords us the privilege to associate with a seemingly ordinary individual who one day, unbeknownst to us at the time, will go on to become famous. For example, my father told me about when in my hometown of Milwaukee he worked with a nondescript gentleman named Lester Polfus. He had no idea that Polfus had a smidgen of musical talent, or did he ever imagine that Polfus would go on to become Les Paul, who pioneered the use of the electrical guitar and had a string of million selling hit records in the early 1950s with his wife Mary Ford.

Such was a similar case with Chick Webb, leader of the house band at the Savoy Ballroom in Harlem in the 1930s. Little did Webb know that one of his young band members who was starting his career with him at the Savoy would go on to make major contributions to jazz, eventually creating a new form of the genre. That originator was trumpeter Mario Bauza. Before we examine the seminal contributions of Bauza, mention of Chick Webb, a truly under recognized and under appreciated big bandleader, is in order.

William Henry "Chick" Webb was born in robust good health on February 10, 1909, in Baltimore to a poor, close-knit family. He remained firmly attached to his mother and grandmother throughout his life. Unfortunately, Webb's physical well-being took a tragic turn for the worse at a very young age. While an infant, he suffered an accidental fall resulting in several shattered vertebrae, leaving him a hunchback less than five feet tall, whose physical condition sentenced him to lead a life of constant, intense pain.

Inspired by watching parade bands in Baltimore, Webb took his first job when he was nine years old selling newspapers to earn a set of drums. He learned the craft of percussion with dispatch, developing prowess for flashy, trick drumming. Joining a local boy's band when he was eleven, he soon graduated to working Chesapeake Bay excursion boats with the Jazzola band.

Webb moved to New York in 1924 and joined Edgar Dowell's orchestra. Armed with a sharp sense of humor, he regularly frequented the famed Rhythm Club at 132nd Street and Seventh Avenue in Harlem. The Rhythm Club was a gathering spot for job-hunting musicians and was patronized by the likes of Benny Carter, Duke Ellington, Sonny Greer, and Coleman Hawkins. It was at the Club that he formed a strong friendship and matched storytelling wit with fellow raconteur Ellington. His ability to tell tall tales became known among his fellow musicians as spinning the Webb.

In 1926 Duke Ellington secured a job for Webb at the Black Bottom in Manhattan and Webb formed his first band for the engagement. It was a five-piece unit that included his very close friend, the great Johnny Hodges, one of the historic big three alto saxophonists along with Benny Carter and Charlie Parker. He moved on to the Paddock Club on 50th Street in 1927 and spent the balance of the 1920s playing numerous spots in New York City including the Cotton Club and Roseland Ballroom before settling in at the Savoy on a near-permanent basis in 1931.

Recognition of the Savoy Ballroom is in order as it holds a hallowed spot in Swing Era annals. The ballroom opened for business in 1926 on the east side of Lennox Avenue between 140th and 141st streets in Harlem. Over its thirty-two-year life it played host to a galaxy of the great big bands and saw its fame spread nationwide through remote radio broadcasts. The Savoy had a second floor dance area that measured fifty by two hundred feet with two bandstands set side by side so there was no interruption in the flow of music for the creatively skilled dancers who originated numerous new dances, including the Lindy hop, named after Charles Lindberg. By the early 1950s the glory days of packed houses had passed, and the Savoy was demolished in 1958 for the construction of the Delano Village housing project. It was truly the end of an era.

Webb added a female vocalist in 1935 that as a gawky sixteen year-old teenager won an amateur night contest at the Apollo Theater in Harlem in 1934. The singer was Ella Fitzgerald, who entered the event as a dancer with the hope of securing a professional booking. When her turn came she froze on stage and couldn't dance. Instead, she saved her big chance by singing "Judy" in the style of her favorite vocalist, Connie Boswell, taking first place in the evening's competition. It was her initial public appearance.

Fitzgerald was formally introduced to Webb at the Harlem Opera House in early 1935 by Bardu Ali, who often fronted the band for Webb. After listening to Fitzgerald sing a few songs in the Opera House's dressing room, Webb decided to give her a tryout at a Yale University dance he was scheduled to play the following evening. She was a smash hit with the college hipsters and Webb hired her on the spot, immediately taking her under his wing serving as her mentor and protector during her stay in the band.

In 1938 Webb entered into his peak period. Fully ensconced at the Savoy, he had a million-selling number one hit in "A-Tisket, A-Tasket" sung by Fitzgerald, landed a half year spot on the NBC *The Good Times Society* radio show, had a gig at the Paramount Theater in Times Square, and became the first African American band to play at the Park Central Hotel. He was on his way to fully making his mark.

Unfortunately, destiny had other plans for Webb. By 1939 his ever-increasing health problems became painfully severe, forcing him to check into John Hopkins Hospital in Baltimore after an opening night performance on a Washington D.C. riverboat. His condition was serious. Surgery was performed, and the little drummer amazed doctors with his stamina, tenaciously clinging to life. Finally, at 8:00 p.m. on June 16, Webb sat up in his hospital bed, and with a wry grin said to family and friends: "I'm sorry, I gotta go." He died seconds later from spinal tuberculoses at thirty years of age.

The legacy of Chick Webb is fourfold. First and foremost, Webb's band truly swung, some say on a par with Count Basie. He had an uncanny ability to urge his band to a fever pitch, frenetically driving the Savoy jitterbuggers to the edge of their dancing limits. An important contributor to the band's fine sense of swing were the arrangements of Edgar Sampson who penned several Big Band Era classics while with Webb including "Don't Be That Way" and "Stompin' at the Savoy," an intended memorial to Webb's stay as the resident Savoy band.

Webb's second legacy involves a miscarriage of musical justice, i.e., the fact that he is overlooked as arguably the best drummer of the Big Band Era. This claim is based on two points of contention, his technical ability and the judgment of his peers. Technically, Webb had an impeccable sense of timing and explosion, fullness of sonority and tone, and an ability to subtly create a charged, swinging atmosphere without being overpowering. As for his peers, both Gene Krupa and Buddy Rich generously acknowledged his skill and influence on aspiring drummers, and Ray McKinley directly sought out Webb as his mentor at the start of his career. Rich was particularly close to Webb, having sat in with him on several occasions at the Savoy. The final proof is in the music. His work on "Lisa," a popular record among drummers themselves, clearly demonstrates the quality of Webb's mastery of the drum and the band's ability to swing.

Third, like a heavyweight champion who is constantly challenged to defend his title, Webb participated with great enthusiasm in defending his Savoy turf in countless Battles of the Bands that were popular during the 1930s. Two are worthy of historical note. In 1937 he engaged the most famous band of the day, Benny Goodman, and according to most accounts won the two-hour contest. A year later he battled Count Basie and suffered a rare defeat by a razor-thin margin. His performance in defeat won him unanimous praise as he went up against what many consider Basie's greatest aggregation that included tenor saxophonist Lester Young, blues vocalist Jimmy Rushing, and the famous All American Rhythm Section of the Count on piano, Walter Page on base, Jo Jones on drums, and Freddie Green on guitar. Thousands were turned away from the packed-to-capacity Savoy Ballroom at both events.

Finally, Webb had an uncanny ability to discover and develop talent. In addition to Ella Fitzgerald, his finds included Taft Jordan, the high-note trumpeter and Louis Armstrong imitator supreme, Louis Jordan, the alto saxophonist and vocalist who went on to form the Tympany Five and influence the development of rock and roll, and an individual who later reshaped the world of jazz, Mario Bauza. A musical prodigy who played clarinet with the Havana Philharmonic at nine years of age, Prudencio Mario Bauza was born in Havana, Cuba, on April 28, 1911. He made a brief visit to New York in 1927 with the Antonio Maria Romeu orchestra, acknowledged to be the first Charanga orchestra. While in New York he saw Paul Whiteman's orchestra perform at the Paramount Theater and was awed by the King of Jazz's C melody saxophonist Frankie Trumbauer. He immediately purchased his own saxophone and took it back to Havana to master and play it in the big hotel show bands.

Fascinated by the vibrant African American community he observed in Harlem during his 1927 visit, Bauza returned to New York to live in 1930 looking for work as a saxophone player. However, dame fortune had other plans in store for the new arrival. In 1931 Cuban vocalist Antonio Machin was in desperate need of a trumpet player for his quartet for a recording date. Bauza offered to learn the trumpet to help the skeptical Machin out. He quickly mastered the brass instrument in two weeks, recorded with the Machin quartet, and unknowingly changed the course of his life and musical history.

After a short stint in 1932 with Noble Sissle, 1933 found Bauza spending three months with the Missourians, who were alternating with Chick Webb at the Savoy. While with the Missourians he was scouted by Webb who had an open trumpet chair when one of his players left to join Duke Ellington's orchestra. Webb was impressed with Bauza's skill and offered him a tryout with his band. Bauza passed with flying colors and joined Webb's organization as lead trumpet player, moving up to musical director in 1934.

Bauza remained with Webb until 1938. In addition to his contributions as first trumpet and musical director, Bauza brought Webb the hauntingly beautiful song "Lona" that he composed in Havana, and provided guidance and support to Ella Fitzgerald in the early stage of her career. He had the highest professional respect for Webb, fully crediting him through the years as an outstanding teacher, swing bandleader, and strong and beloved leader of men, a rare managerial combination.

After leaving Webb, Bauza had short stints with Don Redman and Fletcher Henderson before landing a coveted job in 1939 replacing Doc Cheatham in the Cab Calloway Orchestra, the top-paying African American band of the day. It was while he was with Calloway that Bauza unknowingly made his first contribution to the yet unfounded field of Latin jazz through his influence on a soon-to-be jazz legend.

In 1937, Bauza befriended a young trumpet player named John Birks Gillespie, who was to become better known as Dizzy Gillespie. When Bauza joined Calloway in 1939, Gillespie des-

perately wanted to follow suit. Employing tactics that Machiavelli would envy, he manipulated to
land Gillespie a spot with Calloway. Specifically, he called in sick one evening and sent Gillespie
to take his place. Bauza's clandestine tactic worked. Calloway liked Dizzy's style and asked him
to join the band.

Bauza and Gillespie roomed together during the Calloway days developing a strong, lifelong
friendship. It was at this time that Bauza introduced Gillespie to Afro-Cuban music, and in 1947
he brought Gillespie together with the great conguero and dancer from Cuba, Chono Pozo.
Gillespie incorporated a strong Latin influence in his first successful big band in 1946, generating
his biggest hit with "Manteca" in 1947 and presenting the world premiere of "Cubana Be, Cubana
Bop" at his 1948 Carnegie Hall concert. Gillespie remained an enthusiast of the Latin idiom
throughout his storied career as one of the most influential musicians in the history of jazz.

Bauza left Calloway in late 1940 to join forces with his boyhood friend and brother-in-law
from Cuba, Francisco Raul Guitterez Grillo, the famed Machito. They formed a Latin band that
went by the name the Afro-Cubans, a bold name for the early 1940s, but a name that represented
Bauza's intense pride in his ethnic heritage. The Afro-Cubans immediately set a new standard in
Latin music with a pure, uncompromising, authentic sound that reflected their New York roots.

A major breakthrough for the band occurred in 1943 when Bauza wrote the smash hit "Tanga."
It combined Latin rhythms and percussion with jazz harmonies, breaking new ground by fusing
Afro-Cuban music with modern jazz. It is considered by many to be the anthem of Afro-Cuban
jazz.

With Bauza as the true bandleader and musical architect designing its creative direction, and
the charismatic Machito playing the maracas and performing the vocals with his sister Graciela,
the Afro-Cubans exploded in popularity traveling the globe, introducing the world to Afro-
Cuban jazz. Much of this success was certainly due to Bauza's new concepts in Afro-Cuban
rhythms. In New York City, the Afro-Cubans popularity was of such a magnitude that they were
instrumental in helping establish the Palladium Ballroom as the Mecca of Latin dance in the late
1940s.

The Palladium was located at 53rd Street and Broadway, across from the Letterman Theater,
and but a block away from the renowned jazz club, Birdland, named after the Bird, Charlie
Parker. In 1948, Tommy Martin, ballroom manager and ex-road manager for Chick Webb, invited Bauza to bring the Afro-Cubans to his venue to play on Sunday afternoons to help boost
business. Bauza accepted, and within a year Martin's ballroom was devoted exclusively to Afro-
Cuban music. A year later Martin sold out to Maxwell Hyman who named the increasingly
popular spot the Palladium.

The heyday of the Palladium ran through the 1950s into the 1960s, when the Afro-Cubans,
Tito Puente, and Tito Rodriguez, with their hot and pulsating mambos and cha-cha-chas, filled
the ballroom to its limits with a diverse patronage drawn from throughout the city. In April
1966, Hyman permanently closed the Palladium, marking the end of a unique period of time for
Latin dance enthusiasts in New York.

Bauza left Machito after a thirty-five-year association in 1976. He formed his own band and
in the 1980s had guest appearances in several Latin and jazz albums, and recorded with Graciela.
In 1991 he reunited with Dizzy Gillespie and gave an eightieth-birthday concert at New York's
Symphony Space that was popularly received, paving the way to a contract with the Messidor
label and his very own first album titled *Tanga*. The album won rave reviews and led to concert
tours in both the United States and Europe. Long overdue recognition for his pioneering contributions as the main catalyst for Afro-Cuban jazz was finally received.

Nineteen ninety-three was an ironically bittersweet year for Bauza. On the plus side, his second album, *My Time Is Now*, was released to great critical and popular acclaim and he achieved the dream of every jazz musician by gracing the cover of the June issue of *DownBeat* magazine. However, it all came to an end on July 11, 1993, shortly after completing his third and final album, and but a month after the *DownBeat* article, when Bauza passed away from cancer in his apartment at 944 Columbus Avenue, his home in Manhattan since 1943. His last album, released in 1994, was titled *944 Columbus*.

Thus are the careers of Chick Webb and Mario Bauza linked. Although small in physical stature, Chick Webb was big in contribution to music history. He was a highly skilled drummer, leader of a famous big band, mentor to Ella Fitzgerald, and discoverer of Mario Bauza, who created a whole new type of jazz. Not bad for a severely handicapped, self-taught musician who could not read a note of music, and sadly died when only thirty-years old, on the threshold of fame and fortune.

GERALD WILSON
MASTER OF BIG BAND JAZZ

The Japanese have a mark of distinction called living national treasure. This is the country's way of recognizing their great artists and valued individuals. If we had that honor here in the United States, Gerald Wilson would certainly be one of the first chosen. After eight decades as a jazz musician, arranger, composer, bandleader, educator, and radio personality, he is a master of big band jazz and truly a living national musical treasure.

Gerald Sanley Wilson was born in the small town of Shelby, MS, on September 4, 1918. Still working in the days of the horse and buggy, Wilson's father was the town's blacksmith who played piano and clarinet. His mother was a schoolteacher who graduated from Jackson State University and an accomplished pianist who played at church and school functions. Ironically, she did not approve of jazz and never saw him perform in person.

Drawn to music at an early age, Wilson started playing piano at five, fashioned a wooden baton and pretended he was a bandleader at eight, and switched over to trumpet at ten. The proud owner of a paper route, he read about Louis Armstrong and Earl Hines and all of the great black bandleaders of the day, in the African American papers he delivered such as the *Chicago Defender* and the *Pittsburgh Courier*. He would also stay up till midnight to listen to Duke Ellington radio broadcasts from Harlem's Cotton Club. His life's die was cast.

At the time, Shelby was without a high school for African Americans. After Wilson graduated from grammar school, his mother sent him to live with a family friend in nearby Memphis to attend Manassas High School were Jimmy Lunceford taught music and coached football a few years earlier. With his parent's blessings, Wilson moved to Detroit at the start of his junior year to attend Cass Technical High School and live with old neighbors from Shelby. Little did he know that a life of over seventy years with big bands was about to begin.

Cass Technical High School was nationally renowned for its music program. As proof of that claim, Bobby Byrne, Sam Donahue, Wardell Gray, and Al McKibbon were among Wilson's classmates. Jimmy Lunceford visited Cass Tech to hear the school band whenever he appeared in Detroit. During one of Lunceford's visits, Wilson befriended Sy Oliver who invited him to sit next to him on the bandstand. He got to know Willie Smith and Dan Grissom and Joe Thomas and all the guys in the band. It would prove to be a most beneficial association through the years.

During his senior year at Cass, Wilson joined the Plantation Club Orchestra that played in the basement of Detroit's Hotel Norwood, the hotel that black bandleaders and musicians stayed at when they played at the Graystone Ballroom, one of the fabled venues of the Big Band Era. It was there that he met and developed lifelong friendships with the likes of Duke Ellington, Count Basie, Dizzy Gillespie, and Cab Calloway. Gerald Wilson was now unquestionably on his way to reaching his dream of becoming a bandleader.

Wilson left the Plantation Club in 1939 when he was extended an offer by Chick Carter to join his band in Saginaw, MI, where it was playing after completing a successful engagement at the Apollo Theater in Harlem. It was during his short stay with Carter that he established a lifelong friendship with fellow trumpet player Snooky Young.

The Carter stint was short indeed. Wilson was with him but a few weeks when he unexpectedly received a wire from Jimmy Lunceford, then appearing in New York, to join his band. Luckily, the wire arrived the exact night Carter broke up his band in Dayton, OH, after engaging in a battle of the bands against Erskine Hawkins. The next morning Wilson was on a train to Manhattan to replace Sy Oliver who was leaving Lunceford to take a position as an arranger with Tommy Dorsey.

Jimmy Lunceford's 1939 band was definitely on a par with Basie and Ellington in popularity. In a 1998 National Public Radio (NPR) *Jazz Profiles* feature on Wilson, he commented on the band's formula for success: "We were visual, we just didn't sit there. There was a different outfit for every show. Jimmy was a perfectionist. The arrangements were the most modern in the business and rhythmically swung. It was avant-garde musicianship combined with great showmanship."

The big band community agreed with Wilson's assessment. Arrangers Bill Finegan and Billy May, bandleader Glenn Miller, and the late big band historian George T. Simon were all unabashed Lunceford enthusiasts. Stan Kenton admired Lunceford both personally and professionally, and at one time tried to employ his propulsive drummer, Jimmy Crawford.

Although hired as a trumpet player, Wilson quickly developed his arranging skills apprenticing under William Moore and Edwin Wilcox. He developed an especially close mentor relationship with Wilcox. The results were two hits he wrote for Lunceford, "Hi Spook" and "Yard Dog Mazurka." Wilson also wrote solos for individual musicians and sang in the Lunceford Quartet and Trio along with Willie Smith, Joe Thomas, and Trummy Young. He was a valued, multifaceted member of the band.

In February 1941 the Lunceford band left Chicago by train on a windy, sub-zero day to travel to Los Angeles for a series of engagements booked by the legendary Carlos Gastel, who was in the embryonic stages of launching his career as jazz promoter and personal manager. When Wilson disembarked from the band's private Pullman car at Union Station, the sunny, warm Southern California winter weather made a permanent impression on him, an impression that would eventually result in his leaving Lunceford in April 1942. Wilson talked about it during a recent interview at his home in the View Park area of Los Angeles: "I was classified 1-A and decided to come to LA before I went in the service because I knew I wanted to make it my permanent home. But when I got there I wound up being busier than ever."

Surprisingly, Wilson was not immediately called to duty. He quickly immersed himself in the storied Central Avenue jazz scene and did considerable work playing trumpet for, and writing with, Benny Cater, Les Hite, and Phil Moore before he reported to the Great Lakes Naval Training Base north of Chicago in the summer of 1943. His assignment was to play in the base band at the special request of its leader and former Lunceford band mate, Willie Smith. The Lunceford connection again came into play.

After he completed boot camp, Wilson actually lived in Chicago and commuted to the base daily. He was at home playing in the superb band with his old friends Ernie Royal, Clark Terry, and Smith. It was also a time of professional growth. Wilson had an entire musical organization at his disposal to arrange for and experiment with. He honed his musical craft eight hours a day before he was honorably discharged a year later due to an acute asthmatic condition. Wilson immediately returned to Los Angeles and was soon presented with an unexpected opportunity to achieve his dream of leading his own band.

In October 1944 Herb Jeffries asked Wilson to organize a band for him to front. Wilson quickly formed a band with the best players available that included a young trombonist named Melba Liston and his old friend Snooky Young, who came over from Count Basie. Then a serendipitous turn of events occurred: "We were set to open at Shep's Playhouse, a nightclub at First and San Pedro, when Herb changed his mind and took advantage of another opportunity. Shep's emcee Leonard Reed stepped in and suggested that I open on my own. My dream came true. I was now the leader of my own fifteen-piece big band."

The Gerald Wilson Orchestra was an instant success buoyed by three radio broadcasts a week and a favorable review by noted jazz critic Leonard Feather. They immediately started traveling throughout the country, following Duke Ellington into the Apollo Theater in Harlem in1946. Wilson's old boss, Jimmy Lunceford, in turn, followed them into the Apollo. Their hit performance at the Apollo brought them a ten-week engagement at the El Grotto in Chicago. Wilson's vocalist for the date was Joe Williams. Armed with a record contract on the Los Angeles-based Excelsior label, Gerald Wilson now had the hottest band on the black theater circuit.

Success did not come to Gerald Wilson by accident. He had a hard driving swing band that played harmonically sophisticated arrangements of his own compositions. It infused elements of bebop on up tempo tunes and haunting blues tones on ballads. He also had a quality vocalist in Dick Gray, who also sang with Benny Carter. It was considered the most adventuresome big band of its day. Always striving to develop the best possible ensemble, Wilson's orchestra was integrated and had two female musicians.

By mid 1946 Gerald Wilson's Orchestra was making a then impressive $5,000 a week and was scheduled to accompany Louis Jordan on a thirteen-week nationwide tour. As a point of comparison, Joe DiMaggio was paid $42,000 by the New York Yankees to play baseball that year. Then came the bombshell as described by Wilson: "I realized I reached the top too soon and hadn't even started to do what I wanted to do. I wanted to be able to write all kinds of music, music for the movies, radio, television, and symphony orchestras. After I closed with Ella Fitzgerald in St. Louis, I disbanded and went home to continue my studies. Everyone thought I was crazy."

Once again Wilson returned to Los Angeles, this time to resume his musical explorations, including the works of classical composers, to achieve his goal of becoming a complete musician. However, a short while after he returned he got a surprise phone call. It was from Duke Ellington.

"Duke was in town playing at the Casa Manana in Culver City," Wilson recalled. "He said he needed two arrangements of his own compositions the day after tomorrow for a Columbia recording session. I gladly did them for the Master, that's what I called Duke. I didn't mind the short notice at all. Any call from Duke Ellington is a definite honor."

Those two arrangements led to a three-decade association in which he arranged sixteen of both his own and Ellington's compositions, and on occasion played in Ellington's trumpet section. Highlights included having Ella Fitzgerald singing his composition "Imagine My Frustration" that was in the Broadway show *Sophisticated Ladies* on an Ellington album, having his arrangement of "El Gato" played by Ellington at the Newport Jazz Festival, and playing trumpet with Ellington's orchestra in the film *Anatomy of a Murder*. He developed a particularly close professional relationship with Billy Strayhorn and a lifelong friendship with Ellington, his idol and inspiration.

In 1948 unsolicited good fortune again came Wilson's way when he was asked by Count Basie to fill in for Snooky Young in Basie's trumpet section. So began a two-year involvement with Basie that included Wilson actually living with Basie in his Long Island home while writing the five song "Royal Suite" for Basie's first ever Carnegie Hall concert in 1948. It was an appropriate contribution given Basie's penchant for playing poker. He also wrote for Basie's RCA albums and his nationwide theater tours. As with Ellington, he and Basie became friends for life.

The 1950s was a time of varied activities for Wilson. In 1950 he toured with Billie Holiday and lived in San Francisco for a few years leading a band that produced several recordings, co-owned a grocery store in Los Angeles, played and wrote with Cab Calloway and Benny Carter at Las Vegas Hotels, and performed in Los Angeles in small groups led by his close friends Buddy Collette and Curtis Counce. He also became involved in the cause of racial equality.

There were two separate musicians' unions in Los Angeles in 1950. Local #47 was reserved for whites, Local #767 for blacks. Momentum had been building among black musicians to merge 767 into 47. In stepped Gerald Wilson. At a general 767 meeting, he presented a motion that called for a special meeting to discuss the amalgamation of the two organizations. This was the start of a formal series of events that led to the elimination of union segregation in Los Angeles when both unions merged in 1953.

Gerald Wilson experienced a big band rebirth when he recorded several albums on the Pacific Jazz label in the 1960s. His resurgence was sparked by a successful six-week engagement in 1961 with Earl Grant at the Flamingo Hotel in Las Vegas, where he and Grant became the first African American entertainers to enter the Hotel through the front door and patronize the Flamingo's casino. Wilson received recognition for his cutting-edge work when he won *Down Beat* magazine awards for Best Big Band in 1963 and Best Arranger and Composer in 1964.

This was also the period in which Wilson infused Latin elements into his compositions with several songs dedicated to bullfighting. One of those Latin songs, "Viva Tirado," became a pop hit in 1971 when the El Chicano recording of the song spent five weeks on the charts. Wilson discussed his Latin interest in the NPR interview: "That all stems from my wife, Josefina, who is Mexican. She exposed me to her culture in both Mexico and Spain. I've researched the bullfight and view it not as a sport, but as an art form. It has inspired me to create Latin music."

During the 1960s Wilson's activities extended far beyond recording with Pacific Jazz. He scored for the movie *Where the Boys Are* in 1960, made the first of nine Monterey Jazz Festival appearances with either his own orchestra or conducting Jimmy Lunceford tributes in 1963, contributed to Stan Kenton's 1965 Neophonic concerts, and arranged, orchestrated, and conducted for Al Hirt's 1965 Carnegie Hall concert. The decade ended with Wilson ensconced as a respected dignitary in the world of big band jazz.

Wilson did not pause for breath in the 1970s. He became a radio personality hosting a popular Los Angeles jazz show called *Portraits in Jazz* for five years, contributed symphonic works to the Los Angeles Philharmonic Orchestra conducted by Zubin Mehta, served as musical director for Red Foxx's television show, and began a thirty-two year career as a university-level educator teaching jazz studies at California State University at Northridge. Since 1992 he has been a Professor in UCLA's Department of Ethnomusicology teaching a course titled The Development of Jazz.

In the 1980s, Wilson recorded six critically acclaimed albums on the Discovery and Trend labels. The MAMA Foundation released his *State Street Sweet* and *Theme for Monterey* albums in 1995 and 1998. *Theme for Monterey*, commissioned to celebrate the 40th anniversary of the Monterey Jazz Festival in 1997, earned him his fourth and fifth Grammy nominations. He was thrice commissioned to compose special compositions for Festival celebrations including the Festival's 50th anniversary in 2007. Wilson still remains active leading all-star big bands at jazz events and recording big band albums.

Prestigious awards also came Wilson's way. In 1990 the National Endowment for the Arts presented Wilson an American Jazz Master Fellowship. In 1996 the Library of Congress archived his life works. Wilson celebrated the occasion with a specially commissioned concert at the Library that was broadcast on NPR. That same year MAMA issued *Suite Memories: Reflections on a Jazz Journey*. It is a two-album, spoken-word biography of Wilson's career. His first recognition of the new millennium came when he was presented the Big Band Academy of America's Golden Bandstand Award at their annual reunion in 2001. Wilson was honored in March 2007 at the Kennedy Center along with several of his peers as a "Living Legend of Jazz."

The Wilson musical legacy continues on. His son Anthony has made his mark as a composer, arranger, and jazz guitarist. A graduate of Bennington College in Vermont, he won the Thelonius Monk Institute of Jazz's 1995 Composers Competition and in 1997 received a Grammy nomination for his first album, *Anthony Wilson*. He actively performs at Los Angeles jazz venues. Wilson's grandson Eric Otis is also an accomplished guitarist who played on both his grandfather's MAMA albums. His prowess is not surprising, since in addition to the Wilson lineage his father is guitarist John "Shuggie" Otis, son of the legendary Johnny Otis.

Gerald Wilson commented on his distinguished career with big band jazz while lounging in his comfortable View Park home: "I frequently think about some of the great vocalists I arranged and composed for, Dinah Washington, Julie London, Al Hibbler, Ella Fitzgerald, Sarah Vaughn, Bobby Darin, Carmen McRae, Johnny Hartman, and Jimmy Rushing. They're all gone now and I'm the only black bandleader left from the old big band days. I've tried to be worthy of this great art form and contribute to humanity. I've given jazz the best I have and had the good fortune to be able to devote my life since high school to a pursuit that has brought me pleasure and satisfaction."

1. The Van Alexander Orchestra on the boardwalk in Atlantic City in 1940. Alexander is in the middle in a white jacket.

2. Van Alexander (right) and Butch Stone of the Les Brown Orchestra working on an arrangement in 1943.

3. The Van Alexander Orchestra appearing at the Lowe's State Theater in Manhattan.

4. Left to right: Johnny Mandel, Van Alexander, and Manny Albam in the late 1990s.

5. Benny Goodman at the Hotel Pennsylvania in Manhattan in 1937.

6. The Horace Heidt Orchestra in 1929.

7. The Horace Heidt Orchestra in 1936.

8. The Horace Heidt Orchestra in 1940.

9. The Horace Heidt Orchestra filming *Pot O' Gold*.

10. Horace Heidt around 1940.

11. The Horace Heidt Orchestra at Lowe's State Theater in Manhattan July 1940.

12. Hazel Scott introducing bass player John Kirby and his Sextet at the Café Society Uptown in Manhattan.

13. The Kay Kyser Orchestra in the 1939 film *That's Right – You're Wrong.*

14. Left to right: Roc Hillman, Harry Babbitt, Jack Martin, Sully Mason, and Kay Kyser in the 1940 film *You'll Find Out*.

15. Billy May circa 1950s.

16. Ray McKinley singing and drumming.

17. A smiling Glenn Miller.

18. Alvino Rey and the King Sisters in the early 1940s.
Left to right: Yvonne, Donna, Alvino Rey, Luise, and Alyce.

19. Alvino Rey and the King Sisters in the 1943 film *Larceny with Music*.

20. Alvino Rey and the King Sisters at the Pasadena Civic Auditorium around 1951. Left to right: Yvonne, Luise, Alvino Rey, Marilyn, and Alyce.

21. The King Sisters in the 1965. Left to right top row: Alyce, Yvonne, Luise. Bottom middle: Marilyn.

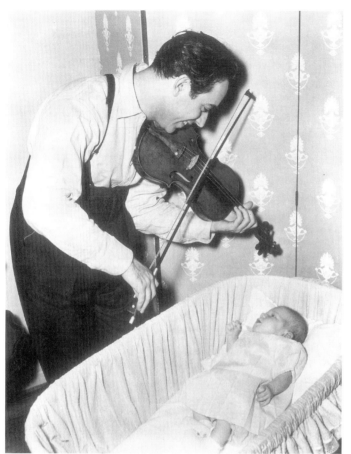

22. Jan Savitt serenading
his daughter.

23. Jan Savitt and his Orchestra
in 1946.

24. Artie Shaw in World War II.

25. Artie Shaw in World War II.

26. Artie Shaw at his Hollywood home in 1944.

27. Artie Shaw and
Roy Eldridge 1944-45.

28. Artie Shaw at the Glen Island Casino in December 1983 with Dick Johnson to the far left.

29. Orrin Tucker and Bonnie Baker
on the bandstand.

30. Orrin Tucker around 1975.

31. Chick Webb and his brass section. Webb third from right standing next to Mario Bauza third from left.

32. Gerald Wilson with the Jimmy Lunceford Orchestra around 1941. Left to right: Wilson, Snooky Young, and Paul Webster.

PART TWO

THE MUSICIANS

ERNANI BERNARDI
A MAN OF MANY TALENTS

In and around Los Angeles, Ernani "Noni" Bernardi, who died on January 4, 2006, at ninety-four, is fondly remembered for the thirty-two controversial years he spent serving on the Los Angeles City Council as a fierce guardian of the tax payer's hard-earned dollar and overall champion of the common man. Few, however, are aware that Bernardi started out in life as an accomplished alto saxophone player for several of the most famous bands of the Swing Era before he went on to business and political success. It is worth taking a few minutes to look at the most interesting and colorful career of Ernani Bernardi, jazz musician, businessman, politician, and successful mail-order marketer.

Ernani Bernardi was born on October 29, 1911, in Standard, IL, a small farming community of three hundred just below the Illinois River a few miles southwest of LaSalle, IL. When he was but a year old his family affectionately started calling him Noni, a nickname that remained with him throughout his life.

Although born to a musical family, Bernardi did not get started in music until he was fourteen years old, when he decided to take up the saxophone. His father, a music teacher, also ran both the town concert band and a country music band that played at local functions.

While in high school, Bernardi played in his father's country band. Immediately after graduation, he moved to Detroit to live with relatives and pursue a business career with Crowley-Milner Department Store.

In his spare time Bernardi studied harmony, taking private lessons from a local musician, and started playing club dates in the Detroit area, spending less and less time on the job at Crowley-Milner. So ended a once-promising career in the retail industry.

By this time it was the early 1930s and Bernardi was ready to expand his musical horizons. He moved to New York to take a job with Larry Funk and "His Band of a Thousand Melodies," replacing Freddy Martin, who left Funk after a short stay to form his own band and eventually become a mainstay at the Cocoanut Grove nightclub in Los Angeles with Merv Griffin as his vocalist.

"I remember Martin's opening night at the Marine Roof of the Bossert Hotel in Brooklyn," Bernardi said during an interview at his home in Van Nuys, California. "The whole Funk band went that night to cheer him on and wish him well."

Larry Funk is most remembered by big band enthusiasts for having employed Helen O'Connell when she was discovered by Jimmy Dorsey at the Village Barn in New York's Greenwich Village in early 1939. Soon after O'Connell left to join Dorsey, Funk gave up band leading and became a highly successful booking agent.

After a year with Funk, Bernardi returned to Detroit to work with booking agents to form his own band that played at the Graystone and Arcadia, Detroit's top two ballrooms. After two years in Detroit he broke up his band in 1934 to return to New York to join the Joe Haymes Orchestra.

It was with Haymes that Bernardi peripherally participated in a major event of the Big Band Era. On Memorial Day of 1935 the Dorsey Brothers Orchestra was playing at the Glen Island Casino in New Rochelle, NY. The constantly bickering brothers had an onstage squabble during their afternoon performance with Tommy abruptly walking out on the spot without saying a word, never to return.

Immediately after the breakup Jimmy took full control of the Dorsey Brothers Orchestra and Tommy took over the Haymes band. Bernardi made an immediate contribution for his new boss penning his first arrangement, "I'm Gettin' Sentimental over You," Tommy Dorsey's theme song and a classic of the Era.

Reflecting on Joe Haymes as a bandleader, Bernardi said: "Haymes looked like a movie star. He always had a good band and was a top arranger, but he was a poor businessman and invariably would have his band taken over by someone else and have to start over again. He was a truly good guy, and I enjoyed working for him."

Toward the end of 1935 Bernardi left Dorsey to join the Bob Crosby band, leaving Crosby to spend the summer of 1936 playing with jazz violinist and madcap Joe Venuti in Detroit. After the Venuti gig he went back to New York for a saxophone chair with Jimmy Dorsey's Orchestra, gaining notoriety by becoming one of the first Swing Era musicians to play with both Dorsey brothers orchestras.

Bernardi thinks that the brothers were as different as night and day: "Tommy was simply overpowering with his trombone playing. He set high standards. He demanded a lot from his musicians and himself, and was a shrewd businessman. Jimmy was more like a sideman in temperament. He wasn't as intense as Tommy; everything was always just fine with Jimmy. He was so easy to get along with."

In 1938, after over a year of heavy traveling, the Jimmy Dorsey band was playing at the New Yorker Hotel in Manhattan when lead saxist Hymie Shertzer left Benny Goodman who was playing at the Hotel Pennsylvania. Dave Matthews immediately left Dorsey to replace Shertzer joined by Bernardi who also went to Goodman replacing Milt Yaner.

While with Goodman, Bernardi arranged several songs for Ziggy Elman that were recorded on the Bluebird label. One of the songs, "Fralich in Swing," a traditional Hebraic folk song, was recorded by Goodman as "And the Angels Sing" in 1939. Featuring a famous trumpet solo by Elman and vocal by Martha Tilton, "And the Angels Sing" was number one on the hit parade for five consecutive weeks.

Bernardi had the highest professional respect for Goodman: "Goodman was very uncommunicative, so you never knew where you stood. He led by musical example. I just sat there every night marveling at how he could play the clarinet. That's all he had to do to get the best out of his musicians. You couldn't help wanting to play better than you could possibly play."

In 1939 Bernardi left Goodman to pursue independent arranging and freelancing in New York. He also had stints with the CBS radio house band and the Raymond Scott Quintet. Then suddenly he was faced with a very pleasant dilemma. Specifically, Bernardi was offered two jobs at once, one by his old boss Benny Goodman to play at the San Francisco World's Fair, the other by Kay Kyser to play in Hollywood. His choice was to join Kyser.

In explaining why he went with Kyser, Bernardi talked about where he wanted to permanently relocate: "A lot of people at the time questioned why I chose Kyser over Goodman. The reason is my wife and I always wanted to settle in Southern California and Kyser was permanently based in Hollywood."

It was indeed a wise choice, as Kyser was at the peak of his popularity with a string of hit records, two popular vocalists in Harry Babbitt and Ginny Simms, a fine trumpet player named

Merwyn Bogue, who played the role of the popular buffoon Ish Kabibble, and his immensely popular radio show, the *Kollege of Musical Knowledge*.

Kyser was also a success in motion pictures. He and his band appeared in several films in the late 1930s and early 1940s achieving Trivial Pursuit fame by having John Barrymore's final movie appearance take place in his 1941 film *Playmates*. There is still a small but devoted following of Kyser's movies attested to by the fact that they are periodically shown on the Turner Classic Movies cable channel.

Finally, insufficient credit is given to Kyser's huge success as a live attraction. The Kyser organization was in constant demand for theater engagements, dances, and concerts, and broke attendance records wherever they appeared. Their only rival as a draw when Bernardi joined the band was Glenn Miller.

While recalling Kyser, Bernardi remarked: "Kay Kyser was one of the nicest fellows I ever worked for. He didn't know one note of music, but he was a sensational promoter and showman, and really knew how to front a band. Kyser's number one asset was Lew Wasserman who took a personal interest in Kyser and helped guide his career."

Bernardi stayed with Kyser during World War II traveling the country entertaining troops in the Armed Forces. He became Kyser's musical director in 1945 replacing George Dunning who went to work for Columbia Pictures to score movies. But Bernardi left Kyser to stay in Hollywood when Kyser moved the band east in 1946.

After Kyser moved on, Bernardi took the members of Kyser's band that remained in Los Angeles and formed his own orchestra playing at the Aragon Ballroom on Lick Pier in Santa Monica, CA. He shared billing with an up-and-comer by the name of Lawrence Welk.

Soon confronted with the necessity to go back on the road and realizing the Swing Era was coming to an end, Bernardi made the decision to dissolve his band after ten weeks at the Aragon and permanently left the music business to become a building contractor, an avid personal hobby for many years. He specialized in building homes throughout the San Fernando Valley under contract to private individuals.

While in business, Bernardi became active in construction association work eventually serving as president of the Southern California Building Contractors Association and had frequent dealings with both the City and County of Los Angeles. With his appetite whetted for politics, he made a run for the Los Angeles City Council to represent the San Fernando Valley in 1957, finishing a close third in the balloting.

Bernardi tried again in 1961 and this time came out victorious. He won every subsequent election to become a City Hall legend retiring from the Council in 1993 with a reputation for being a staunch watchdog of the city budget earning for himself the sobriquet "the conscience of the council."

"My basic philosophy of government was how I would react to proposals before the Council if I was still running my construction business as a taxpaying citizen," commented Bernardi on his Council days.

In 1986 Bernardi launched a new project in his spare time: "I always wanted to recognize the Swing Era's unsung supporting cast, the sidemen, the composers, and the arrangers. The only way that could be done is through a video."

The end result is *The Way It Was*, a jewel of a video that is a sheer delight for big band aficionados. There are eighteen hit songs in their original arrangements, three each from bandleaders Benny Goodman, Glenn Miller, Duke Ellington, Artie Shaw, Tommy Dorsey, and Count Basie. At the start of each piece, the composer and arranger is displayed. During the song, a picture of the original soloist is superimposed while their solo is being played. Over fifty soloists are featured.

The seventeen-member band featured in the video comprised top Hollywood studio musicians, many of whom actually played with the legendary big bands during the 1930s and 40s. These outstanding performers are truly dedicated to the genre and the accurate re-creation of the music. Bernardi, who put the band together, was the leader and played alto saxophone as a sideman.

The Way It Was also serves as a historical record of Big Band Era, as there are few documents extant that list the soloists who performed on the original records. For the purist it's a thrill from yesteryear to see a picture of Harry James while Pete Candoli played his solo on "Don't Be That Way" or a photo of Tex Beneke and Al Klink conducting their famous saxophone battle from "In the Mood" while reprised by Don Lodice and Don Raffell.

Looking back on his career shortly before he passed away, Bernardi mused at his San Fernando Valley home: "I actually had four separate careers, musician, businessman, politician, and now video producer and distributor. Each profession had its own unique challenge. Believe me, it hasn't been boring."

MILT BERNHART
KEEPER OF THE BIG BAND ERA FLAME

Milt Bernhart had a storied career in jazz that included playing trombone with the big bands of Boyd Raeburn, Teddy Powell, Stan Kenton, and Benny Goodman. He was also involved in the formation of Howard Rumsey's Lighthouse All-Stars, played with Nelson Riddle's ensembles on numerous Frank Sinatra recording sessions, and was a fixture in Hollywood movie and television studio orchestras. Notwithstanding those glittering accomplishments, Bernhart has not been sufficiently recognized for his work as keeper of the flame for the Big Band Era. Through his over-quarter-century involvement with The Big Band Academy of America he tirelessly worked to keep the spirit of the big bands alive.

The youngest of six children, Milton Gerald Bernhart was born on May 25, 1926, in Valparaiso, IN, to a family that had no musical talent. His father, who was born in Russia, was the hardworking town tailor who had little time for artistic appreciation. During an interview at his comfortable home in Burbank, CA, Bernhart talked about how he got started in music: "A man named Harold Rogers arrived in Valparaiso very much like Harold Hill in the movie *Music Man*. After he lent me a tuba that I could hardly lift he took to me and allowed me to play his collection of records and taught me how to read music. Even though I wasn't in high school yet, thanks to him, I got to play in the school band."

Unfortunately, tragedy struck Bernhart at an early age; his father died when he was six, his mother when he was ten and a half. Immediately after his mother passed away his brother's family that lived at Lawrence and Western Avenues on Chicago's north side took him in. Soon after arriving in Chicago he switched to trombone and started taking lessons form Forrest Nicola, who taught Bernhart to sight-read, a skill that later proved invaluable in studio work. High school followed in 1939 with Bernhart walking several miles each way to attend Lane Technical High School that had a highly regarded music program. Jazz was a forbidden word at Lane Tech, so Bernhart aspired to play with the Chicago Symphony Orchestra and became involved with the WPA Youth Symphony Orchestra. On a Sunday afternoon during his junior year he met Lee Konitz while playing in a rehearsal of a concert band that was primarily made up of retired musicians who performed with John Phillips Sousa. Konitz and Bernhart quickly became close friends.

Bernhart's career with the big bands was launched while he was still in high school: "I had played with high school jazz bands. Forrest Nicola recommended me for a sub job with Boyd Raeburn at the Band Box on Randolph Street when I was sixteen. Boyd had a Chicago-based swing band, having had a Freddy Martin-style dance band a year earlier at the Chez Paree. He played mostly stock arrangements by Count Basie and a few new hand-written arrangements by Paul Villepigue. As I walked down a flight of stairs into the club the smell of the beer and cigarettes hit me; I froze and couldn't lift my horn to play. Eventually Boyd came over and gave me a few words of encouragement. Thanks to his friendliness I came around and was frequently asked back as a sub, so I got to feel like a regular player on the band. I often wonder what would have happened to my career if he told me to get out, which most bandleaders would have done."

The Lane Tech senior prom provided the launch pad for Bernhart's professional career: "On prom night at the Aragon Ballroom I didn't have any prospects but I gained a lot of confidence working with Raeburn. That night I went up to the leader of the band playing the prom. He was Buddy Franklin, who played all the big hotels in the South for the society people and was a regular at the Aragon. I asked him for a job and the next morning I left with the band to play at the Peabody Hotel in Memphis."

By the time Franklin's band worked its way to Denver three months later Bernhart had become bored playing just dance music, so he left Franklin and joined the Jimmy James band, a slightly hotter local group. Come December, Bernhart felt he was going nowhere and was anxious to advance his career. He decided the solution was to try a new city and accepted an offer to share gas with a fellow James band member who planned to drive from Denver to Los Angeles.

The trip west paid off for Bernhart: "When I got to LA I stayed with my sister who was living in West Hollywood. My first night in town I walked from her house to the Hollywood Palladium where Teddy Powell was playing. He had a good swing band with guys like Charlie Ventura, Pete Candoli, Boots Mussilli, and Marty Napoleon. I walked up to the bandstand as I had done at the Aragon and asked him if he needed a trombone player. He looked me up and down and told me to bring in my horn tomorrow night. I did and sat next to the lead trombone player and sight read my way through several numbers. Teddy was satisfied and I got the job. As soon as I got established with Teddy I was able to get Lee Konitz on the band."

After eight months as third trombonist and part-time Butch Stone novelty-type singer with Powell, two events took place that had a dramatic impact on Bernhart. First, Powell was arrested for bribing a New York City draft board official. He pleaded guilty in Federal court and was incarcerated in a Federal prison a year later. The official eventually committed suicide. Second, Bernhart was drafted into military service.

"I was walking down a street in Detroit with Lee Konitz when we picked up a paper and read that Teddy had been arrested for draft evasion," Bernhart explained. "It didn't surprise me. When I got my draft notice he told me he could pull strings and get me out of the service, but all the guys in the band advised against it. The band immediately broke up and I joined the Army at Camp Hood in Texas where I trained to become a rifleman to fight in Europe. The band at Camp Hood was outstanding. Most of them were the Bob Crosby band with musicians like Ray Bauduc. There were no vacancies so I just stood in front of the band and watched them play."

With the battle in Europe winding down, Bernhart was transferred to Fort Ord in California in early 1945 for retraining for duty in the Pacific Theater. Luckily, the whims of fate once again positively intervened in his destiny. While he was standing in line to be shipped overseas, he was unexpectedly called aside and assigned to replace a trombone player who was just discharged from the base band that had a preponderance of bebop-oriented players. Twenty minutes later his unit left Fort Ord to engage in the invasion of Okinawa. Few returned home.

When the war ended Bernhart was transferred from Fort Ord to play in an Army jazz band at the Presidio in San Francisco. In the band were Red Dorris and Harry Forbes who played with Stan Kenton at his historic 1941 engagement at the Rendezvous Ballroom in Balboa, CA; drummer Jo Jones from Count Basie's legendary All American Rhythm Section; and Wes Hensel who worked with Les Brown and Woody Herman. It was a solid swing band that Bernhart enjoyed playing in.

Upon arriving back in Chicago after his two-year military obligation ended in July 1946, Bernhart had an interaction with Lennie Tristano: "When I got home I got together with Lee Konitz.

He had become enamored of Lennie Tristano and arranged for me to play with him. It was a most unpleasant experience. Lennie unmercifully critiqued my playing and wanted to break down and restructure my method. He was extremely opinionated and I had no interest in that kind of domineering involvement."

Soon after the Tristano episode, Bernhart got a call from Bob Gioga, Stan Kenton's baritone saxophonist and road manager: "Bob asked if I wanted to try out for Stan's band. He said I was recommended by Harry Forbes whom I got to know well in San Francisco. I took a train to Detroit and went straight to the Eastwood Gardens and sat next to Kai Winding in the trombone section. After we finished the evening Stan asked me a few questions and said, 'I'll get back with you.' A few days later Gioga called and asked if I would like to join the band in Indianapolis"

It was in the summer of 1946 when Bernhart joined Kenton's Artistry in Rhythm band that featured the creative arrangements of Pete Rugolo, the vocal stylings of June Christy, and musicians of the ilk of Buddy Childers, Shelly Manne, and Vido Musso. This is the band that laid the groundwork for the Kenton cult that still continues as strong as ever. Unfortunately, the Artistry in Rhythm band came to an end in April 1947 when, on the verge of exhaustion, Kenton disbanded after a concert at the University of Alabama. Milt Bernhart was left without a job and headed back to Chicago. However, his unemployment would not last long.

"I was back in Chicago for just a few hours when Wes Hensel, an old Army band pal, called and said 'I'm with Boyd Raeburn's band in New York. Could you join us?' I was on the next train," Berhhart said. "Boyd was a quiet, unassuming man but had an adventurous, experimental, undanceable concert orchestra. There were good musicians. Buddy DeFranco was featured along with the Candoli brothers and Irv Kluger. We had French horns, six woodwinds, and an elderly bassoonist who played with John Phillips Sousa. Boyd's wife, Ginny Powell, was the vocalist. She was a trooper. It was difficult for her because the backgrounds were not easy to sing against. The book was so demanding that no one could memorize it. It was a daily challenge."

After just a few months with Raeburn, Bernhart joined a rested Stan Kenton's new Progressive Jazz Orchestra in October 1947. It was a concert-oriented band that had a strong Latin influence thanks to Kenton's interest in Latin music stimulated by his close association with Machito and new band members that included Brazilian guitarist Laurindo Almeida and bongocero Jack Costanzo. Bernhart's first solo with Kenton was on the Latin classic "Peanut Vendor" that is still one of Kenton's most popular recordings.

Bernhart stayed with Kenton for about a year, when fatigued from unending one-night stands he left the band and attempted relocation to Denver. The move did not work out, so in 1948 he joined Benny Goodman's new bebop band in New York at the recommendation of Lee Konitz. He was hired because Goodman liked his "Peanut Vendor" solo.

Goodman's band was in transition when Bernhart arrived: "By the time I joined Benny most of the bebop players left and the band was playing the old Fletcher Henderson-style book which really didn't move me. I've always had the highest respect for Benny as a musician but found him extremely difficult to work for. I left him in early 1949 and spent a few months in Denver teaching and playing casuals. Then in December I got a call to join Stan's new Innovations in Modern Music Orchestra."

When Bernhart started his third and final time with Stan Kenton in January 1950 Kenton's Innovations Orchestra had forty musicians, a large string section and a huge payroll. It played symphonic jazz in concert settings only. Although Bernhart left Kenton for the final time in 1952 he maintained a strong association with the Kenton community through the years. He played in Kenton's 1965 Neophonic Program at the Los Angeles Music Center, participated in the 1991

KKJZ-FM's Back to Balboa 50th Anniversary Celebration, toured England in a 1996 Kenton tribute, and was a regular at the Steven Harris annual Kenton Clan Party in Monrovia, CA.

What are Bernhart's thoughts about his six years with Kenton? "Playing with Stan was always exciting. He was open to new ideas, willing to experiment, and truly dedicated to his music. No one worked harder at all aspects of leading a band, including its promotion, than Stan. He took a personal interest in his musicians; not every bandleader did. I wouldn't trade my time with Stan Kenton for anything."

Conversely, what were Kenton's impressions of Bernhart? Audree Kenton recently commented on the matter: "Stan liked Milt personally and respected both his playing and intelligence. When he formed the Progressive Jazz and Innovations Orchestras he immediately sought Milt out. Stan was comfortable with him and they frequently saw each other while they were both at Capitol Records. I've known Milt for a longtime and consider him a good friend. I also have the greatest respect for Milt as musician. He made an exceptional contribution to Stan's career."

After leaving Kenton, Bernhart stayed in Los Angeles and partook in a piece of jazz history. On May 29, 1949, a Sunday afternoon, bassist Howard Rumsey started weekend jazz concerts at the Lighthouse Café in Hermosa Beach, CA. The concerts soon became a nightly feature and set the stage for the establishment of the Lighthouse All-Stars jazz group. In 1952 Rumsey invited Bernhart to join the group that played an important part in the evolution of West Coast jazz. He spent a year playing with the popular All-Stars to a consistently packed Lighthouse and recorded with groups led by fellow All-Stars Bud Shank, Shelly Manne, and Jimmy Giuffre in addition to making recordings with his own small groups. All the while he was unaware that the stage was being set for a dramatic change in the course of his career.

Marlon Brando was a fan of Lighthouse All-Star Shorty Rogers's small jazz group. At Brando's behest, Columbia Pictures executives anonymously stopped by the Lighthouse on several occasions to scout the All-Star musicians to possibly play source music in Brando's new film, the *Wild One*. Bernhart was chosen to play in the film, leading to a quarter of a century of working in over one hundred movies with virtually every Hollywood studio. He also did considerable recording and television studio work during that period.

Thanks again to his association with the Lighthouse All-Stars, Bernhart became a mainstay at Capitol Records through the 50s until the Beatles-led British Invasion changed the face of American popular music in the mid 60s. He prolifically recorded with Nelson Riddle's Orchestra for Nat Cole and Frank Sinatra, and was involved with all of Peggy Lee's Capitol recordings during that period. His trombone solo on "I've Got You under My Skin" is a Sinatra classic. There was also significant television activity.

During the 1960s, Bernhart played in numerous television variety shows such as the *Hollywood Palace*, *Julie Andrews*, *Glen Campbell*, *Jerry Lewis*, and *Smothers Brothers* shows. But by the early 1970s the studio calls were getting fewer and fewer: "What with the growth of rock music and synthesizers, there was a declining demand for large studio orchestras. I saw the handwriting on the wall and in 1973 purchased a travel agency I ran at Hollywood and Vine that primarily worked with the movie studios. Over time I shifted and built a clientele base of people in the music business. I had to; there were too many accounts receivable problems with the studios. My son David took over running it around twenty years ago."

Shortly after purchasing the travel agency, Bernhart was approached by Leo Walker, a successful representative for a paint company and president of the Hollywood Press Club, who had an office in the building Bernhart was located in. He was also the author of two books on the Big Band Era that are still in print, *The Wonderful World of the Great Dance Bands* and *Big Band Almanac*.

What happened next is described by Bernhart: "Leo loved the big bands and wanted to do a big band event. I encouraged him. Drawing on his Press Club contacts he put on a big band reunion at Sorrentino's Restaurant in Toluca Lake in 1976. There was no band, but there was an all-star dais that included Ray Anthony, Russ Morgan, Alvino Rey, and Lawrence Welk. Virtually everyone there had a connection with the music business. It was a huge success and became a highly anticipated annual event by the Los Angeles big band community."

Nineteen eighty-four was a milestone year for Walker's annual Big Band Reunion. That year he established The Big Band Academy of America as a non-profit organization to further the cause of big band music and moved the event that outgrew Sorrentino's to its permanent home at the Sportsman's Lodge in Studio City, CA. He also renamed the annual March gathering The Big Band Academy of America Annual Reunion. However, Walker's days as head of The Academy were coming to a close.

The baton was officially passed in 1986 when Bernhart took over directorship of The Academy by unanimous vote of the board of directors when Walker decided to retire and move to Mesa, AZ, where he passed away in 1995. The Academy formally honored Walker at the 1991 Reunion for his contributions and pioneering efforts.

At the urging of Reunion regular Steve Allen, Bernhart changed the event's format and added live big band music to the program in 1987. He conducted A Tribute to Glenn Miller that featured the Tex Beneke Orchestra and The Modernaires with Paula Kelly Jr. Big band radio personality Chuck Cecil served as emcee and jazz critic Leonard Feather covered the event for the *Los Angeles Times*. The Miller Tribute packed the Sportsman's Lodge's cavernous Empire Ballroom to full capacity. Allen had the right idea.

The following year Bernhart put together A Tribute to Stan Kenton that featured the University of Southern California Stage Band that played the Kenton book. With Bernhart assuming the emcee duties, an impressive array of Kenton alumni attended that included Buddy Childers, June Christy, Bob Cooper, Maynard Ferguson, Anita O'Day, Shorty Rogers, Pete Rugolo, and Bud Shank. Several of the alumni delivered remarks from the dais, creating a nostalgic atmosphere at the sold-out Sportsman's Lodge.

Since 1987 Bernhart has annually held the reunion at the Sportsman's Lodge, featuring live big band music and entertainment by the actual stars of the Big Band Era. No small event to plan and organize, it has evolved to become what is probably the largest annual gathering of Era alumni and enthusiasts in existence. Historically, two of the reunions merit special mention.

In 1997 the Academy began a new chapter in its history when it ventured into the world of achievement with its The Golden Bandstand Award that honored the most distinguished names in big band history, past or present. The first-ever awardees included Van Alexander, Steve Allen, Ernani Bernardi, Les Brown, Frankie Carle, Helen Forrest, Peggy Lee, Abe Most, Martha Tilton, and Bea Wain. All were present at the event. Among the performing highlights was Bea Wain, sounding as good as her Larry Clinton days, singing "The Ladies Who Sang with the Bands" and Frankie Carle, in his early nineties, showing why he was a star attraction with Horace Heidt and his own band, playing a medley of big band hits including his theme song "Sunrise Serenade."

Five years later, the 2002 Reunion celebrated the 60th anniversary of the founding of Capitol Records. The entire history of the storied label was reprised through live performances of Capitol's great big band hits. Two of the performances stood out. Ninety-three-year-old Alvino Rey, who had several top-ten hits with Capitol, played "Cumana," one of his Capitol recordings. Jimmy Dorsey and Kay Kyser guitarist Roc Hillman, who wrote the song with Barclay Allen, was at the Reunion and met with Rey for the first time in thirty years. Continuing with the Alvino Rey-King Sisters connection, Marilyn King, youngest of the six King Sisters, sang her full-of-life version of Capitol's first-ever hit record, Ella Mae Morse's "Cow Cow Boogie." The Capitol Tribute generated one of the reunion's all-time top turnouts.

According to Chuck Cecil, Bernhart created quite a big band legacy: "Milt Bernhart deserves recognition for what he has accomplished. He took over a small social gathering at a San Fernando Valley restaurant and turned it into the premier annual event in celebration of the Big Band Era. Under his guidance it became much more sophisticated and a very entertaining show with Pat Longo leading the house band. Through the reunion Milt has done as much as anyone to keep the spirit of the big bands alive and preserve their history. I've missed only one reunion since he took over and I'm still as excited about attending as if it's the first time."

Milt Bernhart died after a sixty-one year career as a professional jazz musician on January 22, 2004, just a few weeks before the twenty-eighth reunion took place at the Sportsman's Lodge. To what did he attribute his long and multifaceted career? Shortly before he passed away he philosophically mused in his living room: "I was very fortunate. It just seemed that every call I got worked out and led to a new opportunity. All those turning points came about because someone made a business decision that involved me. It doesn't mean that the person who experiences good timing can get away with being mediocre. I was always professionally prepared to take advantage of each turning point that came my way. Favorable circumstances were involved plus a lot of practice on my trombone."

BUDDY CHILDERS
SEVEN DECADES OF LEAD TRUMPET

The demands on a big band lead trumpet player are considerable. A lead player must play with both taste and strength. Ability to constantly play in the upper register while providing an interpretation of the song's arrangement that will be definitive for the rest of the brass section, if not the whole orchestra, is a must. In short, the lead trumpet player is in a position to mold the band. Over the last sixty plus years few have excelled in this challenging capacity with a multitude of big bands as has Buddy Childers.

Marion "Buddy" Childers was born in St. Louis on February 12, 1926, to a family with a distinct musical heritage. His grandfather played cornet and baritone horn in an Army band that once performed for President William McKinley. While growing up Childers spent time in both East St. Louis and Chicago where he took trumpet lessons at age ten from Professor Joseph Fascinato whose son was the respected leader of Chicago radio station studio orchestras. Next came several years of self-instruction in his basement listening to records and faithfully imitating everything he heard on those records. His inspirations were Harry James, Bunny Berigan, and Roy Eldridge during his 1941-43 stint with Gene Krupa's orchestra. By the time he was fourteen he felt confident enough to start performing around St. Louis. Buddy Childers was methodically preparing himself for a career with the big bands.

It is safe to say that those who succeed often take the initiative. Such was the case when Buddy Childers decided to reach for the big-time. He talked about his bold stroke during a conversation at his home in Woodland Hills, CA: "Around September 1942 I went to the Tune Town Ballroom in St. Louis to see Stan Kenton's band and get his autograph. When he came back to town in December I asked him if I could audition for the band. He told me to come to a rehearsal the next Wednesday then called me two weeks later to ask if I was interested in joining the band in South Bend, IN, on January 23, 1943. I jumped at the opportunity and left East St. Louis and high school for good."

But Childers almost blew his big chance: "It was a long wartime train ride from St. Louis to South Bend that involved train changes and when I got there I had to walk almost two miles in bitter cold to the hotel. After I checked in I laid down to rest and fell fast asleep. A little after nine o'clock Stan called and woke me up to patiently tell me to get to work. I achieved my goal of playing for Stan Kenton by the time I was sixteen but was embarrassingly late for my first night on the job. Not all bandleaders would have been as understanding."

Despite his rocky start, Childers spent the next eleven and a half years with Kenton punctuated by stops along with way with several other top tier big bands. Shortly before he joined the Army in 1944, he spent a few free weeks with Benny Carter's band, returning to Kenton after he left military service late that year. When Kenton broke up his Artistry in Rhythm Orchestra in 1947, Childers spent the summer in Chicago at the Sherman Hotel's Panther Room with the Stan Kenton All Stars under the direction of Vido Musso, and the fall touring with Les Brown before he re-associated with Kenton and his new Progressive Jazz Orchestra. After Kenton broke up that band, Childers spent the first half of 1949 in Los Angeles acquiring his Local 47 card and the last half of the year playing in Woody Herman's Second Herd.

Buddy Childers reunited with Kenton once again in his Innovations in Modern Music Orchestra, but he soon received a lucrative offer from Frank DeVol to join his studio band that was playing on Jack Smith's popular radio show featuring Dinah Shore and Margaret Whiting. After spending the fall of 1950 through the spring of 1951 doing radio work, it was back to Kenton. However, there was a misunderstanding with Kenton concerning a pay raise he received that resulted in Childers being fired by Kenton. It was next on to Tommy Dorsey into February 1952 then back to Kenton traveling extensively with his New Concepts Orchestra until the summer of 1954 when he permanently left to spend time with his family and ponder professional opportunities. He did sit in with Kenton one last time at the Tropicana Hotel in Las Vegas and the Crescendo Club in Hollywood in 1959.

During Childer's time with Kenton he had the opportunity to play in several of Kenton's unique musical organizations, each with its distinct mood and style: "The Artistry in Rhythm Orchestra was very challenging. That's when I grew as a trumpet player in order to play the sophisticated music written for the band. Stan liked Machito and the Progressive Jazz Orchestra played a lot of Latin jazz. I remember that the "Peanut Vendor" was a head arrangement. Ray Wetzel and I made the trumpet licks the trumpet section played through the whole song. It was from something we recalled from a chart Gene Roland wrote for the Vido Musso band in Chicago."

Childers continued: "One of the great experiences of my life was playing in Stan's Innovations in Modern Music Orchestra. The thrill of the first concert at the Philharmonic Auditorium in downtown Los Angeles when the whole orchestra came together sent chills up and down my spine. Stan lost a ton of money on that one. We went on the road with a forty-piece orchestra with strings and French horns, two buses, a truck, and a couple of advance men. In those days Stan and I talked a lot and he frequently consulted with me on personnel issues. That was the high of my whole Kenton experience."

Finalizing his thoughts on Kenton, Childers said: "The New Concepts Orchestra was somewhat of a Kenton milestone. That's when the band really started to swing with all those great Bill Holman and Gerry Mulligan charts. They brought a new energy to the band. I'm pleased that Bill, whom I admire very much, is still active and doing exciting work. One of the best things that happened was when Stan Levey joined the band at my suggestion after I convinced Kenton that he had kicked his drug problem. I had to do some heavy lobbying. Stan Levey was a fantastic drummer and a great guy."

What about those other legendary bandleaders Childers worked for? Here are his thoughts: "Benny Carter was one of nature's noblemen. He was such a genius in everything he did musically, whether playing alto or trumpet or writing music. He was one of the sweetest persons I've ever known. I really liked Vido Musso. He was a colorful and unique character, and a superb tenor player."

On Woody Herman, Childers commented: "Woody was wonderful and thoughtful about his people, a great bandleader. I learned something from Woody that still serves me well today. If you have a band that really works let it belong to the band. It's the musician's band, not yours. Frank DeVol was an absolute genius. He had to write all the music for *The Jack Smith Show* five days a week. He would get up at three in the morning and by five have written ten fresh arrangements to give to the copyists who came over to his house to work on them."

"Tommy Dorsey was another superb musician's musician, " Childers said. "I had an automobile accident and cut my lip in two places. On the plane to Rio with the band to perform in Brazil he showed me how to use my horn with an injured lip and by the time we landed in Rio I was able to play. There was a standard myth that Tommy never warmed up. That was false. He would call a set and stand in front of the band and put his trombone to his lips before we started playing and gently blow. He was warming up the whole time."

Buddy Childers still fondly remembers Stan Kenton for giving him his start and has the highest respect for him as a bandleader, musician, and honest and sensitive human being. He remains in awe of Kenton's phenomenal memory and ability to instantly recall the names of fans wherever the band performed In turn, important Kenton alumni appreciate and value Childers's musical and personal contributions to the Kenton bands. Legendary Kenton arranger Pete Rugolo talked about his association with Childers during a telephone conversation from his home in Sherman Oaks, CA.

"The first trumpet chair was in good hands," Rugolo said. "Buddy was a proficient lead trumpet player who was able to skillfully play some very demanding arrangements. He also had a good sense of humor and was liked by everyone in the band. Buddy got along very well with Stan. In fact I always felt that Stan took great pride in discovering him when he was only sixteen years old back in St. Louis. Buddy was a key member of Stan's organizations."

After Childers left Kenton he decided to not take on the myriad responsibilities involved with starting his own big band, instead embarking on an eclectic five year whirlwind of activity. He played for a short time in Georgie Auld's big band and sporadically for three years in Charlie Barnet's quintet, serving as Barnet's best man at his eighth marriage in Las Vegas. As a licensed pilot since 1946, Childers spent three and a half years flying all over the United States in a Beechcraft Bonanza for a commercial charter firm. He also did studio and recording work and made two albums with his own small groups on Liberty Records, *Sam Songs* with a quintet and *The Buddy Childers Quartet*. Both demonstrate Childers's ability as a creatively lyrical soloist. It's easy to get the feeling that both groups were having considerable fun playing together.

In 1959 Childers received an attractive offer to play in Nat Brandywine's house band at the New Frontier Hotel in Las Vegas. He moved there with his family primarily playing in hotel bands, returning to Los Angeles in 1966 for a decade of hectic activity, much of which involved Quincy Jones: "As soon as I got back to LA I did a Supremes album that Quincy and Billy Byers had written most of the music for. During the session Billy, who was sitting in front of me in the trombone section, turned around and said, 'I think Quincy has found himself a bugler.' Billy recommended me to Quincy on everything he did. That got me started back in town and a lot of work at Motown recording sessions. Quincy was so easy for me to work with. His genius is in producing. He knows whom to hire to get the job done. He's very much like Woody was in that respect."

Childers continued to live in Los Angeles throughout the 1970s. Ever the Renaissance man, as an accomplished photographer he actively photographed jazz album covers and musicians as a commercial sideline. Musically, from the late 70s into the early 80s, Childers played with yet another big band, the Toshiko Akiyoshi-Lew Tabakin Big Band. He made several albums and performed at numerous jazz festivals with them. Childers was challenged by the band's complex musical scores and found them stimulating to play.

After considerable professional soul searching, Childers moved to Chicago in 1982. It was there that he recorded his first album as a bandleader, *Just Buddy's*, with a roaring seventeen-piece big band. He played at a jazz club in Chicago for over a year gathering material for the project. Then along came an opportunity for what would prove to be a decade-long association that would be his last activity prior to retiring.

Come 1984 Childers permanently moved back to Los Angeles and accepted an offer from Frank Sinatra Jr. to become a member of his band. He spent the next ten years playing and arranging with the band, the last six of which involved working with Frank Sinatra Sr. as well.

Buddy Childers has always been respected by his peers as a man of sound judgment. As he did with Stan Kenton, Childers became a confidant and sounding board for Frank Sinatra Jr. whom he very much enjoyed working for. His final fulltime gig was a satisfying one for both himself and Frank Sinatra, Jr.

Terry Woodson, record producer and current musical director for Frank Sinatra Jr. commented on Childers's decade-long association with the junior Sinatra at his home in the San Fernando Valley: "I'm very familiar with Buddy's work with Frank. I know that he highly valued Buddy's musical contributions and that they worked exceptionally well together. In my opinion, Buddy ranks among the elite lead trumpet players. He's just a superb musician."

Since the early 1990s Childers remained semi-retired keeping active with his rehearsal big band, flying up until the late 90s, playing for pleasure around Los Angeles, and engaging in projects that sparked his interest. One such project was at the University of Southern California (USC) Thornton School of Music in the late 90s when he ran the USC Jazz Studies Band for a semester while director John Thomas was on sabbatical. Childers also played with the USC Band when it performed at the 1999 Big Band Academy of America Reunion at the Sportsman's Lodge in Studio City, CA.

Another project involved the recording and release of three new albums, *Come Home Again*, *Buddy Childers West Coast Quintet*, and *It's What's Happening Now*. *Come Home Again* features Childers's musical soft side on flugelhorn playing classic ballads backed by Russ Garcia's lush strings and arrangements. *Buddy Childers West Coast Quintet* was recorded at the Local 47 and includes venerable valve trombonist Jimmy Zito in the quintet. *It's whats happening now* is another swinging seventeen-piece big band album that contains three vocals by Tierney Sutton, who teaches in the Jazz Studies Department at USC and in June 2005 won *Jazz Week's* Vocalist of the Year Award. The two have collaborated for over ten years.

Sutton and Childers originally met at the 2nd Baha'i World Congress in New York in 1992. Since then Sutton has sung with Childers's quintet and big band at numerous engagements around Los Angeles including a 1997 American Jazz Institute *Tribute to Stan Kenton* at the Crowne Plaza Hotel in Redondo Beach, CA, while Childers has performed on three of her albums.

"Buddy is one of my heroes and mentors," Sutton recently stated during a telephone interview. "I've learned that he is a rare commodity as one of the few trumpet players who is as strong a jazz trumpet player as he is a lead trumpet player. He's at home in both worlds. Buddy is an incredibly loved person who helped me develop as a musician. He is a special person to me."

Buddy Childers celebrated his seventy ninth birthday in February 2005 at The Back Room at Henri's located in Canoga Park, CA. A first-rate group that included pianist John Hammond, drummer Kendall Kay, bassist Jim Hughart, trombonist Scott Whitfield, and Chiders on flugelhorn and trumpet played to a packed house. After the quintet finished performing a finely decorated birthday cake was served to the appreciative audience, capping off an evening's celebration befitting a jazz icon who has led a full life.

Significant recognition came Buddy Childers's way when on November 6, 2005, the Los Angeles Jazz Society presented him their Lifetime Achievement Award at the Society's 20th Anniversary Jazz Tribute Awards Dinner and Concert. The event was held at the Millennium Biltmore Hotel in downtown Los Angeles and hosted by Leonard Maltin. Merv Griffin served as Honorary Chair.

The Los Angeles Jazz Society's recognition is enthusiastically supported by the jazz community. Jazz trumpet player and educator Don Rader who played with the likes of Count Basie and Woody Herman talked about Childers during a visit to Los Angeles from his home in Sidney,

Australia: "Buddy and I are good friends. I saw him with Kenton and was always amazed at how he became a great lead trumpet player at such an early age. As his career evolved he also became a fine jazz trumpet player and arranger. We had some great times playing together with Percy Faith's Orchestra on Percy's tours to Japan and with Bill Holman and several other big bands around Los Angeles. He's a wonderful person and truly deserves the Society's Lifetime Achievement Award."

While relaxing at his home a few months before he passed away on May 24, 2007, Childers reflected on his life: "I'm grateful to God for giving me the talents and opportunities to accomplish what I've achieved in my lifetime. It's a gift and I've nothing to do with it. At best I'm a vehicle. I was fortunate to have started my professional career at sixteen with Stan Kenton. I've had the opportunity to travel the world playing music, and my five children are the joy of my life. From the time I was a little kid I wanted to be a pilot and I spent over fifty years flying commercially and for fun. I couldn't be more thankful for being blessed with a full life."

JACK COSTANZO
MISTER BONGO

If ever asked the question who introduced the bongo to American music the correct answer would be Jack Costanzo. Dubbed Mr. Bongo by the late jazz writer Leonard Feather, Jack Costanzo was instrumental in bringing the bongo to public recognition through his ground-breaking work with the innovative Stan Kenton Orchestra in the late 1940s. He went on to a storied musical career playing bongos and congas with Nat "King" Cole for five years and, in the 1950s and 60s, building a notable body of work in film, live entertainment, television, and the recording industry with his fiery Latin jazz albums. But now Mr. Bongo is prominently back on the music scene thanks to a pair of hot tropical albums he recently recorded. They have been critically acclaimed and are selling extremely well. Here is the story of his prolific seven-decade career in big band and Afro-Cuban jazz.

In their *The Biographical Encyclopedia of Jazz* Leonard Feather and Ira Gitler list James Costanzo's birth date as September 24, 1922. He was born of Italian heritage in Chicago at St. Michael's hospital and grew up on the Windy City's north side living in both the Irving Park Road area and an Italian neighborhood located around the intersection of North and Cleveland Avenues. Costanzo acquired the nickname Jack in honor of his paternal grandfather.

When a teenage Jack Costanzo decided to stop by a local thrift shop, he had no idea his life was about to forever change. While rummaging through the merchandise, he found and purchased a RCA album recorded by the eleven-piece Cuban band Orquesta Casino de la Playa that featured the legendary sonero Miguelito Valdez, who had the first ever hit recording of "Babalu" in 1939 and gained fame in the United States singing with Xavier Cugat. He was mesmerized by the complex Afro-Cuban rhythms and quickly became a Latin music devotee.

Costanzo started frequenting Chicago's north side Merry Garden Ballroom when he was only fourteen years old. It was there that two career-shaping events took place. First, a Puerto Rican band played a two-week engagement at the Ballroom. It was the first live Latin band Costanzo ever saw. He was awestruck by the band's bongo player and decided to learn the instrument while he was watching the drummer perform. However, there was a problem. He did not have a set of bongos.

What happened next was described by Costanzo in a 2001 interview with Jose Rizo on his Friday night KKJZ-FM *Jazz on the Lain Side* radio show: "I made my first bongos using wiped out butter tubs with bass drum heads as covers. We used to heat the skins to tighten them. I can't tell you how many skins I burned. I started out by copying the bongo players on the Casino de la Playa record. At first I didn't know where my hands would go. I'd fake it and eventually came up with my own technique. I finally got comfortable and progressed beyond straight rhythm."

The second event that impacted Costanzo's career occurred when the Ballroom owner, a Mr. Rice, who later became active in Chicago politics, introduced him to Marda Saxon. She was a professional singer, five years his senior, who was singing at the Merry Garden with Carlos Molina's Tango Orchestra that worked the society circuit at hotels and ballrooms. They paired up and entered a regional dance contest sponsored by the *Chicago Examiner*, winning the fox trot competition. The prize was a trip to New York to work at the Paramount Theater. However, Costanzo had other ideas. He boldly talked the paper into giving them cash instead, using the money to buy a wardrobe for their newly formed dance team. He refined his bongo skills while playing during Marda's solo numbers, following her footwork, accenting with the bongos.

Costanzo and Saxon married during World War II while he was serving in the Navy as an aviation ordinance petty officer. After he was discharged in 1945, the couple settled in Los Angeles and taught dance lessons at the Beverly Hills Hotel. Then, while jamming at a Hollywood nightclub, he was discovered by popular Los Angeles orchestra leader and singer Bobby Ramos who had just landed a contract to play at the prestigious Trocadero on the Sunset Strip. But Ramos did not have a bongo player in the band. He liked what he saw at the jam session and in January 1946 hired Costanzo. His professional career as a bongocero was officially launched.

Nineteen forty-six was also a landmark year in the musical development of Stan Kenton. Late that year he met Frank Grillo, better known as Machito, in New York. Kenton immediately became enamored with Afro-Cuban music, so much so that in a 1966 interview with Chuck Cecil on his *Swingin' Years* radio show he stated that he seriously considered changing his name to Stanley Martinez. In early 1947 Kenton recorded the Pete Rugolo arrangement of "Machito" as a tribute to the great Cuban bandleader who was instrumental in the development of Latin jazz. The two became admirers of each other's music and close friends.

While Kenton was immersing himself in Afro-Cuban jazz, Jack Costanzo was building a reputation as an exceptional bongo player. In late 1946 he left Bobby Ramos to join the Lecuona Cuban Boys, appearing with them at the Million Dollar Theater in Los Angeles, the Tracedero, and the Copacabana in Manhattan. It was with the Lecuona Cuban Boys that Costanzo played the conga drums for the first time. Today, he plays congas almost exclusively. Next came a stint with veteran Cuban bandleader Rene Touzet. Little did Costanzo realize that with each move he was better positioning himself for a major breakthrough to wide spread recognition.

It all came together in July of 1947 at the Masquerade Club in Hollywood where Costanzo was drumming and dancing with Marda in Touzet's band. Much to his surprise, in walked Stan Kenton who was looking for a bongo player to feature in the new band he was forming and offered him the job. He jumped at the chance to join what would become both *Down Beat* and *Metronome* magazine's big band of the year. Jack Costanzo was on his way to joining the elite of the jazz world.

What followed next was a magical year-and-a-half run with Kenton's Progressive Jazz Orchestra that did indeed make Jack Costanzo a household name. He was featured on numerous Latin songs that were arranged by Pete Rugolo. For Costanzo to showcase his skills as a percussionist, Rugolo specifically wrote one number, "Bongo Riff." His work during that period was of such excellence that he won the public admiration of no less than Machito and Leonard Feather, who anointed him Mr. Bongo while they were standing on the platform of the 30th Street Station in Philadelphia waiting for a train to go to New York to play the Paramount Theater.

One particular Kenton recording stands out for its historical significance in the archives of Afro-Cuban jazz. On December 6, 1947, at the RKO-Pathe Studios in New York City, Kenton recorded Rugolo's arrangement of "Cuban Carnival" and a head arrangement of a Cuban tune "The Peanut Vendor," first introduced in America by Don Azpiazu's Havana Casino Orchestra at New York's Place Theater in 1930. Included in this recording session along with Costanzo on bongos were Machito and Rene Touzet on maracas, Jose Mangual on timbales, and Carlos Vidal on congas. With "Artistry in Rhythm" and "Intermission Riff," the "The Peanut Vendor" would be one of the most requested melodies from the Kenton book through the years. A few weeks later Machito and Vidal again collaborated with Costanzo and Kenton to record "Bongo Riff," "Introduction to a Latin Rhythm," and "Journey to Brazil." According to Latin jazz historian Max

Salazar, Machito was impressed by the ability of Kenton's musicians to adapt to Latin rhythms and frequently reminisced about his association with Kenton as a memorable part of his career.

Pete Rugolo spoke highly of his thirteen-month association with Costanzo during a recent interview: "Jack did not know how to read music when he joined the band, but he learned fast. He was easy to get along with and all the guys in the band chipped in and helped him out, especially Shelly Manne and Eddie Safranski, his roommate on the road. Jack had a good ear, excellent technical skills, and was blessed with a natural sense of rhythm. He was an important contributor to Stan's Progressive Jazz Orchestra."

In December of 1948 Kenton disbanded to embark on an extended sabbatical from the music business. It marked the end of his Progressive Jazz Orchestra and the beginning of a five-year association for Costanzo with Nat "King" Cole and his Trio. He talked about the humorous misunderstanding that occurred when Cole hired him on Rizo's show: "After Kenton broke the band up I went to Miami for a vacation. While I was there my brother called and said there was an ad in *DownBeat* by Nat stating that he was looking for Stan's bongo player. When I got back to California my brother called again and said that Nat thinks he hired you. So he went to see Nat at the Blue Note nightclub in Chicago where he was playing and showed him my picture. Nat immediately realized he hired the wrong person. It got straightened out and I joined Nat in February, just in time for the Trio's tour with Woody Herman."

Thanks to "Nature Boy," a 1948 number one million seller for eight consecutive weeks, Nat Cole was a full-fledged star when Costanzo joined the trio. However, Cole always had a restless eye toward expanding the Trio's musical growth. With the addition of Costanzo, Cole was now able to develop new rhythmic approaches that included forays into bebop.

After the Progressive Jazz Orchestra broke up, Capitol Records quickly hired Pete Rugolo as a producer. He frequently arranged for Cole and had an opportunity to observe the impact Costanzo had on the Trio: "I always thought that Nat's playing style served as a link between Earl Hines and bebop pianists like Bud Powell. With Jack on board Nat was able to branch out and make some sophisticated bebop recordings in 1949 like "Bop Kick" and "Laugh! Cool Clown." Nat also ventured into calypso music that year with Jack doing excellent percussion work on "Calypso Blues."

The truth be told, Costanzo was most comfortable participating in the bebop movement. In the early 50s he would frequently jam at the Monday evening professional musician's jam session at Birdland with the likes of Miles Davis, Dizzy Gillespie, Charlie Parker, and Bud Powell. Costanzo commented on his friendship with Powell from his home near San Diego: "Bud gave me one of the greatest compliments I ever received. We were cooking one night at Birdland when he came up to me and said, 'What a great feeling it is to have a guy who knows how to play conga drums to jazz.'"

Cole frequently spent after hours on the road with Costanzo. Sammy Davis Jr. would join them whenever he was in town. As a result of this personal association, they confided in each other and developed a lifelong friendship. Costanzo was also close to Cole's wife Maria. They often discussed a variety of topics ranging from events of the day to the latest developments in fashion and the arts.

Costanzo enthusiastically discussed his relationship with Cole: "The two greatest persons I have ever known and worked for were Stan Kenton and Nat Cole. Nat was a perfect gentleman and very loyal to his friends. He once volunteered to help me promote a new line of conga drums that my friend Pepe Martinez was putting on the market. He did that purely as a personal favor. I remember some great times hanging out together and I'm still honored that Nat hired me because he thought I was the best man for the job."

In October of 1953 Costanzo and Cole came to an amicable parting of their ways as told by Costanzo: "I was planning to leave Nat because there was nothing more for me to accomplish. He evolved to become a vocal personality and the only work I did was on "Calypso Blues," and he and I did it all alone. While we were at the Fairmont Hotel in San Francisco he told me he would like to talk to me. We went to the Libra Lounge and he explained that he wanted to try a regular drummer. I said 'Nat, I'm so glad you told me because I was thinking of leaving anyway.' We parted the best of friends."

The stage was now set for Costanzo to branch out into myriad entertainment idioms. He kept active working with musicians by touring with Peggy Lee over the next three years. He also established himself in the movies. Through the 50s and 60s he appeared in eleven films as a musician. His single talking role was in *Harum Scarum* with Elvis Presley. Costanzo was also involved in more sound tracks than he can actually remember. One of the more memorable was his bongos background in the film noir classic *Touch of Evil*.

Then there was television. During that period Costanzo appeared on numerous television shows. The most prominent were the *Ed Sullivan*, *Dinah Shore*, *Art Linkletter*, and *Frank Sinatra* shows, and more than a few jazz specials. His friend Judy Garland made a special trip to a Hollywood nightclub he was performing at to ask him to dance and play bongos on her GE special. He also played background music on many TV shows. It is Costanzo's bongo work that sets the dramatic tone to the *Mission Impossible* theme.

During the 50s, the time of the Beat Generation, it became popular to learn how to play the bongos. Thanks to his Hollywood associations, Costanzo became known as the "Bongo Teacher to the Stars." It was a well-deserved sobriquet that developed from his personal tutelage of movie stars who included Gary Cooper, James Dean, Betty Grable, Zsa Zsa Gabor, Van Johnson, and Hugh O'Brian. Costanzo and Gabor would go on to become close personal friends. He also taught bongos to Carolyn Jones to prepare her for her film role in *Hole in the Head* and Jack Lemon for his in *Bell, Book and Candle*.

Finally, in the mid-1960s Costanzo became the top-recording percussionist in Los Angeles. However, his work was not restricted to just jazz. He recorded with numerous pop singers and rock 'n' roll groups, including Bobby Darin and the Supremes. In fact, Costanzo was the first Latin drummer to play rock 'n' roll music.

All this exposure made Costanzo well known in entertainment circles. As a result, he would often rub elbows with many famous movie stars of the day. Three in particular stand out: "I knew Ava Gardner, Betty Grable, and Marilyn Monroe very well. All three were very down to earth and seemed to have the feeling that they were given more than they were talented enough to deserve. They were all a pleasure to work with, not the least bit temperamental."

But the jewel of Costanzo's post Kenton-Cole period was his work as a bandleader. Between 1954 and 1971 fourteen of his own tropical music albums were released. However, his first album, *Afro Cuban Jazz North of the Border*, was recorded live by Costanzo as told on *Jazz on the Latin Side*: "I put together a great pickup band with guys like Zoot Sims, Joe Comfort, Bill Holman, and Herbie Steward to play at the California Club in West Los Angeles. A friend of mine came in with a home recording set and recorded us. I took it to Norman Granz and told him I'd like to record it for an album. He said, 'You don't have to, we'll release it as is.'"

A year later, in 1955, Costanzo recorded his first album with his own band. Produced by Gene Norman and released on GNP Crescendo Records, it was titled *Mr. Bongo Jack Costanzo and his Afro Cuban Band*. Among the musicians in his first group were pianist Eddie Cano, with whom he would frequently collaborate over the years, and trumpeter Paul Lopez, who over the last fifty years has crafted myriad sizzling Latin jazz arrangements for him.

After twenty-five years in the fast lane, Costanzo decided to slow down and smell the roses. In 1972 he moved with his then wife, former Playboy bunny Gerrie Woo, to San Diego. They continued to entertain through 1987 with their show band, which debuted at the Sahara Hotel in Las Vegas in 1966, at nightclubs, and on USO tours in Southeast Asia during the Vietnam conflict. Costanzo then segued into semi-retirement playing occasional engagements until 2000, the year he jumpstarted his spectacular comeback.

Jack Costanzo's return to public recognition started with the release of *Chicken and Rice* by GNP Crescendo, his first album in twenty-nine years. Next came two blockbuster albums that firmly propelled him back to national prominence in the world of jazz.

Thanks to the exposure he gained from having several of his recordings included in three albums of the late 1990s Capitol Records *Ultra-Lounge* series, Costanzo put together a band comprising San Diego-based musicians that recorded *Back to Havana* on the CuBop label. It was released in 2001, followed by *Scorching the Skins*, also on CuBop, in early 2002. Both were produced by world-class timbalero Bobby Matos. With two new smash albums, and national media exposure, Jack Costanzo was back.

Contributing to the popularity of Costanzo's band is his vocalist, the striking Marilu. Born in Panama, she was discovered by him while singing with a San Diego salsa band. Constantly active on stage with sinuously graceful dance movements, she patterns her vocal style after Celia Cruz but sounds very much like La Lupe. Costanzo has put together a crowd-pleasing combination that rhythmically cooks.

With his current popularity, not to be overlooked is Costanzo's influence on contemporary Latin jazz musicians. Classically trained violinist Susie Hansen has a popular Los Angeles Latin jazz band that incorporates a strong dose of classic Cuban charanga. At a recent private engagement in Burbank, CA, she commented on the effect Costanzo has on the current scene: "Jack Costanzo influences the musicians of today to stay true to the traditions of Latin jazz. He plays jazz with all its improvisation, and it's also dance music that is really swinging. He is respectful of the music of the past and brings it into the present, reminding us all of our musical roots."

What do other members of the Latin jazz community have to say about Costanzo? Legendary Los Angeles Latin music disc jockey Lionel "Chico" Sesma is now retired and lives in East Los Angeles. He recently assessed Costanzo's musical impact: "Starting in 1954 for almost twenty years I promoted monthly dances called Latin Holiday at the Hollywood Palladium. Jack was always a big draw. Historically, he played an important part in establishing what the huge popularity of Latin jazz is now."

Finally, Costanzo's role in Latin jazz history is cited in scholarly research. Several books such as Isabelle Leymaire's *Cuban Fire*, John Storm Robert's *Latin Jazz*, and Scott Yanow's *Afro-Cuban Jazz* document his contributions to the genre. He also made presentations and played at major jazz symposiums such as the International Association for Jazz Education National Conference in 2005 and the Los Angeles Jazz Institute's Latin Jazz Festival in 2008.

Over sixty years have gone by since Jack Costanzo joined Stan Kenton's Progressive Jazz Orchestra. When asked to reflect on his wide-ranging career he said: "I've had some great memories, four Carnegie Hall appearances with Kenton and Cole, seven trips to Cuba to jam with their best musicians, and personal friendships with many of the greats of Latin jazz like Perez Prado and Cal Tjader. But my utmost compliment came from my good friend Max Salazar when he once said to me, 'Jack, you are the pioneer. You are the guy who opened the door for bongo players to the music business.'"

ROSALIND CRON AND THE
INTERNATIONAL SWEETHEARTS OF RHYTHM

Sadly underappreciated in jazz history are the contributions of the all-female big bands that first came to public attention during the 1930s. These women ensembles peaked during World War II, experienced a postwar slump in activity, and then made a comeback starting in the 1980s. Alto saxophonist, clarinetist, and flutist Rosalind Cron spanned both eras playing with the International Sweethearts of Rhythm during the war and co-founding the contemporary Maiden Voyage Orchestra in 1978. She has played a significant role in the annals of all-female big band jazz.

Rosalind Cron was born in Boston on April 23, 1925, to a musically talented Jewish family. Her father, a Russian immigrant who left school in the third grade to help support his mother, played violin and her American-born mother studied piano. Cron's late brother also carried on her family's music tradition as a folk singer and guitarist. A published author, he was a devotee of both jazz and classical music.

While Cron was growing up in Newton, MA, late night big band remote radio broadcasts played an important part in influencing her direction in music. She talked about those days at her apartment in the Horace Heidt Estates in Sherman Oaks, CA: "When I was nine years old my dad decided it was time for me to take music lessons, but he knew I didn't have the temperament for the violin, so he suggested I listen to the big bands play at the hotels on our Atwater Kent radio. One evening I heard a sound that I loved and it happened to be a saxophone. So my dad looked in the paper and discovered that in nearby Waltham, for $3 a month, you could rent a silver saxophone and take lessons from a Mr. Steele. That's how I got started."

And what a start it was. Cron entered seventh grade lugging her saxophone to band rehearsals and quickly developed a schoolgirl crush on the ninth grade first clarinetist, Serge Chaloff, who became her mentor until he graduated from Newton High School. Chaloff would later become a member of Woody Herman's Four Brothers Band and a legendary jazz baritone saxophonist. During her junior year she met classmate George Wein who founded the Newport Jazz Festival in 1954. Wein had just started a Sunday afternoon rehearsal band in the basement of his parent's home. It was with Wein's band, sitting between Hal McKusick on lead alto sax and Chaloff on baritone sax, that Cron learned the fundamentals of section work.

An eye-opening experience occurred during Cron's junior year when Eddie Durham's All-Star Girl Orchestra played at the Raymor Ballroom in Boston. Cron relates: "I went to see the band play with my horn in hand. During a break I asked Eddie if I could sit in. He said sure. After sitting in for most of the night, I was asked by him to join the band. I thanked him but told him I had to finish high school first. I knew that night that I was determined to go on the road with a big band as soon as I graduated from high school."

Cron also experienced a surprise brush with the authorities: "During my junior and senior years I worked quite regularly around Boston, frequently with my friend, pianist Nat Pierce. The war made inroads in the ranks of young musicians and I found myself in demand by all-male big bands. I played quite a bit with George Graham who had a magnificent local big band and with small groups at supper clubs during the summer. In my senior year I was playing with a trio five nights a week in a cellar club doing my homework on the bus and subway and between sets until one night I was discovered by the Alcohol Beverage Control Commission. They asked me to leave immediately because I was under age."

A few weeks after high school graduation in 1943 Cron received an unexpected telephone call from Murray Rose, manager of Ada Leonard's popular Chicago based All-American Girl Orchestra. Leonard put together an all-female big band that debuted in Chicago at the State Lake Theater on December 20, 1940, followed by successful USO tours in 1941 and 1942. Rose extended an offer to Cron to join the band before its opening at the Oriental Theater in Chicago. To this day she does not know how her name was brought to Leonard's attention.

"My association with Ada Leonard gave me the opportunity to work with fine women musicians from around the country for the first time," Cron said. "I really enjoyed working with Ada. She was a great lady on and off the stage and ran a classy organization. But after we finished playing at the Oriental we went on a few months of one-nighters through the South traveling on hot and dusty trains and eating in greasy cafes. I came down with trench mouth twice and after only three months with Ada I was sent home. I was crushed."

As soon as Cron arrived back in Newton she started working in her father's waste paper business driving his truck and helping manually bale the paper brought to his shop. Then late in 1943 an unexpected opportunity materialized to join the International Sweethearts of Rhythm, a racially mixed ensemble that is still considered to be the best all-women swing band of its time. Cron tells how it came about.

"George Graham dissolved his successful big band in Boston and was playing with Vido Musso's band at the Strand Theater in Manhattan," Cron explained. "He had heard about the Sweethearts, who were playing up at the Apollo Theater in Harlem, and went to hear them between sets. George was so taken aback by their playing that he went backstage to congratulate everybody. That's when the Sweethearts's manager, Mrs. Rae Lee Jones, told him that they had an opening for a lead alto player because Margie Pettiford, Oscar Pettiford's sister, became ill and had to go back home to the Midwest. George suggested me to replace her and then he and Mrs. Jones phoned me at home to make an offer. After consulting with my parents I called Mrs. Jones back a few hours later at the Hotel Theresa in Harlem to tell her I'd accept and I joined the band a few days later in New Britain, CT."

The International Sweethearts of Rhythm Orchestra was organized in 1937 by Laurence Clifton Jones (no relation to Rae Lee Jones), an educator and graduate of the University of Iowa who founded the Piney Woods Country Life School in 1909. It is one of the few remaining black boarding schools in the United States. Located near Jackson, MS, Piney Woods provides disadvantaged African American youth the opportunity for excellence in education with a broad curriculum. Jones was a featured subject on the late Ralph Edwards *This Is Your Life* television show in the 1950s.

A shrewd observer of current trends in entertainment, Jones regularly listened to Phil Spitalny's all-female Hour of Charm Orchestra on their network radio show that debuted in 1935 and in 1937 saw Ina Rae Hutton and her all-female Melodears perform in Chicago. Recognized for his astuteness in promotion and public relations, he opportunistically decided to take advantage of the fame those bands enjoyed and in 1937 formed an all-girl orchestra from the students at Piney Woods to tour and raise funds for the school. All the young girls he selected to learn an instrument and play in the band were in their early teens. Jones named the group the International Sweethearts of Rhythm because in addition to African-American musicians there were band members of mixed African American parentage that included young women with Chinese, Hawaiian, Italian, Mexican, Native American, and Puerto Rican backgrounds.

The Sweethearts developed into a solid swing band and in 1939 branched out from Mississippi and started to tour through the South and Midwest. However, by April 1941 they became dissatisfied with their relationship with Piney Woods and left the institution to strike out on their own with assurances from Washington, D.C., businessman Daniel Gary. With assistance from Gary they moved their base of operation to a home in Arlington, VA, that became known as the Sweetheart House. Boxing immortal Joe Louis was a frequent visitor to the House.

A few months after the Sweethearts moved north they fully established their reputation playing with Jimmy Lunceford-like power and drive at a record breaking performance at the Howard Theater in Washington, D.C. Successful engagements followed at the Apollo Theater and Savoy Ballroom in New York along with tours of the top black theaters, traveling in their own bus fitted with overnight sleeping accommodations. There were also battles of the bands with Erskine Hawkins, Fletcher Hendrson, and Earl Hines. Louis Armstrong and Count Basie took an interest in the band and frequently watched them perform at the Apollo. With solid arrangements provided by musical directors Eddie Durham and Jessie Stone the Sweethearts were the nation's top all-female big band when Rosalind Cron became the second white musician to join them at the end of 1943. The first was Toby Butler who played trumpet. Butler was actually orphaned at five years of age and brought up by an African American family in a small town in Virginia. It is interesting to conjecture how this adoption was managed given the Jim Crow laws that existed at that time.

The week after Cron came aboard, Detroit arranger and composer Maurice King, who later wrote and arranged for numerous Motown artists, took over as musical director and a whole new world opened up for her. Rehearsals were long and hard and the music became challenging to play. King, who wrote the band's theme song that featured Cron, also started writing original ballads for the alto saxophone to further showcase her. His rigorous rehearsing paid off. The Sweethearts became stronger and tighter and were soon positively compared in the African American press to Fletcher Henderson's band.

In addition to being rigorously rehearsed by King, the Sweethearts had outstanding musicians as told by Cron: "Anna Mae Winburn, who was a trained musician, fronted the band and sang. She had a terrific stage presence and was an excellent vocalist as was Evelyn McGee. Vi Burnside was a marvelous tenor saxophonist who was recognized in a *DownBeat* poll, something unheard of in those days for a woman musician. I always enjoyed the work of Pauline Braddy, a superb drummer who could hold her own with any percussionist, male or female. Even Sid Catlett and Jo Jones admired her skill. Two hundred fifty pound Tiny Davis played a powerful trumpet and had the ability to spark the band with her music and personality. At one point Louis Armstrong unsuccessfully tried to hire her for his band. They were all fine musicians."

In the summer of 1944 the Sweethearts headed west to Los Angeles to play at Joe Morris's Plantation Club in Watts. They made their way performing at numerous military bases, starting in the Ssouth on through the Ssouthwest. The wildly enthusiastic morale-boosting reception they received from GIs, along with extra rationed gas stamps and food they were given by base personnel, sustained them on their several-week trek west.

After considerable success at the Plantation Club small gigs were interspersed by a three week stay at Curtis Mosby's Club Alabam on Central Avenue. Herb Jeffries was with them for the last week and their show was broadcast on a nightly fifteen minute radio program. However, there were problems at the Alabam as told by Jeffries during a telephone conversation from his office in Palm Desert, CA: "I remember that the Club Alabam was padlocked shut by the IRS because of tax problems the last day of our gig. I got paid because I always arranged for payment in advance. The Sweethearts didn't do that and as a result they didn't get paid."

Jeffries commented on his experience with the Sweethearts: "The Sweethearts were not a novelty act. They were a very good swing band with excellent soloists, including Rosalind Cron. I enjoyed listening to them play. The customers at the Alabam were always hard to please and the Sweethearts passed the test. The patrons enthusiastically responded to their sound."

During this time Cron and the Sweethearts' trumpeter Jean Star decided to catch Benny Carter and his band who were playing Sunday afternoons at a club on Hollywood Boulevard: "For two straight Sundays we took our horns and traveled on the Red Car to sit in with the band for a couple of sets. Playing next to Vido Musso is a treasured memory. What chutzpah we had in those days. At the end of Carter's gig Jean was invited to join his trumpet section and left town with the band."

The Sweethearts spent nearly two months in Los Angeles performing at the Plantation and Alabam and appearing on four Armed Forces Radio Services *Jubilee* shows that featured the irrepressible Ernie "Bubbles" Whitman as emcee. They also experienced a dose of discrimination that was costly to them when they lost an opportunity to play at the Orpheum Theater in downtown Los Angeles because a major country western star refused to share billing with them. All in all, 1944 proved to be a good year for the Sweethearts with the annual *DownBeat* poll ranking them as America's number one all-female orchestra from among the myriad women bands that were active during the war years.

A major highlight of Cron's time with the Sweethearts was their six month USO tour of Europe from July 1945 to January 1946. The tour came about as a result of their *Jubilee* broadcasts that prompted black GIs overseas to write to see them perform live. They landed in Le Havre, France, and went to Paris for three weeks where they played at the Olympia Theater and then on to Germany attached to the Third and Seventh Armies. The Sweethearts played all through Germany traveling in three trucks, one with a hole in the roof, to venues ranging from the Stuttgart Opera House to military bases and airfields. Cron recalled the weather conditions: "That winter was bitterly cold. We were provided only one uniform that included two shirts, two skirts, a jacket, a pair of slacks, and a cute little cap. I don't know what we would have done without the black soldiers who were base quartermasters. They came to our rescue providing us long johns, pants, boots, mittens, and woolen caps."

Notwithstanding positive experiences performing in Europe and Los Angeles, life on the road with the Sweethearts was not without problems. Cron remembers that traveling through the South as a white girl in a black band was not easy and that there were many close calls with the authorities.

"It was very difficult and an eye opener because coming from the area of Boston I grew up in I was not aware of racial prejudice," Cron recalled. "When I first heard of Jim Crow I thought it was a person I would meet, not the name for segregated laws. I actually spent a night in jail in El Paso in a darkened cell for walking in public with a black soldier who was in uniform. In the South I disguised that I was white on stage with makeup and different wigs to avoid trouble when the local sheriff came to check if there were any white musicians in the band. I will always remember the many wonderful black families that had me in their homes to spend the night when there were no public accommodations at great risk to themselves."

Rosalind Cron's association with the Sweethearts was an experience she has not forgotten: "My years with the Sweethearts shaped my life. I learned about the depth of racial prejudice and segregation that existed and personally experienced both. I also formed long-lasting friendships that I continue to cherish. Many of us still talk on the phone sharing our experiences and keeping up with each other. It's a unique bond that I haven't been able to replicate with many others over the years."

When the International Sweethearts of Rhythm returned from their USO tour in January 1946 Cron decided to leave the organization. Two factors came into play. She was disillusioned because she and the band members felt they were being exploited with substandard pay plus she was exhausted from the constant travel. The time had come to move on so Cron set out with her best friend from the band, saxophonist Helen Saine: "Everyone called her Saine. She was five feet seven, half black and half Italian, striking in looks, and went out several times with both Joe Louis and Sugar Ray Robinson. She was loved by everyone for her sweetness of character and kindness."

The pair rented a cold-water, fourth floor apartment in Spanish Harlem. Cron played in a four-piece combo led by Estelle Slavin in a piano bar while Saine attended modeling school. In April they went their separate ways when Saine moved to Chicago to be closer to her fiancé. Cron returned home to Newton where she spent an unhappy few months working as a book-keeper in a bank and occasionally playing in local rehearsal bands due to limited professional opportunities in music, as most work went to male musicians who returned from the war. She also studied clarinet with former principal clarinetist in the Boston Symphony, Emile Arcieri, and experienced a change in the course of her personal life.

In 1948 Cron became inactive in music when she married a visiting non-musician from California. They had two sons in the 1950s. She and her husband spent 1949-1950 in Arizona where he studied at the American Institute for Foreign Trade then moved to the New York area before they permanently settled in Los Angeles in 1953. Cron studied Portuguese at the Institute while her husband was enrolled there. There was a health issue when she was struck with polio shortly after they moved to Southern California. After fully recovering in 1959 Cron launched a musical comeback when she started playing in the clarinet section of the Santa Monica Concert Band and the sax section of their big swing band. Next to come was a decade of musical satisfaction.

"The 1960s were a very good time for me musically," Cron enthusiastically commented. "I married trombonist Bob Pring after I divorced my first husband and started to teach clarinet to beginners and played with the concert band until 1970. Through answering an ad in the Local 47 *Overture* I also spent seven years with Kay Carlson's weekly rehearsal band which was eventually taken over by the late Dick Cary, who was a superb arranger and played several instruments. That was a high spot of my musical life. I sat side-by-side with Herbie Steward for a few years and played with great musicians like Teddy Edwards, Bill Perkins, Rex Stewart, and Zeke Zarchy. During that period I was doing the best playing I had ever done."

Unfortunately, Cron's musical activities were interrupted in the early 1970s when she experienced an accident caused by her hypoglycemic condition. That incident brought about the end of a quintet she had just formed. She did continue her career as an executive secretary in the insurance industry in which she had been working since 1967. Cron did not seriously return to involvement in the world of music until 1978, thanks to a social gathering she held for the legendary pianist Marian McPartland.

"When my brother was in New York on business in the mid 70s he stopped by The Carlyle Hotel to listen to Marian McPartland play," exclaimed Cron. "He sketched her and during a break showed her his work and gave her my phone number because he knew that we were both interested in writing about women musicians. She called me and we talked on the phone several times over the next few years. I provided her contact information for all the Sweethearts and she called them whenever she worked the cities in which they lived. In 1978 Marian phoned to tell me she was coming to LA for a gig, so I put on an open house for her in my apartment in Koreatown that was attended by female musicians from all over the West Coast. We had a fantastic time."

Marian McPartland vividly recalled the event from her home in Port Washington, NY: "I enjoyed Roz's gathering and very much appreciate all the work she did putting it together. We became friends for life and she was of great help in providing me material for the chapter on the Sweethearts in my book *Marian McPartland's Jazz Life*. She's a fine musician and one of my favorites."

Soon after the McPartland soiree, Cron resumed playing alto and clarinet and formed an all-female rehearsal band with Los Angeles drummer Bonnie Janofsky, whom she met at an upstairs club on Lincoln Boulevard in Santa Monica. It was the band that in the early 1980s evolved to become the seventeen-piece all-female Maiden Voyage Orchestra currently led by jazz saxophonist and flutist Ann Patterson. Eventually, burdened with juggling an onslaught of secretarial jobs with temp agencies, Cron turned the band over to Janofsky. Today, Maiden Voyage, along with the Diva and Kit McClure bands in New York, are the premier contemporary all-female big bands in the country. Then as the 70s came to a close Cron formed her own short-lived big band and in 1980 participated in her final formal involvement with the International Sweethearts of Rhythm.

Immediately after World War II the demand for all-female big bands came to an end, and the Sweethearts were no exception to their decline. Following numerous postwar personnel changes and the death of Rae Lee Jones, the organization disbanded in 1949. It was not until thirty-one years later, in March 1980, that fifteen remaining Sweethearts reunited one last time at the Third Annual Women's Jazz Festival at the Crown Center Hotel in Kansas City.

The theme of the Festival was "Commemorating Decades of Female Achievement in Jazz." At the urging of Marian McPartland, on the third day the Festival hosted a two hour salute to the International Sweethearts of Rhythm. Music was provided by the Bonnie Janofsky-Ann Patterson Big Band. Jazz critic and historian Leonard Feather served as narrator and several Sweethearts shared their current personal activities from the stage. National Public Radio's *Jazz Alive* program covered the event.

The Festival proved to be well worth the trip to Kansas City for Cron: "We had not seen each other for over three decades. It was truly a pleasure renewing old friendships and a special thrill when Leonard Feather closed the program reading congratulatory telegrams from President Carter and Norman Granz. A few weeks after the Festival Leonard wrote an extensive review of the salute along with a history of the Sweethearts that was published in the *Los Angeles Times*. No other all-female band had ever been so honored at an event of such stature."

Renewed interest in the Sweethearts was sparked by the Festival. Until then very little was available on the Sweethearts as they made only a few 78 rpm records, film shorts, and radio broadcasts that were extremely difficult to find. That all changed in 1984 when Rosetta Reitz released the first complete long playing album of the Sweethearts, consisting primarily of air checks, on her Rosetta Records label. Nat Hentoff wrote glowingly of the album in the *Wall Street Journal* in January 1985. A thirty minute documentary on the Sweethearts followed the album. Titled *The International Sweethearts of Rhythm*, it was screened at the New York Film Festival in 1986 and tells the Sweetheart's story through rare archival film clips and oral history interviews. The film has been shown at over one hundred film festivals world-wide and frequently airs on public television stations. Long sought audio and visual material on the Sweethearts was finally available.

The afternoon Cron returned home from Kansas City in 1980 she received a telephone call asking if she would play in an all-black rehearsal band in Compton, CA: "That was the beginning of two years of playing with all-male black rehearsal bands. It was really a fantastic experience, I met such wonderful musicians. Then by 1982 I had risen in the corporate world and had to give up playing and concentrate on my business career until I retired in 1993."

Since Cron retired she has remained active in the milieu of music. One activity involved a jazz history project dear to her heart. In the early 90s she developed a friendship with Dr. Sherrie Tucker while working with Tucker on her highly acclaimed 2000 book *Swing Shift "All-Girl" Bands of the 1940s*. Cron reviewed Tucker's work for Local 47 and 802 publications and appeared on television on a *CBS Sunday Morning News* show feature on the book. Four years later she was interviewed for Women's History Month on a *Riverwalk Jazz* radio program that saluted the Sweethearts.

In 1996 Cron was in Washington, D.C., with four original Sweethearts when in celebration of African American Music Month the International Association of African-American Music awarded the International Sweethearts of Rhythm their Diamond Award for the Sweethearts' work during the 1940s as the finest all-female black band in the country. She also consulted with Kit McClure on McClure's *The Sweethearts Project* CD which was released in 2004. Cron even returned to performing, playing with the Los Angeles Valley College Wind Ensemble from 2002 through 2004 after surgeries that replaced arthritic joints in both her hands.

At her apartment on a sunny San Fernando Valley afternoon Cron reflected on her career in music that innocently began with saxophone lessons in Newton in 1934: "My involvement with the Sweethearts was one of the great experiences of my life. It influenced how I raised my sons and formed my political views. A particularly fond memory is my association with the superb musicians I've met and worked with through the years and the many friendships I formed with them. Looking back at my adventures in music and accomplishments in business I feel I have led a full life. I consider myself a very lucky lady. I can still play my horns and I'm loved by four fantastic men, my two sons and two grandsons!"

ALAN GREENSPAN
BIG BAND ERA ALUMNUS

Arguably the most powerful person in the United States next to the four Presidents he served under was Alan Greenspan, former chairman of the Federal Reserve Board, and alumnus of the Big Band Era. In his capacity as chairman, Greenspan was responsible for the direction of the world's most powerful economy by controlling our nation's money supply and credit conditions. He was capable of generating economic expansions and recessions. His every utterance was scrupulously analyzed and could cause violent fluctuations in the stock market.

In his youth Greenspan gave no indication that the fate of our free enterprise system would rest in his hands. He was born in New York in 1926 and raised by his divorced mother in Manhattan's Washington Heights neighborhood. At an early age he demonstrated an exceptional facility for numbers by computing complex mathematical problems in his head and memorizing the batting averages of virtually every major league baseball player. Greenspan also loved to play sports. He was active in tennis and a natural left-handed first baseman in baseball.

Greenspan began his brilliant scholastic career graduating from George Washington High School, located at 191st Street and Audubon Avenue, a veritable factory of the famous at that time. Among those who attended George Washington High School in the pre-World War II era were Secretary of State Henry Kissinger, United States Senator Jacob Javits, movie star Paulette Goddard, NBC Television news host and moderator Edwin Newman, bandleader and composer Van Alexander, Benny Goodman's vocalist Helen Ward, jazz drummer Shelly Manne, and Les Brown's longtime saxophonist and vocalist, Butch Stone. New York Giant's shortstop Buddy Kerr and heavyweight contender Bob Pastor who gave Joe Louis two of his toughest fights were also prewar products of Greenspan's alma mater. Notable postwar athletes include baseball stars Rod Carew and Manny Ramirez.

While in high school, Greenspan played the clarinet and tenor saxophone. He was sufficiently accomplished to win admission to the Julliard School, but soon moved on to try his hand as a professional musician with Henry Jerome's band.

Trumpeter Jerome was an established bandleader in the New York area during the 1940s. In the early 40s his sixteen-piece dance band was dubbed "Henry Jerome and His Stepping Tones" and played sweet music in a style very similar to Hal Kemp. In 1944 he changed over to a more bop-oriented format. Even though the band had some fine musicians such as saxophonist Al Cohn and drummer Tiny Kahn along with arranger Johnny Mandel, it was somewhat ahead of the times and met with little success. Jerome eventually gave up bandleading and moved on to a lucrative career as a record producer in New York working with Coral and Decca Records.

Leonard Garment, advisor to President Richard Nixon, who was also in the Jerome organization as a saxophone player, recalls that Greenspan kept the bands books (they always balanced), and helped the musicians with preparing and filing their income taxes. Garment also remembers the future Fed chief voraciously reading books on finance and the stock market between sets.

Although quite a good musician, Greenspan soon realized he would never be great. After about a year, he left Jerome to a obtain bachelor's and master's degrees in economics from New

York University, and with William Townsend opened his own economic consulting firm. He eventually received his Ph.D. in economics from New York University in 1977.

In 1966 a chance meeting set the stage for Greenspan's career in government. While taking a lunchtime stroll on Broad Street in Manhattan's financial district he encountered his old friend Leonard Garment, who was working as an attorney in the same law firm that employed Richard Nixon. They had lunch at the Bankers Club and as they parted Garment suggested that Greenspan meet the future President.

Meet they did. Nixon was highly impressed with Greenspan's views on the federal budget, so much so that, as chief executive, he appointed him Chairman of the President's Council of Economic Advisers in 1974. Greenspan returned to his consulting practice in 1977, and was called back to government by President Ronald Reagan who appointed him as chairman of the Federal Reserve Board in August 1987. He served in that capacity through January 2006. It is frequently said that one of the main keys to success is being in the right place at the right time. Alan Greenspan was certainly in the right spot when he unexpectedly ran into Leonard Garment in 1966 after not seeing him for several years.

Of all the Big Band Era alumni who have gone on to achieve non-musical success, in terms of position and power Alan Greenspan ranks at the top. He was constantly in public view and had the ability to affect business conditions worldwide through his steerage of the United States' economy. However, the next time you read of or hear about Greenspan, keep in mind that he received his first paycheck on his first job not as an economist, but as a saxophone player with Henry Jerome's big band.

JAKE HANNA
60 YEARS OF SWING

Few jazz drummers command the respect of their peers that Jake Hanna does. For example, Mel Lewis commented in a 1985 *Modern Drummer* interview that there were four major living big band drummers: Louie Bellson, Jake Hanna, Buddy Rich, and himself. In referring to Hanna, the British publication *The Rough Guide to Jazz* states, "Although he emerged too late to achieve quite the reputation of Buddy Rich, his talents are comparable." Over a professional career spanning seven decades Jake Hanna has established himself as a popular and superior percussionist who is a skilled artist with the brushes and comfortable playing with both big bands and small groups.

John Hanna was born in Boston's Dorchester area on April 4, 1931. He acquired the nickname Jake while growing up in Dorchester thanks to a strong resemblance to his uncle Walter who was referred to as Jake. There was musical talent in the Hanna family. His father played cymbals in the *Boston Herald Traveler* newspaper band and his older brother Willie, who tutored Hanna on the drums, had a reputation around Boston as a drummer who kept perfect time.

Hanna started to play drums in the Catholic Youth Organization band at St. Brendan's parish in Dorchester when he was six years old. However, a conflict soon developed. He loved baseball and spent as much time playing the game as he did practicing the drums. In 1939 his father took him to his first major league baseball game at Fenway Park to see the Red Sox play the New York Yankees. Hanna surely never dreamed that thirty-five years later Yankee centerfielder Joe DiMaggio, whom he saw that day, would personally request to meet him when both were dining at the Irish Pub in Atlantic City.

During a visit at his home in Los Angeles, Hanna talked about his extensive career. A master raconteur, he started out commenting on his activities during the World War II Big Band Era scene in Boston. Specifically, during the war years he spent a lot of time at the RKO Theater in downtown Boston watching the great big bands play: "The RKO is where I got my musical education. All I had to pay was thirty-five cents to get in and I had a free pass to go backstage from my father's newspaper. I saw a lot of great drummers. There was Buddy Schutz with Jimmy Dorsey and Buddy Rich with Tommy Dorsey. Woody Herman appeared a lot with Don Lamond. Count Basie, Benny Goodman, Lionel Hampton, Louie Prima, they all played there. My favorite act was the Mills Brothers. They were the best of all the vocal groups."

With seeing all the great Swing Era bands perform at the RKO it was only natural that Hanna would emulate their drummers: "While I was growing up Gene Krupa was my biggest influence. I loved Buddy Rich's playing. I also paid close attention to Buddy Schutz who in my opinion is a much underrated drummer. Later on in my career Denzel Best with his wire brush work had a major impact as did Kenny Clarke and Jo Jones."

Hanna started performing professionally at a very early age; he had his first paid job when he was only thirteen. It was the war years and there was a lot of work available with both combos and big bands. He also started hanging around with skilled Jewish musicians from Ruby Braff's neighborhood who were playing pure jazz. Their association served as a good learning experience. Hanna continued to play all over Boston whenever he could get work during high school and until he left home to join the Air Force in 1950.

After Hanna left the Air Force in 1953 he played with a series of big bands that included Tommy Reed, Ted Weems, Buddy Morrow, Maynard Ferguson, and in Toshiko Akiyoshi trios. He commented on how they were to work with: "It's never worth it if you're not having fun, and I had a lot of fun working with all of them. Tommy Reed was out of Chicago. He had a very good band. Buddy Morrow and Maynard were truly great guys to work for. They always took responsibility for everybody else's mistakes. If somebody hit a clam they would immediately say it was their fault. Ted Weems was hilarious He and Woody were the two funniest guys I ever worked for. I had a great time with Toshiko. I played with her trio for five straight summers at the Hickory House in New York. She's a superb musician and we became good friends. While I was playing with all those bands I was able to squeeze in some work at Berklee. It was a busy time."

In 1958 Hanna returned to Boston and started a year's run playing in the house band at the Hub City's Storyville night club: "That was absolutely the best band I ever played with. Lou Carter and Champ Jones and I were the rhythm section. The front line was Buck Clayton, Vic Dickenson, "Pee Wee" Russell, and Bud Freeman. The vocalist was Jimmy Rushing, one of the all-time great jazz singers and a fantastic human being. We just opened and played the intermissions and everything always went perfectly. Can you imagine? That was just a house band. George Wein owned the club and occasionally played a little piano in the band. Everyone loved George. He and the Marienthal brothers who ran the London House and Mr. Kelley's in Chicago were the best of all the club owners."

After Storeyville, Hanna went on the road for a couple of years with Marian McPartland. How that job came about is an interesting story. Anita O'Day happened to be singing at Storyville one evening with her own group. Her drummer, Johnny Pool, got sick and Hanna filled in for him. McPartland was at the club that night and sat in on the piano for just a few songs. It just so happened that everything she played blended together perfectly with Hanna. During the break they had a friendly but innocuous little chat and then, to his surprise, she called him the next day to ask him to go on the road with her starting out in Milwaukee.

Hanna truly enjoyed working for McPartland. In fact, it was a career highlight: "Marian was the all time greatest, the easiest of them all to work for. Without a doubt the classiest person I ever played for and a trip to hang out with when we were on the road. We had many laughs together."

Next came the start of a long association with one of the best-loved of all bandleaders, Woody Herman. Hanna played with Herman for a very short time in the late 1950s then joined his Swingin' Herd for about two years in 1962. He was with that edition of Herman's many Herds from its inception.

"It was January 1962 and I had just finished a short stint with Harry James," Hanna said. "Gus Johnson left Woody to stay in New York and I was hired to replace him in a sextet that was supposed to go out on the road. But before the road trip we were booked to play the Metropole in Manhattan with a big band Woody put together just for that engagement. That was a powerful band. Shelly Manne came in on our third night and we were really roaring. He called everyone in town and by the second set you couldn't get in and by the end of the evening we were booked all across the country."

Hanna added: "That ended Woody's plans for the sextet. Gene Williams, the bartender, spread the word and every night the place was packed with musicians. Bob Haggart and Zoot Sims showed up a lot as did Joe Cronin, Woody's buddy from the Red Sox. Nat Pierce rewrote the book. We played the history of the Herman band, the 40s hits, the Four Brothers Band, and the Third Herd. As time went on we started playing our own arrangements of other songs like "The Days of Wine and Roses." Hank Mancini told Woody that it was the best arrangement of the song he ever heard. What a band and what a bandleader."

Herman and Hanna had a great relationship: "I worked with Woody a lot over the years. I was with him at his 40th Anniversary Carnegie Hall concert and put together a great little combo for him that played the Rainbow Room for a month in early 1984. That was the first time Scott Hamilton and Warren Vache worked with Woody. Polly Podewell was the vocalist. I loved Woody and we had a great relationship. My wife Denisa and I went out with him a lot socially to have dinner and to go to clubs to hear bands play. He was quite a guy."

Not long after leaving Herman, Hanna spent almost ten years playing in the *Merv Griffin Show* starting in 1965. In fact, he permanently relocated to Los Angeles with the show around 1970: "Television work was fun and Merv was a real nice guy. Everyone respected him because he was a very good musician. The band itself was excellent; we had the best players available. But the music wasn't stimulating. All in all it was an interesting experience but not one I would want to repeat unless Merv ran the show. He took care of everyone very well."

After Hanna left the Merv Griffin Show in the 70s he spent the balance of his career freelancing. Hanna also did some freelance work while he was with Griffin in Hollywood that led to an involvement with a historic jazz album. He reminisced about that period of his career: "Around the time I was thinking of leaving Merv I got involved with the start of Supersax [a Charlie Parker tribute band from 1972]. Buddy Clark and Med Flory were instrumental in getting it going. I remember that after a Saturday afternoon rehearsal out in the Valley Jack Nimitz dropped a bomb when he unexpectedly told us we were booked to play the next Monday night at Donte's in North Hollywood. Wally Heider came by and saw us. He liked our sound and set up an audition at his studio for executives from three record companies to come and hear us play. Two of them weren't interested. They insisted we play Burt Bacharach songs. Then Mauri Lathower from Capitol jumped up and said 'I'll take them.' A few days later we recorded *Supersax Plays Bird* and we were off and running."

During his freelance days Hanna spent a lot of time with Concord recording for Carl Jefferson, going all the way back to the start of the label. His first Concord album was with Herb Ellis and in 1975 he did *Live at Concord* with a septet he and Carl Fontana co-led. It was the label's biggest seller ever up until that point. Hanna is proud of the fact that he was instrumental in getting Rosemary Clooney, Scott Hamilton, and Woody Herman to record with Jefferson. In fact, in 1977 he put together Clooney's first Concord album, *Everything's Coming up Rosie*. Hanna picked the songs and selected the musicians. That album played a big part in her late 1970s comeback.

Continuing with his freelance work, Hanna spent a few years touring with Bing Crosby until he passed away in 1977. Much has been written about Crosby, both pro and con, and Hanna has definite impressions of him as a vocalist and a person: "We had a good quartet with Bing in front swinging away. The job itself was a piece of cake. There were no problems with the music and you couldn't hang out with a better group of guys. Bing was the best singer I ever heard or worked with. He had perfect, swinging time and could do anything and sing everything, any type of song. Great stage presence, boy could he work the audience and they loved him. I was amazed by his photographic memory. Bing could glance at a lyric and memorize it in seconds. What a top-notch gentleman. He treated everyone with dignity and respect. Thanks to him we flew first class on Pan Am on a special plane they named The Bing Crosby. There'll never be another Bing Crosby. I miss him."

While reflecting on his career, Hanna spent some time explaining why he never aspired to be a bandleader. He said that there were too many hassles and responsibilities that were unrelated to music such as taxes, securing bookings, and the inevitable personnel problems that confront the boss. He emphatically stated that he just wanted to play the music and never had any interest in running a band. It was obvious that he is a musician, not a businessman.

Musical preference was the next topic. Although Hanna came to prominence in the Bebop Era, he has a clear-cut partiality for music of the Swing Era: "My basic love is the music of the 30s and 40s, the days of the big bands. That was the time of the great American songbook, Cole Porter, George Gershwin, Harry Warren, and Richard Rogers. I especially admired the work of Jerome Kern. I still listen to CDs of all those great big bands and songs. That's the music I grew up with and it's still what I most enjoy playing and listening to."

Through the years Hanna played myriad jazz festivals. Several came to mind: "I got off to a great start. My first festival was the Newport Jazz Festival with Toshiko. The Concord Festival was always tops. The Nice Festival in France was another good one. The sound was excellent at both those places. I played Blackpool in England a bunch times. It's well organized and always a lot of fun. I very much liked the Sweet and Hot Music Festival here in LA that took place every Labor Day weekend. I've played it almost every year. Wally Holmes, the late trumpet player, ran it and did a good job putting it together."

What is Jake Hanna up to these days? Just to keep in shape he occasionally plays for a night or two with small groups around Los Angeles. He's still interested in the local scene and gets out to the clubs now and then to check out what's going on. He has an extensive record collection that he listens to and gives lessons to experienced drummers who are interested in improving their technique. Travel is on the agenda as he occasionally participates in educational clinics at jazz conferences and still plays at jazz festivals around the country. He has no trouble keeping busy.

In line with his interest in mentoring percussionists, Hanna closed with passing along his thoughts on how they can improve their skill and technique: "I would recommend listening to CDs of the great drummers, Krupa and Rich, Dave Tough for cymbals, Denzel Best for brushes, and Jo Jones for anything. Also get film of them and watch them play. Don't try to copy any one of them. Just practice religiously and what you heard and saw will kick in and you'll come up with your own style. I feel very fortunate that when I was starting out I was able to see and hear in person all those famous drummers at the RKO in Boston. That's how I learned. Those big band days with all the many outstanding drummers were a unique period of time that we'll probably never see again."

ROC HILLMAN
WITNESS TO THE DORSEY BROTHERS BREAKUP

Guitarist Roc Hillman had the good fortune to participate in many of the historic occurrences of the Big Band Era, including the Memorial Day afternoon in 1935 when the Dorsey Brothers Orchestra broke up, propelling Jimmy and Tommy Dorsey to go their separate ways. Before we take a look at that major event in big band history, a few words about Roc Hillman, a giant of the classical and jazz guitar, are in order.

Roc Hillman was born on July 13, 1910, in Arvada, CO. After World War I, his family moved to nearby Denver where he grew up in an Italian neighborhood, acquiring the nickname Rocky, which was soon shortened to Roc.

Hillman was part of a musical family. Although his father was a printer and newspaper editor by trade, he also appeared on the vaudeville circuit as a banjo player and tap dancer. His oldest sister, with whom he donned a blond wig and female dress to do a dance act in high school, won Charleston dance contests in Denver and danced professionally in vaudeville. His youngest sister was a ballerina who appeared in the New York theater.

During an interview at his home in Woodland Hills, CA, Hillman recalled the impact of his high school theatrical activities on his friends: "I dressed as a girl in a theater act with my sister. However, I never dared let my buddies know it was I."

While attending the University of Colorado, Hillman worked as a cub reporter for the *Denver Post* and played guitar in both college- and Denver-based bands. He gained local journalism fame by doing a major feature on Babe Ruth and Lou Gehrig when the then World Champion New York Yankees played an exhibition game in Denver.

January 1934 found Hillman playing with the Vic Schilling band at the Broadhurst Hotel in Denver. Also playing in Denver was the Smith Ballew band with a young trombone player by the name of Glenn Miller. Miller approached Hillman in a Denver music store and asked him to join the Ballew band just as the band was about to head east to New York City.

Hillman has fond memories of his association with Miller: "A lot of people thought Glenn Miller was formal and intimidating. I found him to be one of the boys, a great guy, and a pleasure to work with. I owe my career to being discovered by him."

Soon after arriving in New York the Smith Ballew band broke up. Thanks to Glenn Miller's recommendation, Hillman and several other band members joined the new Dorsey Brothers Orchestra. It was a solidly swinging band. In addition to Jimmy and Tommy Dorsey, it featured the arrangements of Miller, the hard-driving drumming of Ray McKinley, and the hot trumpeting of Bunny Berigan.

In the spring of 1935 a young crooner from Hoosick Falls, NY, who had just won an amateur singing contest on Fred Allen's *Town Hall Tonight* radio show, joined the band as its male vocalist. His name was Bob Eberly, older brother of Ray Eberle, who later became Glenn Miller's vocalist.

Although the Dorsey Brothers band was doing quite well and securing top bookings, trouble loomed on the horizon. The problem was the constant fighting between Jimmy and Tommy Dorsey. Recalling the situation, Hillman explained: "Everyone knew that Jimmy and Tommy squabbled since they were little kids. But it had gotten so bad that Glenn Miller couldn't conduct rehearsals. He was so frustrated that he left to help Ray Noble put together his band."

Just a year after the band was formed, the Dorsey Brothers landed the top spot in the country as the lead band for the 1935 summer season at the Glen Island Casino in New Rochelle, NY. With a romantic view of Long Island Sound, the venue was considered the most prestigious and popular dance spot in the East with remote radio broadcasts beamed nationwide. Hillman's old friend Lou Gehrig attended the band's opening night performance along with several Yankee teammates.

The Dorsey Brothers conflict came to a head on Memorial Day during an afternoon performance. As bandleader Tommy Dorsey counted off the tempo for "I'll Never Say Never Again Again," Jimmy Dorsey called out 'Isn't that a little fast, Mac?' Without saying a word, Tommy glared at Jimmy and walked off the bandstand never to return.

Hillman was not surprised at what happened: "The Dorseys were different as night and day. Tommy was a high-strung perfectionist. Jimmy was unaggressive, laid back, and always needling Tommy. Both had short fuses. It was just a matter of time."

After the breakup, Jimmy continued to lead the original Dorsey Brothers band. He achieved huge success peaking in 1941 and 1942 with a series of million-selling hits featuring vocalists Bob Eberly and Helen O'Connell, the biggest of which were "Green Eyes" and "Tangerine."

Tommy immediately took over the Joe Haymes band and went on to develop what many think was the greatest all around band of the Big Band Era. He hit the big time in 1937 with "Marie" and "Song of India" and in the early 1940s featured a skinny kid from Hoboken, NJ, by the name of Frank Sinatra as his vocalist along with Connie Haines and Jo Stafford and the Pied Pipers.

The Dorsey Brothers eventually buried the hatchet and got together to form a new band in 1953. They met with huge success securing a national television show. Unfortunately, fate intervened as the two brothers died within six months of each other. Tommy choked to death in his sleep in November 1956 in his home in Connecticut. Jimmy died of throat cancer in a Manhattan hospital in June 1957.

As for Roc Hillman, he stayed with Jimmy Dorsey until he switched over to Kay Kyser's band in the spring of 1940. Commenting on his time with Kyser, Hillman noted: "Kay was good to his musicians. He had a great sense of humor, loved selling swing music, and always catered to the dancers."

While with Kyser, he appeared in several movies with the band and became a successful songwriter penning two major hits in "My Devotion" and "Cumana." "My Devotion," sung by Vaughn Monroe, was on the hit parade for 14 weeks in 1942 and earned a gold record. "Cumana" was recorded by numerous bands including Freddy Martin's and Alvino Rey's. Hillman actually started writing songs in the early 1930s while he was with Vic Schilling in Denver. He originally specialized in novelty tunes, but soon graduated to popular arrangements. Over thirty of his songs were published and recorded.

In 1942 Hillman was drafted into the Army. His first assignment was to lead the Headquarters Western Defense Command Band. The band played swing music at over one hundred military locations throughout Southern California and made several appearances at the famed Hollywood Canteen. His pianist and arranger was jazz legend Gil Evans who after the war arranged for Claude Thornhill and collaborated with Miles Davis on the seminal 1949 *Birth of the Cool* and 1959 *Sketches of Spain* jazz albums.

Hillman was given a new assignment in 1944 that lasted for the duration of the war. He was assigned to the Beachcomber's Band special unit in the South Pacific. The band often performed under enemy fire on nearly fifty islands, including Guam and Iwo Jima. Several famous personalities were part of the entertainment unit. The Commanding Officer was British actor Maurice Evans; the second in command was radio and television personality Alan Ludden. Carl Reiner was the group's comedian.

After the war Hillman briefly rejoined Kay Kyser and then went on to spend the late 1940s and early 1950s playing in television and motion picture studio orchestras. In fact, he led the first ever Los Angeles studio television orchestra on KLAC TV. A highlight of his movie career was working with Fred Astaire.

"Fred Astaire was my idol," Hillman said. "He was a definite perfectionist, but always pleasant and gracious to the cast. He would spend hours preparing for a dance number without ever losing his sense of humor and patience."

Since the 1950s Hillman has spent his time teaching guitar, playing at clubs and special events, and owning a music store in the San Fernando Valley for a number of years. Patty Duke, Gary Crosby, Hugh O'Brian, and Dennis Weaver are among the Hollywood celebrities he tutored. As a dedicated sports fan, he regularly played in a Dixieland combo on Sunday afternoons at Los Angeles Raider's football games until the team relocated to Oakland in 1995. Blessed with superb health, he remains in good spirit and enjoys talking about the Big Band Era.

Roc Hillman looks back on his career with great satisfaction: "I have no complaints. I played with the top big bands, was in television and the movies, and wrote several hit songs. Most important, I'm the last person still alive who was playing on the bandstand the day the Dorsey Brothers broke up."

LEGH KNOWLES

FROM GLENN MILLER TO THE NAPA VALLEY

Many Big Band Era sidemen faded from public view when the Era came to a close after World War II. Such was not the case with Legh Knowles, whom big band authority George T. Simon referred to as "a good all-around trumpet player" in his biography of Glenn Miller. Knowles played for Miller, Red Norvo, and Charlie Spivak before the war and after the conflict segued into the wine industry eventually becoming the chairman of Beaulieu Vineyard located in California's Napa Valley. Here is the story of Legh Knowles's journey from Glenn Miller's trumpet section to business success in the rich wine fields of the Napa Valley.

Legh Francis Knowles was born in Danbury, CT, on June 18, 1919. At an early age the Knowles family moved to nearby Bethel where his father worked as a hatter and owned a restaurant called the Log Cabin Buffet. There was musical talent in the Knowles family back in England and his father always desired to be a trumpet player in the United States. To vicariously achieve his musical dream he bought his son a trumpet when he was nine years old and arranged for lessons with a former trumpeter in and expatriate from the British Army named Bill Dalton who was also somewhat of a temperamental individual. Dalton insisted to be driven to the Knowles home by taxi to provide his lessons, an expensive demand at the time. Knowles was a quick study. By the time he was eleven he could transpose from one key to another, sight read, and play symphonic music.

An uncommonly intelligent individual, Knowles skipped two grades and graduated from high school at fifteen in 1935. It was the end of his formal education. Around this time he started to teach the trumpet in his parent's home in Bethel and in the city's 1937 phone directory was listed as a professional musician, an unusual accomplishment for someone his age.

Warren Lafferty is a lifetime Bethel resident who took trumpet lessons from Knowles starting in 1937 and is currently active in the Legh Knowles Bethel Scholarship for the Performing Arts: "My mother was a good friend of Legh's mother. At one of my lessons Legh's father asked him if I practiced that week. Legh shrugged his shoulders and his father said to me, 'If you do a good job next week you got a hot dog and soda coming at the restaurant.' Legh was a very good teacher. I've been playing for seventy years now and I owe my musical foundation to him."

The repeal of Prohibition in 1933 set the stage for Knowles's first nightclub job and the start of his professional career. The day after Prohibition ended he played with a small band led by NBC staff pianist Lou Catone at the Blue Ribbon Casino in Brewster, NY, for eight dollars a night, earning more each week than his father did working at the hat factory and running his restaurant. He also joined the musicians union and played with local groups all through high school. Knowles's first job after graduation was playing in a band at a show featuring the notorious fan dancer Sally Rand at Lake Hopatcong in New Jersey. After that he played with big bands in New Haven and as far away as Albany and Boston in addition to continuing to teach music at home. Then in early 1938 came a gig in Westchester County and his first encounter with Glenn Miller.

Knowles was playing lead trumpet and singing in the glee club in Ray Keating's band at Murray's, located in Westchester County on the Bronx River Parkway in Tuckahoe. The band had fifteen coast-to-coast radio broadcasts a week on the Mutual Broadcasting System and was heard by Glenn Miller who was putting together his second band, the band that made it. The indefatigable Miller needed a trumpet player and immediately drove to Bethel to talk to Knowles's mother in an attempt to locate him. He knocked on the Knowles's door interrupting her PTA card party. She invited him in for a glass of apple cider and told him he could find her son at Murray's. Little did the ladies of the Bethel PTA realize that they were meeting the person who would soon become the most famous bandleader in the world. Knowles and Miller met at Murray's with Miller offering Knowles a job in his trumpet section. However, as their conversation progressed the eighteen-year-old Knowles became intimidated by the no-nonsense Miller and turned him down.

After the Murray's engagement ended Knowles briefly played in Billy Rose's Aquacade in New York then moved on to Red Norvo. Knowles enjoyed his time with Norvo and thought that the band truly swung with drummer George Wettling and pianist Bill Miller of Frank Sinatra fame in the rhythm section. He got along well with Norvo and his volatile wife and vocalist Mildred Bailey, regularly riding with them to engagements in their deluxe LaSalle automobile accompanied by Bailey's maid and two dachshunds. Those trips gave him an opportunity to observe the Norvo's legendary domestic battles. A musical highlight was playing at the Famous Door on 52nd Street alternating with the John Kirby Sextet. But by late-1938 Norvo's band was experiencing severe financial difficulties. All the while Glenn Miller patiently remained interested in Knowles. Spurred by advice from Miles Rinker, Bailey's brother and manager, Knowles decided to leave the about-to-go-bust Norvo group and join Miller's band which was on the threshold of breaking through to worldwide fame.

On December 15, 1938, Knowles joined the Glenn Miller Orchestra at the Ricker Gardens in Portland, ME, playing for $75 a week. However, that salary did not last long as told by Knowles in an interview on Don Kennedy's *Big Band Jump* radio program: "I joined Glenn for $75 a week. One night we were playing at Duke University and he called me over and said, 'Who do you think you are? I'm paying real good musicians fifty bucks and you're holding me up for seventy-five. You're going to get fifty dollars starting now.' You know, he unsettled me so much that I didn't say a word and that's what happened."

Miller's adjustment of Knowles's salary substantiates his reputation as an excellent businessman. But how creative was Miller? Knowles talked about Glenn Miller's creativity on Kennedy's show: "Glenn Miller was highly creative. His creativity showed up when he had the vision to construct a harmonization which became the Glenn Miller sound, which was enjoyable, memorable, and loved by the public. We had Bill Finegan and Jerry Gray doing the arrangements. He gave them the pattern and they wrote them."

Glenn Miller did become the most famous bandleader in the world during the summer of 1939 playing at the Glen Island Casino in New Rochelle, NY. It was also the year that his classic "In the Mood" broke into the record charts. Knowles recalled the part he played in shaping the song on Chuck Cecil's *The Swingin' Years* radio show: "The song was 248 in the books. We were rehearsing after the job at the Glen Island Casino around five in the morning. In the trumpet section was Mickey McMikle, Clyde Hurley, and I. We played the song for the first time and we all thought that it was awful. The first thing Glenn asked was how we would get to a high D. Mickey and I suggested a few things then Clyde suggested the passage he eventually played on the record. Glenn turned around and said to Chummy MacGregor, 'Write that.' We played it the next night for the first time and it became a classic."

What was Knowles's most memorable experience with Glenn Miller? There was one and he talked about it in December 1986 on Bob Holmes's *Vintage Sounds* San Francisco radio show that he appeared on several times during the 1980s: "The first time we came out of the pit at the Paramount Theater in 1939 playing our theme song, Moonlight Serenade, I got permanent goose bumps all over, hearing those kids scream. It's something I'll never forget. Plus, I had a great time during the summer of 1939 at the Glen Island Casino rooming in New Rochelle with Al Klink, Mickey McMickle, and Al Mastren. I just wish that we all weren't so tired from working our non-stop schedule when we played Carnegie Hall in October 1939. We were exhausted and I didn't appreciate the historic impact of what we were doing."

Knowles also talked about his good friend and Glenn Miller vocalist Ray Eberle's arm wrestling prowess on a May 1984 *Vintage Sounds* program: "Arm wrestling was popular in bars in the East back then. Ray had an innocent smile but was as strong as an ox. Our regular group would walk into a bar and if any arm wrestling was going on Ray would casually ask how it goes. The guys in the bar thought they had a live one and would challenge him to a match with the loser buying a round of drinks. Ray would always toy with them for thirty seconds then take them down. We got a lot of free drinks with that routine. Ray and I had some great times together. The interesting thing is he was planning to visit and stay with us in Napa when he died."

After making 122 records and ready for a recuperative break, Knowles left Miller on May 17, 1940. He valued the experience and responsibility he gained working in the organization and thought that Miller was the best executive he ever worked for. In a 1979 article in the *Los Angeles Times* that was quoted in his obituary in *Miller Notes*, Knowles credited Miller with teaching him about business fundamentals and leadership: "The discipline I learned back then has come in handy in the wine business. Music is discipline, and you can't get much more disciplined than working for Glenn. I remember one year, it was 1939, and we worked 359 nights. I don't know what I did the other six nights that year. It was a great training ground, because it taught me that even if you were sick or tired or whatever, once you were out there and everybody had paid their money, you just had to produce."

Zeke Zarchy replaced Knowles in Miller's trumpet section. He reminisced about him at his pleasant home in Studio City, CA: "I spent a few weeks with Legh in the Miller band before he left and we became very good friends. When he got to be an executive at Beaulieu he would frequently send me cases of fine wine. We saw each other several times at music and social functions over the years. I particularly remember that in 1987 Milt Bernhart's Big Band Academy of America conducted a Glenn Miller alumni tribute. We were both there and had a great time together. Legh was a happy fellow and well liked by everyone he played with."

Without any firm plans in mind, Knowles returned home to Bethel. He resumed giving trumpet lessons and eventually took over a big band that started playing at the Seven Gables Inn in Milford, CT, after Frankie Carle finished his engagement there. Then in the middle of 1941 he was approached one evening at the Seven Gables by Charlie Spivak's brother, who told him Spivak would like him to join his band. An admirer of Spivak's musicianship, he took the job and went back on the road for a year with Nelson Riddle as his roommate until he was drafted into the Army Air Corps in 1942. According to Warren Lafferty, Spivak was fond of Knowles and presented him with an engraved trumpet when he left for the service in appreciation for his work in the band.

Garry Stevens was Spivak's vocalist while Knowles was with the band and is still actively singing in his nineties with big bands in Northern California. He shared his memories of Knowles while chatting at his home in Benecia, CA: "Legh was a bit of a clown and kept the guys, including Charlie, loose, especially on those long bus rides. He had everyone in stitches trading jokes with the bus driver, Harry Huter, a lovable character who just recently passed away in Florida. Legh was a very good trumpet player and played in the band when I recorded many of my hit records. He was definitely colorful and I would have loved to have seen him again after the war."

During his time in the military Knowles served in the Army Airways Communication Squadron after completing a sixteen-week course in Morse code and radio technology in Sioux Falls, SD, in only six weeks. He was selected for communications duty as musicians were recognized for showing a natural aptitude for learning and working with Morse code that came from their musical training. As for music, he occasionally played with local bands near the military bases he was stationed at. Knowles valued his military experience in that it taught him for the first time in his life that he could achieve success in something other than music. After the war he briefly played with a small band near Bethel. Then, although he felt he was playing better than ever, he put down his trumpet for good, to leave music and seek a new career path.

Legh Knowles's postwar fortunes did not get off to a blazing start. He ran an appliance store in Bethel, then sold MGM records for a New Haven-based record distributor throughout several eastern states before he moved to Washington, D.C., to work in the milieu of government contracting as a product representative. Then in 1948 he spotted an ad in a Washington newspaper that would change his life. The advertisement said "Wanted: individual who is accustomed to appearing before large groups of people."

The ad was placed by the Wine Advisory Board, a promotional arm of the state of California's Department of Agriculture, to hire an individual who had the qualifications to improve wine's then low-grade image and promote its use as a mealtime beverage and in restaurants. At the job interview Knowles told the Board that he was comfortable appearing in front of large groups as he did just that playing with Glenn Miller and would enjoy public speaking. He was immediately hired for a salary of $350 a month. Armed with only on-the-job training, Knowles quickly excelled in the position and was soon promoted to eastern division manager covering the whole eastern United States. Then in 1953, while trying to persuade Cornell University's School of Hotel Administration to include oenology studies in its curriculum, he was offered a job by the Taylor Wine Company based in New York's Finger Lakes region.

Taylor's marketing office was located in the Empire Sate Building where Knowles started work as assistant national sales manager. He made an instant impact when he persuaded the famous 21 Club in Manhattan to stock Taylor Wines. Knowles next moved on to the E & J Gallo Winery in 1958 as the Cincinnati area sales manager with the mission of building up the state of Ohio. After several moves across the country with Gallo, in 1961 he wound up at their corporate headquarters in Modesto, CA. Knowles enjoyed his personal association with the late Ernest Gallo and was proud of his involvement with the firm for which he wrote the company's first sales manual and introduced advanced merchandising concepts. But he grew increasingly frustrated with their reluctance to venture into the premium wine market. Sensing his displeasure, a friend suggested he approach Beaulieu Vineyard (BV).

In the early 1960s BV was in its golden age, setting the standard for quality California wine. The prestigious winery was owned and managed by Madame Helene de Pins, daughter of aristocratic Frenchman Georges de Latour who founded it in 1900 at Rutherford in the heart of the Napa Valley. The legendary Andre Tchelistcheff was the winemaker and the winery's principal label, Georges de Latour Private Reserve Cabernet Sauvignon, was widely considered the best cabernet made in America. BV was among the elite of premium American wines.

Knowles took the initiative and wrote Madame de Pins a letter saying that he admired BV's wines and business operations from his first day in the wine industry and that he thought he could contribute to the organization. Madame de Pins was impressed by his letter. After she met

Knowles she called a board of directors meeting and the board voted to hire him as BV's first national sales manager.

The hiring of Legh Knowles in 1962 proved to be a wise decision for BV. He moved up the corporate ladder to general manager, president, and chairman in 1984. Knowles led the firm through its takeover by Heublein in 1969, the same year he successfully introduced their Gamay Beaujolais by placing it on American Airlines flights, and consistently kept BV's return on investment among the tops in the industry. He was also a staunch advocate of point of difference marketing, a concept he learned from Glenn Miller.

In an interview in *The Wine Spectator California Winemen Oral History Series* Knowles discussed his view on point of difference marketing: "I'm a point of difference nut. I learned the importance of that back in the 30s and 40s when I was playing trumpet for Glenn Miller, who made a different but thoroughly enjoyable sound. When you listened to Glenn Miller, you didn't think you were listening to Tommy Dorsey or Shep Fields or Duke Ellington. You knew you were listening to Glenn Miller, because he created that distinctive sound."

A highlight of Knowles's career at BV occurred when he decided to start advertising their wines on radio in the mid 1970s. He went to BV's ad agency who recommended Yves Montand or Vincent Price as spokespersons. However, the extreme compensation they requested for their services shocked Knowles and he decided to do the ads himself. Knowles quickly became a celebrity thanks to his down to earth ad-lib radio commercials that ran for several years and were pointed at demystifying wine and parodying the description-laden verbiage that wine critics tend to use. One of his favorite on the air sayings was "If you think the best wine is the most expensive, let me know and I'll charge you more."

Bob Chiacco was a successful salesman in the wine industry and knew Legh Knowles well. Here is what he had to say about his association with him from his home in Carmel: "Next to Andre Tchelistcheff, Legh was the best authority on salesmanship and gaining brand exposure and markets that I ever saw in my thirty-three years in the wine business. I first met him when I was with Gallo in Cincinnati and he and his wife Margaret had me over for dinner three or four nights a week. Later on we saw each other weekly when we worked together at BV. I knew Legh had it the first time I saw him. He drove an elegant car and dressed with tailor-made suits and cashmere topcoats and beautiful hats and gloves. He loved golf and was good at it but he could never best his wife Margaret who was a natural athlete. I remember Legh loved eating the day after cold spaghetti. I'm Italian and I never saw that before. When he died Margaret gave me his white 1989 Cadillac Brougham sedan that had a maroon leather interior. It's in mint condition and I still drive it several times a week. Margaret and I stay in contact, I call her weekly."

Legh Knowles also had a wide circle of friends from outside the wine industry. One was Sam Spear, a television and radio commentator on horse racing in Northern California who covers the Bay Meadows in San Mateo and Golden Gate Fields in Berkeley along with all area summer racing fairs. He reminisced about Knowles from his office in Walnut Creek, CA.

"I met Legh around 1985 at Bay Meadows where BV was sponsoring Ascot Day," Spear said. "We enjoyed horse racing, wine, and big band music and quickly became good friends. Legh and I regularly visited wineries in the Napa and Sonoma Valleys. When we walked into a winery they would roll out the red carpet for him. He was a great ambassador for wine from the Napa Valley and he did a tremendous job of raising the profile of red wine and selling cabernets to the American public."

Spear added: "I remember that one of the great times we had occurred when I brought Joe DiMaggio out to the wine country and we met Legh for lunch at the original Piatti's restaurant in Yountville. Legh and Joe had a great time talking about New York during the period when

Joe was playing with the Yankees and Legh with Glenn Miller. I just sat back and listened. Their conversation was fascinating. When Legh passed away I was personally chosen by Margaret to preside over his church service. At the conclusion of the funeral Mass at St. Apollinaris Church in Napa I called up the elite of the California wine business to speak, Brother Timothy of Christian Brothers, Robert Mondavi, and Ernest Gallo. Even though they were all competitors it was evident that they had great affection and respect for Legh both personally and professionally. That was a special moment."

Shortly before he retired from BV on January 1, 1989, Knowles was honored as one of twelve Napa Valley Living Legends of Wine at a banquet in San Francisco conducted by the Napa Valley Vintners Association. After Knowles left BV he developed a program called *Wine and All That Jazz* that he presented at sales conferences and universities and did consulting work in the wine industry. A heavy smoker, Legh Knowles died from cancer of the esophagus on August 15, 1997, in a Napa nursing home. A few weeks later United States Congressman George P. Radanovich read a tribute to him on the floor of the House of Representatives.

What was Legh Knowles's private life like? In 1950 he married Margaret Taylor, a Nashville native who was working at the Pentagon when he met her. She currently lives in Tuckahoe where Knowles first met Glenn Miller. They had a daughter Barbara who works as an archivist at the New York Public Library for the Performing Arts at Lincoln Center and resides in Manhattan. She talked about her father by telephone while vacationing at Disneyworld in Orlando: "My father was very intense. He came from a family that struggled financially and never went to college, and that was part of what drove him to excel. My dad had a great sense of humor. He loved to go to Disneyland in Anaheim and admire how well it was run. I'm sitting here now at Disneyworld. The reason I continue to come here even without my kids is because I had such a great experience going on the rides with him while I was growing up. That and our going to the beach to listen to the crash of the waves were my two favorite things. My parents had a wonderful marriage and he was an amazing, supportive dad, as well as a very generous grandfather to my two kids."

Life sometimes works in strange ways. While Legh Knowles was sitting in Glenn Miller's trumpet section with Mickey McMickle and Clyde Hurley during the summer of 1939 at the Glen Island Casino, the odds are high that he gave little thought to his future plans yet alone visualized that in a few years he would be giving up music to eventually become the chief executive of a major corporation. He also most certainly was not aware of all he was absorbing about the fundamentals of managing a commercial enterprise and committing to excellence while observing Miller run his band. As it turned out, Legh Knowles's employment with the Glenn Miller Orchestra proved to be his formal business education. It was an education that served him well.

JOHN LAPORTA
FROM HERMAN TO MINGUS TO BERKLEE

Jazz master John LaPorta's career spanned the entire spectrum of jazz from 1934 until he passed away on May 12, 2004. He played with Woody Herman during the Big Band Era and with Charles Mingus during the post-Bebop Era. He studied with Lennie Tristano, associated with Gil Evans, performed his own works at the Newport Jazz Festival with his own quartet, worked in national band camps with Stan Kenton, taught for a nearly a quarter of a century as a fulltime professor at the Berklee College of Music, and authored numerous educational texts. LaPorta has been an esteemed musician, prolific composer, and respected educator who made jazz albums and played a weekly gig at a Sarasota, FL, supper club until a few months before his death. Here is the story of an accomplished jazz artist who serendipitously became a dedicated jazz educator and passed his extensive experience and knowledge on to a whole new generation of eager jazz students.

LaPorta was born in Philadelphia on April 13, 1920, to parents of Italian heritage who had no special musical talent. He grew up in a six room attached brick house in a working class, multicultural northeast Philadelphia neighborhood where altercations among ethnic groups were the order of the day. The course of his life fortunately embarked on a detour from the mean streets when, at eight and a half, he started studying clarinet under Herman Pade and at eleven played in Pade's German Band at Sunday community picnics. When LaPorta was twelve he started to practice on the tenor saxophone and joined the Polish American Band that played weddings and social events and performed in the prestigious annual Philadelphia New Year's Day Mummers Parade. His formal musical training took a more serious turn at fourteen when he started to study clarinet with the respected Joseph Giglioti who taught at the Settlement Music School in South Philadelphia.

Wider musical horizons awaited LaPorta at Philadelphia's Northeastern High School. He launched his professional career earning money playing at cafes and nightclubs during his freshman year and performed classical music in the American Youth Symphony Orchestra under Leopold Stokowski during his sophomore year. While a junior he played six nights a week from 9:00 p.m. to 2:00 a.m. at Marty's Grill in northeast Philadelphia and carried a full academic major. With just a few hours of sleep each night, his studies suffered. The time had come to make a career decision. Finding music more appealing than academics, LaPorta decided to not return to Northeastern for his senior year and instead transferred to Mastbaum Vocational School that offered the city's best music program. Also attracted to Mastbaum around that time were clarinetist Buddy DeFranco and trumpeter Red Rodney.

During the summer of 1939 LaPorta played with a band in Ocean City, MD, made up primarily of Mastbaum students. Sadly, the day before Labor Day he received a wire that his father had suffered a fatal stroke. He immediately returned home to his family in Philadelphia where over the next few years he played in small groups and frequently jammed with African American musicians at the Showboat Club and other cafes located just a few blocks east of Broad Street.

Two of his many engagements briefly took him out of town, one to Albany, GA, and the other to upstate New York. However, Philadelphia remained LaPorta's base where he was unknowingly positioning himself for his first job with a big band.

The Big Band Era was at its peak in 1942, the year that Jimmy Dorsey, Woody Herman, Harry James, Kay Kyser, Glenn Miller and Alvino Rey dominated the record charts. Nonetheless, often overlooked in big band history is the fact that in addition to the top tier, big name bands there were hundreds of territory bands spread across the United States that roamed specific areas. One such band was the Philadelphia-based Buddy Williams Orchestra. It was actually a very good band that included former Glenn Miller drummer Bob Spangler and future Woody Herman trombonist Bill Harris who was working as a bill collector by day in Philadelphia when he joined Williams's orchestra.

That spring LaPorta connected with the Buddy Williams Orchestra that consisted of seven brasses, five saxes, piano, bass and drums. They played a summer engagement at Wildwood, NJ, and then moved on to the Lantz's Merry Go Round Bar in Dayton, OH, that was popular with the personnel working at nearby Wright Field. Just as the band was starting to make a name for itself with nightly broadcasts over 50,000-watt Cincinnati radio station WLW, Williams was drafted into military service effectively bringing his band to a close and providing an opportunity for LaPorta to move up the big band ladder.

Sandwiched between the first tier bands and the territory bands were the second tier bands that for whatever reason did not quite make the big time. One of those was the Bob Chester Orchestra. Chester never had to be concerned with financial matters. Born in 1908, he came from an extremely wealthy family in Detroit where his stepfather was a high-level executive in the automobile industry. In 1939 Chester's good friend Tommy Dorsey had a business dispute with Glenn Miller and in spite sponsored a new Chester-led band to compete with Miller, playing in the Miller style. The band had seven minor charted hits in the early 40s, two featuring the attractive and talented Dolores O'Neill, one of the sadly unrecognized female vocalists of the era. Chester finally gave up band leading in the early 50s and moved back to Detroit where he carved out a successful business career. He passed away in 1975.

A month after Williams broke up his band in late 1942 LaPorta received an offer to join Chester's orchestra thanks to a recommendation by Bill Harris who was already with the Chester organization. LaPorta commented on his involvement with Chester's band from his home in Sarasota, FL: "By the time I joined Bob he had given up the Miller imitation and developed a solid swing dance band. We had some outstanding musicians. Irv Kluger was an excellent drummer who would go on to do a lot of work with Artie Shaw. Herbie Steward was a very talented tenor saxophone player. He was quite mature for a seventeen year old. Manny Albam played third alto, but it was obvious that his first love was arranging. Betty Bradley, an eye-catching and capable vocalist who was well liked by the band, replaced Dolores O'Neill who left after she married one of the trumpet players, Alec Fila. Bob himself, a tenor saxophone player, rarely played with the band. By mid 1944 the band started to slip because of heavy turnover and raids from better-known bandleaders. After eighteen months on the road traveling from coast to coast I decided it was time to move on."

LaPorta and his new wife, the former Virginia Trisler, whom he met playing with Chester at the Topper Ballroom in Cincinnati, moved into a second floor spare room in his uncle's Italian grocery store in Brooklyn in mid-July 1944. However, the confined space lacked toilet facilities. Fortunately, the neighborhood bar accommodated their needs.

Shortly after settling in Brooklyn LaPorta went to a theater in Newark to see Woody Herman's band perform. After the show he went backstage and met with Bill Harris and Ed Kiefer, old friends from his Buddy Williams and Bob Chester days. Kiefer introduced him to Herman's lead alto saxophone player, Sam Marowitz, who offered LaPorta the open third alto chair. It was September 1944 and LaPorta joined the band while it was playing at the Café Rouge in Manhattan and doing the weekly *Old Gold Show* on CBS radio that featured Alan Jones of "Donkey Serenade" hit record fame.

The First Herman Herd that LaPorta spent twenty-eight months with is considered to be one of the great orchestras in the history of jazz. It powerfully swung with aggressive young musicians playing new songs with fresh and sometimes humorous arrangements carefully crafted by the ilk of Ralph Burns and Neal Hefti. Although there were brilliant soloists like high note trumpeter supreme Pete Candoli and innovative trombonist Bill Harris, the band's hallmark was its sterling ensemble playing. Providing leadership and inspiration thanks to a climate in which creativity was encouraged was the much-revered Woody Herman. All in all, it was a hard driving, progressive band with a bop tinge and big sound that thrilled its audiences playing with sheer joy and abandon.

LaPorta had several interesting observations to offer on individuals he worked with in the Herman band: "When Conrad Gozzo joined the band he was already considered the best lead trumpet player in the business but had to become comfortable with the head arrangements. The trumpet section was very competitive. He and Pete Candoli initially became rivals and for a short time had a personality clash. But once Conrad established himself they developed a fond mutual respect for each other that continued after they left the band."

Head arrangements were indeed the trademark of the First Herd: "During the first set Woody would often leave the bandstand and mingle with the crowd. Chubby Jackson would seize the opportunity and yell out 'Let's make a head.' Neal Hefti often provided a creative spark with a melody line then all the other sections would kick in and contribute. After two or three weeks a fully developed piece of music would evolve."

Herman was blessed with two outstanding female vocalists: "Frances Wayne had a dignified bearing and a gorgeous, controlled voice of operatic quality. It was so pure that Duke Ellington tried to hire her. Mary Ann McCall was a hip, free spirit with a husky voice that sang with emotion and passion. Frances came from an Italian family in Boston that enjoyed the opera. Mary Ann was from Philadelphia and was a true student of the blues and jazz."

Personal idiosyncrasies abounded in the Herman Herd: "Flip Phillips, whose real name was Joseph Filipelli, was a superb tenor saxophone soloist who lived for eating Italian food and would order it any time he could at any hour. Whenever we got back to New York from a road trip, he would call his wife from Grand Central Station regardless of what time it was. She would immediately boil water to make pasta and have a full home-cooked Italian dinner ready for him by the time he got home to their apartment in Brooklyn, even if it were 3:00 am."

Pianist Jimmy Rowles provided much-needed musical relief for LaPorta: "Jimmy really ignited the rhythm section and was great at backing up the soloists. He also did me a big favor. After playing lead alto and soloing with Bob Chester I became a bit frustrated playing third alto with no solos for Woody. From time to time he would find a bar with a back room and piano and spend hours accompanying me while I improvised. He didn't have to do that."

Although he did not solo with Herman, LaPorta continued to develop the writing skills that he originated at Mastbaum High School when he was seventeen years old. While the band was based in Los Angeles, he studied music theory with Dr. Ernest Toch who had a profound impact on the development of his arranging style. His composition "Non Alcoholic" became a permanent part of the Herman book. It was a swing piece that was inspired by the weekly *Wildroot*

Show on CBS radio that featured the First Herd. Wildroot hair tonic's claim to fame was that it was non-alcoholic.

When asked what in his opinion was the key reason that made the First Herd a great musical organization, LaPorta commented that it was the band's timing: "The time of the First Herd was the great thing. As lead men, Gozzo, Harris, and Marowitz played time right down the middle. Some musicians play on top. Dixieland players tend to play on top a lot. With those three guys leading their sections the band couldn't help but have swinging time."

After a December 24, 1946, engagement at Castle Farms in Cincinnati, Woody Herman broke up his tremendously popular First Herd and headed home to Hollywood to spend quality time with his wife Charlotte and daughter Ingrid. At the time, little did LaPorta realize that he was about to embark on a sixteen-year odyssey through the New York jazz scene that would begin with a year of study with groundbreaking pianist, composer, and educator Lennie Tristano.

LaPorta met Tristano while the Herman band was playing in Chicago in late 1946. Tristano was immediately impressed by LaPorta's ability to read his complex music. When Tristano moved to New York in early 1947 the LaPortas and Tristano and his first wife Judy developed a social relationship. This affiliation led to a year's study with Tristano during which LaPorta recorded an album and played in a series of weekly jazz radio broadcasts called *Moldy Figs versus Moderns* with him. LaPorta also became acquainted with saxophonist Lee Konitz through Tristano and developed a friendship with Gil Evans who was arranging for Claude Thornhill. But there were storm clouds on the horizon.

"Lennie lived in his own world and developed a cult-like following among his students," LaPorta said. "While I studied with him he would negatively analyze my playing without offering any positive suggestions. His comments would breakdown my confidence, so I gradually stopped seeing him."

LaPorta commented on the end of their relationship: "*Metronome* Editor Barry Ulanov was conducting a Monday evening English class for musicians at his apartment in the Village. After one of the classes he suggested I see Lennie again. I did, and at the end of our discussion, Lennie, who spoke in the third person, said 'Lennie sees things different from you. Perhaps it's best we go our separate ways.' I was greatly relieved."

Involvement with big bands continued when LaPorta played with Boyd Raeburn and Claude Thornhill in 1949. His reputation in the jazz world soared when he was asked to play with the Metronome All Stars in 1951 and was called by Charles Mingus to make an album on his Debut label in 1954. The album, *The John LaPorta Quintet*, was positively reviewed by Ulanov in *Metronome* and Nat Hentoff in *DownBeat*. Nineteen fifty-four was also the year of the Jazz Composers Workshop.

In the fall of 1953 *Metronome* music critic Bill Coss approached LaPorta and several other musicians about forming a group of composers to perform music written by them in a concert setting. This was the genesis of the Jazz Composers Workshop that included Charles Mingus. The group gave three concerts in 1954 that were accorded extensive articles in *Metronome* by George T. Simon and Barry Ulanov before it dissolved late that year.

Shortly after the Jazz Composers Workshop broke up, Mingus called LaPorta to record with a nucleus of the original Workshop. The results were two landmark free-form, experimental albums titled *Jazz Composers Workshop* and *The Jazz Experiments of Charles Mingus*. They have made a huge impact on the nefarious recording business over the years as several overseas record companies have pirated them. Unfortunately, the musicians who recorded the albums have never received a dime for their efforts.

After the Jazz Composers Workshop came to an end, LaPorta continued to play and record with Mingus in small groups. He talked about the great bass player's propensity for on-stage histrionics: "Mingus rarely rehearsed a composition from beginning to end. As a result, musicians playing them for the first time could easily get lost, resulting in a concert performance bordering on the chaotic. Whenever this happened Mingus would launch a tirade at the suspected musicians and with great flamboyance shout to the audience that he was starting the piece over."

Mingus and LaPorta developed a strong professional rapport. The volatile bass player frequently recommended LaPorta for recording sessions as he did in 1956 when he suggested LaPorta to pioneer modern-jazz drummer Kenny Clarke to play in Clarke's *Klook's Clique* album. It was recorded in record producer Rudy Van Gelder's home studio in Hackensack, NJ, and featured LaPorta on the cover.

The 1958 Newport Jazz Festival that was immortalized in the documentary film *Jazz on a Summer's Day* marked another milestone in John LaPorta's career. Festival founder George Wein and jazz educator Marshall Brown created the International Youth Band comprised of teenage musicians from sixteen different countries to play at the 1958 Festival. The band was a big hit, garnering a rave review in *Variety*. LaPorta played an important part in its success by auditioning and rehearsing the reed section and writing the band's book with Jimmy Giuffre and Bill Russo. LaPorta also played the Festival with his own quartet, receiving compliments from *DownBeat*, *Metronome*, and his peers. After he came off the stage at the end of his set Cannonball Adderley said to him: "John, you really have a pretty tone, especially on that beautiful ballad of yours." That beautiful ballad was La Porta's piece "The Most Minor" that spawned an album by his Quartet of the same name.

LaPorta continued his work with young musicians in 1959 when he participated in the first National Stage Band Camp for students at Indiana University in Bloomington, IN. Stan Kenton, whom LaPorta first met in the mid 40s at the Bradford Hotel in Boston while the Herman Herd was playing the New England area, headed the camp. LaPorta would be associated with the camps for the next twenty-five years.

The milieu of jazz education always attracted LaPorta. He started private instruction at his studio in Manhattan in 1948, the year he joined the faculty of the Parkway School of Music in Brooklyn where he taught fulltime for two years. Through the late 40s and the 50s he worked with Long Island high school concert jazz bands. As a student, he attended the Manhattan School of Music where he received a bachelor's degree in clarinet in 1956 and a master's degree in music education in 1957. John LaPorta was without a doubt fully prepared to evaluate an unexpected opportunity for a major career change that would involve the world of academia that came his way in 1962.

Lawrence Berk founded the Berklee College of Music in Boston in 1954. Berklee is the world's largest independent music college and the premier institution for the study of contemporary music. Toshiko Akiyoshi, Kevin Eubanks, Quincy Jones, Diana Krall, and Branford Marsalis are but a few of its noted alumni. LaPorta accepted an offer from Berk to teach as a tenured professor at Berklee starting in June 1962. He would go on to spend twenty-three years at the institution, retiring as professor emeritus in 1985. Part of his legacy was the development of a structured four-year Instrumental Performance diploma program that lowered the school's dropout rate and helped students develop their performance skills. He kept active by playing with and writing for fellow faculty member Herb Pomeroy's Jazz Orchestra and performing with the Berklee Faculty Saxophone Quartet.

John LaPorta did not languish after he retired in 1985 to Sarasota, FL. With a continuing strong interest in jazz education he returned to Boston every summer through 1999 to work with students in the Berklee summer program and tutored the Riverview High School jazz band in Sarasota for five years. In recognition of his educational contributions, in 1994 the International Association of Jazz Educators presented him their distinguished Humanitarian Award that honors educators whose love for teaching jazz surpassed conventional academic standards. They also named their Jazz Educator of the Year Award in his honor in 2006. LaPorta is a founding member of the organization.

Most jazz musicians do not start recording new albums and re-releasing previously recorded material at 78. John LaPorta did. In 1998 he released the *John LaPorta Quartet Life Cycles* album that he recorded with Berklee faculty that year. Next came *Theme and Variations* in 2002 that consisted of two parts, his unissued 1956 composition for octets "Theme and Variations" and a reissue of his 1957 *Concepts* album that included his "Concertina for Clarinet" that dramatically showcased the clarinet's jazz solo possibilities. His most recent work was *I Remember Woody*, a tribute to the leader of the Herds for whom he still holds the highest professional respect. It was his first musical involvement with Herman's music since 1959 when he recorded the clarinet solo on Stravinsky's "Ebony Concerto" with a band led by Elliott Lawrence that included several Herman alumni. Both Herman enthusiasts and the music world in general have very well received the tribute album he recorded in 2002.

John LaPorta has led a fascinating musical life as documented in his Cadence Jazz Books biography *Playing it by Ear*. When asked to comment on his diverse career just a few months before he died from complications of a stroke he said: "I'm very lucky. I played through the Big Band Era and the 40s and 50s New York jazz scene and was involved for thirty-seven years with Berklee in jazz education. I got to personally know many of the great musicians of my day from Herman and Kenton to Mingus and Gillespie and Parker. Most important, at eighty-three I'm still actively playing at jazz festivals and recording new albums, have many friends, continue to be happily married to Ginnie for sixty years, and enjoy keeping up with all that's currently going on in jazz."

WILLIE SCHWARTZ AND PEGGY CLARK
A BIG BAND ROMANCE

Clarinet, saxophone, and flute player Willie Schwartz was a key contributor to the distinctive sound that made the Glenn Miller Orchestra the most popular of the Big Band Era. Peggy Clark was one of four Clark Sisters that sang as The Sentimentalists on a string of Tommy Dorsey hit records in the mid 1940s. They met while performing with Bob Crosby's band at the Strand Theater in Manhattan in early 1948 and married in Los Angeles on September 17 of the same year after a whirlwind courtship. Their idyllic forty-two-year marriage was truly a big band romance.

The Schwartz's extraordinary story starts with Wilbur "Willie" Schwartz, who was born in Newark, NJ, on March 17, 1918. He was naturally attracted to music at an early age and quickly became proficient on the clarinet, saxophone, and flute. Schwartz soon developed to the point that while still a high school student he would frequently cross the Hudson River to play professional engagements in Manhattan. However, he surely never imagined while honing his craft that he would play a significant role in shaping the musical course of the Swing Era, playing with the most famous of all the big bands.

Trombonist and arranger Glenn Miller failed in his first attempt to lead a band in 1937. His unsuccessful venture cost him in the neighborhood of $20,000, far more money than most major league baseball players of that time made in a single season. By the spring of 1938, with financial backing from his wife Helen's parents, he decided to try a second time and was on the hunt for new musicians. Enter his good friend, then *Metronome* staff writer, George T. Simon.

Simon unremittingly scoured the metropolitan New York area jazz scene to uncover material for his *Metronome* column. While reviewing the Julie Wintz band at the Top Hat nightclub in Union City, NJ, he discovered Willie Schwartz playing saxophone and recommended him to Miller for his new band. Miller went to the Roseland Ballroom where Wintz next played to hear Schwartz. It was April 1938. He liked Schwartz's saxophone sound but detected something distinctive in his clarinet work that led to his hiring him to play lead clarinet over four saxophones. This creative blend was the unique sound that made the Glenn Miller orchestra famous.

In his book, *The Swing Era*, Gunther Schuller discussed Schwartz's contribution to Miller's success: "But by April 1938, Miller had organized and rehearsed a new band, with an expanded five-man saxophone section and two personnel additions crucial to Miller's future—Tex Beneke and Wilbur Schwartz. Beneke, as the most featured soloist and sometime vocalist with Miller during the band's heyday, was to become world-famous. But Wilbur Schwartz has been little recognized for his unique contribution to Miller's success, even though it was Schwartz's warmly pulsating lead-clarinet sound over the four saxophones that established Miller's fame with both musicians and the public. Miller had found "the sound," but it was twenty-year-old Schwartz, a remarkably consistent and musical player, who had put it across."

Schwartz played clarinet and saxophone with Miller's band until the patriotic leader dissolved it to join the Army as a captain after its last performance at the Central Theater in Passaic, NJ, on September 27, 1942. Schwartz had the highest respect for Miller and always felt proud to be part of his organization. He was also a part of Miller's golf contingency as recently explained by Miller trumpeter Zeke Zarchy who frequently met with Schwartz and Billy May for breakfast at the still-in-business Patys Restaurant on Riverside Drive in Toluca Lake, CA: "I introduced golf to the band and Glenn immediately became a golfing enthusiast. He would play whenever possible. Willie, Frank D'Annolfo, Dale McMickle, and Jack Lathrop, whose mother played in golf tournaments, were also active golfers. Willie was a great guy with a tremendous sense of humor. Everyone in the band loved him."

Glenn Miller trombonist Paul Tanner and Willie Schwartz were good friends. Tanner commented on his days with Schwartz in the Miller band from his home in Carlsbad, CA: "Willie and I did a lot together. We rented an apartment on Pelham Road in New Rochelle with Rolly Bundock while we were playing at the Glen Island Casino during the summer of 1939 and went in together to buy a car that Willie's dad over in Newark fixed up for us. Willie was definitely on the mischievous side and a bit of a Peck's bad boy who was always ready for a practical joke. But Glenn liked him and valued his playing, as did all the guys in the band. Things were never dull when Willie was around."

After Miller broke up his band, Schwartz joined the Merchant Marines and toured with the U.S. Maritime Service Band. The Schwartz family has a photo collection of him playing with the Band at Santa Catalina Island in 1943. When the war ended, he moved to Los Angeles and did radio and studio work and played with a variety of big bands. Come early 1948 he was with the Bob Crosby band performing at the Strand Theater in New York when he met Peggy Clark.

Few would think of North Dakota as a bastion of the big bands. Surprisingly, the state does have a strong Swing Era tradition. Lawrence Welk hails from Strasburg. Norma Egstrom, who was born in Jamestown, got her start singing with accompaniment by an organist at the Powers Hotel Coffee Shop and on radio station WDAY in Fargo. The station's program director, Ken Kennedy, suggested she change her name to Peggy Lee. The Crystal Ballroom in Fargo was a major stop on the big band circuit. It was there, on November 7, 1940, that a Duke Ellington engagement before a capacity crowd was recorded and issued by the Book of the Month Club with a booklet written by Stanley Dance. It is considered to be one of the best of Ellington's many location recordings and featured a brilliant tenor saxophone solo by Ben Webster on "Stardust." And seventy-five miles north of Fargo, situated on the banks of the Red River of the North, is Grand Forks, home of the States Theater and Ballroom where all the great big bands played and the home of the singing Clark Sisters.

There were four Clark sisters born two years apart in Grand Forks: Jean in 1920; Ann in 1922; Peggy in 1924; and Mary in 1926. Their singing career was sparked by their father William Jennings Bryan Clark, a local businessman, who had a rich baritone voice. Contributing to their natural talent was their mother Hilma, who was an accomplished pianist. Their primary form of family entertainment, during the bleak days of the Great Depression that was particularly unkind to North Dakota, was harmonizing together.

During a recent interview at her home in Encino, CA, Peggy Clark talked about the sister's early start as entertainers: "I remember appearing with my sisters in public for the first time when I was five years old. We were always singing around Grand Forks, especially at the University of North Dakota. We sang at University events and all the fraternity and sorority parties. While I was in high school we had our own daily radio program."

Richard King practiced law for fifty-seven years in Grand Forks before he passed away at eighty-five in 2006 and in 1976 founded a popular seventeen-piece territory band called Dick King's Classic Swing Band that is still active. In 2004 he recalled working with the Clark Sisters:

"I first heard the Clark Sisters back when they were little kids. In 1940 there were twenty-two farmers and businessmen running for Grand Forks county sheriff. The candidates always had entertainers when they made campaign appearances. At one of the candidate's rallies I played saxophone and sang with my sister on the same program with the Clark Sisters who were just a sensational singing group with great stage presence. Even then it was clearly evident that they had the ability to go far."

The Clark Sisters did indeed go far. In fact, they went straight to New York with no stops along the way thanks to the counsel of a family friend. Peggy Clark tells how it all happened: "Bob Ryan was an established marimba player in New York who was from Grand Forks. On a Christmas visit home he suggested we think about going to New York. We all agreed and he introduced us to a manager, Alan Ruppert, who set us up in the McAlpin apartment hotel on 34th Street in Manhattan. All this suddenly happened at the beginning of 1942 when I was seventeen years old."

Ruppert quickly landed the sisters their first job traveling up and down the East Coast for three months with Major Bowes's *The Original Amateur Hour* radio talent show. Bowes wanted a female vocal group on each show so the sisters changed their group's name for each program to compete as an alleged new contestant. Next, came a year with a USO tour of military bases that provided valuable radio air time. They worked their way from New England down to Florida and across the country to California. George T. Simon saw them sing in New York during July 1942 and gave them a good *Metronome* review. When the tour ended they returned to New York to sing at Manhattan venues. Then came Tommy Dorsey and a breakthrough to nationwide fame.

How Tommy Dorsey hired the Clark Sisters is a noteworthy story. Peggy Clark recounted the particulars: "Tommy wanted to hear us sing but we couldn't go to do an audition because Jean was recovering from an illness and was unable to walk. So he and Sy Oliver came over to our apartment and we sang for them. He asked us to join the band right there and we opened with him as The Sentimentalists at the Café Rouge of the Hotel Pennsylvania in the fall of 1943."

The Café Rouge engagement in Manhattan was the start of a breathtaking two-and-a-half-year run with Dorsey, singing at the top theaters and hotels across the country. The four sisters were also with the band when it appeared in the film *Thrill of a Romance*. Unfortunately, their song was left on the cutting room floor. But there was also recording stardom. They charted six hit records with Dorsey, the most popular of which were the top ten hits "On the Atchison To-peka, and the Santa Fe" in 1945 and "Until" that included a Harry Prime vocal and was released in 1948. Their exuberant version of "On the Sunny Side of the Street," arranged by Sy Oliver, was a particular swing favorite of George T. Simon.

Superb musicians were always a hallmark of Tommy Dorsey's bands. Peggy Clark talked about two great drummers she worked with: "Both Gene Krupa and Buddy Rich played with Tommy while we were part of the band. Gene was a consummate showman and just a real nice guy, a true gentleman. Buddy was exceptionally adept technically but he had an unpredictable and touchy personality. They were the best percussionists I ever worked with."

There were others that made an impression on Clark: "Jess Stacy played piano in the band for a while. He was one of the funniest men I ever met. Buddy DeFranco was on clarinet and so talented. He was a superb musician and a sweet man. When we got there, Nelson Riddle was playing trombone and starting out as an arranger. He had a junior high school sense of humor back then. Sy Oliver was a big influence on Nelson."

What about the volatile Dorsey himself? "Tommy did like to have a drink now and then. But with us he was polite, patient, and very paternal; he kept a watch on us. He took an interest in us and went out of his way to work with us to broaden our development. Tommy was a wonderful musician and we learned so much from him both musically and about the band business."

The Dorsey–Sentimentalists Era came to a close in mid 1946 when Mary left the group to marry Bruce Branson, who was with the Dorsey band. The remaining Clark Sisters immediately discussed their career options and decided the time had come to strike out on their own. They held auditions in New York to replace Mary, hiring Lillian Ventimiglia, who was a perfect fit vocally and in personal compatibility. She would eventually marry Sy Oliver.

The reconstituted Clark Sisters spent 1947 primarily doing radio work on several shows on both the East and West Coasts and reunited with Tommy Dorsey for a December recording session. In early 1948 they joined Bob Crosby's band at the Strand Theater in Manhattan, where Peggy Clark met Willie Schwartz, and continued to tour with Crosby on the East Coast through the spring. Willie and Peggy first spoke to each other during a rehearsal and it was love at first sight. Nevertheless, the days of the Clark Sisters performing together as a vocal group were rapidly coming to a close.

In the summer of 1948 the three remaining Clark sisters moved to Los Angeles to do the *Jack Smith Show*; Willie Schwartz also came west to do radio work on the *Club 15 Show*. Lillian Ventimiglia decided to stay in New York. Jean had already married. Ann married soon after they arrived in Los Angeles as did Peggy to Willie at the Chapman Park Hotel in Los Angeles's mid-Wilshire area on September 17. After considerable deliberation, the sisters agreed that the time had come to discontinue the group and move on and raise their families. Throughout the years they would occasionally reunite to record albums. But they did not publicly appear together until 1990.

Notwithstanding the Clark Sister's dissolution, the Schwartz's actively continued their careers in musical entertainment. Willie Schwartz flourished professionally for the next forty years. He would go on to achieve a distinguished and varied career in music, playing for several years in the NBC Orchestra and in numerous radio and television shows and the movies. In the 1950s he branched into classical music, playing with the Los Angeles Philharmonic Orchestra at the Hollywood Bowl and in 1966 spent three weeks touring Japan with the Percy Faith Orchestra. Thanks to his associations with Billy May and Nelson Riddle he was involved with myriad record albums that featured major vocal artists such as Rosemary Clooney, Ella Fitzgerald, Peggy Lee, and Frank Sinatra.

Glenn Miller-related activities were always high on Willie Schwartz's agenda. He played in the 1954 *The Original Reunion of the Glenn Miller Band* concert at a filled-to-capacity Shrine Auditorium in Los Angeles and at the Queen's Theater in Sydney in conjunction with the Australian opening of the popular 1954 film *The Glenn Miller Story*. There were additional trips to Australia and appearances with Tex Beneke's Orchestra at numerous Glenn Miller concerts and reunions over the years. In 1989 he toured England and Scotland with Miller alumni and performed in the 1989 PBS television show *The Glenn Miller Big Band Reunion* that was held before a live audience at Hollywood's Aquarius Theater. Still an avid golfer, while in Scotland Schwartz got to play at the famous St. Andrews Golf Course with Miller trombonist Jimmy Priddy. Schwartz also remained close to original Miller band members. In addition to May, Tanner, and Zarchy he kept in contact with Trigger Alpert, John Best, Ernie Caceres, and Dale McMickle.

Willie Schwartz remained active and was a fixture in the Hollywood studio and recording scene until he became ill in the late 1980s. He passed away on August 3, 1990. Schwartz's close friend Billy May delivered an emotional eulogy at his final service. The Big Band Academy of America posthumously presented their Golden Bandstand Award to Schwartz and inducted him into their Hall of Fame at their 2002 annual Reunion in Studio City, CA.

Peggy and Ann were the only two Clark Sisters that remained professionally active. Peggy prolifically sang as a group vocalist on television shows and in the movies. Her film work included several Disney pictures and classic musicals such as *Brigadoon*, *My Fair Lady*, *Seven Brides for Seven Brothers*, and *The Music Man*. She was also active with the Johnny Mann Singers for twenty years and had the honor of singing at functions for two presidents, Gerald Ford and Richard Nixon. The affair for President Ford was held in Palm Springs in 1990; she was joined by her three sisters and old friend Lillian Ventimiglia who flew out from New York.

The Schwartz family's legacy in the entertainment industry is being capably perpetuated by the three Schwartz children. Nan is a composer and arranger who has been nominated for two Grammies and is highly respected by no less than Johnny Mandel. Karen is a talented vocalist who has carried on the family tradition of group singing in television and film. Doug does sound restoration and engineering at his studio in North Hollywood, CA. He was nominated for a Grammy for album mastering.

Peggy Clark started performing in 1929. Looking back through the years she has no second thoughts: "My sisters and I had a great career with the big bands and I had a tremendous time working with the all the studios. I saw Hollywood inside and out. Willie and I always enjoyed getting together socially with Billy May, Hank Mancini, and Nelson Riddle. Most important, we had an ideal marriage and raised a wonderful family. All of us had so much fun together and we're still as close as ever."

CHICO SESMA
FROM BIG BANDS TO LATIN JAZZ

Although thriving in New York since the early 1940s when introduced by Mario Bauza and Machito, Latin jazz was virtually unknown in Los Angeles in 1949, the year former Big Band Era trombonist Chico Sesma launched his career in Southern California radio. Such is not the case today. Thanks in large part to both Sesma's pioneering radio work and Latin Holiday dances at the Hollywood Palladium, Los Angeles has evolved to become one of the major centers of Latin jazz in the United States. If there was a Los Angeles Latin Jazz Hall of Fame, Sesma would be among the first inductees for his contributions as a Big Band Era musician, Latin jazz radio personality, and Salsa dance promoter who consistently featured the top names in Tropical music.

Today East Los Angeles is home to the largest Hispanic community in the Los Angeles area. It abounds with colorful murals, outstanding Mexican restaurants, and the lilting strains of Mariachi music. When Lionel Sesma was born in East Los Angeles on March 29, 1924, it was a diverse community composed of Mexican, Japanese, Jewish, and Russian residents. Sesma, who grew up in a Mexican American family with no special musical talent, attended Hollenbeck Junior High School, where he learned to play trombone, and later Roosevelt High School.

During a conversation at his home in the Hollenbeck Park area of East Los Angeles, Sesma reminisced fondly about his time at Roosevelt: "The music program at Roosevelt was something that is hard to find at high schools today. We had a ROTC band, a symphony orchestra, and a dance orchestra. There were three music theory classes taught by three different music teachers who also ran the bands. I took every theory class and played in all three groups. Music was my life in high school and I loved the big bands. It was a thrill listening to Paul Whiteman play at our senior prom at the Florentine Gardens in Hollywood."

After graduating, Sesma attended Los Angeles City College: "That was a great experience. At that time they had what they called a studio staff orchestra which was a dance orchestra. We used to have musicians from the studios and name big bands come in and rehearse us and lead us through charts. I recall that Murray McEachern spent a lot of time with us. Everything was very high tech. The professor was an engineer and had a lot of sophisticated recording equipment so we made a lot of records. George Weidler, who went on to play alto sax with Les Brown and Stan Kenton and marry Doris Day, was in the orchestra. From time to time we talked about what was going on with the big bands."

It was actually while attending high school that Sesma started to professionally develop his skill on the trombone playing with East Los Angeles-based fifteen-piece dance orchestras led by popular Mexican American bandleaders. He started out with Phil Carreon and moved along to Sal Cervantes, Tilly Lopez, and Freddy Rubio. The most prominent of the four was Phil Carreon, who had musicians of the quality of Billy Byers, Teddy Edwards, Herb Geller, and Lennie Niehaus play in his band during the 1940s. By late 1943 Sesma progressed to fulltime trombonist with drummer Ken Baker's respected swing band that operated on the West Coast and gave

Liz Tilton, Martha's younger sister, her start as a vocalist a few years earlier. It was an opportune gig, one that would lead to a step up the ladder to a higher-profile big band, the Johnny Richards Orchestra.

Definitely worth examining is the personal history of musical prodigy Johnny Richards who was born Juan Ricardo de Cascales on November 2, 1911, in Queretaro, Mexico. His mother was a concert pianist who studied under Paderewski. Richards's family moved to Schenectady, NY, in 1912 where he spent his early years. At eight, the gifted multi-instrumentalist joined a vaudeville act called The Seven Wonders of the World and in his late teens played saxophone and was the house orchestrator in Philadelphia's Mastbaum Theater pit band. In the early 1930s Richards composed film scores for the Gaumont Film Studios in London and then moved on to Hollywood where he served as Victor Young's assistant at the Paramount Studios. Richards formed his first orchestra in 1940 and as 1943 came to a close it was playing at the Club Del Rio in San Pedro, CA, when Sesma came aboard thanks to the recommendation of Richard's lead alto player, Joe Glorioso. Sesma's fellow Roosevelt High School alumni and popular Swing Era vocalist Andy Russell was playing drums in the band that night.

Following the Club Del Rio date, the band played at the Hollywood Casino nightclub and appeared on Phil Baker's *Take It or Leave It* quiz show and the *Jack Carson Show* network radio programs. Richards then took the band east, performing at Jerry Jones's Rainbow Rendezvous in Salt Lake City, Elitch's Gardens in Denver, and the Roosevelt Hotel in Washington D.C. before arriving in New York in late 1944. While in the New York area, Sesma and the band had bookings at the Hotel Lincoln and Walter's Larchmont Post Lodge. They also recorded for Musicraft and appeared on the Armed Forces Radio Service's *One-Night Stand* and *Victory Parade of Spotlight Bands* radio shows. After a month's break in Manhattan the band backed up comedian Eddie "Rochester" Anderson on tour at the Rialto Theater in Boston and the Oriental Theater in Chicago. During his short stay in Chicago Sesma ran into fellow Los Angelino Gerald Wilson, whose big band was also playing in town. As soon as the two week Oriental Theater engagement ended Richards decided to break up his band and in mid-1945 Chico Sesma headed back home to Los Angeles. It was the conclusion of his association with Johnny Richards.

What were Sesma's impressions of Johnny Richards? "Johnny's charts were challenging and interesting to play although they were not overly appealing to dancers. He certainly was a brilliant musician, but I found him somewhat aloof as a bandleader. I respected him professionally and was not surprised that after the band broke up in Chicago he went on to a notable career as an arranger and composer with several well-known vocalists and big bands, especially Stan Kenton. In fact Johnny did fine work on Stan's *Cuban Fire* album. I remember I was saddened when I heard he died from a brain tumor. He was young, only fifty-six."

Over the next few years Johnny Richards would indirectly play a part in Sesma's career on two occasions. The first involved twenty-one-year-old Tom Talbert's first recording session as a big bandleader on June 25, 1946, at the Radio Recorders studio in Los Angeles. Talbert talked about the session from his home in Beverly Hills shortly before he passed away in 2005: "I heard about Chico from Johnny Richards. When I started rehearsing I immediately selected him for the first trombone part and it worked out well. He was a very good player and was popular with everyone in the band."

In addition to playing lead trombone on all the recordings alongside Ollie Wilson, a favorite of Artie Shaw, Sesma sang a vocal refrain in Spanish on Richards's and Ralph Yaw's composition of "Down in Chihuahua." Sesma and Richards collaborated on writing the dialogue. Several critics have viewed the Talbert version of the song as superior to the Stan Kenton adaptation with vocal work by the Pastels that was recorded in early 1947.

Sesma spent the next three years working exclusively with big bands: "After the Talbert recordings I played on the road and in Los Angeles with big bands led by Chuck Cascales, Johnny Richards's brother whom I knew through Johnny, Jimmy Zito, Les Brown's superb trumpet player, and Floyd Ray, a popular African American bandleader who went on to become a recording industry executive in the 60s. I was also with Boyd Raeburn and Russ Morgan locally in Los Angeles. I truly admired Russ; he was a fine musician and a strong person who knew how to run a band. We did a lot of recording work for Decca and on motion picture sound tracks. Russ Morgan has all my respect."

As a benchmark, the Big Band Era is considered to have officially ended in December 1946 when within a few weeks of each other several top bandleaders disbanded, albeit temporarily, because of a dramatic postwar decline in business. According to the late big band historian George T. Simon, the group included Les Brown, Benny Carter, Tommy Dorsey, Benny Goodman, Ina Ray Hutton, Harry James, and Jack Teagarden. Unfortunately, industry conditions continued to deteriorate as the decade progressed. By 1949 opportunities for big band sidemen became fewer and fewer, prompting Chico Sesma to ponder his future, a future that would soon lead to a four-decade career in radio.

"I had a childhood friend named George Baron who was an account executive for KOWL in Santa Monica, a station that focused on specialized markets," Sesma said. "He went to radio school and had aspirations of becoming a radio announcer that he set aside because working as an account executive was more lucrative for him. We crossed paths and he and the station management came up with the creation of the *Chico Sesma Show* because they had enjoyed considerable success with a music program designed to reach the African American market in the person of a black disc jockey, Joe Adams, who following his radio career had a longtime association with Ray Charles. They wanted to duplicate that success with a Mexican American bilingual format as opposed to a Spanish only format which had dominated the Los Angeles market up to that point. George gave me a two week crash course in radio announcing and I got the job immediately after a fifteen minute audition. It was at that time that I acquired the nickname Chico."

What started out as a half hour show grew quickly by popular demand to a three hour program that attracted both Hispanic and non-Hispanic listeners. With his deep, rich, baritone voice, Chico Sesma was now an established radio personality playing big band music of the likes of Duke Ellington, Woody Herman, Stan Kenton, and Jimmy Lunceford. However, Sesma's program format was about to experience an unexpected and sudden change.

Soon after he went on the air Sesma started to roam through the many record stores that were then concentrated on Pico Boulevard to search for new material. He made a startling discovery. For the first time Sesma heard the sounds of Machito and Tito Puente and Tito Rodriguez. It was a shocking revelation, and he immediately started playing their pulsating, infectious music on his program. The response was overwhelmingly positive and within six months *The Chico Sesma Show* became an all-Latin music program. Thanks to Sesma's rummaging through record bins in the back of record stores, Afro-Cuban-based Latin jazz was played on a Los Angeles radio station for the first time and the new sound became an instant sensation.

Another milestone in Sesma's career occurred in 1954. It was the year he started his legendary Latin Holiday dances at the Hollywood Palladium: "George Baron suggested that I try to promote a dance for the Hispanic youth. I was able to get the Hollywood Palladium for a Sunday evening, which was its off night, for $800. It was a huge success; we drew almost 4,000 the first night. Within less than three years it became a well-attended monthly event. I kept going until 1973. Even though we were still doing well I sensed that the dance scene in Southern California was starting to change."

The first Latin Holiday dance featured Perez Prado and Joe Loco, who happened to be in Los Angeles. Through the years Latin music giants such as Celia Cruz, Jack Costanzo, Machito, Benny More, Johnny Pacheco, Charlie and Eddie Palmieri, and Tito Puente were among the many that headlined programs. A highlight occurred on a magical Sunday in 1958 when More and Puente appeared together on the same bill. Starting in 1965 the popular East Los Angeles rock and roll band Thee Midniters, whose live recording of "Land of a Thousand Dances" hit the charts that year, played the Latin Holiday dances for two years. They were well received and by the end of their run had moved up to become a headline act.

Bongo superstar Jack Costanzo recalled his Latin Holiday experience from his home near San Diego: "Chico Sesma and I are good friends, we go back a long way. I have fond memories of playing at his Latin Holiday dances. Chico knew how to run a class event and the Hollywood Palladium was always packed. The kids loved the music and could really dance. Those were great times and great Latin music."

The 1950s were a busy time for Sesma. In addition to developing Latin Holiday he continued at KOWL along with fellow disc jockeys Adams, Jim Ameche (Don Ameche's brother), and Frank Evans until 1957 when the station changed ownership and was renamed KDAY and converted to a Top 40 format. After short stints with a local FM station and KNOB, Sleepy Stein's jazz station, Sesma was briefly off the air until September 1959 when he landed an evening show with KALI. He was with the station until 1967 at which time he fell victim to another change of hands. His departure from KALI proved to be a blessing in disguise as it allowed him to start an entirely new professional career.

In February 1969 Sesma decided to take a chance and answer an ad in the *Los Angeles Times* for a job with the State of California's Employment Development Department. He was accepted and in a very short period of time worked his way up from a position in the human relations division to become a public information officer working with the electronic and print media and organizing and conducting special events. His background on radio and running the Latin Holiday dances were perfect training for the job.

Come1979 Sesma's career with the State of California was on the fast track and it appeared that after nearly twenty years as a fixture on Los Angeles radio he was permanently off the air. Then along came New York-based Fania records, often referred to as the Motown of Salsa, and a surprise return to KALI: "In early 1979 Fania entered into an arrangement with KALI to do a show featuring their records. I was asked to return to KALI to host the evening program. I didn't have programming latitude but that didn't bother me because I loved Fania's format. Who could complain about playing songs by artists like the Fania All Stars, Celia Cruz, Larry Harlow, and Willie Colon? I could go on and on. I found Jerry Masucci, who formed the label with Johnny Pacheco, and the entire Fania organization a pleasure to work with."

It was a hectic period for Sesma, what with his Fania radio show and demanding professional position with the State. As the 1980s unfolded he decided the time had come to slow the pace. In May 1982 he left KALI when Fania ended their program and in December 1983 retired from a distinguished fifteen-year career with the State of California's Economic Development Department. However, Sesma has not faded from public view. Through the years he has kept active in music, playing trombone with the Hispanic Musicians Association, and has remained in contact with his childhood friend and fellow Roosevelt High School graduate, Paul Lopez, a distinguished trumpet player, arranger, and composer who attended Julliard. He also has appeared as a guest on several radio shows.

Well-deserved recognition has also come Sesma's way. In 1991 The Hispanic Musicians Association celebrated their Spirit of Music Awards at the Sportsman's Lodge in Studio City,

CA. Over 600 Latin music enthusiasts crammed the Lodge's Empire Ballroom to full capacity. Among the event's five honorees was Chico Sesma, who received the Association's Spirit of Music Award for his impressive life-time contributions to music, radio, dance promotion, and community service in Los Angeles. The award was presented to Sesma by Association president Bobby Rodriguez. He was also recognized by the International Latin Music Hall of Fame in 2002 and honored at a star-studded tribute.

Chico Sesma is still an icon of the Latin jazz community. Jose Rizo's popular *Jazz on the Latin Side* radio show is a longtime fixture on KKJZ-FM. He discussed Sesma's contributions from the station's Chuck Niles studio in Long Beach: "We all owe Chico a debt of gratitude. He introduced Latin jazz to Los Angeles through his radio show and Latin Holiday dances. He also had a definite impact on contemporary musicians. My good friend Poncho Sanchez grew up listening to him. Today we have a vibrant Latin jazz scene here in Southern California with the best artists in the country playing at a host of clubs and concerts. We can thank Chico for getting it started."

In closing, two other aspects of Sesma's career deserve mention. First, he was a sociological trail blazer. When he went on the air in 1949, the impact of the notorious World War II Los Angeles Zoot Suit Riots had not been forgotten. Thanks to his bi-lingual radio show featuring new Latin music talent that had wide appeal and to his trendy concerts at the Hollywood Palladium, he set the tone for greater cultural appreciation in Los Angeles.

Finally, there is the matter of professional accomplishment. Most of us would be satisfied to achieve success in one single field of endeavor. Chico Sesma succeeded in four. He was a Big Band Era musician who played with the top bands, a popular radio disc jockey, a successful concert promoter, and a senior public affairs specialist with a state government agency. That's not a bad resume to reflect on while enjoying a well-deserved retirement.

BUTCH STONE'S SENTIMENTAL JOURNEY

What musician has spent sixty plus years of his eight decade career in the music business with the same big band, has traveled the world with Bob Hope, has become an acquaintance of presidents, and is still entertaining in his nineties? The answer is Butch Stone, who has had the good fortune to experience the entire Big Band Era and participate in every facet of the post-World War II musical entertainment industry.

Henry Stone was born in New York City on August 29, 1912. Nicknamed Butch by his maternal Uncle Leon when he was two months old, he lived on 183rd Street in Manhattan's Washington Heights district, graduating from George Washington High School in 1930.

Stone reveled in growing up in the New York of the 1920s and became passionately dedicated to the New York Yankees, then led by Babe Ruth. He spent many an afternoon atop Coogan's Bluff watching Yankee games in the old Polo Grounds before they moved into Yankee stadium in 1923, and was a fan in the stands at Yankee Stadium on June 1, 1925, the day Lou Gehrig made baseball history replacing Wally Pipp in the Yankee starting lineup to become their starting first baseman without missing a game until May 3, 1939.

Nineteen twenty-five was a milestone year for Stone. Shortly after his thirteenth birthday, he developed a strong interest in music and started taking baritone saxophone lessons. Stone quickly mastered the instrument and gained notice playing in the George Washington High School concert orchestra and the school pep band that played at all athletic events, experiencing his first taste of entertaining.

After graduating from high school in 1930, with the Great Depression in full force, Stone landed a job working for Consolidated Film Industries in Fort Lee, NJ, delivering the film Consolidated developed and printed to the Paramount, Strand, and other leading Manhattan theaters. He launched his professional musical career two years later when he joined the ten-piece Frank Rysen Band that was playing Jimmie Lunceford arrangements four nights a week at the Club Fordham located at Fordham Road and Jerome Avenue in the Bronx. Stone received $7 a night and like all the band members, including Rysen himself who drove a truck for a brewery, kept his day job.

In 1934, soon after he secured a short stay at the famed Roseland Ballroom, Rysen broke up his band due to scheduling conflicts with the member's fulltime jobs. Stone's next move was to quit his job with Consolidated in late 1938 and go to work for his high school classmate and lifelong friend, bandleader Van Alexander, a move that was to set the tone for the rest of his career.

It was with the Van Alexander band that Stone started singing novelty tunes and developed the style that earned him the appellation The White Louis Jordan. His breakthrough came performing in Alexander's band at the Raymor Ballroom in Boston when he introduced his signature song, "A Good Man is Hard to Find." According to Stone, the Raymor was a twin ballroom uniquely divided into two dance floors separated by a walled partition. Playing opposite the Van Alexander band that night was Woody Herman's band, then billed as The Band That Plays the Blues.

In the late 1930s Stone became immersed in the New York big band scene. He, Alexander, and bandleader and vocalist Peter Dean became fast friends with Swing Era historian George T. Simon. They took sorties to the Savoy Ballroom in Harlem to hear Chick Webb and Ella Fitzgerald, and as diehard baseball fans regularly attended games at Yankee Stadium, the Polo Grounds, and Ebbets Field.

At his home in Van Nuys, CA, Stone recalled a game at Yankee Stadium when Simon, a rabid Dodger fan, paid the price for rooting against the Yankees: "Simon needled us about the Yankees all afternoon. When they unexpectedly lost to the last place Saint Louis Browns, Alexander and I grabbed his prize fedora and threw it off the top deck."

Jack Teagarden, with backing from MCA, put together his own band in 1939. One of his first moves was to recruit Stone, who has fond memories of their association: "I thoroughly enjoyed the year I spent with Teagarden. He was a fine man to work for and a superb trombone player. Jack was a big man with a tremendous appetite. While we were in Milwaukee playing at the Riverside Theater he ate two huge pork shanks in one sitting at Mader's German restaurant. If you were able to eat the first one, they gave you the second one free. The waiters couldn't believe it."

However, life with Teagarden was not easy. The traveling was intense, several hundred miles a night, seven days a week, and it took its toll on Stone. In 1940 he left to join Larry Clinton, who had extended him numerous previous offers.

In late 1941, the Clinton band was playing at the Loew's State Theater at 45th Street and Broadway when Les Brown stopped by to hear Stone sing "My Feet's Too Big" and "Nagasaki." Knowing that Clinton was preparing to break up his band after the Lowe's State engagement to join the Air Force as a flight instructor, Brown asked Stone and Irv Cottler, Clinton's drummer, to see his agent, Joe Glaser, about a job with the Brown band.

Joe Glaser, who ran Associated Booking in a plush office at 57th Street and Fifth Avenue, was a big man around the New York music scene, handling Louis Armstrong among others. Cottler and Stone decided to ask for $125 a week, an impressive sum for that time. Glazer countered with $75 a week, Brown's standard salary for his band members. Cottler refused and signed up with Claude Thornhill for his desired $125 weekly wage, and eventually wound up spending twenty-seven years as Frank Sinatra's drummer. Stone accepted Glaser's offer and immediately went to Chicago to join Brown at the Black Hawk restaurant, launching a fairy-tale career with The Band of Renown.

Stone's career with Les Brown was indeed varied and never dull. There were myriad recording sessions for Brown's numerous hits. Stone was in the studios playing for all of them, including band vocalist Doris Day's blockbusters capped by her 1945 Swing Era classic, "Sentimental Journey." Stone enjoyed working with Day: "Doris was just a sweet, cute person. So easy to get along with. I didn't know anyone in the music business who didn't like her."

There were also engagements in Las Vegas, television work on the *Steve Allen, Dean Martin,* and *Hollywood Palace Shows*, and appearances in two movies, *Seven Days Leave* starring Lucille Ball and Victor Mature in 1942, and Jerry Lewis's original *Nutty Professor* in 1963. But the bulk of Stone's postwar activity involved Les Brown's longtime association with Bob Hope.

In 1947 Les Brown became Bob Hope's official band, playing on all of Hope's radio and television shows from that time on. The band and Stone also made eighteen Christmas trips to Korea and Vietnam with Hope to entertain our troops between 1950 and 1972. One trip in particular stands out to Stone.

"We were stationed in Saigon during the Vietnam War," Stone said. "The hotel next to us was bombed and hundreds of servicemen were injured. The blast was so powerful that it blew out our power and all toilet facilities. The Army moved us up to Bangkok for security and we flew back and forth to Saigon daily to put on shows for the boys."

Over the years, Stone got to know Thailand and its Monarch, His Majesty Bhumibol Adulyadej, quite well: "We frequently played for the King of Thailand at his Palace. He was a great jazz fan and in the 1950s composed a song for a Broadway musical. The King played saxophone and loved to join in with the band, jamming with us for hours at a time."

Notwithstanding his involvement with Hope, Brown and his band regularly toured the country, coast to coast, well into the 1970s. Stone commented on their hectic pace: "We would play four weeks at the Hollywood Palladium with a radio broadcast to New York and them spend two months doing one-nighters traveling by chartered bus to the Hotel Pennsylvania in Manhattan where we would play the Cafe Rouge for eight or nine weeks. Every night we did a radio broadcast from the Pennsylvania back to Los Angeles. On the way, we would always stop in Chicago to play the Panther Room at the Hotel Sherman with a radio hook up. We still hold the Panther Room record for the most appearances by a big band."

Stone further commented: "Touring was an important part of the big band business. At that time a band made its money playing one-nighters. We'd always pack them in because they heard the band on the radio and wanted to see us in person since there was no television. Even after television came in we still continued to tour the country by bus."

Although Les Brown passed away in 2001, the band still continues under the direction of his son Les Brown Jr. Even though Stone is long retired as a saxophonist, he sang with the band in October 2007 at a concert in Thousand Oaks, CA, bringing down the house with his patented, lusty rendition of "A Good Man is Hard to Find." Butch Stone was always a crowd pleaser.

Through the years Stone has received numerous honors for his contributions to the world of entertainment. In spite of the fact that he has been recognized by Presidents Gerald Ford and Richard Nixon, and General William Westmoreland, two events stand out. In 1996 at the Ventura Club in Sherman Oaks, CA, an eighty-fourth birthday party was held for Stone with Steve Allen as emcee, Bob and Dolores Hope performing, and Les Brown's Band of Renown playing for a packed house of entertainment greats. However, the ultimate in professional recognition came when the Big Band Academy of America presented him their the Academy's Golden Bandstand Award along with Patty Andrews and Pete Rugolo before six hundred swing music supporters at their 1998 annual reunion at the Sportsmen's Lodge in Studio City, CA.

It's been quite a ride for Butch Stone. In reflecting on his life and multifaceted eight-decade career in entertainment, he said, "No one can argue that wealth and recognition are not important, but the greatest gifts in life are health and happiness. Fate has blessed me with those gifts. I love performing, I'm in great health, couldn't be happier, and am blessed with sixty-five wonderful years of marriage to my wife Shirley whom I luckily met on a blind date at the Hippodrome Theater in Baltimore. No man can ask for more."

PAUL TANNER
FROM SKUNK HOLLOW TO GLENN MILLER
TO UCLA

T here were only four musicians in Glenn Miller's band who participated in every RCA Bluebird and Victor recording, radio program, movie, and live appearance. One of that elite group was trombonist Paul Tanner, who rose from the hollows of Kentucky to stardom with the most popular big band in history, to a professorship at a prestigious university.

Paul Tanner was born in Skunk Hollow, KY, a hamlet so small that it does not exist on any map, on October 15, 1917. He was the third of six Tanner sons, all of whom went on to successful careers in either business or music. His father, an Army colonel, was the school master of the local one-room schoolhouse and an outstanding piano player.

When Tanner was three-years old the family moved to Onancock, VA, and then on to Wilmington, DE, where Tanner's father was appointed superintendent for the sate reformatory for boys. The Tanner family took up residency in the reformatory itself where Tanner lived through high school.

Little did Tanner know that his days residing in the reformatory would serve to shape the direction of his life. When he was eleven years old, two reform school students introduced him to the trombone. Although he met with little success on the piano, he instinctively took to the brass instrument, quickly mastering it. A musical calling was born.

Tanner's professional career in music actually began while he was still in high school. In 1933 he joined the family band, The Kentuckians, that spent the summer playing at the Pier Ballroom in Wildwood, NJ. The next summer, they graduated to Atlantic City, playing the Palais Royale where they backed up a chorus line of 300-pound dancing ladies called the Beef Trust.

After high school, Tanner enrolled at the University of Delaware where he had a short lived academic career, showing little interest in scholastic matters. Immediately after leaving the university, he joined the Kentuckians full time and spent a grueling two years touring the southern United States as told by telephone from his home in Carlsbad, CA: "We had some very unique experiences. It seemed we played numerous gambling clubs that were regularly raided by the police with their guns drawn, and one night on the road when we couldn't find a hotel all of us slept in a bordello, with our clothes on."

The Kentuckians broke up in 1936 and Tanner traveled to New Jersey for a brief stint with Frank Dailey's band. It was indeed the Frank Dailey of Meadowbrook Ballroom fame. He then connected with his family in Atlanta where they had relocated and played with a local band. Realizing he was going nowhere, he decided to move back to Wilmington where he once again found work playing locally. After a brief gig with a Texas territory band, he returned to Wilmington and made a calculated decision that would change the course of his life.

Tanner tells the story: "In the summer of 1938 I decided to go back to Atlantic City where there were always six or seven prestige bands playing. I got a job with Marty Carouso's band at a local strip tease establishment, the Swing Club, hoping to get lucky and be discovered by a big time bandleader on his night off. One evening I looked out into the audience while I was playing and there was Glenn Miller, sitting right up front with his wife Helen who was elegantly dressed with white gloves on."

After the show Tanner summoned all the courage he had and went over to Miller's table to ask him for a recommendation. Miller apparently liked what he saw. He told Tanner he was impressed with his high register and offered him a job instead of a recommendation. Tanner accepted on the spot and embarked on a fairy-tale four-year run with the Miller organization. To quote Tanner: "Every night was New Year's Eve."

Paul Tanner joined Miller's band wondering how it all came about. The Swing Club was not the kind of establishment Miller frequented. Someone must have told Miller about Tanner, and Tanner himself never felt comfortable discussing the situation with his new boss. In any event, Miller immediately christened the relaxed and laid-back Tanner "Lightnin."

What was Glenn Miller really like? According to Tanner: "One of the first things I learned about him was that he was willing to work brutally hard to achieve perfection. Glenn was also an extremely knowledgeable musician, an astute businessman, a great organizer, a chronic workaholic, and extremely patriotic. He was also a very good athlete. There were those who thought he had no sense of humor, but he most certainly did whenever business did not come first. I thoroughly enjoyed working for him, and he made me a better all-around trombone player."

How about Glenn Miller the musician? "He was a fine trombone player, very underrated. Glenn had a good solid tone, played well in tune, had a respectable upper range, and was very consistent. He was a superb arranger who could uncannily judge whether or not a song was worth his while. If it was, he would often spend hours reworking the entire score to achieve a sound conforming to his standards, quite often deleting as much as he retained. A perfect example is how he rewrote Joe Garland's "In the Mood" to turn it into a huge hit."

It all came to an end on September 27, 1942, at the Central Theater in Passaic, NJ, when the band gave its last performance before Miller joined the Army with a captain's rank. Tanner remembers the evening. "Marion Hutton choked up and had to run off-stage. The Modernaires couldn't finish their numbers and the kids in the audience were sobbing uncontrollably. Glenn, aware that continuing would be futile, had the stage hands ring down the curtain. It was the end of an era."

After Miller's band broke up, Tanner refused lucrative offers from Horace Heidt and Sammy Kaye, joining former Miller associate Charlie Spivak's band. After nine months with Spivak he enlisted in the Army spending the duration of World War II in New York playing in wartime radio shows and films, and recording V-Discs.

As the conflict was coming to a close, Tanner thought about his postwar career. He consulted with his old friend Frank Dailey who advised him to join Les Brown's Band of Renown. He took Dailey's advice, and after a satisfying but short stint with Brown, he reunited with his old friend Tex Beneke and his Orchestra where he spent the next five years.

By now it was 1951 and Tanner faced a critical decision. The summer of 1951 was the last date Tanner could enroll in college under the G.I. Bill. After considerable deliberation, he decided to give up the big bands and matriculate at UCLA. He chose UCLA over cross-town rival University of Southern California because he could get a better parking spot on campus.

It took Tanner seven years to achieve his BA because of concurrent obligations as a staff musician with the American Broadcasting Company. Upon graduation, he was offered a faculty position and spent the next twenty-three years as a professor of music, picking up his Masters Degree and Ph.D. along with writing with educator and musician David McGill the most widely used textbook on jazz titled *Jazz*, now in its eleventh edition. He estimates he has taught music to over 75,000 students during his tenure ship at UCLA along with writing twenty other books on the theoretical aspects of music and the trombone.

While at UCLA Tanner held a unique position in the Music Department. He was the only faculty member ever to teach all four areas of scholastic musical discipline: performance, theory, history of music, and music education. Tanner was also able to travel throughout the world as a classical trombone soloist with the UCLA Concert Band.

Tanner's last day of class at the Westwood campus in 1981 was one he will never forget: "I was truly surprised. My students hired Tex Beneke's band with all the old Miller alumni to play and set up bleachers and food stands. It's the only time in UCLA history that the student body gave a going away party for a retiring professor. It was all a surprise, reminiscent of the film *Mr. Holland's Opus*. However, that wonderful sendoff did not affect my objective grading."

While ensconced in academia at UCLA, Tanner still carried on as an active trombonist. He spent from 1951 to 1977 as an American Broadcasting Company staff trombone player and did extensive freelancing with Frank Sinatra, Nat "King" Cole, and David Rose, playing on Rose's two big hits, "Ebb Tide" and "The Stripper."

Tanner was even a precursor to the synthesizer. The Theremin is a boxlike musical instrument invented by the Russian scientist Lev Theremin that physically resembles a radio receiver and produces musical tones through electronic circuitry. Tanner tinkered with the instrument and wound up playing it for three years on the *My Favorite Martian* television show staring Bill Bixby. He even dabbled in rock and roll playing the Theremin on the Beach Boys smash hit "Good Vibrations." They were so pleased with Tanner's manipulation of the instrument that they invited him to tour with them. He graciously demurred. Tanner accomplished all this while teaching at UCLA.

Since his retirement, Tanner has kept active participating in the annual Glenn Miller Birthplace Society Festival in Clarinda, IA, acting as an expert witness in court cases involving the music business, and attending Glenn Miller functions in England and Japan where the Miller name is more famous than ever.

Earlier we asked what Glenn Miller was really like. Now its time to ask what Paul Tanner is really like.

Who better to render an opinion than highly respected big band historian George T. Simon who knew Tanner since 1938? In 1999 he said: "Paul Tanner is a truly outstanding person. Not only was he a fine musician and academic, he is a gracious and courteous soul blessed with a fine sense of humor who treats everyone with dignity and respect. As a human being, they don't come any better than Paul Tanner."

ZEKE ZARCHY
THE LIFE OF A SIDEMAN

The truly unsung heroes of the Big Band Era were the sidemen, members of the band that played a specific musical instrument. They were the backbone of a band, largely toiling in anonymity while the bandleader basked in fame. What was the life of a sideman like? One need look no further than the career of lead trumpeter Zeke Zarchy, whom Big Band Era historian George T. Simon referred to as "one of the most respected big band musicians and one who has maintained that respect throughout his career."

Rubin Zarchy was born in Harlem on June 12, 1915, to parents who immigrated to the United States from Russia during Russia's war with Austria in the late 1800s. His father was a house painter who worked for a variety of painting contractors. As a result, the Zarchy family was constantly on the move, relocating throughout New York City.

Musical ability was definitely coded into Zarchy's genes. His father was an accomplished mandolin and accordion player, while his mother's father was a professional musician in Russia. Her sister, who stayed behind in Russia, became a concert pianist and professor of music at Leningrad University.

Notwithstanding his genetic pedigree, Zarchy's musical career started somewhat inauspiciously. He began violin lessons when he was eight years old but soon succumbed to fanatically playing stickball on the streets of Manhattan. The lessons lasted but two years. Then came a twist of fate that would serve to shape the direction of Zarchy's professional life.

When he was eleven years old, Zarchy's mother took him to visit her first cousin whose son happened to be rehearsing his four-piece band and playing the trumpet. Zarchy was mesmerized by what he saw and immediately took up the instrument thanks to the largesse of his older brother who bought him a trumpet with a mouthpiece for $25. It was a leftover from a volume sale the local music store made to the New York City public school system. That store was located in Brooklyn's Brownsville section at Saratoga Avenue and Sterling Place, and was owned by the portly Sam Ash, founder of the Sam Ash music store chain.

After six months of lessons from his cousin's music teacher, Zarchy started to practice on his own. He was soon offered his first job playing in a band at a local women's auxiliary lodge run by his neighborhood drummer friend's mother for the princely sum of $1 for a four-hour engagement. He continued to play functions traveling the subways around New York until 1933 when he graduated from Brooklyn's Samuel Tilden High School, where he spent his senior year lunch hours listening to the Scott Fisher band with its lead trumpeter Chris Griffin broadcasting from the Park Central Hotel. It wasn't long before he landed his first fulltime position. It was with Nat Martin's ten-piece band at Lum's Chinese restaurant at 59th Street and Lexington Avenue in the heart of Manhattan.

Lum's was a well known celebrity hangout thanks in part to the reputation of Martin who was the pit orchestra leader for several of the Marx Brothers Broadway shows. Zarchy was paid $25 per week to play three sets staggered from 12 noon to 1:00 a.m., seven days a week. With little demand for housepainters during the depth of the Great Depression, Zarchy's father was out of work and at eighteen he became the family breadwinner.

As Zarchy tells the story at his home in Studio City, CA, it was during his four month stay at Lum's that he acquired his nickname Zeke: "The band's saxophone player and I regularly did a comedy sketch called Len and Zeke, sporting false mustaches and straw hats singing "Put on Your Old Gray Bonnet." I spent my three-hour lunch break hanging out with all the musicians around Broadway and got to know everyone very quickly. Since the band's turnover was asstonishly high due to the brutally long hours and low pay, the new musicians found it easier to identify me as Zeke rather than Rubin."

Zarchy's next move was to advance up to the then-popular Manhattan taxi dance halls, where for ten cents a ticket a patron could dance with a hostess while a six-piece band played a tune for two choruses. He proceeded to make the rounds of the taxi dance halls upping his weekly salary by $2 or $3 with each switch. Incidentally, it was those Times Square-area taxi dance halls that were the inspiration for the 1930 hit song "Ten Cents a Dance" sung by Ruth Etting.

From the world of taxi dance halls, Zarchy took a succession of steps up the musical ladder when he went on to play with various bands in New York night clubs. He graduated to more prestigious ballroom bands, culminating with landing the lead trumpet chair in Bert Block's band in 1934. Block's was a fresh new swing band that included arranger Axel Stordahl, second trumpeter Joe Bauer, and vocalist Jack Leonard, all three of whom eventually joined Tommy Dorsey's orchestra. In fact it was Dorsey who would indirectly influence Zarchy's next move.

After the Dorsey brothers famous breakup at the Glen Island Casino in 1935 on Memorial Day, Tommy Dorsey hired twelve of the fourteen musicians from the Joe Haymes band to form his own organization. Haymes immediately regrouped and put together a new band. His first move was to offer Zarchy the lead trumpet chair. To Zarchy's delight, he played alongside his high school idol, Chris Griffin.

Zarchy was with Haymes for about a year when he got a surprise call from Benny Goodman at the recommendation of Griffin who was now in The King of Swing's trumpet section. The call came while Haymes's band was playing at the Coney Island Amusement Park in Cincinnati. He accepted Goodman's offer and stayed with the most popular big band in the country until December 1936 when he left to join Artie Shaw. Zarchy was attracted by Shaw's band that had a novel combination of a string quartet, two violins, cello, viola, jazz rhythm section, and only one saxophone and three brasses. It was an enjoyable experience for Zarchy, albeit a short one of but three months, as Shaw disbanded in early 1937 after playing a one-month engagement at the Adolphus Hotel in Dallas. Contrary to Shaw's cantankerous image, Zarchy found him a pleasure to work for.

On his first night back in New York, Zarchy went to see his old friends in the Benny Goodman band playing at the Hotel Pennsylvania's Madhattan Room. Goodman warmly greeted Zarchy and took him to a table occupied by seven members of the Bob Crosby band, including its manager Gil Rodin, who immediately offered Zarchy a job as lead trumpet player based on Goodman's recommendation. Zarchy accepted on the spot and at nine the next morning was at the Pennsylvania Station with Crosby and the band, boarding a train to play a fraternity party at Cornell University. Playing Crosby's unique style of big band Dixieland music was a new and career-broadening experience that would serve Zarchy well later in later years. On a personal note, he learned how to drive by squiring Crosby between one-night stands in Crosby's brand new Packard convertible.

In early 1938 Zarchy decided to return to New York after Crosby's band completed an engagement at the Palomar Ballroom in Los Angeles. Two days after he got home he received a call from legendary MCA booking agent Willard Alexander, who asked him if he would like to join Red Norvo's band that was opening at the Commodore Hotel. He started the next day. Zarchy reveled in playing Norvo's book and associating with Norvo and Mildred Bailey, notwithstanding the pairs constant bickering between themselves. Commenting on Norvo's musicianship, Zarchy said: "Red was a superb musician and bandleader with a unique ability to gently swing. And don't forget Mildred Bailey. To this day she does not get sufficient recognition for her singing ability."

Zarchy decided to return to Crosby in mid 1938, staying until the fall of 1939 when he went over to Tommy Dorsey's Orchestra, meeting up with the band at the Palmer House in Chicago. Playing with Dorsey was a rewarding professional experience for Zarchy: "Tommy was a true musical inspiration. Everyone who played for him became a better musician, including myself. Just look at the impact he had on Frank Sinatra's vocal phrasing. I was with Dorsey when Sinatra joined the band at the Riverside Theater in Milwaukee. I couldn't believe it when I heard him swing 'East of the Sun' that first night. I immediately knew he was a unique talent."

After working virtually non-stop since his days at Lum's restaurant, Zarchy decided to take a break. In early 1940 he left Dorsey and took three months off to tour Florida and Cuba. Before he left he went with friends to see the latest big band sensation, Glenn Miller, at the Pennsylvania Hotel. Zarchy explains how it turned out to be a most fortuitous visit: "I ran into my old friend Mickey McMickle, who was playing trumpet in Glenn's band. He suggested to Miller that when I get back I substitute for him so he could have a cyst taken out of his lip. Glenn thought it was a good idea, so when I returned from Florida I joined the Band at the Wardman Park Hotel in Washington D.C.."

Zarchy soon developed a close association with Miller that would last until the bandleader's death in 1944. That association was based on Miller's respect for Zarchy's acumen and their mutual interest in the sport of golf: "Glenn was a very good golfer. He and I played whenever we could, even once in pouring rain with the caddies holding umbrellas over us."

At the end of 1940 Zarchy left Miller to take the lead trumpet chair with the NBC radio orchestra in New York. It was the ultimate step up for Zarchy because at the time it was considered to be the most prestigious job a big band trumpet player could aspire to. The staff, including Arturo Toscanini's symphony, had an impressive 148 musicians. Playing alongside them provided him experience that was to prove invaluable to his professional development. Zarchy stayed at NBC until September 1942 when he drove to Miami along with nine other NBC musicians to enlist in the Army. After basic training they were assigned to a brand new band being formed at the Boca Raton Air Base. Six months later orders came through transferring him to a post band in Atlantic City.

"As I was reporting for duty after three days of driving I was told that they had no notice of anyone coming in, least of all another sergeant," Zarchy said. "But not to worry, it would be straightened out in the morning. At that moment Captain Glenn Miller walked in and everyone saw the light. He had stopped by on his way from Knollwood Field in North Carolina where he was based, to see his wife at their home in Tenafly, NJ. We went out to dinner and he told me of his plans to organize the best service band he could and eventually take it overseas where it would do the most good. I was surprised when he said, 'And you're the first one.'"

Zarchy was immediately tasked by Miller to form and front a dance band identical to his pre-war band in Atlantic City. It would be the nucleus of the famous Glenn Miller Army Air Force Band and play fourteen mess halls for lunch and dinner with forty-five minute sets. Trunks containing the Miller library and music stands were shipped within the week, and the program quickly became a huge success.

Due to unsatisfactory facilities in Atlantic City, Miller decided to transfer operations and started to form his Army Air Force Band at an Army base at Yale University in March 1943 with Zarchy as both his lead trumpet player and First Sergeant in administrative charge of the band. They maintained a close personal and working relationship until Miller's ill-fated plane trip across the English Channel. In fact, Zarchy was one of the last persons to talk to Miller before he boarded the single engine aircraft with two military personnel.

"I finished lunch at the Duke of Bedford's estate that served as one of the Eighth Air Force headquarters bases," Zarchy explained. "I knew Glenn was leaving for Paris ahead of us, so I went to the estate's main building and there he was with Don Haynes and Paul Dudley, his second and third in command. They were getting ready to accompany him to the airport a mile away. We chatted for a few minutes, and then a staff car arrived to take them all to the plane. After he got in he turned around and said, 'See you over there Zeke.'"

After his death, the Miller Army Air Force band continued under the official command of Don Haynes with Ray McKinley, a bandleader in his own right before the war, fronting the band and arranger Jerry Gray directing radio broadcasts. In Zarchy's opinion the well liked McKinley did a superb job and Gray's talent was ever-present. Zarchy continued to play lead trumpet until he left the Army exiting at Andrews Field outside of Washington, D.C. on November 23, 1945. The war was over and now he was about to embark on the second phase of his professional life, driving cross country to Los Angeles, arriving on December 5, 1945.

It was in Los Angeles where Zarchy settled and started a five-decade career in freelance studio work interrupted only by a ten year fulltime stint with the NBC staff orchestra during the 1950s. His studio radio and television projects included the *Edgar Bergen and Charlie McCarthy*, *Burns and Allen*, *Johnny Carson*, *Bing Crosby*, *Frank Sinatra*, *Red Skelton*, *Smothers Brothers* and *Your Hit Parade* shows among many others to numerous to mention.

In addition to studio work, Zarchy found time to do numerous casuals, motion pictures, and recordings, including several singles and albums with Crosby and Sinatra. He also frequently toured overseas, appearing in big bands in Australia, England, Europe, Japan, and South America. In fact, he has made thirty-two trips to Japan, where he has a strong fan base, since 1973.

It was earlier mentioned that Zarchy's days with Bob Crosby would prove of later value, and indeed they did. Throughout much of the 1980s, he played solid trumpet in Bob Ringwald's Great Pacific Jazz Band, a seven-piece traditional jazz band that evoked memories of the best of Louis Armstrong, who inspired Zarchy early in his career.

It should be noted that Zarchy's accomplishments are not only musical in scope. A man of many talents, he has been a professional photographer with a home studio and a skilled woodworker who designed and built much of the furniture in his Studio City home that overlooks the San Fernando Valley. Each table, chair, and cabinet he created was based on historical architectural themes.

On Sunday, March 7, 1999, Zarchy was given an honor bestowed on few sidemen. In front of 500 big band enthusiasts at the Sportsmen's Lodge in Studio City, CA, he was installed into the Big Band Academy of America's Golden Bandstand as part of the class of 1999 along with his old friend from his Glenn Miller days, Tex Beneke.

Still active and in good health, Zarchy commented on his over seventy years as a musician. "In his book *The Big Bands*, George Simon said the lead trumpet player was the unsung hero responsible for the band's sounds. I'd like to be remembered for my contributions in doing that job in both the big bands and the studios. I have no complaints. It's been a rewarding and exciting musical career that gave me an opportunity to see the world and work with the greats of the entertainment business. When I started out at Lum's working just to help out my family I never dreamed all this would happen."

33. Ernani Bernardi far right playing with Benny Goodman at the Paramount Theater in Manhattan in January 1939.

34. Ernani Bernardi fourth from right in the middle of the saxophone section
playing with Benny Goodman at the Paramount Theater in Manhattan in January 1939.

35. Milt Bernhart around 1950.

36. Milt Bernhart in 1954
at the Radio Recorders
Studio in Hollywood.

37. Milt Bernhart left with trumpeter
Manny Klein in the late 1980s.

38. Milt Bernhart
around 2000.

39. Buddy Childers with June Christy in Miami Beach June 1945.

40. Buddy Childers with the Stan Kenton softball team in Encinitas, CA, in 1946. Childers is second from the right in the bottom row.

41. Buddy Childers in the Stan Kenton trumpet section in 1951.

42. Jack Costanzo with Nat "King" Cole.

43, 44, 45. Jack Costanzo
at the Hollywood Palladium
in the late 1950s.

46. Rosalind Cron in 1942 far left with Nat Pierce playing piano.

47. Rosalind Cron in 1944.

48. The 1944 International Sweethearts of Rhythm's saxophone section. Rosalind Cron is in the middle.

49. Rosalind Cron playing in the middle of the International Sweethearts of Rhythm's saxophone section in 1944.

50. Henry Jerome's saxophone section rehearsing in 1944.
Alan Greenspan is at the far right and Leonard Garment at the far left.

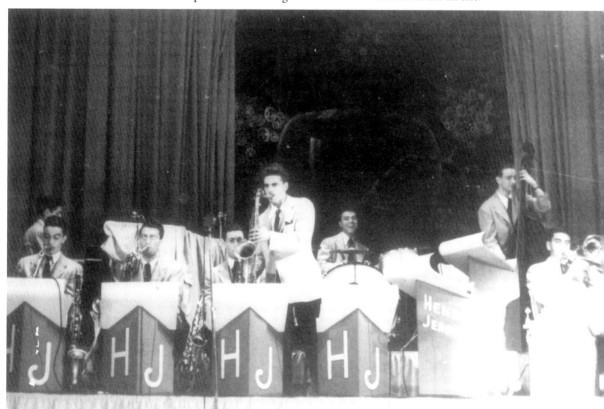

51. The Henry Jerome Orchestra playing at the Lowe's State Theater in Manhattan in 1944.
Alan Greenspan is in the saxophone section at the far left.

52. Jake Hanna in 1961.

53. Roc Hillman playing guitar with the
Jimmy Dorsey Orchestra.

54. Roc Hillman playing bass during World War II.

55. Legh Knowles playing with the Ray-John Orchestra at a wedding reception at the Ridgefield, CT, Italian Hall in 1933. Knowles is second from right.

RAY-JOHN orchestra 1933

56. Legh Knowles with the Glenn Miller Orchestra.

57. Legh Knowles playing trumpet with the Charlie Spivak Orchestra at the Strand Theater in Manhattan in 1942. Spivak is standing next to Knowles's right.

58. The Charlie Spivak Orchestra appearing at the Strand Theater in Manhattan in 1942. Spivak is playing trumpet at the far right with Knowles standing and playing immediately behind him.

59. At Piatti's Restaurant mid to late1980s. Left to right: Legh Knowles, maitre d', Joe DiMaggio, and Sam Spear.

60. John LaPorta second from left in the Woody Herman saxophone section in the mid 1940s.

61. Igor Stravinsky conducting a rehearsal of his "Ebony Concerto" with the Woody Herman Orchestra. Woody Herman is to the far left playing clarinet. John LaPorta is second from right playing saxophone.

62. Left to right: John LaPorta, Virginia
LaPorta, and Woody Herman at the
Berklee College of Music circa 1970s.

63. John LaPorta in 2000.

64. Tommy Dorsey's Sentimentalists (Clark Sisters) in the mid 1940s.
Top left to right: Mary and Ann. Bottom left to right: Jean and Peggy.

65. The Sentimentalists.

66. Willie Schwartz sitting at the far left of the saxophone section conversing with Glenn Miller.

67. Chico Sesma with the Johnny Richards Orchestra at Elitch's Gardens in Denver in 1944. Top row third from left.

68. Chico Sesma and Celia Cruz at a Latin Holiday dance at the Hollywood Palladium.

69. Butch Stone at George Washington High School in Manhattan.

Paramount Theater

Yankee Stadium

May 1 1944 through September 1946 was one of the happiest periods of my life. Whether sitting next to you on the bandstand or playing shortstop next to you at 3rd base, we never had a harsh word between us.

I love you like a brother, Butch

Ted Nash

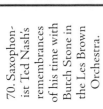

70. Saxophonist Ted Nash's remembrances of his time with Butch Stone in the Les Brown Orchestra.

71. Butch Stone visiting with Bob Hope.

72. Paul Tanner to the far left of the Glenn Miller trombone section behind the Chesterfield box.

73. Professor Paul Tanner

74. The Tommy Dorsey brass section in 1940. Zeke Zarchy trumpet middle of top row. Tommy Dorsey lower right bottom row in white jacket.

PART THREE

THE VOCALISTS

BOB EBERLY
JIMMY DORSEY'S HITMAKER

Any nostalgic return to the music of the Big Band Era would be incomplete without re-
membrance of the rich baritone voice of Bob Eberly. As Jimmy Dorsey's male vocalist
from the spring of 1935 through the end of 1943, he generated fifty-eight hit records
according to *Joel Whitburn's Pop Memories 1890-1954*. Thirty of those hits charted in the top
ten. Twelve reached number one and became Era standards. Bob Eberly was categorically Jimmy
Dorsey's hit maker and a Swing Era legend that was considered by many to have the best natural
voice of all the big band male vocalists.

It all started in upstate New York when opera singer John "Jack" Eberle and silent film pianist
Margaret "Peg" O'Brien met while performing at the Lyric Theater in Hoosick Falls, a picturesque village of 4,800 northeast of Albany near the Vermont border. They married in 1907 after
a brief courtship and eventually moved to nearby Mechanicville, where Robert John Eberle was
born on July 24, 1916. He was the oldest of their eight surviving children and the only one who
used a different surname. The name change occurred in 1938 when Eberle altered the spelling of
his last name to Eberly while singing at the Paramount Theater in New York with Jimmy Dorsey
because his original Eberle family name was continuously mispronounced and often confused
with Milton Berle. Dorsey's manager Billy Burton suggested the conversion to Eberly to avoid
the frequent mix-ups.

The Eberle family permanently returned to Hoosick Falls in the early 1920s when Jack left his
position as a policeman in Mechanicville to purchase and operate Jack's Hotel and Restaurant at
the corner of Elm Street and Railroad Avenue. A dedicated New York Yankee fan, Jack Eberle
faithfully posted World Series scores on a large chalkboard he displayed on the outside porch of
the hotel.

Music was an important part of the Eberle family's life in Hoosick Falls. All the Eberle children
regularly helped out in the hotel kitchen with everyone involved singing together in close harmony. They also sang in St. Mary's Academy plays, the Immaculate Conception Church choir, and
at community events. Bob frequently harmonized at home with his younger brother Ray, who
retained the family name and went on to considerable fame as a vocalist with the Glenn Miller
Orchestra. He also played banjo and guitar, performed around town accompanied by his mother
on the piano, and was an Immaculate Conception altar boy and St. Mary's cheerleader. Scholasti-
cally, Eberly won regional oratorical contests and graduated as president and valedictorian of the
St. Mary's Academy class of 1934.

After graduation, Eberly worked in the family business and sang locally. Sensing uncommon
talent, his father encouraged him to try out for the amateur competition segment of Fred Allen's
popular radio show, *Town Hall Tonight*. In early February 1935 Eberly decided to vie for a spot
on the Allen program and took an evening boat from Albany to New York City to try his luck.
Four weeks later, on March 6, he appeared on *Town Hall Tonight* and won first prize that included $50 in cash and a week's engagement at the Roxy Theater in Manhattan. After his week at

the Roxy ended Eberly returned home to Hoosick Falls with no prospects and no idea that Bob Crosby, Bing's younger brother, was about to play an important role in determining his future.

Bob Crosby joined the Dorsey Brothers Orchestra as their male vocalist in 1934 and from the outset had problems getting along with Tommy Dorsey. Roc Hillman was a guitarist with the Dorsey Brothers at the time. He lives in Woodland Hills, CA, and is still keeps track of the music business. During a recent interview at his home Hillman talked about the Crosby situation.

"For reasons unknown to me Tommy did not care for Bob Crosby and made life difficult for him," Hillman said. "Even though Bob seemed to get along with Jimmy Dorsey reasonably well he was definitely unhappy and left the band around February of 1935 when Gil Rodin got him a job fronting a new group made up of musicians that quit Ben Pollack's band. It was structured as a cooperative and became the Bob Crosby Orchestra that included the Bob Cats. Bob's departure created an opening for a new male vocalist."

It all came together in April 1935 in Troy, NY, when Eberly auditioned in borrowed tuxedo and dress shoes with the Dorsey Brothers Orchestra when they played the Troy Police and Benevolent Association's annual ball. He received a sensational ovation when he finished singing and was asked by the Dorseys that same night to accompany them on a four-state eastern tour that started in North Adams, MA, followed by recording and radio tests in New York. All went well, and on May 16, 1935, he sang as the band's male vocalist when it opened at the Glen Island Casino in New Rochelle, NY, for the summer season. At only 18 and less than a year out of high school Bob Eberly was firmly established with one of the top big bands in the country, a band that would soon come to its end.

The Dorsey Brothers were notorious for constantly fighting among themselves. On Memorial Day 1935 one of their recurrent clashes spontaneously erupted at the Glen Island Casino. Roc Hillman saw it happen: "Tommy called for 'I'll Never Say Never Again.' Jimmy immediately questioned the tempo. Tommy instantly turned around and walked out for good without saying a word. It was the end of the Dorsey Brothers Orchestra."

The two brothers went their separate ways. Jimmy inherited the Dorsey Brothers Orchestra on the spot and played out the Glen Island Casino summer engagement. Tommy essentially took over the Joe Haymes band and with it built the Tommy Dorsey Orchestra. Bob Eberly and Jimmy Dorsey had already developed a solid friendship, so Eberly did not think twice about remaining with what overnight became the Jimmy Dorsey Orchestra, an Orchestra that would break through to national recognition in 1936.

From late December 1935 to July 1937 the Jimmy Dorsey Orchestra was based in Hollywood playing the hugely popular Thursday evening *Kraft Music Hall* radio show that starred Bing Crosby. Crosby was most generous to those he liked, and he liked Bob Eberly. Although Eberly did not regularly sing on the show, Crosby gave him numerous on air plugs enthusiastically referring to him as the Hoosick Falls Hurricane. However, Eberly did sing with the band and became a popular attraction when it played West Coast venues starting with the Palomar Ballroom in Los Angeles in January 1936. He also did extensive recording work with Dorsey in Hollywood. His first number one hit record, "Is It True What They Say about Dixie?," was recorded there on March 29, 1936. The Dorsey band's eighteen-month stay in Southern California served Bob Eberly well.

While in Hollywood the Dorsey Orchestra worked on three movie sound tracks. One of the films provided Eberly an interesting experience that he related during a March 1978 interview taped by Chuck Cecil at the Pantages Theater in Hollywood that was broadcast on his *Swingin' Years* radio show: "I decided to stop by the RKO studios where the band was working on *Shall We Dance* with Fred Astaire and Ginger Rogers just to see what was going on. As soon as I got there I got a call from someone who asked me if I could take a minute and come to his office and sing 'You Can't Take That Away from Me,' a song he just finished writing for the film. He was very unassuming. When we were done I told him I thought he was a nice guy and played pretty good piano. While I was talking to him Jimmy was in his car waiting to drive us to the Palomar where we were working that night. He started honking his horn and then came in the studio to get me. As we left he said 'Why are you bothering George Gershwin?' Silly me. I had no idea that it was George Gershwin who asked me to sing."

During the summer of 1937 the Jimmy Dorsey Orchestra left the *Kraft Music Hall* show and Hollywood to embark on a three month cross country tour of one-niters, arriving in New York in time for fall bookings at the Hotel New Yorker and Paramount Theater. Through the balance of the 1930s Dorsey's popular band that featured Bob Eberly performed at prestigious ballrooms, hotels, and theaters. The hotel engagements and several appearances at Frank Daily's Meadowbrook in Cedar Grove, NJ, were particularly significant as they provided valuable radio air time. The band also gained exposure appearing in Paramount and Warner Brothers film shorts in which Eberly was generously showcased. All the while he continued to generate hit records crafted by the band's chief arranger, Tutti Camarata.

Few have accomplished as much in the Big Band Era as the versatile Salvador "Tutti" Camarata who was born May 11, 1913, in Glen Ridge, New Jersey. Camarata took up the violin at eleven, wrote for his brother's local Verona, NJ, dance band while a teenager, and spent time studying at Julliard. He went on to play trumpet and arrange for Charlie Barnet and Joe Venuti before he joined the Jimmy Dorsey Orchestra in Hollywood as lead trumpet player and arranger in early 1936. In 1938, with Dorsey's blessing, he occasionally arranged for Paul Whiteman. However, Tutti Camarata's greatest achievement came when he crafted the band's phenomenal early 1940s recording success that involved Bob Eberly and the band's female vocalist, Helen O'Connell.

As the decade came to a close, a significant event took place when Helen O'Connell joined the Dorsey Orchestra in January 1939. O'Connell was born May 23, 1920, in Lima, OH, and grew up in Toledo where she started dancing at ten and singing at thirteen to help support her family when her father died. She left home at sixteen with the Jimmy Richards band and after over a year and a half on the road with them landed a spot on Russ David's KSD radio show in St. Louis. In her spare time O'Connell occasionally stopped by the Chase Hotel to sing with a group led by her sister and brother-in-law that was performing at the Hotel's Steeplechase Lounge. It was there that she was discovered by bandleader Larry Funk. She joined Funk and His Band of a Thousand Melodies and was singing with Funk at the Village Barn in New York's Greenwich Village when Jimmy Dorsey's secretary heard her on a radio broadcast from the Barn and recommended that Dorsey go see her. He did, and immediately hired her away from Funk, a common personnel practice during the Big Band Era. With her infectious dimpled smile, upbeat personality, and good humored kidding with Eberly she became an instant hit. The stage was set for Bob Eberly, Helen O'Connell, and Tutti Camarata to make big band history with a unique musical format.

In mid 1940 the Dorsey band was playing on a radio series sponsored by Twenty Grand cigarettes. However, there was a program scheduling problem. Shortly before he passed away in April 2005 Tutti Camarata explained how he handled the situation during an interview at his home in Studio City, CA: "There wasn't enough time for Bob, Helen, and the band to each do their own number because the show had a lot of individual acts. I was allotted just three and a half minutes at the end of the show to get everyone in so I came up with the concept of a three tempo arrangement. It was a product of necessity."

So was born the famous Jimmy Dorsey three tempo hit songs that dominated the charts from the spring of 1941 through 1942. The format consisted of a ballad beginning by Bob Eberly, then a saxophone solo by Jimmy Dorsey followed by a Helen O'Connell finish with an up-beat vocal. Their first three tempo hit was "Amapola" that held the number one spot for ten straight weeks, longer than any other record during 1941. It was followed by "Green Eyes" and "Yours" in 1941 and "Tangerine" and "Brazil" in 1942.

It didn't stop there. Eberly added five number one Camarata-crafted hits of his own in 1941. They were in chronological order, "I Hear a Rhapsody"; "High on a Windy Hill"; "My Sister And I"; "Maria Elena"; and "Blue Champagne." Counting both the three tempo and his own individual hits, Bob Eberly recordings spent twenty-seven weeks in the number one position that year. Eight of those number one records ranked in the year's Top 40 and for five consecutive weeks during the summer he had five of the Top 10 hits on the *Your Hit Parade* radio show. With blockbuster recordings and appearances with the band in several three-minute movie shorts called "Soundies" that were shown on special movie jukeboxes, Bob Eberly was the most successful big band vocalist of 1941 and a household name.

Thanks to Eberly and O'Connell's huge popularity and their movie-star-quality looks, it was inevitable that rumors of romance would surface. There was constant speculation aswirl about an involvement. O'Connell clarified the question of a romantic relationship in a 1989 interview on Don Kennedy's *Big Band Jump* radio show: "Oh, no. Not at all. Bob already had a girl friend when I joined the band, but they'd had a tiff and I didn't know that, but I did have a crush on him. We were really just very good friends. He married her and stayed married to her until he died."

The girl friend O'Connell referred to was Florine Callahan, a beauty contest winner from Knoxville, TN, who danced in the Rodgers and Hart musical *Too Many Girls*. Eberly and Callahan first met in 1938 at the Bon Air Country Club located north of the Chicago suburb of Wheeling where the band was playing and she was dancing in a review. Upon introducing himself, Eberly boldly told her that someday he would marry her. His prognostication proved to be correct as they exchanged wedding vows on January 28, 1940. The couple permanently settled in Great Neck, Long Island, in the early1960s and had three children, Bob Jr., Rene, and Kathleen.

Through the Swing Era there was an avalanche of movies that featured the name big bands, and for good reason. Few who lived away from major metropolitan areas were able to see the great big bands perform in person. As a result, they were regularly featured in motion pictures providing an opportunity for their fans in towns like Hoosick Falls to watch them on the silver screen. Eberly was prominently featured in two popular films with the Jimmy Dorsey Orchestra in 1942 and 1943, *The Fleet's In* (Paramount) and *I Dood It* (MGM). His performances were well received and there were rumors that after the *The Fleet's In* was completed, Paramount was interested in having Eberly replace Dick Powell in a film. He did receive numerous attractive offers at that time to go out on his own, but not an aggressive risk taker by nature Eberly stayed loyal to his good friend Jimmy Dorsey, never bothering to sign a formal contract. The two remained close for life with Eberly spending considerable time with Dorsey before he died in New York at fifty-three on June 12, 1957, seven months after his brother Tommy passed away in late 1956 at fifty-one.

In Hoosick Falls, the Big Band Era was a unique period of time in the village's history. Eberly's younger sister Pat Knap commented on what it was like growing up there in the late 30s and early 40s during a telephone conversation from her home in Bradenton, FL: "It was an exciting time. Every night the whole town would be glued to their radios to listen to Bob sing with Jimmy Dorsey or Ray with Glenn Miller. The old New Theater on Church Street was packed whenever

PART THREE: THE VOCALISTS

their movies played there. It was something we took for granted. We thought it would never end."

Inevitably, the end did come. As 1943 began, change loomed on the horizon and Bob Eberly's time with Jimmy Dorsey started to wind down. Helen O'Connell left the band to get married and Tutti Camarata joined the Air Force as a flight instructor. O'Connell's replacement was Kitty Kallen with whom Eberly had two smash hits, "Star Eyes" and "Besame Mucho." "Besame Mucho," his last hit record, broke into the charts in January 1944 and was number one for seven straight weeks. Both were reminiscent of the old three tempo format. Then while still at the peak of his popularity and vocal prowess, Eberly departed from the band in December to join the Army. The eight-and-a-half-year Jimmy Dorsey-Bob Eberly Era that was so much a part of Americana officially came to a close.

During his two-plus-year stay as a sergeant in the Army, Eberly kept musically active entertaining troops at military hospitals and facilities with a service unit led by The Waltz King, Wayne King, which was based in Chicago. Notwithstanding the fact that he received a personal letter of encouragement from his old friend Bing Crosby, after his military discharge Eberly returned to a new world of entertainment that did not eagerly embrace former Big Band Era vocalists. He did unsuccessfully tryout for a spot on the *Chesterfield Supper Club* radio show while, according to big band historian George T. Simon, suffering from the handicap of a slight brain concussion. But the reality was that the Era had ended, and Eberly adapted by striking out on his own as a single act. Although his days as an established star were over, he did sporadically return to public attention.

In 1947 Eberly made his last movie, reprising "Green Eyes" with Helen O'Connell in the film *The Fabulous Dorseys* (United Artists). With his matinee idol features, engaging personality, and still recognizable name and voice he was a natural for television. Through the years he made appearances on several network TV shows that included the *Steve Allen, Perry Como, Jackie Gleason, Arthur Godfrey,* and *Jack Parr* shows and the Dorsey Brothers *Stage Show*. He also filled in with Helen O'Connell for the vacationing Perry Como on the CBS television show *TV's Top Tunes* during the entire summer of 1953. Eberly was always popular as an attraction on Public Television big band fund raisers, frequently performing with Helen O'Connell.

Eberly also had an active postwar recording career according to Tom Cullen, veteran Madison, WI, big band and popular music researcher and record collector. He was also Bob Eberly's personal friend. Cullen's studies have revealed that Eberly made numerous recordings with Decca in the late 40s and Capitol in the 50s. His Capitol output, that included 6 songs with Helen O'Connell, consisted of more contemporary arrangements by his good friend Harold "Hal" Mooney and continued to emphasize Eberly's romantic voicing.

There were also record albums. In the late 1950s Eberly made two albums for the Grand Award label with another friend, Enoch Light, and closed out his commercial recording career with a 1961 Warner Brothers Records album with Helen O'Connell under the direction of Lou Busch who was also known as Joe "Fingers" Carr. Unfortunately, none of those albums or records made the hit parade although they added to his sizable body of recording work. But the Bob Eberly name still captured the magic of the big band days, providing him the opportunity to launch his own career as an individual performer after he returned from the war.

Blessed with an innate sense of showmanship, natural ease, witty humor, and an engaging manner that charmed audiences, Eberly was ideally cut out for performing in public. From the end of World War II through the 1960s he sang at supper clubs in the East and Midwest, occasionally traveled to California to appear at the popular Disneyland Big Band Series, and starting December 20, 1963, sang with the Glenn Miller Orchestra led by Ray McKinley for three weeks at the Wagon Wheel in Lake Tahoe. *L.A. Jazz Scene* writer and staff photographer Bob Comden performed with Eberly at Disneyland: "In the late 60s I played lead trumpet in Jimmy Dorsey's band fronted by Lee Castle that backed up Bob Eberly and Helen O'Connell at Disneyland's Carnation Plaza. They drew a tremendous crowd for each performance that always included a lot of younger people. I remember Bob as gracious and patient with his fans and a pleasant and cooperative person to work with. He was well liked by all in the band."

The 1970s proved to be a productive decade of golden nostalgia for Bob Eberly. He toured with the Jimmy Dorsey Orchestra under the direction of Lee Castle, sang at the Rockefeller Center's Rainbow Room and at the Waldorf Astoria Hotel, headlined numerous big band re-union concerts and appeared, frequently with Helen O'Connell, at Disneyworld's prestigious Top of the World super club in Orlando. It was also at the Top of the World where he appeared for the only time with his brother Ray one evening in 1976. Nineteen seventy-seven marked two specific highlights. First, he filled the St. Mary's Academy gymnasium to capacity when he returned home to sing at the Hoosick Falls 150th Anniversary Ball. Second, Eberly starred with Helen O'Connell and Tex Beneke and his Orchestra in the cross-country *Sounds of the Summer of '42* tour that sold-out nationwide. But as the decade came to a close so did the career of Bob Eberly.

Professionally, 1980 started out on a high note for Eberly when on February 1 he appeared in the still-talked-about *One More Time* production at the Hollywood Palladium. It was hosted and produced by Peter Marshall and in addition to Eberly included the Tex Beneke Orchestra, Helen O'Connell, and The Modernaires with Paula Kelly Jr. Personally, it was another matter. That spring he was diagnosed with lung cancer followed just a few months later by the removal of his cancerous right lung at St. John's Hospital in Queens. Bob Eberly suffered the consequences of a lifetime of heavy smoking. He would never sing again.

After his surgery Eberly was transferred to the Manhasset Medical Center and from there to the Memorial Sloan-Kettering Cancer Center in Manhattan with Frank Sinatra picking up a good portion of the medical bills. Sinatra also frequently called Eberly to talk about the big band days. The next several months were difficult times for Bob Eberly as he underwent intensive chemotherapy and suffered a series of heart attacks. Eberly had a history of heart problems, suffering a coronary thrombosis in the early 1960s. By late summer of 1981 he was back at Sloan-Kettering when Tom Cullen saw him for the last time.

"I was visiting in New York on September 19, 1981, and got permission to see Bob at Sloan-Kettering," Cullen explained. "Although he was adorned with several tubes he still spoke clearly and coherently as we talked about his condition and career highlights. Bob kidded that he should have been a folksinger, referring to the huge crowd coming to see a free Simon and Garfunkel concert a few blocks away in Central Park. We knew this was our last meeting even though Bob would not admit the end was near. I left with the satisfaction of having seen him in brave spirits one last time."

Shortly after Cullen's visit, Eberly was released to spend his final days with his daughter Kathleen at her home in Glen Burnie, MD, where he passed away on November 17, 1981, preceding Florine by six years. He received the last rites of the Catholic Church and was buried at Pinelawn Memorial Park in Farmingdale, Long Island, after a public service.

Bob Eberly was certainly one of the significant contributors to and major personalities of the Big Band Era. His three tempo hits with Helen O'Connell stand out as enduring Era highlights and positively impacted wartime morale. He was also acknowledged as a superior vocalist who was exceptionally popular with the entire big band community.

Gifted with a rich, distinctive intonation and the ability to perfectly phrase and sing with emotion Bob Eberly was among the elite vocalists of the Swing Era. Both his vocal style and stage presence were of such significance that he had a developmental impact on numerous singers including Mike Douglas, Dick Haymes, and Mel Tormé. He also influenced the career direction of Frank Sinatra as told by Sinatra in George T. Simon's book *Simon Says*: "I don't think I ever told anybody this before, but the reason I started on my own when I did was because I wanted to make sure I got there as a single before Bob Eberly did. I knew that if that guy ever did it first, I'd never be able to make it the way I did. That Eberly, he sang so rich and pure, it used to frighten me. Even today, guys who sing in his fashion can't even sit in the same room with him. That guy has always been too much, and I knew he'd be too much for me if he ever got started on his own before I did."

As for popularity, in the highly competitive world of the big bands of the 30s and 40s many who succeeded were not necessarily well liked. Such was not the case with Bob Eberly. George T. Simon discussed Eberly's reputation in his book *The Big Bands*: "Eberly was immensely popular with everyone who knew him. Whereas musicians generally were rather critical of band vocalists, those in Jimmy Dorsey's band swore by Bob. It is doubtful whether the entire Big Band Era ever turned out a more beloved person than Bob Eberly, and even today those associated with him during his Dorsey stay recall with great reverence and enthusiasm the man's honesty, humility, wonderful values, and terrific sense of humor."

Eberly was also a favorite of businessmen who conducted commerce with the big bands as told by radio personality and good friend Dick Waco from his home in Canton, OH: "When I was living in Cleveland and producing big band concerts in Ohio that Bob performed in he always stayed at our house. We had some great times. Bob was a beautiful person and a very talented cartoonist who parodied our home life in cartoon form. There was no one easier and more enjoyable to work with."

A place in American cultural history, the peak of professional accomplishment, and the respect and affection of his peers sum up the career of Bob Eberly. It's safe to say that's far more than he expected to accomplish that cold February night in 1935 when he took a boat from Albany down the Hudson River just to try out for Fred Allen's radio show. It turned out that it was well worth his staying up late and taking the trip.

HERB JEFFRIES
THE BRONZE BUCKAROO

It's time for a two-part big band trivia quiz. First, what do Dick Haymes and Frank Sinatra have in common? The answer is both were successful big band singers before they became movie stars. Here is the second part. What soloist still actively performing gained fame as a movie star before he became known to the public as a headlining big band vocalist? The answer is Herb Jeffries, "The Bronze Buckaroo."

Umberto Balentino, who would later gain worldwide fame as Herb Jeffries, was born of Ethiopian, French-Canadian, Irish, and Italian decent in Detroit on September 24, 1911. He came from an artistic, theatrical family. Jeffries' Irish mother, who ran a boarding house frequented by Duke Ellington when he appeared in Detroit, was also a clothes designer. She designed theatrical costumes and wedding dresses for the Ford family and other magnates connected to the automotive industry. His was an artistic world of music and the theater.

Jeffries grew up in an integrated, multi-cultural Detroit neighborhood near the border of the then all-Polish city of Hamtramck. It was a close-knit community that freely shared cultures allowing him to learn to speak fluent Italian and Yiddish. He was highly athletic as a youth and at eight learned to become an expert horse rider while spending summers at his grandfather's dairy farm in Port Huron, MI. This was a skill that would serve him well later in his career.

When he was twelve years old Jeffries discovered the power of what would become his rich baritone voice that would allow him to record jazz, popular, western, and Jamaican folk songs with equal ease as told during a telephone interview from his office in Palm Desert, CA: "As soon as I started singing in my church choir the choir master moved me from the front to the second and third lines. Then he finally moved me to the back line and said 'I can still hear you, Herb.'"

From the church choir Jeffries moved on to sing at church functions, private parties, and Polish weddings in Hamtramck. After a short stay in New York when he was seventeen, he graduated to performing at clubs in and around Detroit. Then came 1933 and his big break. Jeffries tells the story: "I was working in a Detroit cabaret called the Michigan Democratic League when Louis Armstrong came in one night and heard me sing. He gave me a note to give to his friend Erskine Tate who had a big band in Chicago. Louis said the World's Fair would be opening in a few months and it would be a good chance for me to progress career-wise."

Jeffries acted on Armstrong's advice and boarded a Greyhound bus for Chicago to join Tate's band. To supplement his income while singing with Tate, he sold flags at a concession stand at the World's Fair. Then good fortune stuck once again, validating Armstrong's council.

In early 1934 Jeffries was discovered by Earl "Fatha" Hines while singing with Tate at the Savoy Ballroom, located at South Parkway and 47th Street on Chicago's South Side. Hines offered Jeffries a substantial raise to become his vocalist along with the lure of a coast-to-coast radio hook-up at the Grand Terrace nightclub. Hines was well into his eleven-year run as the house band at the South Side nightspot that was patterned after Harlem's Cotton Club. Al Capone was a frequent visitor to the Grand Terrace and had a reputation for great generosity as a tipper. He was also a big fan of Hines.

Commenting on Hines, Jeffries said: "He was a great gentleman and a fine man to work for. He was truly compassionate. When I came to Chicago I had the suit on my back and one in my suitcase. He immediately outfitted me in a tuxedo and gave me a brand new wrap-around coat. He was very much like Duke Ellington in sensitivity, a brilliant musician, and superb bandleader. He could work magic with a piano."

Jeffries would go on to spend over a year with Hines. He gained valuable experience singing at the Grand Terrace and occasionally going on the road with the band touring the South playing in ballrooms in larger cities and old, tin-roofed tobacco warehouses in smaller towns. He acquired a national reputation thanks to steady radio exposure, and recorded his first hit song, "Blue Because of You," written by Dunlap and Carpenter.

By late 1935 Jeffries was ready to head to California. He joined Blanche Calloway's band as it toured west, leaving her after a few months to board a bus for Los Angeles, arriving in mid 1936. The vibrant Central Avenue jazz scene was at its peak, and Jeffries immediately immersed himself in the setting, performing at the Street's top spot, the Club Alabam, and consorting with celebrated bandleaders such as Jimmy Lunceford and Don Redman at the Dunbar Hotel.

After settling down in Los Angeles, Jeffries frequently thought about what he observed while touring the South with Hines: "I saw how blacks could see only white cowboys in segregated movie theaters. That was particularly hard on the kids who did not have a cowboy role model to look up to. I thought why not put movies about black cowboys in those theaters? It could be good for business and for the kids."

He headed back to Detroit and Chicago and tried to raise money for a black cowboy film from local policy barons who ran the cities number rackets. They weren't interested, so Jeffries returned to Los Angeles and luckily read about *The Terror of Tiny Town*, a western with an all-midget cast. The article gave Jeffries new hope: "If a western could be made about little people, why couldn't one be made about black cowboys? I went to see Jed Buell, the producer of *The Terror of Tiny Town*, at his Gower Gulch office. He was known for producing B-westerns. I wasn't there fifteen minutes before he started talking to Alfred Sack, his film distributor in Dallas, who said 'I'll take all you have.'"

The initial film was *Harlem on the Prairie*, the first of four all-black westerns from 1937 to 1939 in which Jeffries stared as Bob Blake, the lead singing cowboy. He had a sidekick named Dusty, a white stallion he called 'Stardust', and a vocal group patterned after the Sons of the Pioneers titled The Four Tones. Spencer Williams Jr. who would later star as Andy in *Amos and Andy*, was a regular in all four films.

The movies were immensely popular in black theaters nationwide and made Jeffries a bona fide movie star. To promote his films, he regularly toured the country in spectacular fashion in a Cadillac outfitted with steer horns on the front and a gold rope with "Herb Jeffries" in script on the back. Local kids in all the towns his tours hit ritually followed him down the street in Pied Piper fashion. Black children now had their own western star they could look up to.

Unfortunately, Jeffries's first movie fell prey to the vagaries of film preservation, as there are no known prints of *Harlem on the Prairie* in existence. *Two Gun Man from Harlem*, *Bronze Buckaroo*, and *Harlem Rides the Range* are now considered classics and are available for rent in specialty video stores and are periodically shown on the Turner Classic Movie cable television channel. The prints for these three films were found in a cellar in Tyler, TX, covered with dirt.

Gene Autry, Jeffries's cowboy idol at the time, complimented him on the quality of his film work in 1939. Today, there is an exhibit featuring Jeffries in the world-class Autry Museum of Western Heritage in Los Angeles.

As 1939 drew to a close, Jeffries triumphantly returned to visit Detroit. His first item of business was to see Duke Ellington's band at the storied Graystone, Detroit's premiere ballroom, where in the late 1920s he paid a ninety-five cents admission charge to see Jean Goldkette with Bix Beiderbecke and the McKinney's Cotton Pickers perform.

In a 1979 interview on Chuck Cecil's *Swingin' Years* radio show, Jeffries tells how his life changed from that of a movie star to a big band singer that night at the Graystone: "I was standing in front of the bandstand in full western regalia including a ten gallon hat. Duke had just finished playing at the Harlem Opera House where they were showing the *Bronze Buckaroo*. He saw me and suddenly said 'Here's the Bronze Buckaroo. Why don't you come up and sing a few songs?' To my surprise, he called me backstage after the show and said, 'What are your plans?' I said I guess I will go back to Hollywood and make more movies. He said 'Too bad, I was going to offer you a job.' I said, 'I'll change my plans,' thinking it would be great exposure for my films and a once in a lifetime opportunity to work with the Great Band."

Jeffries joined Ellington's band at its finest hour. It was propelled to new big band-style rhythmic heights with the addition of St. Louis bassist Jimmy Blanton in 1939 and Kansas City tenor saxophonist Ben Webster in 1940. With propulsively swinging classics such as "Jack the Bear," "Ko Ko," and "Cottontail," it would become known as the Blanton Webster Band, or more commonly the Great Band.

In 1940 Jeffries had his first hit record with Ellington, "You, You, Darlin.'" Later that year he added to his stature recording with an all-star band led by Sidney Bechet. Then came his close friend Billy Strayhorn's arrangement of "Flamingo," one of the great Big Band Era classics. Jeffries recounts the recording session on Cecil's show: "It was December 28, 1940. We were in Chicago and it was kind of a fluke. I was in my hotel room when I got a surprise phone call from the governor. We all lovingly called Duke the governor. He said hurry over to the studio. We've got twenty minutes left for a recording session we're doing and I'd like to record "Flamingo." It was exciting for me because we were trying out the song on theater dates and it was quite successful. I hurried in unusually heavy traffic to the studio that was normally ten minutes away. I got there with five minutes left and recorded the song just as time ran out, improvising some of the lyrics."

"Flamingo" would go on to sell well over a million copies through the years. Most important, it marked a significant turning point in Ellington's orchestral direction in which more sophisticated vocal arrangements were crafted by Strayhorn to support both the singer and the band.

A highlight of Jeffries's tenure with the Great Band was his participation in Ellington's musical revue with a socially significant theme, *Jump for Joy*. It starred Ivie Anderson, Dorothy Dandridge, and blues singer Big Joe Turner, in addition to Jeffries, who recalled a unique nightly occurrence: "Duke was hidden in the pit conducting the orchestra during the entire show. The public's demand for him was so great that after each performance he had to do a forty-five minute jam session. "Flamingo" had broken loose by that time and I came down to the pit to join the band and sing it. That was a great experience."

Jump for Joy opened at the Mayan Theater in Los Angeles and had a twelve-week run, closing on September 27, 1941. It never made it to Broadway. According to Jeffries: "There were too many chiefs and no Indians. All the show's many backers wanted a well-meaning say in policy leading to confusion and bickering. That caused financial problems and in the end killed it."

What does Jeffries have to say about Duke Ellington the person? "Two aspects of Ellington are little appreciated. He was a deeply spiritual man who constantly read the Bible. Just listen to his Sacred Concerts for proof. At one time Duke was also one of the ten best-dressed men in the world. He was always elegant in attire and impeccable in bearing and speech. He made me what I am and I think about him every day."

Jeffries left Ellington in mid 1942 to join the Armed Forces Radio Service, spending World War II recording V-Discs and entertaining troops. After he completed his military obligation Jeffries returned to Los Angeles's still-active Central Avenue milieu and formed a band with master trumpeter Gerald Wilson. It was Wilson's first band.

New Orleans reared songwriter and owner of Exclusive Records, Leon Rene, the brother of Otis Rene, approached Jeffries in 1947 to record "When I Write My Song." It was adapted from Saint-Saens's "Samson et Dalila." Accompanied by Buddy Baker and his orchestra, the recording became a huge hit, landing Jeffries an executive position in the firm that was headquartered at Sunset and Vine in Hollywood.

Exclusive was known for tapping fresh, new talent. An example was Los Angeles Compton area resident and Rhythm and Blues pianist Joe Liggins and His Honeydrippers, whom they discovered playing at the Samba Club in Los Angeles. His first record for Exclusive was "The Honeydripper (Parts 1 & 2)." It was the number one R & B hit nationally for a record eighteen consecutive weeks.

Hits continued for Jeffries in 1947 with the emotionally moving *Magenta Moods*, named top album of the year by *Look* magazine. This recording success set the stage for a lucrative nightclub career for Jeffries through the late 40s at Ciro's and the Macombo in Hollywood, along with prestigious venues in Florida and New York. He closed the decade with another charted hit record, "The Four Winds and the Seven Seas."

In 1951 Jeffries moved to France and became a sensation singing on the Cote d' Azure. He went on to open his own nightclub in Paris, the Flamingo, that he ran for ten years, taking time out to entertain GIs in Korea. Rita Hayworth and Ali Kahn were frequent visitors along with a constant stream of Hollywood celebrities. Armed with the fluent French he learned at an early age, he made numerous appearances on French radio shows. A man of eclectic pursuits, while in Europe Jeffries became an accomplished sports car racer and an avid mountain climber

After he sold the Flamingo around 1961, Jeffries returned to the States and spent the decade performing at nightclubs up and down the East Coast. He relocated to Hawaii for seven years during the 70s, frequently appearing at Tu Tu's Plantation, his brother's nightclub on Oahu, returning to the mainland to live in Woodland Hills, CA. Jeffries made his last move soon after the millennium, settling in Idyllwild, CA. All the while he continued to appear in nightclubs, concerts, and Ellington events in the United States and overseas.

With his powerful voice in full force, Jeffries recently recorded two albums, *Herb Jeffries—The Bronze Buckaroo* in 1995 and *Herb Jeffries—The Duke and I* in 1999. *The Bronze Buckaroo* was recorded with several guest artists, including The Mills Brothers and Rex Allen, Jr. It was critically acclaimed and led to his enthronement in the Festival of the West's Cowboy Spirit Hall of Fame in 1997. Like fine wine, his vocal quality has aged and improved with time.

An overlooked aspect of Jeffries's career is his postwar body of work in television and the movies. Starting with the 1951 film *Disc Jockey* that starred a host of famous big band personalities, he appeared in twelve pictures, four of which were made for television. His most recent film appearance was in the 1999 American Movie Classic television documentary on film preservation entitled *Keepers of the Frame*.

Notable TV guest appearances included *Gunsmoke, Hawaii Five-0, I Dream of Jeannie, The Virginian,* and as the voice of Freight Train in the 1970 cartoon series *Where's Huddles*. He also composed songs for several motion pictures.

Now in his late 90s, Herb Jeffries remains in amazing health and still actively performs at Southern California jazz festivals. At the Ellington 2000 Festival held at the Hollywood Roosevelt Hotel over the 2000 Memorial Day weekend, he commented on his pace that would tax a person far younger than he: "1999 was my busiest year ever in traveling and performing at concerts. It was the Ellington centennial, and I'm the last surviving member of the Great Band. It's nice to know that Duke, the Master, is as popular as ever and that I'm remembered as a part of that great organization and as his first male vocalist."

Jeffries started the new millennium in style when he was enshrined in the Big Band Academy of America Golden Bandstand in March 2000 before a packed house of 600 big band enthusiasts at the Sportsmen's Lodge in Studio City, CA. In 2004 he was honored with a star on the Hollywood Walk of Fame. They were fitting tributes to a true giant of the Big Band Era who shares his mentor Duke Ellington's vision of a world in which we all live together in peace and harmony, a world of which Jeffries has frequently said: "There is only one race, the human race."

JACK LEONARD
BIG BAND CROONER AND
HOLLYWOOD BUSINESSMAN

Few Big Band Era stars achieved success in the music industry as both performer and businessman. One who did was Jack Leonard, a handsome vocalist for Tommy Dorsey with a seemingly effortless style, who, after the Era ended, became a successful business representative for a host of music stars and entertainment corporations. His was a dual career that spanned six decades.

John Joseph Leonard, nicknamed Jack to distinguish himself from his father of the same name, was born in Brooklyn on February 10, 1913, to Irish-American parents who were also born in Brooklyn. He lived on Lincoln Road and attended St. Francis of Assisi grammar school. When he was ten years old his family moved to Freeport on Long Island, to a home at 48 South Long Beach Avenue that his father inherited from his uncle. At the time Freeport was a residential haven for the New York vaudeville community, and the eventual home of bandleader Guy Lombardo.

Leonard graduated from Holy Redeemer parochial school, where he served as an altar boy, and later attended Freeport High School, leaving after his junior year to take a clerical position with the New York Life Insurance Company in Manhattan. While in elementary school he took three years of formal violin lessons from then Nassau County Philharmonic Conductor George Porter Smith. It was his only formal music training.

After six months with New York Life, Leonard took a step up to an office position with a Wall Street investment firm. However, post-stock-market-crash conditions were not good, and he was gone less than a year later. With the Great Depression raging, jobs were hard to come by. Leonard felt fortunate to land an outdoor public works project job to build a miniature golf course at Jones Beach in bitter winter weather that one day reached a numbing seventeen degrees below zero. While working outside in bone-chilling conditions, little did Leonard know that his fortunes were about to take a dramatic change for the better thanks to being in the right place at the right time.

Samuel L. Israel was a Freeport attorney and Leonard's friend. In early 1934 he convinced Leonard to join him one evening and visit the Roadside Rest at nearby Oceanside to hear Israel's friend Bert Block and his band. During an intermission Block came to the pair's table and informed them he needed a new vocalist. Israel immediately told Block about Leonard's local reputation as a singer, and in turn encouraged Jack to try out at an audition Block was holding the next Monday. Leonard was apprehensive about his chances because he was scheduled to compete against an applicant who could sing and play guitar. It turned out that he had no worries. The band took a vote and at the urging of arranger Axel Stordahl unanimously selected him as their vocalist. He was now officially a professional big band singer earning $10 a week and no longer had to worry about facing the elements at Jones Beach.

According to Block's lead trumpet player, Zeke Zarchy, Leonard quickly fit right in the band: "Although Bert Block did not play a musical instrument, he had a good solid local Long Island band that featured a book of fresh arrangements by Axel Stordahl who also played trumpet. It was a very musical band that was popular with the dinner crowd and highly thought of by my fellow musicians. I remember that Jack teamed up with Stordahl and second trumpet Joe Bauer to form a vocal trio called the Three Chips. Jack was a great guy, well liked by everyone in the band. He was definitely one of the boys."

In the fall of 1934 fate once again interceded on behalf of Leonard while Block's band was playing a two week engagement at Ben Marden's Riviera overlooking the New Jersey Palisades. The Dorsey Brothers were scheduled to follow Block at the Riviera. One evening Tommy and Jimmy stopped by to check out the facility and listen to Block's band. Tommy Dorsey left that evening strongly impressed by Jack Leonard's singing ability.

Immediately after the Dorsey Brothers break up at the Glen Island Casino on Memorial Day of 1935 Tommy Dorsey formed his own band. In need of a male singer, he lured Leonard, Stordahl, and Bauer from Block to join his organization soon after the Block band's first recording session on October 3rd. In that session, Leonard did a superb job of adroitly styling the lyrics on "Almost," played at an impossibly fast tempo.

It wasn't a bad deal for Dorsey. In one fell swoop he picked up his desired vocalist, an arranger who would later play an important part in his band's success, two trumpet players, and the old Block vocal group he renamed the Three Esquires.

Leonard recorded his first record for Dorsey, "A Little Rendezvous in Hawaii," on February 3, 1936. It was also his first hit. But a year later he and Dorsey struck gold with "Marie," one of the most memorable recordings of the entire Big Band Era. In a 1978 radio interview with big band broadcast personality Chuck Cecil, Leonard recounts how it all came about.

"We were playing Nixon's Grand Theater in Philadelphia and were having a battle of the bands with a superb black band called the Sunset Royal Serenaders," Leonard said. "Tommy and I were in the wings with our arrangers Axel Stordahl and Paul Weston watching them perform "Marie" with a jazz version with just the band singing without a straight vocal lead. That gave Tommy the idea to update "Marie" which was a great old song. Axel, Paul, and our first alto man, Freddie Stulce, went to work on it and came up with the arrangement."

Leonard continued: "Let's not overlook one thing. My vocal was good and the arrangement with the patter background was unique, but the big thing that that made 'Marie' a hit record was the magnificent trumpet solo by the immortal Bunny Berigan. He had no chart in front of him. He just stood up after I got through singing and blew. It was really something to see."

Ironically, "Marie" was on the B-side of its record. The expected major hit on the A-side was "Song of India," an adaptation of classical music by Nikolai Rimsky-Korsakov that was suggested to Dorsey by RCA Victor recording chief Eli Oberstein. It did get to number five at its peak position, but did not come close to achieving the popularity of "Marie." Both songs were recorded on January 29, 1937.

For the first time in history a big swing band would have a million selling record. "Marie" would be one of an incredible forty-two hit records Leonard would record with Dorsey, twenty-four of which made the top ten with four ranking number one. With his recording popularity at a peak along with regular radio appearances with the Dorsey band, he was one of the most popular big band vocalists of the late 1930s. He consistently ranked near the top of the annual *Metronome* and College Editor polls, leading the *Metronome* poll in 1939 in a close vote over second place Bing Crosby.

With all his success, Leonard never forgot Freeport. Lifetime Freeport resident and former Nassau County Housing Commissioner Raymond Malone's parents knew Leonard's parents in Brooklyn. He got to know Leonard well starting in grammar school: "Whenever a group of us would take dates to the Hotel Pennsylvania to see Tommy Dorsey, Jack would always bring Tommy over to our table during intermissions to say hello. He treated us like royalty and we were the envy of the crowd. It was impressive. I'm sure the well-to-do patrons wondered how kids like us could get Jack and Tommy to come over and sit with us."

Edna Leonard Woods, Leonard's sister, lived in Freeport. She recalled the deluge of fan mail Leonard received: "My mother and I used to keep quite busy sending Jack's picture to his fans. He had a lot of fan clubs in United States and Canada. They used to correspond and exchange photographs with each other and have contests among themselves to see who could recruit the most new members. The kids were big fans of Jack."

Leonard frequently relaxed from the pressures of the band business by playing golf with Bud Freeman, Axel Stordahl, and Dave Tough. But by late 1939, exhausted from four years of non-stop work with Dorsey, Leonard contemplated striking out on his own. It all came to head in November at an engagement at the Palmer House Hotel in Chicago when Leonard took exception to the high-strung Dorsey's offensive treatment of his friend trumpeter Jerry Blake during a late night rehearsal. In a show of allegiance to his friend, he walked out never to return. His eventual replacement? Ironically, Frank Sinatra, whom he brought to Dorsey's attention a few months earlier when they were driving to Dorsey's twenty-eight room home in affluent Bernardsville, NJ, after an evening's work at the Pennsylvania Roof in Manhattan.

Just as Leonard was leaving Dorsey, his last number one song with the Dorsey band hit the charts. It was "All the Things You Are," from the Oscar Hammerstein and Jerome Kern Broadway musical *Very Warm for May*. The blockbuster recording officially marked the end of the Leonard-Dorsey Era.

Jack Leonard did not have much time off to recuperate. He immediately signed a radio contract with CBS, making regular appearances on several shows, most frequently on Raymond Scott's *Concert in Rhythm*. He also played theater dates, charted three hits on the Okeh label, and ranked fifth in the January 1941 *Metronome* poll. Then in May 1941 tumult struck.

That month Leonard was about to score a major breakthrough. He had just signed a then lucrative $500 per week contract to appear at the Paramount Theater in Manhattan and passed a Twentieth Century Fox screen test with flying colors. He also received another contract in the form of a draft notice ordering him to immediately report to duty at Fort Dix, NJ, where he spent the next three years entertaining troops with his own band and appearing as a featured personality on the *This Is Fort Dix* radio show for WOR-Mutual. It was the Army's first radio show and ranked in the top ten of radio's most popular variety shows of 1943.

It was also in 1943 when Leonard had his biggest post-Dorsey hit with "I Never Mention Your Name" that placed in the top ten and was on the charts for thirteen weeks. The next year he recorded V-Discs and was transferred overseas to entertain troops in England and France, performing before as many as 8,000 servicemen a day. His efforts won the admiration of Dinah Shore, who upon returning from a USO tour was quoted as saying "Jack Leonard is doing a marvelous job over there. Why, he's singing to the boys out in the forests and even without a piano."

Leonard was discharged from duty on October 6, 1945, at Fort Lewis, WA. He signed a record contract with the Majestic label and resumed signing in night clubs and theaters. Exposure from successful engagements at the Copacabana and Paramount in New York along with a tour of

Midwest theaters with Jane Fromon landed him a 1947 contract with Columbia Pictures where he made three films, *Swing the Western Way*, *When a Girl Is Beautiful*, and *Glamour Girl*, that also starred Gene Krupa.

Then in the early 1950s, with the Big Band Era but a historical footnote, Leonard decided to change the course of his career and move over to the business end of the music scene. Over the next twenty five years he went on to serve in various management capacities with Nat "King" Cole, Percy Faith, and Jack Jones. He also held publishing positions with Warner Chappell Music, Paramount Famous Music, and Screen Gems Columbia Music. However, it was his association that began in 1953 with Cole through his death in 1965 that would define Leonard's business career.

Nick Sevano, longtime associate of Frank Sinatra and Hollywood personal manager, was a close friend of Cole as well. During a luncheon discussion at a restaurant near his home in Beverly Hills he said: "Nat adored Jack and truly valued his services. Jack did superb work as Nat's musical promoter and assisted his manager Carlos Gastel. He played a definite role in Nat's huge success. They had a marvelous relationship."

Sevano also commented on Leonard's business career. "Jack had an ideal temperament and was a perfect gentleman. He was astute, hard working, and knew the business. He also knew the right people and was able to put together special events like the Hollywood Celebrity All Stars baseball game at Dodger stadium. With a combination like that he never had to worry about finding work."

Jack Jones acknowledged Leonard's contribution to his career: "Jack Leonard was my first manager and a wonderful person. I was nineteen at the time and asked him how I could become a better singer. Jack said 'You sing fine now but if you fall in love with a girl it would help.' A short while later I came to him and told him I found a girl I liked a lot. He immediately said 'Wonderful. Now, if she would only leave you you'll know the meaning of the words you are singing.'"

Leonard also kept up with his friends from the Big Band Era through the years as documented by Duke Ellington's vocalist Herb Jeffries, who immortalized Ellington's classic recording of "Flamingo": "Jack was a sweet guy. We frequently met for lunch at Schwab's drug store to reminisce about the big bands and would occasionally hit the clubs together. Jack did not loose his popularity. He was frequently called up to sing and always sounded as good as his Dorsey days."

Even though he was involved in the commercial sector of the music business, Leonard made occasional club appearances in Los Angeles and New York and cut a few records with Tommy Dorsey in the 50s. He flew to New York from Los Angeles in late 1956 to sing "Marie" on a television tribute organized by Jackie Gleason in honor of Dorsey who choked to death that year in his sleep on the Sunday evening after Thanksgiving. Just a few weeks before he died, Dorsey discussed doing a brand new record album with Leonard. They had gone so far as to select twelve songs to record.

Jack Leonard retired from Screen Gems in the late 1970s. He made his last public appearance on a 1987 PBS special on Tommy Dorsey that was hosted by Jack Jones before he passed away at the Motion Picture and Television Hospital in Woodland Hills, CA, on June 17, 1988. In her Westlake Village, CA, home his wife Marilyn recalled his achievements during a 2000 visit.

"Jack never stopped receiving letters from his fans," she explained. "They would even send him gifts. For years we used to receive kielbasa every Christmas from a couple in Pennsylvania. He had a lot of accomplishments both as a big band singer and businessman. However, his greatest triumph was as a human being. Everyone who worked with Jack liked him and respected him. That's his legacy that I like to remember."

DOLORES O'NEILL
THE BIG BAND ERA'S BEST KEPT SECRET

Few Big Band Era song stylists gained the respect of their peers as did the talented and attractive Dolores "Dodie" O'Neill, who was billed as the Katherine Hepburn of Swing due to her physical resemblance to the four-time Oscar Award-winning movie actress. Her standing in Swing Era annals is well documented and firmly fixed. In his classic 1967 book *The Big Bands* historian George T. Simon referred to O'Neill as "an absolutely sensational singer." Currently, on his nationally syndicated *Big Band Jump* radio show Don Kennedy recently called her "one of the finest vocalists of the Era." Here is the in-depth and long-overdue story of Dolores O'Neill, a truly outstanding big band singer whose sultry voice conveyed a uniquely sensual and provocative quality.

Dolores Coletta O'Neill, the oldest of six children, was born on August 25, 1914, in Scranton, Pennsylvania. She acquired the nickname Dodie from the Sisters of the Immaculate Heart of Mary while a student at St. Cecilia's grammar school. There was musical talent in the O'Neill family as her mother along with her grandmother and aunt regularly sang at home together in close three-part harmony. However, the O'Neill's were not well off and constantly moved from house to house. Her father, Red O'Neill, was at times a farmer and general contractor who was prone to buying rounds of drinks for the house at the local tavern. Due to his ongoing financial mismanagement, O'Neill's mother worked as a charwoman in downtown Scranton office buildings to support the family.

During her senior year at Scranton Technical High School, where she played basketball and took business courses, O'Neill made an impulsive decision that would launch her career as a big band vocalist. She talked about what took place during a telephone conversation from her home in Wingdale, NY: "At a whim I went into radio station WGBI in Scranton while I was waiting for my younger sister to finish her dancing lessons in the same building and boldly asked them if I could have my own program. I sure had an awful lot of nerve. They said do you play anything and I said no. But there was a chap in the office whose name I don't remember who played piano and had his own sustaining radio show. I asked him if he could play for me. He said sure and asked me what key and of course I had no idea what a key was. I sang "Don't Blame Me" and the station owner instantly offered me a once-a-week fifteen-minute program with the piano player accompanying me."

On the strength of her WGBI radio show, after graduating from high school, O'Neill was offered a job singing at a night club called the Airport Inn in nearby Wilkes-Barre. She eschewed an opportunity to work in a local attorney's office and took the Airport Inn proposal because it offered better pay. For the next year O'Neill sang at the Airport Inn during the week for $25 plus room and board, returning home to Scranton by train on the Reading Railroad for the weekend. Upon her arrival back home she would immediately turn over her paycheck to her mother to help support her family.

The year O'Neill spent with the Leslie Hobbs band at the Airport Inn served her well. She learned how to sing before a live audience and developed stage presence. It also led to a year of international travel: "A couple of agents who booked acts into the Airport Inn kept telling us we were too good for Wilkes-Barre and should give New York a try. So we loaded Leslie's car up with instruments and arrangements and my belongings and drove to New York to spend the night with a girl we knew who used to perform at the Airport Inn. When we woke up the next morning the car was stripped and the all the music and instruments were stolen. I lost everything I owned."

Stranded in New York with no work, O'Neill decided to accept an offer to join a packaged tour of Central and South America: "I spent a year singing in Buenos Aires, Havana, Rio de Janeiro, and Panama City. In Panama City there was a large naval base and when the fleet was in, the club was packed, so I was able to make extra money working as a hostess after the show was over. It was a good financial deal. The job offered free room and meals so as I was able to send a good portion of my paychecks home to help out my family."

By now it was 1935 and O'Neill decided to give New York another try. She left the tour and started singing at clubs in and around New York. One late summer 1937 engagement stood out: "I was at a club called the Parkview Tavern in Newark singing requests accompanied by a piano player. Artie Shaw was there one night because he had just gotten a new car and wanted to take it out for a drive. He requested a song that I wasn't familiar with so I told him I didn't know it and asked him what his next choice was. I sang his second selection and caught his attention."

O'Neill did indeed spark Shaw's musical interest. Shaw hired her and she sang and recorded with the band for the last few months of 1937. Even though Shaw tried to change her first name from Dolores to Penny, O'Neill enjoyed her time with him and still has the highest respect for his intellect: "Artie Shaw was the most intelligent person I ever met. When we traveled to engagements I always sat in the front seat of his car with him. I was introduced to his brilliance when he spent an hour explaining the aurora borealis and various scientific theories of the creation of the universe while we were driving through Vermont. I had never heard of the aurora borealis before."

Conversely, what was Shaw's opinion of Dolores O'Neill? Shortly before he passed away in December 2004, Shaw expressed his professional respect and positively commented on his experience with her: "Dodie was a damn nice woman and a good singer. She had a real feel for a song and could deliver it with strong emotion. A fine person, I enjoyed working with her."

Come 1938 O'Neill decided to return to the night club circuit headlining in both New York and Philadelphia. By mid-1939 she was primarily working in Philadelphia establishments and doing a sustaining radio show on WCAU with then seventeen year old Kitty Kallen when MCA secured a position for the both of them with the newly formed Jack Teagarden Orchestra. Kallen was to do ballads, O'Neill the jump tunes. Musically, it was a first-class band with quality musicians such as lead trumpeter Charlie Spivak who was also a quasi-partner with Teagarden, saxophonist Ernie Caceras, jazz trumpeter Lee Castle, guitarist Alan Reuss, drummer Dave Tough, and the leader, legendary trombonist and blues-tinged vocalist Jack Teagarden.

Kallen and O'Neill joined the Teagarden Orchestra at the Blackhawk Restaurant in Chicago and were roommates on the road. After leaving Chicago the band embarked on a one-month tour of the Midwest and Canada followed by an August booking into Frank Dailey's Meadowbrook in Cedar Grove, NJ. Featuring recurrent remote broadcasts along with its proximity to New York, the venue was considered a prestigious booking. But soon after the band opened at the Meadowbrook O'Neill decided to accept an offer to join another newly formed band, the

Bob Chester Orchestra. It was a decision that would dramatically change the course of her life both professionally and personally.

Bob Chester formed his orchestra during the summer of 1939. Although the sadly under recognized ensemble never achieved huge financial success primarily due to the easy going Chester's relaxed leadership, it did tastefully mix sweet and swing songs to provide popular dance music. In his book *The Swing Era* Günther Schuler discussed the Chester organization: "Among the hundreds of bands that populated the swing landscape of the late thirties to early forties, Bob Chester's band can be singled out as one of the more polished, thoroughly professional, eminently listenable, and committed to jazz with a high degree of musical integrity."

Sometime around September 1939 Dolores O'Neill came to the Bob Chester Orchestra from Jack Teagarden's band replacing vocalist Kathleen Lane. During the year she spent with the band O'Neill regularly sang on its radio broadcasts and made numerous Bluebird recordings, three of which became smash hits. Those hits were "With the Wind and the Rain in Your Hair," "Now I Lay Me Down to Dream," and "May I Never Love Again." "With the Wind and the Rain in Your Hair" is a particular favorite of big band radio personality Chuck Cecil. The novelty song "Pushin' the Conversation Along" that she sang with trumpeter Al Stuart was one of the band's two most requested songs at dance dates. However, O'Neill's time with Chester was marked by not only professional success, but also dramatic personal change thanks to her ardent relationship with the band's brilliant young lead trumpet player, Alec Fila.

Born of Polish ancestry in Passaic, NJ, on January 29, 1921, Alec Fila was urged by his father, who was a trumpeter in the Passaic American Legion band, to take up the trumpet when he was ten years old. Fila made rapid progress and over the next few years appeared on several local New York radio shows and played in the Catskills with Henry Jerome's band. At fifteen, he was both featured on the popular Major Bowes's *The Original Amateur Hour* radio show and awarded a full four-year scholarship to study at Juilliard. Formally trained as a classical musician, he was striving for a career in symphonic music. However, a future in symphonic-orchestral work turned out to be a short-lived goal.

One evening in early 1939 Fila had a trumpet lesson scheduled with a Julliard faculty member who failed to keep the appointment. Suddenly a man excitedly came by from a room down the hall to ask Fila if he could sit in for a trumpet player that did not show up for a band rehearsal. The band turned out to be the newly formed Jack Teagarden Orchestra. Fila did sit in and immediately became enthralled by the jazz music they were playing. So much so, that he wound up accepting an offer of $75 a week to join the band and gave up his Julliard scholarship. Fila's reputation soared and after just a few months with Teagarden he was offered $100 a week by Bob Chester to become his lead trumpet player. The stage was set for what turned out to be an inauspicious first meeting between Dolores O'Neill and Alec Fila.

"Right after I left Teagarden I got together with the Chester band in Minneapolis," O'Neill said. "After I sang a few songs Bob took the band aside and asked what they thought of my work. They all liked me except Alec who said, 'She stinks. Send her back to New York.' That's how I met Alec."

Notwithstanding their acrimonious introduction, the handsome Fila, who was an inch shorter than the statuesque five feet nine inch tall O'Neill, started to meet with her for a late night snack after work. Sparks flew and they soon became an item. The two married in January 1940 while the band was playing a hotel date in Virginia. Musically, all went smoothly with Chester until later in the year when Fila started to receive offers from the top name bands. His association with Bob Chester was about to come to a close.

Benny Goodman was a huge Alec Fila fan. He once said that he was happy playing the clari-net but if he could ever play trumpet he would like to play like Alec Fila. Goodman desperately wanted Fila in his band. He finally got his wish in the summer of 1940 when he hired Fila to play in his trumpet section. Fila did go on to do outstanding work with Goodman as exemplified by his hauntingly beautiful solo in "The Man I Love" sung by Helen Forrest. As for Dolores O'Neill, she left Chester soon after Fila did. However, O'Neill struck out on a brand new career path, network radio.

While Fila stayed with the big bands, O'Neill segued into radio: "Right after I joined Bob Chester I performed with the band at the New York World's Fair Dancing Campus. Dinah Shore always used to come there with George Simon, whom she was casually dating at the time, to hear me sing. We became good friends and she recommended me to replace her on NBC's *Chamber Music Society of Lower Basin Street* program after she left it to go to Hollywood to be featured on the *Eddie Cantor Show*. Doing the *Basin Street* show was a great experience and we aired some very good swing music. I stayed on it until Gregory, the first of my five children with Alec, was born on May 5, 1941. That's when I stopped working to raise our kids."

During 1941 the Fila family lived in New York City in a penthouse on Riverside Drive while Alec Fila received top sideman's pay performing with the Goodman, Will Bradley, and Glenn Miller orchestras. They frequently entertained musicians from the Miller band at the penthouse. Fila also played lead trumpet in Fletcher Henderson's Orchestra during a recording session, an uncommon occurrence in those racially unenlightened times. Then in late 1941 disaster struck when Fila's lips gave out and he could no longer play the trumpet. His big band career was sud-denly halted and the Fila's moved to West Philadelphia to be near where several of O'Neill's siblings had relocated from Scranton.

Through the 1940s the Fila's continued to live in Philadelphia and were semi-active in the mu-sic business. Dolores had her own radio show on WCAU during 1943 and when Alec's embou-chure improved he played with the WCAU staff orchestra and the new innovative and critically acclaimed Elliott Lawrence Orchestra in 1946 and 1947. In 1948 he formed his own band with Dolores featured as vocalist. Unfortunately, Fila was a very poor businessman. His attempt at band leading did not last long. Domestically, as the decade progressed marital problems unfortu-nately developed and intensified. In early 1949 the Fila's agreed to divorce and go their separate ways.

Alec Fila spent much of the 1950s playing in his old friend Henry Jerome's band at New York's Hotel Edison. He also played in the orchestra on Tallulah Bankhead's weekly hour-and-a-half *The Big Show* radio show in the early 50s. Fila formed his own four-piece combo in 1959 and played for about six months at a Manhattan club called the Keyboard. Dissatisfied with the group, he gave it up and retired from music to live in Manhattan and mange his personal invest-ments. He passed away on December 31, 2001, after forty-three years of marriage to his second wife, Joan Harrison of Pontiac, MI, who established a scholarship at Julliard in his name. So far three students have studied at Julliard thanks to the scholarship.

After her divorce, Dolores O'Neill moved in with her sister and brother-in-law in Collings-wood, NJ, and returned to work. She briefly sang with Elliott Lawrence and in New York and Philadelphia clubs. In 1950 O'Neill reunited with Artie Shaw to spend several months on the road with his band. They played at numerous military bases where she was very well received by the GIs. O'Neill closed out her career with the big bands in 1951 singing with Gene Krupa's Or-chestra. She made one recording with the band, "I Remember Harlem," which was never released because Krupa disbanded before she could record the second side.

For the next two years O'Neill worked in Philadelphia performing at smart clubs and occasionally appearing on WCAU. But health problems surfaced: "In 1954 I was diagnosed with TB and spent the entire year at the Lakewood Sanitarium in Blackwood, NJ. I got a big moral booster one evening when I was listening to Ella Fitzgerald being interviewed on a radio show and heard her say that I was one of her favorite vocalists."

O'Neill's old boss Gene Krupa helped her out with her stay at the sanitarium. Harry Fleitman played saxophone in the Krupa band and explained what happened from his home in Lindenwold, NJ: "Dodie and I were with Gene for most of 1951 until he broke up the band that fall. She did all the locations and traveled on the band bus with us. Dodie was very well liked by everyone in the band and got along great with Gene. In 1954 Gene did a benefit for her in Philadelphia with a small combo and donated the entire proceeds to her to assist with her financial obligations."

After her illness O'Neill resumed performing until she married Linton Weil in 1956. Weil was a jazz lover who at one time had an interest in the Riobamba Room on East 57th Street, the chic nightclub where Dean Martin made his New York debut in 1943. When they married he had just received a Ph.D. in psychology from New York University and was a successful stockbroker with Bache & Co. at the firm's Rockefeller Center office.

"Right before I went with Artie Shaw in 1950 I was working 52nd Street singing at the Three Deuces and staying with George and Beverly Simon in Greenwich Village," O'Neill commented. "That's where I met Linton. He started following me around wherever we played. In fact, the guys in Krupa's band would say 'Here comes your fan club again'. Linton's wife died in childbirth and left him a son. After we married I effectively retired. We combined our children and moved to his family's fifteen room estate in Wingdale and I've been there ever since. We had a wonderful marriage until he suddenly died in 1974."

Since relocating to upstate New York, O'Neill occasionally sang at small private gatherings and local benefits. In 1971 she made her last appearance with a big band substituting for her ailing daughter Alexa who was scheduled to appear with the Jimmy Dorsey Orchestra led by Lee Castle at the Fireman's Ball in Milford, CT. Alexa is a gifted vocalist who began performing as a teenager and has sung at the Smithsonian Institution and with the Sammy Kaye Orchestra. She currently teaches music in the New York City school system and appears with jazz combos at Manhattan clubs. The O'Neill legacy of accomplished vocalists continues.

Dolores O'Neill had quite a remarkable life. She extricated herself from the humblest of beginnings, succeeded as a successful big band singer and radio star, suffered personal sadness, raised six children from two families, and lived a comfortable life on a country estate enjoying her ten grandchildren, eight great-grandchildren, and one great, great-grandchild until she passed away on December 12, 2006. O'Neill also significantly contributed to the history of the Big Band Era. Legions of fans of that period still remember her for having one of the outstanding pure voices of all the female vocalists. And it all started in her senior year in high school when she had the temerity to walk into WGBI in Scranton to ask for her own show while she was waiting for her little sister to finish her dancing lessons.

ANDY RUSSELL
EAST LOS ANGELES'S CONTRIBUTION
TO THE BIG BAND ERA

Sweeping eastward from downtown Los Angeles is the Mexican-American barrio of East Los Angeles, better known to native Angelinos as East LA. It runs from Boyle Heights to Monterey Park and is home to one of the largest Mexican populations in the world outside of Mexico City, a population that is rapidly growing in political importance in the nation's most ethnically diverse city.

A visit to Los Angeles would not be complete without a drive through East Los Angeles. One feels electricity in the air as the streets are filled with passersby and children of all ages. There are artistically unique and vividly colorful murals painted on walls throughout the area. Restaurants abound that serve richly flavored Mexican cuisine ranging from the ever-popular home of the giant Manuel's special burrito at El Tepeyeac to the sophisticated La Serenata de Garibaldi that draws the chic Hollywood movie crowd led by frequent patrons Bette Midler and Michelle Pfeiffer. Sounds of mariachi bands fill the air. Vibrant thoroughfares and commercial centers such as Caesar Chavez Boulevard, First Street, and Whittier Boulevard visually transport the onlooker to Mexico City. Classic boxing gyms that have spawned the likes of Oscar De La Hoya and a host of other great pugilistic champions dot the community and impart a unique Runyonesque flavor.

The East Los Angeles of 1919 was a dramatically different community than it is now. The Boyle Heights section, with its center of activity at the intersection of what is today Caesar Chavez Boulevard and Soto Street, to be sure had a significant Mexican population. But there was also a strong Jewish community along with more than a smattering of Japanese and Russians. This was the rich cultural kaleidoscope that produced East Los Angeles's contribution to the Big Band Era, percussionist and romantic vocalist Andy Russell.

Andres Rabago Perez was born in Los Angeles on September 16, 1919. Early in his singing career his name would change to Andy Russell at the suggestion of his first big name boss, veteran bandleader Gus Arnheim.

One of ten children, Russell grew up in a bilingual household in Boyle Heights. His father, who earned a good living as an extra in Hollywood films, was from the Mexican State of Durango. His mother originally hailed from Chihuahua, Mexico. Throughout his entire professional career Russell maintained pride in his 100% Mexican ethnicity.

Although his parents regularly listened to Mexican music, from an early age Russell was drawn to American music, especially that of the big bands. Tommy Dorsey was his favorite band closely followed by Artie Shaw. He also liked Benny Goodman and Glenn Miller. His singing idols were Bing Crosby and Dorsey's crooner Jack Leonard. With his interest in contemporary American music combined with his strong Mexican culture, Russell always considered himself a mixture of both Mexican and American heritages.

Russell attended Roosevelt High School in East Los Angeles, now the nation's largest high school with 5,200 students. While in high school, he sang with Don Ramon's Orchestra that played at dances in East Los Angeles. In an attempt to cut costs, Russell was asked by Ramon to learn an instrument to add to his singing duties. He chose the drums, and after only three weeks of practice in his parent's basement he became a proficient, self-taught swing drummer.

Fate smiled on Russell while he was a student at Roosevelt when he had the opportunity to audition for Gus Arnheim's band as a drummer and singer. Arnheim's was one of the West Coast's top dance bands, ensconced for years at the Cocoanut Grove nightclub in the Ambassador Hotel on Wilshire Boulevard. Both Bing Crosby and Russ Columbo rose to fame by singing with Arnheim. Russell passed his audition with ease.

Arnheim was responsible for major changes in Russell's public image and singing style. It was commonplace at the time for entertainers to change their names. For example, Benjamin Kubelsky became better know to the public as Jack Benny. While playing an engagement at the Peabody Hotel in Memphis, TN, Arnheim suggested Andres Rabago Perez change his name to one with a better "ring." Since he reminded him of his old vocalist Russ Columbo, Arnheim suggested Andy Russell.

Russell indeed had a rare talent for his time. He had the ability to speak impeccable English and Spanish; it was Arnheim who saw opportunity in this bilingual skill. Specifically, he convinced Russell to sing in both English and Spanish to distinguish himself as a vocalist. This strategic change in style immediately paid dividends as dancers crowded the bandstand to watch the handsome Russell croon in both languages.

After his stint with Arnheim, Russell joined Vido Musso and His Orchestra that was in essence run by Musso's pianist, Stan Kenton. A truly unrecognized Swing Era musician, Musso has sadly never received his due acclaim.

Born in Sicily in 1913, Musso had little formal education, never learned to read music, and was renowned for butchering the King's English. A brilliant and exciting tenor saxophonist with a powerful tone and throaty rock-and-roll type growl, he joined Benny Goodman in 1936 and became an instant crowd pleaser. He moved on to Gene Krupa, led his own band with Kenton's involvement, then worked with Harry James, Woody Herman, Tommy Dorsey and Kenton from 1945-1946, reuniting with Kenton in 1956 to contribute classic solos to the *Kenton in Hi-Fi* album that quickly climbed *Billboard's* pop album chart immediately after its mid-year release. From the late 1940s on he led bands on the West Coast and in Las Vegas lounges, relocating to Palm Springs in the mid 1970s after hip surgery. Musso remained mildly active until he succumbed to a heart attack in 1982, and was always considered by Frank Sinatra to be one of the all-time great tenor saxophone players.

Exempt from the military draft due to a broken arm he suffered while playing handball as a child, Russell spent much of 1942 with the Johnny Richards Orchestra. While performing with Richards at Joe Zuccca's Show Case in Hermosa Beach, CA, Russell was approached by Tommy Dorsey to see if he was interested in replacing his drumming idol Buddy Rich, who was scheduled to join the Marines Corps. He thanked Dorsey but declined when Dorsey told him he could only play drums and not sing because he already had a vocalist under contract. That vocalist was Frank Sinatra.

Following his tenure with Richards, Russell moved on to join Alvino Rey and the King Sisters. Rey was a superb guitarist who gained a measure of fame in the early 1940s with the four King Sisters vocal group that Horace Heidt discovered while they were singing on a radio show in Salt Lake City, UT. Then came December 1943, and a recording session that was to propel Russell to celebrity status overnight.

Record retailer Glenn Wallichs, and songwriters Buddy DeSylva and Johnny Mercer founded Capitol Records in Hollywood in 1942 with a combined investment of $10,000. It was the first major record label ever headquartered on the West Coast and was highly innovative from the start, being the first to provide disc jockeys with records, recording masters on tape, and issuing records in all three speeds.

Mercer asked Russell to record for Capitol paying him $150 for both sides of his first record. The recording, "Besame Mucho," hit the top ten in April 1944 and went on to sell a million copies. The song was a signature Russell recording combining his singing in both English and Spanish, and its huge success prompted legendary personal manager George "Bullets" Durgom to urge him to give up the drums and concentrate on a solo singing career.

Russell followed up "Besame Mucho" with a January 1944 recording of "Amor" that went on to crack the top ten in June 1944. His success dramatically continued with an impressive twelve records breaking into the charts between April 1944 and September 1948 a phenomenal eight of them in the top ten. He was not only an established star of the Era, but recognized as a unique contributor as well with his bilingual singing style that opened up the international market for Capitol.

The famed radio show *Your Hit Parade* provided Russell one his greatest thrills of the Big Band Era. *Your Hit Parade* ran from 1935 through 1958 on radio, and 1950 through 1959 on television. Sponsored by Lucky Strike cigarettes, the show was a Saturday night institution featuring the top ranked songs of the week performed by the show's vocalists.

Groomed as a replacement for Frank Sinatra, who left *Your Hit Parade* to concentrate on the *Max Factor Presents Frank Sinatra* radio show, Russell joined *Your Hit Parade* in June 1946 for an eleven month engagement. Soon after he started, Russell had the number 1 and 2 hit songs on the show, "They Say It's Wonderful" and the record's flip side "Laughing on the Outside." He sang them both, one of the few times in the history of *Your Hit Parade* that the program's vocalist had the top two songs and actually sang them on the program. Russell did considerable radio work during the 40s and had his own mid-decade show with his good friend Bing Crosby as an occasional guest. He also made guest appearances on several television variety shows in the early 1950s.

With his good looks and engaging personality, Russell was a natural for the cinema. Between 1945 and 1947 he appeared in four films, the last of which was *Copacabana* that starred Groucho Marx and Carmen Miranda. A typical period musical comedy, Russell had a significant role and was provided an opportunity to amply display his impressive vocal talent. The film has historical significance as it was Marx's first solo acting effort without his brothers and is periodically shown on the Turner Classic Movie cable network.

After the Big Band Era came to a close, Russell moved to Mexico City in the mid-1950s and launched a new international career becoming a major celebrity throughout Latin America. He starred in Latin films; toured extensively performing in Mexico, South America, Spain, Portugal, and Cuba; and served as the host of *The Andy Russell Show* on Argentine television from 1956 to 1965. During this nearly twenty year Latin American period he won numerous awards including The Pioneer of Argentine Television, The Showman of the Americas, and in 1974 the Eagle of the Americas, conferred on him by Mexican journalists.

Russell's Latin American touring engagements provided many colorful experiences. Two are of note. First, he was invited to sing for Francisco Franco in Spain on three occasions and was personally presented with numerous awards from the dictator. Second, Russell regularly appeared in Cuba during the Fulgencio Batista regime and was performing at the Havana Hilton when Fidel Castro took over generating a massive celebration that swept him onto the streets of Havana.

In the mid 1960s Andy Russell professionally returned to the United States to reunite with Capitol to record two albums and again later in the decade to headline a show at the Sahara Hotel in Las Vegas. Then after eighteen years of entertaining in Latin America interspersed with engagements in Europe and the Orient he moved back to Los Angeles from Mexico City. Russell continued to make personal appearances and new recordings, eventually retiring in 1989 to Sun City, AZ, where he developed a close friendship with big band historian Leo Walker who died in 1995. In February 1992 Russell suffered a paralyzing stroke, followed by a second stroke two months later. He passed away at Saint Joseph's Hospital in Phoenix on April 16, 1992. A public memorial service was held six days later at Saint Juliana's Catholic Church in Fullerton, California.

Certainly one aspect of a person's legacy is how they are remembered by their peers, and in this regard Russell ranks right at the top. Famous big band disc jockey and authority Chuck Cecil remembers Russell as always willing to lend him a hand with his popular syndicated radio show the *Swingin' Years*, along with the incredibly high level of energy Russell exhibited during his live performances. Guitarist Roc Hillman, who played for Jimmy Dorsey and Kay Kyser, recalls Russell as a natural who was born to entertain and a performer who was truly loved and admired by all in the business. Vocalist Bea Wain sang for Larry Clinton and performed on *Your Hit Parade* for several years. She frequently comments on her high level of professional respect for Russell. Not bad testimonials for a self-taught musician and singer from the barrio of East Los Angeles who went on to become a Swing Era celebrity and international star.

East Los Angeles has a rich music tradition that includes mariachi, salsa, and rock and roll with the internationally popular Mexican-style rock band Los Lobos that gained fame in the 1987 film *La Bamba*. That tradition also extends to jazz. The Roosevelt High School Jazz Band that opened the 1995 Playboy Jazz Festival at the Hollywood Bowl has been long recognized as one of the top high school jazz bands in the country. The late East Los Angeles jazz pianist Eddie Cano blended jazz harmonics and Latin rhythms; admired by Ella Fitzgerald, Cano recorded with Les Baxter and Cal Tjader and had a hit record with "A Taste of Honey" in the early 1960s. Lionel "Chico" Sesma distinguished himself as a Swing Era trombonist and pioneering Los Angels Latin jazz radio personality. And of course there was Andy Russell, East Los Angeles's gift to what many consider to be the Golden Age of jazz, the Big Band Era, a unique period of time in our nation's cultural history.

JO STAFFORD
AN AMERICAN MUSICAL ICON

Who do you think is the number one ranked female vocalist of the 1940 to 1954 pre-rock era? The answer is Jo Stafford, one of the most admired song stylists in the history of American popular music. Singing either solo, as lead singer for the Pied Pipers, or in duet with both Frankie Laine and Gordon MacRae, and under several pseudonyms, she recorded an incredible 110 Top Forty hits during her storied career. Her body of work includes the Broadway show tune, folk, jazz, novelty, pop, and religious genres. In addition to her recording success, she appeared on radio and television, in the movies, and was dubbed GI Jo by servicemen thanks to the sentimental ballads she sang during World War II. Jo Stafford is truly an American musical icon.

In 1916 Stafford's father, Grover Cleveland Stafford, moved to California from Gainsboro, TN, to seek his fortune. He settled in Coalinga, a small town in the San Joaquin Valley southwest of Fresno, to work for the Southern Pacific railroad. After a few months with the railroad, he was hired by the Shell Oil Company to work as a roughneck. He would spend the rest of his working life with Shell, eventually becoming a foreman with his own company car supervising a dozen rigs.

Stafford returned to Gainsboro in September 1917 to bring his wife, Anna York, a distant relative of World War I hero Sergeant Alvin York, to Coalinga. On November 12, 1917, Jo Elizabeth Stafford was born in Coalinga in a company-owned house on a site called lease 35. She was the third of what would be four Stafford sisters. Other than the fact that Anna played the five-string banjo, there was no history of any notable music accomplishment in her parent's families.

Jo Stafford commented on her start in singing during a telephone interview from her home in Los Angeles's Century City area: "I had two older sisters, Chris and Pauline. They were eleven and fourteen years older than I. We were a spread out family; my younger sister was seven years younger than I am. My oldest sister, Chris, always told me that I started singing back in Coalinga before I can even remember."

In 1921 the Stafford family permanently moved to Long Beach, CA, when the nearby Signal Hill oil field opened. It was in Long Beach where Jo Stafford formally studied opera while she was at Polytechnic High: "I did classical singing as a coloratura soprano. I remember singing the aria "Caro nome" from Verdi's *Rigoletto* at the Long Beach Terrace Theater while I was still in high school. Unfortunately, talent scouts weren't scouring for sopranos, so I had to go to work when I graduated in 1935."

Work meant joining her older sisters who were already singing as the Stafford Sisters on their own KHJ radio show in Hollywood. The trio also regularly performed on the station's *David Brockman's California Melodies* and KNX's *The Crockett Family of Kentucky* shows. *The Crockett Family* was on nightly during the week and featured a special barn dance show on Saturdays. They were a pure country group that provided Stafford her initial introduction to the world of country music. The sisters rounded out their whirlwind schedule by singing background music for films at several movie studios.

After three years of apprenticeship doing radio and film work around Hollywood, Stafford unknowingly started on the road to musical fame and fortune in 1938 when one of the Big Band Era's most famous vocal groups, the Pied Pipers, was serendipitously formed. She talked about how it all came about on Don Kennedy's *Big Band Jump* radio show in 1999: "I was on what we used to call a cattle call at 20th Century Fox for a musical that starred Alice Faye and Don Ameche called *Alexander's Ragtime Band*. Just about every singer in Southern California was on it; there was a huge singing chorus. That's when I met a quartet called the Four Esquires and a trio called The Rhythm Kings. All seven of them were young men. We started fooling around singing on the set between takes and wound as a group of eight that we decided to call the Pied Pipers."

During the summer of 1938 the Tommy Dorsey orchestra was based in Los Angeles. His arrangers Axel Stordahl and Paul Weston, popular male vocalist Jack Leonard, and Herb Sanford, producer of the *Raleigh-Kool* network radio show that featured Dorsey, rented a house on Colgate Avenue in Beverly Hills for the duration of the stay. Shortly after they all moved in they invited several vocal groups over for a party. At the urging of Alyce and Yvonne King, who were dating Weston and Stordahl, the Pied Pipers were invited. It was the first time Jo Stafford met Weston, whom she would marry in 1952.

No account of Jo Stafford's career would be complete without mention of Paul Weston. Born in Springfield, MA, on March 12, 1912, Weston graduated from Dartmouth College in 1933 as a Phi Beta Kappa with a degree in economics. While at Dartmouth he led a popular campus dance band. With little demand for economists during the Great Depression, he abandoned his graduate studies at Columbia University and by 1935 was established in the music business providing arrangements to Joe Haymes, Rudy Vallee, and the popular *Fleischmann Hour* radio show. When Tommy Dorsey took over Joe Haymes's band that September he hired Weston as a staff arranger. Weston remained with Dorsey until 1940 when he left to go to Hollywood to freelance, working with Dinah Shore, Lee Wiley, and Bob Crosby's band when it played in the 1942 movie *Holiday Inn* that starred Bing Crosby and Fred Astaire.

While he was writing arrangements for *Holiday Inn* at Paramount, Weston met Johnny Mercer who was also at the studio working on *Star Spangled Rhythm*. They quickly developed a close association that led to Mercer hiring Weston as the musical director for his newly formed Capitol Records. Weston broke through to public recognition in 1944 when he recorded his first mood music album, *Music for Dreaming*. It was the first of several albums in which he incorporated the lush use of strings with romantic big band sounds, earning him the sobriquet Master of Mood Music.

The 1938 vocal group soiree in Beverly Hills hosted by the four Dorsey-associated bachelors provided the Pied Pipers their big break. Impressed by the group's sophisticated harmony and Jo Stafford's crystal clear voice, Herb Sanford recommended them to Dorsey who in turn offered them a one-night tryout on the *Raleigh-Kool Show* in New York. There was, however, a catch. All eight Pied Pipers had to get to New York on their own.

During a feature on the Pied Pipers on Chuck Cecil's *Swingin' Years* radio show, the late Dick Whitinghill, one of the original Pied Pipers and longtime Los Angeles radio personality, told how they arrived at the decision to go to New York in December 1938: "Here we were in Los Angeles and had to go to New York to take a chance on a one-night stand. We sat around and decided if we should do it. Someone sent out for a jug of wine and by the time the gallon jug was done we said let's go. So the eight of us got into two cars and drove all the way to New York for an audition. I dread to think what would have happened if we blew it because we would not have had enough change left between us to get back to Los Angeles."

The Pied Pipers did indeed not blow their one shot chance. They landed a spot on Dorsey's show, appearing for the first time on December 23, 1938. However, the program's England-based sponsor did not like what they heard and the Pied Pipers were unceremoniously off the air after eight shows. Now unemployed, they kicked around New York, but after a few months started to return to Los Angeles one by one when nothing developed. Then in December 1939 Dame Fortune intervened.

"I was living in the Glendale area and the exact day my unemployment benefits ran out I got a collect call from Chicago," Stafford said. "It was Tommy Dorsey asking us to join the band as a quartet. So John Huddleston, Chuck Lowry, Billy Wilson and I took the first train to Chicago to join up with Tommy."

The rest is big band history. Starting with their nostalgically romantic 1940 million seller "I'll Never Smile Again," sung with Dorsey's new vocalist Frank Sinatra, the Pied Pipers turned out hit record after hit record. Many of those recordings were sung with Sinatra; two were with Connie Haines. Stafford had a definite first impression of Frank Sinatra: "The Pied Pipers joined Tommy at the Palmer House in Chicago, and then we went on to our next engagement at the Riverside Theater in Milwaukee. We heard on the train that we were getting a new boy singer and were anxious to hear him. The Pipers always sat on stage in front of Buddy Rich's drums. When he came out all we saw was his profile and back, but eight bars into his first number I knew this was something new, exceptional, and very good."

While with Dorsey, Stafford scored with numerous solo hits of her own, the biggest of which was the rhythmic Sy Oliver arrangement of the gospel oriented "Yes, Indeed!" in 1941. Oliver wrote the composition and recorded it with her. She also appeared with the Pied Pipers in three Tommy Dorsey films and established herself as a household name. Then, due to a snap decision by the impulsive and volatile Dorsey, it all suddenly came to an end in Portland in December 1942.

"It was a silly kind of argument," Stafford explained. "Tommy ran across Chuck Lowry at the train station and asked what track the train was on. Chuck gave him the wrong information and Tom got lost. By the time he got to the train he was hopping mad and exploded at Chuck. We all got up and left the train and that was it. We were never out of work again."

Johnny Mercer, who was a big Tommy Dorsey and Pied Piper fan, immediately snapped them up for Capitol Records. They became regulars on his *Johnny Mercer Music Shop* radio show and hit the charts with blockbusters such as "Candy" and "The Trolley Song." However, all was not roses working for Mercer: "John would occasionally lose his temper with his musical artists and then regret his actions and send them roses the next day. He was always very kind to me, but one night it looked like it would come to an end. Before he got started I said, 'John, I do not want to receive a dozen roses tomorrow morning.' It worked."

Come 1944 Stafford had never given any thought to striking out on her own. She was happy and contented as lead singer for one of the Big Band Era's most popular vocal groups. However, many of her personal friends and professional associates began to urge her to go it alone. The final prod came from the only manager she ever had, former General Artist Corporation executive Mike Nidorf. After several lengthily conversations, Nidorf convinced her that she could build a successful solo career. Late that year she made the big move and left the Pied Pipers. Her replacement was June Hutton, who came over to the Pipers from Charlie Spivak's orchestra.

With Paul Weston as her arranger, Stafford embarked on an incredible seven-year run of hits at Capitol records. However, her first million seller was ironically recorded with another group,

Red Ingle and The Natural Seven as told on Cecil's *Swingin' Years*: "In June of 1947 I ran into Red Ingle walking down the hall at Capitol right after I finished mapping out a record date with Paul in his office. The girl singer Red lined up couldn't make his recording session. Just for fun I filled in and recorded "Tim-Tayshun" hillbilly style under the name Cinderella G. Stump. When it came out no one could figure out who Cinderella G. Stump was. Even though it hit number one and was on the charts for fifteen weeks, I never earned a dime of royalties from it."

In the late 1940s, Stafford had ten smash hits singing duets with Gordon MacRae. "My Darling, My Darling" was on the charts for seventeen weeks and their inspirational song "Whispering Hope" sold over a million copies in the South alone. Stafford also started recording albums with Capitol. Over the years she would record a wide variety of albums with several record labels that included American folk songs, Scottish folk songs, the blues, jazz standards, popular music, religious songs, and show tunes. In commenting on her *Jo + Jazz* album in the liner notes, legendary jazz critic Leonard Feather wrote: "This album is something very special."

Stafford was also a fixture on radio throughout the 40s, starting with the *Johnny Mercer Music Shop* show. She starred on Tuesday and Thursday evenings on the *Chesterfield Supper Club Show* from 1945 to 1950, made guest appearances on *The Carnation Hour* and *Club 15*, and had her own network *Jo Stafford Show* that was sponsored by Revere Camera from 1949 to 1951. For a five-year period into the early 1950s she broadcast to over 300 million listeners worldwide on Radio Luxembourg from Hollywood and the Voice of America from New York. Her strong overseas popularity, generated in part by those broadcasts, led to an engagement at the London Palladium in 1952.

The close of the 40s was also a time of romance for Jo Stafford. From Kennedy's *Big Band Jump*: "Paul and I were good friends for quite a few years before we ever got serious about each other, mainly because we were on opposite coasts most of the time. We would run into each other only two or three times a year. Then in 1947 I brought my Chesterfield radio show to California from New York and Paul became my conductor. We started going out and wound up getting married in 1952."

In 1950 Stafford followed Weston when he moved over to Columbia Records. It was a good move, one that led to four gold records from late 1951 to early 1954. Those million sellers were: "Shrimp Boats," "You Belong to Me" (her biggest-selling hit), "Jambalaya," and "Make Love to Me." She also had eight hit records singing with Frankie Laine and one, "Indiscretion," accompanied by Liberace. By 1955 she had sold 25,000,000 records for Columbia and was presented their prestigious Diamond Award. To fully appreciate her recording popularity, that count of 25,000,000 did not include her sixty charted hits with Capitol.

Stafford continued her success on the airwaves in the 1950s. Only this time the medium was television, not radio. She frequently appeared on *Club Oasis* and The *Voice of Firestone* shows. Her own musical variety series, *The Jo Stafford Show*, ran from early 1954 well into 1955.

Nineteen fifty-seven marked another musical milestone for Jo Stafford with the creation of Jonathan and Darlene Edwards: "For years Paul played a silly version of "Stardust" at parties. Then there was a Columbia Records convention in Key West. Paul went as West Coast head of A & R. One night after the meetings they all went to a bar and Paul played this goofy version of "Stardust" just for fun. A couple of the fellows, George Avakian and Irving Townsend, suggested he make an album. On the way back to Los Angeles on the plane he thought I have to have a partner to make this work."

Thus *The Original Piano Artistry of Jonathan Edwards* was released in 1957. There were a total of five Jonathan and Darlene Edwards albums, with their second album, *Jonathan and Darlene Edwards in Paris*, winning a Grammy for Best Comedy Album in 1960. What with Weston play-

ing piano out of tune and Stafford singing off key and purposefully missing notes, the hilarious
novelty albums quickly attracted a cult following that exists to this day.

Just as Benny Goodman kicked off the Big Band Era in 1935 with his famed engagement at
the Palomar Ballroom in Los Angeles, Bill Haley is considered to have launched the Rock Era
in 1955 with his hit record of "Rock Around The Clock." Rock and roll quickly took over the
music business and in 1957 Jo Stafford had her last charted hit, "Wind in the Willows," which
incorporated a definite rock tinge. After her own television series she did in London during the
summer of 1961 that was broadcast throughout the British Commonwealth, Stafford decided to
wind down and spend more time with her children, Amy and Tim. She continued to occasionally record albums on a variety of labels into the mid 1960s and sporadically engaged in special
projects. Her album *Sweet Hour of Prayer* garnered her a Grammy nomination in 1964.

One special project involved recording show tunes for a Readers Digest compilation in the late
1960s. Another involved the formation of Corinthian Records in 1977. It was with Corinthian
that she recorded for the last time, not as Jo Stafford, but with Weston as Jonathan and Darlene
Edwards. On June 15, 1979, her recording career came to a close when they waxed a parody
single of "Saturday Night Fever" and "I Am Woman."

Corinthian is actually the product of Paul Weston's interest in religious music. Of Catholic
faith, he wrote a Mass in the style of Gregorian Chant. That led to the formation of Beverly
Hills-based Corinthian records that now reissues Stafford and Weston albums from Columbia
masters she now owns and others leased from various labels. Her son Tim manages the enterprise.

During the 1980s and 90s Stafford devoted her efforts to community service. She was presi-
dent of SHARE, an organization that assists handicapped children, and was active in the So-
ciety of Singers. Her last public appearance was at a Society of Singers event. In 1990 she sang,
"I'll Never Smile Again" with the Hi Lo's at the Society 75th birthday tribute for her good friend
Frank Sinatra. However, the Stafford musical legacy is kept alive and well thanks to her daughter
Amy, who carved out her own career as an accomplished professional singer.

Paul Weston was also active in philanthropic activates during that time period as three-time
past president of the Los Angeles Crippled Children's Society, an organization he was affiliated
with for over thirty years. In 1971 he was honored as a founder of the National Academy of Recording Arts and Sciences. Weston passed away on September 20, 1996. The inscription on his
tombstone at Holy Cross Cemetery in Culver City, CA, simply reads MY FRIEND.

After Weston's departure, Stafford kept busy until her passing at her Los Angeles home on July
16, 2008, attending to her four grandchildren and studying World War II history. An acknowledged expert on the conflict, she won numerous friendly debates with military officials concerning battle details. Her interest in World War II stemmed in part from the affection servicemen
bestowed on her as GI Jo.

When asked to sum up her Big Band Era experiences on Cecil's *Swingin' Years* show, Stafford
gave a somewhat surprising answer: "I would like to recognize the musicians. I consider them
the nicest persons on earth. They are gentle and kind people. They are sometimes a little nutty,
but that's fun too. I always found them to be wonderful and easy to work with. There would have
been no Big Band Era without them."

Jo Stafford's recordings still continue to sell. In fact, her 1995 three CD *Jo Stafford: The Portrait
Edition* album has become a somewhat hard to find collector's album. What is the reason for her
ongoing popularity? Certainly one must consider her voice with its perfect pitch and emotional
melancholy that can whimsically transport the listener to a nostalgic world painted by the lyrics of the song she is singing. This skill of projecting lyrics in a manner to create total personal

involvement with a song is no doubt one reason why Stafford is one of the enduring vocalists of our time—the only vocalist to have three stars on the Hollywood Walk of Fame in recognition for her body of work in records, radio, and television.

KAY STARR — BIG BAND STAR AT 15

Let's see if you can answer a trivia question that covers two musical eras. What singer from the Big Band Era had the first number one single by a female in the Rock Era? The answer is Kay Starr, who sang for big band legends Joe Venuti, Bob Crosby, Glenn Miller, and Charlie Barnet. She achieved that distinction when she hit the top of the *Billboard* charts in 1956 with "Rock and Roll Waltz." Starr's is a multifaceted career that spans eight decades as an accomplished vocalist in the blues, country, jazz, pop, religious, show tune, and even Calypso genres. She has sung them all with style.

Katherine Laverne Starks was born into a non-musical family on July 21, 1922, in Dougherty, OK. At the time, Dougherty was a small railroad stop in south-central Oklahoma with one community telephone. Her father Harry was an Iroquois Indian, her mother Annie was Irish.

Harry Starks was a highly respected, master installer of ceiling fire sprinkler systems for the Texas Automatic Sprinkler Company. When Starr was three years old her father was transferred to Dallas. Soon after the family arrived there, she started her career in song, singing to the family chickens.

"My mother raised chickens and sold eggs to supplement the family income," Starr said during an interview at her Bel Air home in Los Angeles. "After school I used to go out in the coop all by myself to serenade them. They were a very polite audience."

Starr's aunt, Nora Hughes, heard her singing to the chickens and encouraged her mother to enter her in a 1931 yo-yo contest at the Melba Theater in Dallas: "I did all the yo-yo tricks like Walk The Dog and Around The World while I sang "Now's The Time To Fall In Love." I won third place. The girl who won first place deserved it. She sang, did yo-yo tricks, and performed acrobatics."

The Melba Theater talent contest led to a weekly fifteen-minute radio show on Dallas station WRR that lasted until the family moved to Memphis when Starr was eleven years old. She arrived in town as a country singer with a modest following she acquired performing in Texas and Oklahoma both as a solo act and with country groups such as the then yet-to-be-famous Bob Wills and the Light Crust Doughboys. Thanks to her reputation, Starr landed a twice-weekly fifteen-minute show singing requests with a female piano accompanist on WREC while she was going to school. Since Starks was constantly misspelled in fan letters, the station suggested a name change. She decided on Kay Starr and her show was renamed *Starr Time*. She also frequently sang and tap-danced on *Saturday Night Jamboree* on Memphis's WMPS.

After four years of radio work in Memphis, fate smiled on Kay Starr when Joe Venuti came to town in 1937 to play at the Peabody Hotel. A classically trained violinist who grew up in Philadelphia with his close boyhood friend guitarist Eddie Lang, Venuti played with Jean Goldkette, Roger Wolfe Kahn, and Paul Whiteman in the 1920s before starting his own band in the 1930s. A legendary practical joker, Venuti is recognized as one of the great jazz violinists.

Starr tells how her big break came about: "I was still a student at Technical High School when Joe Venuti came to Memphis. His contract with the Peabody Hotel called for a girl singer. He didn't have one in the band at the time and the hotel people wouldn't let him appear without one.

Joe's road manager, Elmer Beechler, heard me on the radio and called and asked if I would like to sing with the band at the Peabody. I was astounded that they picked a local girl to sing with Joe; I thought I was going to faint."

This unexpected turn of events led to work with Venuti during the summers of 1937, 1938, and 1939. When the band traveled, Starr was chaperoned by her mother Annie who pretended to be her sister. Annie had no trouble passing as a sibling because she was only seventeen years older than Starr and looked quite young. The two were extremely close, spending time cutting out different styles of paper dolls and making scrapbooks of their favorite movie stars. The pseudo-sister relationship was an extension of their growing up together and discouraged questions about Starr performing as a minor.

Kay Starr learned a lot singing for Venuti: "Joe Venuti was loved by all his musicians. One thing Joe did for me was to not try to make me into something he wanted me to be. He just tried to correct my idiosyncrasies and let me evolve my own style. Joe always said if you forget the words to a song make them up and keep singing. I must have made up more lyrics in my career than Johnny Mercer. He gave me the strength to think that I could do anything I wanted to do."

Bob Crosby's manager Gil Rodin heard Starr singing on a remote broadcast with Venuti from the Peabody in June 1939. In between female vocalists at the time, he asked Venuti if Crosby could borrow Starr as a temporary replacement. She tearfully left Venuti who assured her that an association with Crosby would be to her career interests and boarded a train with her mother to join him in Detroit. She toured Canada with Crosby and sang "Memphis Blues" on his *Dixieland Music Shop* radio show that also featured Johnny Mercer on June 27, 1939.

Starr had an amusing experience during her stay with Crosby: "I used to sit next to Irving Fazola on the bandstand. He had a big jug of booze, and when he nodded off the guys would sneak it from him and empty it and fill with water. He always called me little sister and gave me his jug to hold when he soloed because he trusted me and knew that I didn't drink. The guys in the band thought that was cute. I had a lot of fun joking with Irving while the band was playing."

When Starr's short stay with Crosby was over she was in New York preparing to return to Memphis with her mother by bus. However, her plans suddenly changed when she got a surprise call from Glenn Miller.

Miller's popular female vocalist Marion Hutton had just collapsed on stage from exhaustion and was hospitalized. He was in desperate need of a singer to fill in until Hutton was able to return. Starr stepped in and sang with Miller at the prestigious Glenn Island Casino, receiving national radio exposure, and recorded two songs, "Love with a Capital You" and "Baby Me." They were her first recordings. She also celebrated her seventeenth birthday while she was singing with Miller.

What was it like singing for Glenn Miller? Starr commented: "Although Glenn was very strict he would fondly pat me on the head when I was done singing. The guys in the band were sweet and dear to me because I was only an inexperienced sixteen-year-old. They saw I had good pitch and the first night tested me by going eight bars from key to key. I went right with them and earned their respect. Glenn Miller taught me professionalism, to be on time, and to be totally prepared to perform at my best at all times. The musicians clowned around and laughed, but when Glenn walked to the bandstand it wasn't more than a minute before everyone was on the bandstand ready to play. I definitely learned structure working for him."

Miller trombonist Paul Tanner recalled Starr's filling in for Hutton with the Miller Orchestra: "I remember Kay's stay with the band very well. What struck me was the poise she exhibited for someone as young as she was. She was very easy to get along with, all the guys in the band liked her, and she sang very effectively."

After her brief engagement with Miller, Starr returned to high school in Memphis, graduating in 1940. Realizing she had to leave home to further her career, she went to Los Angeles and reunited with Venuti, living with him and his wife Sally in their San Fernando Valley home. The childless Venuti's were delighted to have Starr stay with them. After Venuti broke up his band at the start of World War II, she joined one-armed New Orleans-style trumpeter and vocalist Wingy Manone's band, singing with him until Charlie Barnet discovered her in early 1944.

Starr talked about how Barnet discovered her: "I was rehearsing with Wingy Manone at Wallichs Music City in Hollywood. Wallichs was a record store and recording studio at Sunset and Vine where all the bands would come to rehearse and record. I've always been a loud singer, and Charlie Barnet's manager, Charlie Weintraub, heard me singing through the sound proof room. He offered me a tryout with Charlie, who was also rehearsing at Wallichs, and I thought Wingy, who had quite a hot temper, would go after him. I walked down the hall and peeked in the room Charlie was rehearsing in. I couldn't believe how powerful his band sounded. He saw me and asked me to sing ahead of four or five other girls who were standing in line with their sheet music. After a few songs, in which I made up some of the lyrics, he said 'you got the job'. I thought my God, who's going to tell Wingy?"

The twelve or so months Starr spent with Barnet were a whirlwind of constant activity. She recorded several Decca records, V-Discs for distribution to troops overseas, and sang on Saturday night Armed Forces Radio Service shows at military camps and hospitals across the country, frequently flying to radio show locations on cramped military planes ferrying paratroopers. All this singing over Barnet's thunderous band took its toll when Starr lost her voice in early 1945 and left the band to recuperate. She had developed polyps on her vocal chords and actually considered surgery. When informed that an operation might permanently change her vocal quality and ability to sing, she opted to rest her voice and take a break from the music business.

What are Starr's impressions of working with Manone and Barnet? "Wingy commanded respect, loved Dixieland music and his work, and his musicians loved him. I did a lot of overnighters with Wingy and learned about life on the road. I think that he is underrated as a bandleader and a musician."

"Charlie was a very handsome man from a well-to-do family who I thought liked to party more than lead an orchestra. The band members were a wild bunch. We were thrown out of more hotels than you could imagine. When they got to partying they used to draw less than proper pictures on the hotel walls and Charlie wound up paying," Starr concluded.

After a several month recuperation from her throat problem during which she rarely spoke, things started happening for Kay Starr in mid-1945. She had a successful appearance at the Streets of Paris nightclub in Hollywood followed by a sold-out engagement with Herb Jeffries at the nearby El Morocco. As told by Jeffries, he and Starr became lifelong friends: "Kay Starr is a sweetheart. I could fill the pages saying nice things about her. She's a great lady with a wonderful sense of humor, one of the finest woman singers as a person. I love her to death."

At the same time Starr's nightclub career started to grow in 1945, her recording career began to develop in earnest on three different fronts. First, she ran into Capitol Records A&R man Dave Dexter and popular Los Angeles disc jockey Gene Norman in Hollywood while they were having coffee. This chance encounter led to a Capitol all-star jazz recording date that included Nat "King" Cole and Coleman Hawkins, among others, and a series of appearances on Armed Forces Radio Service and Gene Norman-produced jazz concerts. Norman also later recorded Starr on his GNP Crescendo label.

Second, Starr started recording on two independent Los Angeles record labels, Jewel (owned by bandleader Ben Pollack), and Lamplighter. The seventeen sides she did with Lamplighter are highly respected jazz works that were recorded with Barney Bigard, Red Callender, Vic Dickenson, Allen Reuss, Zutty Singleton, and Willie Smith. Mel Powell is reported to have played piano on some of the tracks. Her entire body of work with Lamplighter is available on the Baldwin Street Music label.

Finally, Starr began an involvement with Standard Transcriptions that would last through the decade. Her first recordings included ten sides with her old boss Joe Venuti and Les Paul. She went on to record several dozen songs that would be distributed nationwide to radio stations to use to put together a show on Kay Starr. The majority of her transcription work is available on the Soundies label. Then came 1947 and Capitol Records.

Thanks to her growing popularity and previous work with the label in 1945, Starr signed a contract with Capitol Records in 1947. However, she had trouble competing with Capitol's great stable of female vocalists—including Peggy Lee, Ella Mae Morse, Jo Stafford, and Margaret Whiting—in getting good songs to record prior to the 1948 musicians strike.

Luckily, Starr found those songs: "I was just starting out with Capitol and had to come up with tunes to record before the strike because Peggy, Ella Mae, Jo, and Margaret were established stars and had first pick. I was down in the dumps and stopped at a little place on Vine Street we nicknamed The Hymn and Hangover Club because you would go there to hangout and pray to get a job. Red Nichols was performing when I walked in. When Red took his break he came over and asked me if I was dying. I explained to him what was going on. He said to come out to his house in the Valley and he would show me a piano bench full of old songs that have never been recorded. I thought they were great. One of them, "The Lonesomest Gal in Town," became my first regional hit with Capitol. I still sing it at nightclubs."

Notwithstanding her initial travails, Starr went on to become one of Capitol's most successful recording artists. Between 1948 and 1954 she had twenty-nine charted hits, thirteen of which made the top ten. In 1952 she had a gold record with "Wheel of Fortune" that was on the hit parade for twenty-five weeks. It spent nineteen weeks in the top ten, with ten consecutive weeks at number one. "Wheel of Fortune" was the second best selling record of the year. During her phenomenal seven-year run, she had three of the year's Top 40 hits in 1950, and one each in 1952, 1953, and 1954. Her popularity was such that during that period that she made three movies, and had several guest appearances on Danny Thomas's television show and Spike Jones's radio show. She even had a number one hit in England in 1952 with "Comes A-Long A-Love" and headlined at the London Palladium in 1953.

While Starr was at Capitol, she was instrumental in helping keep Tennessee Ernie Ford from leaving the label: "Around 1950 Ernie was unhappy and was thinking of leaving Capitol. He said he was tired of singing church songs and wanted to sing country songs like they did in Nashville. The executives were concerned because he was one of their few male stars. Peggy, Ella Mae, and Jo didn't want anything to do with country music so they asked me if I was interested and I said yes. That's how I got started singing country music. Ernie and I became great friends and he stayed at Capitol."

The result of Starr and Ford collaborating as a duet were two smash 1950 hits. "I'll Never Be Free" made the top five on both the country and pop charts, and ranked thirty-one on the year's Top 40 hits. They followed it up with "Ain't Nobody's Business but My Own" that hit the top five on the country list, and made two appearances together at the Grand Ole Opry. Tennessee Ernie Ford was now a contented Capitol employee.

Starr moved over to RCA in 1955: "When EMI bought out Capitol I decided to accept an offer from RCA. One of the first songs they gave me was "Rock And Roll Waltz." I thought Oh God, what have I gotten myself into? I asked if they were sure they wanted me to do this. I sing songs about blood and guts and unrequited love, and this is a mom and pop song. They said just be yourself and I thought okay, if that's what they want I'll get into it up to my knees. After I recorded it I went to the Bahamas for a vacation. I had just got there and my attorney called and said I had to turn around and fly back to LA right away. He said "Rock And Roll Waltz" is going through he roof and it looks like it will sell a million."

"Rock And Roll Waltz" did indeed sell a million. It was on the charts for twenty weeks, six at number one, and was the fifth-best seller for 1956. It also helped shape the future of RCA, as its rock-oriented success was instrumental in the label's decision to promote a then unknown country-rock singer also from Memphis. His name was Elvis Presley.

Starr would record ten charted hits with RCA, two of which made the top ten. She even recorded a Calypso song, "Jamie Boy," that made the top 100 for five weeks in 1957. Starr also did four albums with RCA that included songs popularized by Count Basie (she was a favorite of Basie blues shouter Jimmy Rushing), Duke Ellington, and the Ink Spots. A deeply spiritual person, she is especially proud of her 1959 RCA album *I Hear the Word*, a compilation of religious music.

After her contract with RCA ran out in 1959, Starr returned to Capitol for a five-year rendezvous. Although she recorded three Top 100 singles in 1961 and 1962, her return to Capitol is noted for arguably her greatest period for producing quality albums. Those albums covered a wide range of music that included the blues, Broadway show tunes, country music, and jazz standards. Several of those album's songs reflected her vocal resemblance to her close friend Dinah Washington. Starr was extremely saddened by the great blues singer's death in 1963.

Big Band Era bandleader and renowned arranger Van Alexander arranged and conducted four albums for Starr during her second stay at Capitol. One of the albums, *Losers, Weepers*, incorporated the lush use of strings that perfectly complemented Starr's voice. He talked about his association with Starr: "Kay was a delight to work with and was blessed with a sound that was immediately identifiable. She was a great blues singer who naturally tended to always do things in a blues style. She had a slight rasp in her voice that all the great blues singers seem to have. I always arranged for her with the blues in mind."

After Starr left Capitol, she continued to sporadically record albums on various labels. A personal highlight occurred in 1968 when she did an album, *Kay Starr and Count Basie*, with her good friend Count Basie. She recorded her last studio album in 1981. Starr's final album was her only album that featured a live performance. Released in 1997, it was recorded at Freddy's Supper Club in Manhattan in 1986. The album, *Live at Freddy's*, shows her unique ability to entertain a cabaret audience with both her conversation and singing.

In the 1960s, Starr's career took a dramatic twist when she started to concentrate on singing at live performances. She became a top headliner at the Flamingo in Las Vegas, the Riverside in Reno, and Harrah's in Lake Tahoe. Her hotel successes opened the door to numerous big band tours through the years and the lead role in *Annie Get Your Gun* in Houston. Her last overseas performance occurred in 1993 when she appeared in the United Kingdom as part of Pat Boone's April Love tour.

Starr also reunited with Bob Crosby, singing with him at the 1979 Hoagy Carmichael Newport Jazz Festival tribute held at Carnegie Hall. They were also regulars appearing at the big band concert series at Disneyland: "I loved working at Disneyland. I'm a family oriented person, and I got a big kick out of seeing grandfathers dancing with their granddaughters."

In August 1981 Starr joined the popular *Four Girls Four* review that during its history included in addition to Starr, Kay Ballard, Rosemary Clooney, Rose Marie, Helen O'Connell, Martha Raye, and Margaret Whiting. The group performed for several years touring the United States and Canada and appeared on several television shows. Whiting and Starr became close friends as told by Whiting: "Kay originally tried out for *Four Girls Four* after Rose Marie left. Rose Marie was a tough act to follow, but with her charm and talent Kay did a great job and was loved by us all. It's funny. While I lived in Los Angeles I lived close to Kay as well as Nelson Eddy and Peggy Lee. We would all run into each other at the supermarket."

In spite of two hip replacements, Kay Starr is still keeping active. In October 2000 she participated in a benefit for the Tuskegee Airmen in Palm Springs organized by her old friend Herb Jeffries. January 2001 found her following Margaret Whiting at Libby's, a Cabaret in Atlanta. She was appointed to the Big Band Academy of America's Golden Bandstand at their annual reunion held in March 2001 at the Sportsman's Lodge in Studio City, CA. The power in her voice was still evident when she wowed the 600 plus audience singing "Crazy," "You Got to See Momma Every Night," and "Wheel Of Fortune." Her two daughters proudly accompanied her to the event. Soon after her appointment to the Golden Bandstand Starr participated in Tony Bennett's CD *Playin' with My Friends: Bennett Sings the Blues*. She recorded her songs for the album at her old haunt, the Capitol Studios in Hollywood.

Starr has always been in active in community service work. As a member of the Society of Singers, several years ago she donated the proceeds of a two-week engagement at the Hollywood Roosevelt Hotel to the Society. A supporter of Native American causes, she worked with Jim Thorpe's daughter to help establish D-Q University, a tribally controlled community college in Davis, CA. She has twice taught voice training through singing at the Eugene O'Neill Theater Center in Waterford, CT, with Margaret Whiting, who frequently stays with Starr at her Bel Air home when she visits Los Angeles.

What do her peers say about Kay Starr? In his highly respected book *Jazz Singing*, author Will Friedwald devotes an incredible twelve consecutive pages to Starr, speaking with near awe about her gifts as a blues, country, and jazz singer. Jazz critic Nat Hentoff wrote in a 1999 *Wall Street Journal* review of her *Live at Freddy's* album: "Her most transcendent performances are of equal rank with classic sessions by Lee Wiley, Mildred Bailey, and even Billie Holiday." In the late jazz historian Barry Ulanov's voluminous *A History of Jazz in America*, he refers to Starr as "a natural jazz singer, with rhythmic imagination and a larynx that is at least a second cousin to Bessie Smith's." No less than Patsy Cline, Billie Holiday, Helen Humes, Mahalia Jackson, John Lennon, and Lester Young have listed Starr among their favorite singers. In 2001 the Bravo cable television channel featured her comments in their *Popular Song: Soundtrack of the Century* series. As the ultimate in professional recognition, Starr is one of a select few female jazz artists to have her albums available for purchase at the Music Shop store located in the Smithsonian Institute's American History Museum in Washington, D.C..

Now in her seventieth plus year as a professional singer, what are Starr's thoughts as she looks back on her career? Here is her answer: "A few years ago I was having dinner at a Palm Springs restaurant with friends sitting near a table with Frank Sinatra and his group. All of sudden Frank came over, tapped me on the shoulder and whispered in my ear, 'Get smart kid. You and I are just a couple of saloon singers.' I've had a great life, and if I can just be remembered as a down-to-earth, old saloon singer who did her best to be a good entertainer I'd be satisfied."

GARRY STEVENS
FROM CHARLIE SPIVAK TO TEX BENEKE
TO A LIFE WITH THE BIG BANDS

In December 1942, when he received his Greetings from Uncle Sam, Garry Stevens was on the verge of stardom with three top ten hits singing as the male vocalist with the popular Charlie Spivak Orchestra. After World War II he returned to the big bands singing with the Glenn Miller Orchestra led by Tex Beneke for over two years before he moved to upstate New York to carve out a successful business career and entertain locally. In 1998 he came back to public attention when a British music magazine published an article titled "What Ever Happened to Garry Stevens?" Ironically, Stevens never stopped performing and is currently more active than ever. His has truly been a life with the big bands that started with his first paid gig in 1933.

Garry Stevens was born in Los Angeles on October 21, 1916. He inherited his musical talent from his father who was an accomplished yodeler. The Stevens family moved nine times throughout Los Angeles during his youth, eventually settling into a home in the shadow of the University of Southern California (USC) campus. While he was growing up, he would take a short walk to the nearby Los Angeles Coliseum on fall Saturday afternoons where he ushered USC football games.

It was while in elementary school that Stevens unknowingly began a life in music. He talked about his background by telephone from his home in Benecia, CA: "When I was nine years old I thought I'd be interested in joining the school band. They lent me a coronet to get started. Six months later my mother, who thought it would be a good idea to be a musician, bought me an expensive, brand new $100 Conn 22B trumpet. They were a popular band instrument for school children because they were very sturdy and durable."

Stevens matriculated to Manual Arts High School, adjacent to the USC campus, in 1930. It was the summer of 1933, prior to his senior year in high school, when he got his start as a professional musician.

"I went with a group of high school kids to play in a ten-piece band at Wheeler's Hot Springs Resort in Ojai up near Ventura," Stevens said. "We got paid $5 a week plus room and board, and fifty cents a week to clean the pool. It was a sulfur water pool that made it really slimy, so I had to scrub extra hard to earn that fifty cents. Prohibition was still in effect and the two stunt men who ran the Caliente nightclub in the Resort made bootleg booze. They taught us how to drink whiskey from a jug. That's when I decided to become a musician."

After Stevens graduated from Manual Arts in 1934 he enrolled at Los Angeles City College (LACC) that at the time was highly respected for its outstanding music department. It was at LACC that he started consorting with Leroy Holmes, with whom he had worked in the past on casual one-night dates around Los Angeles. Holmes would go on to a distinguished career as an arranger for Vincent Lopez and Harry James before the war, and arranger and conductor for MGM and United Artists after the war. He won one of his four Academy Awards for his score of the song "The High and the Mighty" from the film of the same name that was on the charts for fourteen weeks in 1954.

In the fall of 1935 Stevens unexpectedly became a fulltime musician: "In October I went with Leroy Holmes to play for a month at the Westward Ho Hotel in Phoenix. By the time I got back to LA I had fallen so far behind in my studies I decided to leave school and try to establish a career as a musician."

As frequently happens in the game of life, being in the right place at the right time can mysteriously determine one's fate. In early 1936 Stevens was playing trumpet in a band at Omar's Dome near Pershing Square in downtown Los Angeles when Paul Kain, a saxophone player who had a popular seven-piece local band, heard him. He accepted an offer by Kain to join his group, setting in motion a series of events that would determine the course of both his career in music and personal life.

Kain's band soon left to play in Salt Lake City then went on to spend the summer season performing at the Saint Catherine Hotel on Catalina Island. That fall Kain headed east to spend eight months in Albany, New York's State Capitol. It was there that Stevens met his first wife with whom he raised a family of three children.

Cupid was quite active while Kain was playing in Albany. In addition to Stevens, Kain himself, bass player Ted Alexander, and drummer Sammy Ferro met and eventually married their wives during the band's eight-month stay.

After the Albany engagement, Kain's band stayed on the East Coast for the next year and a half playing venues such as Cape Cod and Saratoga Springs in the summer, New York City hotels in the winter, and occasional dates at the Statler Hotel in Detroit. It was while appearing at the Brook nightclub in Saratoga Springs that Stevens exhibited Lou Gehrig-like stamina.

"The Brook was directly across the street from the Piping Rock night club where big names like Fanny Brice, Joe E. Lewis, and Sophie Tucker always performed," Stevens explained. "We played seven days a week from 10:00 p.m. to 7:00 a.m., including a floor show that started at 5:00 am. Our stay at the Brook lasted for the month long racing season, nine hours a day, without one day off. It was exhausting. I gave Kain my notice to quit every night."

Paul Kain settled to permanently play in the Washington, D.C., area in late 1938. Stevens moved to Washington to work with Kain and take a job as a staff trumpet player with radio station WTOP where he also started singing a few songs on the air. The station's program manager, Lloyd Dennis, liked what he heard and suggested to Stevens that he try concentrating on becoming a vocalist to advance his career. Stevens sang on a variety of the station's shows and was very well received. Dennis's assessment was indeed correct. A new career in music was born for Garry Stevens.

After a four-year stint with Kain, in the summer of 1940 Stevens decided to go on the road with Don Bestor, one of the popular veteran bands from the 1920s that, starting in 1934, played on Jack Benny's radio program. However, Stevens did not stay with Bestor very long.

"Don Bestor had a nice hotel-type band and was a good friend of Jack Benny," commented Stevens. "But we traveled in our own cars. The problem was that our jobs were unbelievably far apart. You would be in St. Louis today and New York tomorrow. I decided that I shouldn't be driving the wheels off my car so when the summer was over I went back to WTOP as a vocalist."

While working around Washington, Stevens got to know Harry Klee, the lead alto player for Bill Downer's popular local band. Shortly after Downer sold his entire band to sweet trumpet stylist Charlie Spivak in 1940, Klee recommended to Spivak that he hire Stevens as his vocalist. The sale worked out not only to Stevens's benefit, but Downer's also. He would go onto a successful career as a music publisher and executive with Decca Records and MCA Music, passing away in Los Angeles in 2000 at eighty-six.

In a 1972 interview on Chuck Cecil's *Swingin' Years* radio show Spivak talked about how he got his start as a bandleader: "Glenn Miller was responsible for the whole thing. He was my guardian angel. He put up all the money for me so I could get started and put me in the Glen Island Casino in New Rochelle, NY. That was my starting out place. I was fortunate to go in there and with Glenn's help make some kind of name for myself."

Stevens joined the Spivak organization in February 1941 at the fabled Glen Island Casino: "When I joined Charlie we did as many as twenty-seven broadcasts a week from Glen Island. It was called the cradle of the name bands and we had great exposure on NBC's blue and red networks, CBS, Mutual, and New York's WNEW. It was a thrill to start out there."

During Stevens's nearly two year stay with Spivak, the band was staffed with outstanding musicians that included drummer Dave Tough, trumpeter Les Elgart, and alto saxophonist Willie Smith. There was also formally trained pianist Dave Mann who earned a degree in music from the Curtis Institute in Philadelphia and wrote the Vaughn Monroe hit "There I've Said It Again," and Glenn Miller's entire trombone section headed by Paul Tanner who came over to Spivak when Miller disbanded in late 1942 to join the Army at a the rank of captain. Sonny Burke was the chief arranger assisted by an up-and-coming trombone player named Nelson Riddle who at the time was studying arranging under Bill Finegan.

Shortly after Stevens came aboard, the Stardusters joined the band as its vocal quartet. Their lead singer was June Hutton, all-girl bandleader Ina Ray Hutton's younger sister. In his classic book *The Big Bands*, the late big band historian George T. Simon profusely praised Stevens, Hutton, and the Stardusters. The quality of the musicianship in the sweet style Spivak band left nothing to be desired.

Stevens's first hit with Spivak came in late 1941 when "This Is No Laughing Matter" made it all the way up to number eight on the charts. Then in September of 1942 came one of the biggest selling two-sided hits of the Big Band Era. On the A-side was "My Devotion" that was on the charts for twelve weeks hitting the number the two spot two weeks in a row. It was the fifteenth-most popular hit of 1942 and to this day is remembered as a World War II sentimental classic. The B-side was "I Left My Heart at the Stage Door Canteen" from the Broadway musical *This is the Army*. It too hit the top ten, rising to number eight. Garry Stevens was now an established big band star ranking as the fourth-most-popular male vocalist in the country on the 1942 *Billboard* poll. He closely followed Frank Sinatra, Dick Haymes, and Bob Eberly in the voting.

In late 1942 Stevens had his last hit with the Charlie Spivak Orchestra before he joined the service. It was "White Christmas," and it rose to number twelve on the charts. Although Bing Crosby's version sold the most records, Stevens's was the most popular on jukebox selections and would sell over a million copies with repeat Holiday sales over the years. Freddy Martin also had a recording with the vocal by Clyde Rogers, but it was on the charts for only one week. Nelson Riddle was paid the princely sum of $15 to arrange "White Christmas," Stevens $10 to record it.

Roc Hillman was a guitar player for Jimmy Dorsey and Kay Kyser, and a close friend of Charlie Spivak. Now well in his nineties he is retired in Woodland Hills, CA, and recalls how he wrote "My Devotion": "While I was with Jimmy Dorsey I was a good friend with Johnny Napton, one of his trumpet players. We were warming up one evening in the dressing room at a theater in Detroit before we went on. We started playing a few licks and came up with the melody. A few months later I added the lyrics and called it "My Devotion." Right after I joined Kyser I must have taken it to a dozen publishers in New York without any success. Then one night while I was on the bandstand playing with Kay at a hotel in New York I received a telegram from Santly-Joy, one of the big publishers at the time, saying they liked my song. All the top bands started to record it, but I must say that I couldn't be happier than with Garry Stevens's interpretation."

It was a bitter cold day in Fall River, MA, where the Spivak band was playing in December 1942 when Stevens received his draft notice in the mail. The notice had seven changes of addresses marked on it over a six weeks period thanks to Stevens constantly moving to new locations with Spivak. The next day, with two records in the top ten, he took the train to New York to enlist in the Army Air Corps at the Grand Central Palace building and embark on a new phase of his professional career.

What was Gary Stevens's impact on the Spivak band? In an interview on Skitch Henderson's *The Music Makers* radio show six weeks before he died from cancer on March 1, 1982, Spivak discussed Stevens's contributions: "The kids in those days looked at the vocalists as idols. Garry was a very collegiate type; he looked like a kid just out of college. The girls went out of their minds when they saw him. He was a good-looking young man and sang very well. He sold a lot of records for us."

Stevens reported for active duty in March of 1943 to the Fourth Air Force Band headquartered at Lemoore Air Station near Fresno, CA. Lemoore was a B-24 training command that covered California, Oregon, Washington, Nevada, and Idaho. The band appeared at numerous Air Force bases throughout those states, playing as many as ninety engagements a month including USO shows six to seven nights a week at Officer's Clubs, Non Commissioned Officer's Clubs, base parades, and the famous Hollywood Canteen where Stevens once shared the stage with Ezra Stone of "Henry Aldrich" radio show fame. The band also made several recordings for the Office of War Information Band Tours. His military involvement not only gave Stevens an opportunity to sing, it also allowed him to return to playing trumpet for the first time since his Washington D.C. radio days.

When Stevens separated from the service in March of 1946 he was offered a transfer in grade to join the Air Force Band in Washington D.C., then a very talented and respected organization. With little deliberation, he opted for a return to civilian life with the hope of recapturing the popularity he enjoyed during his Spivak days. He was discharged at Fort Lewis in Tacoma, WA, and immediately returned home to Los Angeles.

Soon after arriving in Los Angeles, Stevens found work with Freddie Slack and primarily Garwood Van, who was headquartered in the City of Angels. In his book *The Big Band Almanac*, Leo Walker referred to Van as an excellent hotel-style band that played all the top hotels throughout the country. Stevens appeared with Van at prestigious venues such as Ciro's on the Sunset strip and the popular Arrowhead Springs Hotel nestled in the San Bernardino Mountains.

While Stevens was reestablishing his career as a vocalist in Los Angeles, Tex Beneke was starting his career as a bandleader on the East Coast. In late 1945, at the request of Helen Miller, Glenn Miller's widow, Beneke assumed leadership of the postwar Glenn Miller Orchestra. The band debuted under his direction in New York at the Capitol Theater on January 17, 1946. Come September, Artie Malvin and the Crew Chiefs decided to leave Beneke to individually strike out on their own. In need of a singer, Beneke extended an offer to Stevens to join the Glenn Miller Orchestra he was now leading

Stevens accepted Beneke's offer and immediately found himself back in the recording studio. During his two-and-a-half year stay with Beneke he would record twenty-eight songs. His biggest hit with Beneke was the "Anniversary Song" that was on the hit parade for eleven consecutive weeks in 1947, reaching the number three position.

In December 1947 Stevens participated in a historic big band event when the Beneke band played a Hollywood Palladium engagement. The Hollywood Palladium was a glamorous venue that at the time was frequented by big name movie stars such as Rita Hayworth and Lana Turner. Betty Grable could usually be seen in the audience when her husband Harry James was a headliner.

During that engagement, Beneke set a new one-night Hollywood Palladium attendance record of 6,750. The Armed Forces Radio Service transcribed several of the band's Hollywood Palladium radio broadcasts during their December 1947 date for their *One-Night Stand* show. The band's appearance on *One-Night Stand* was so successful that it was asked to perform on the Air Force's *On the Beam* radio recruiting show in early 1948. It also led to additional appearances on *One-Night Stand* over the next several years with Peggy Lee, Stevens's favorite female vocalist.

Once again Garry Stevens was associated with a band in which romance was in the air. The Mello-Larks vocal group joined Beneke at the same time Stevens did. One of the Mello-Larks was Ginny O'Connor, who grew up in Los Angeles and would go on to eventually serve as the founding president of the Society of Singers, an organization structured to help singers who have fallen on hard times. She immediately hit it off with the band's young piano player, Henry Mancini, who was arranging under the direction of the band's chief arranger, Norman Layden. They married in 1947.

Paul Tanner played in Beneke's trombone section. He commented on his experience of working with Stevens in the band: "Garry Stevens was one of the nicest guys I ever worked with. He was a great singer, a definite asset to the band. Everyone liked him, including Tex who always had good things to say about him in interviews with the press."

Although Stevens thoroughly enjoyed his stay with Beneke, the travel and time away from home was becoming a burden. He was sometimes on the road with the band for as long as three straight months without a night off. In April of 1948 he decided to leave Beneke and settle down to start a family. Little did he imagine that he was about to also start a new career in both commercial and entertainment business ventures in Albany.

"Right after I left Tex, my wife and I took a trip to Albany to visit her family with no definite plans for work in mind," Stevens said. "While I was getting a haircut I ran into Bob Snyder, a local disc jockey on WROW who is now retired in Florida. He suggested I contact WROW that had an opening, to audition for a job. I tried out an wound up staying there as a disc jockey for fifteen months."

With his radio popularity in full swing, Stevens was contacted by television station WRGB in nearby Schenectady in the summer of 1950. WRGB, founded and owned by General Electric, was the first television station in the United States and the only station in the Albany area. That call led to a nine-year association for Stevens with WRGB: "We did a half-hour show five nights a week. I was the head honcho. I was the leader of a seven-piece band, trumpet player, vocalist, emcee, interviewer, and associate producer. Without realizing it at the time, it turned out that back in 1950 we were really the forerunner of the Mike Douglas-Merv Griffin type show before they even thought of going on the air. Any time a famous personality of name value came through we got them on the show for an interview. We had Helen Forrest, Stan Kenton, Woody Herman, Spike Jones, and Billy Butterfield. Actors Ed Begley, Edward Everett Horton, and Metropolitan Opera star Mimi Benzel were on. Bob Eberly stopped by a lot. Celeste Holm was a regular when she did summer theater."

After his television show went off the air in 1959, Stevens took an executive position in the moving industry. In 1964, armed with the experience and connections he gained in the moving business, he switched over to selling real estate. Stevens opened his own Albany real estate firm, Garry Stevens Realty, in 1975, retiring from business in 1995.

While he was engaged in commerce, Stevens managed to stay active in the Albany music milieu: "I did a lot of local work with my own seven-piece band. Then in 1977 Al Cavalieri came into my real estate office and asked if I'd like to sing with his big band. It was a good fifteen-piece band, and I sang with him locally until we left Albany to move to California in 1998. I actually took over the band when Al passed away in 1993."

Stevens and Judy, his second wife of over twenty-five years, settled in Benecia, a small town rich in California history located thirty-five miles east of San Francisco on the East Bay shoreline:"I always wanted to come back to California for the climate. We took a look at San Diego and even put a deposit on an apartment in La Mesa. But I wasn't use to the heavy traffic and was overwhelmed by the freeways. Then we flew up to San Francisco and found Benecia. The next day we went to a real estate office and bought a house."

"Since sailing is one of our prime recreational activities, one of the major considerations that sold us on Benecia was that we were able to keep our twenty-seven foot sailboat *Bandsinger* at the Benecia Marina that's only one mile from our home. Henry Mancini used to describe me as a band singer, hence the boat's name."

Benecia has provided Stevens a whole new world of musical opportunities. Thanks to the local Rotary Club, he was introduced to Virl Swan, past conductor of the Vallejo symphony orchestra, and his seventeen-piece big band. Stevens sings with Swan's band monthly at the local Elk's Club. However, his association with the Benecia High School jazz ensemble is his pride and joy.

"Right after we moved I went over to Benecia High School and introduced myself to Roxanna Macheel, the jazz band director," Stevens commented. "She said she'd love to have me sing and work with the band. When I started, the kids didn't relate to the 40s at all. Now they're very accomplished and love to play classic big band music. I've appeared with them over a dozen times and have taught five classes on jazz. A highlight was in March 2005 when I sang with them at the California Music Educators annual convention in Pasadena. We've played for seniors, at private parties, and school concerts.

"Although I haven't worked with the school's marching band, they made me an honorary member and gave me one of the jackets they wore when they played in the Rose Parade in Pasadena on News Years day. It's been a great experience, I truly enjoy working with the students, and a few of them show real promise. We are even planning to make a CD."

Stevens's involvement with Benecia High School also extends to the world of technology. He organizes classes for student volunteers to teach computer usage to seniors at the Rancho Benecia Mobile Home Park where he lives and is vice president of the 213-member homeowners association.

Long overdue recognition is finally coming Garry Stevens's way. His scrapbook is in the Glenn Miller archives at the University of Colorado and his own CD, *Then and Now*, that covers his music from 1942 to 2004, is out. He performed at the 2000 Big Band Academy of America's annual Reunion at the Sportsmen's Lodge in Studio City, CA, and was inducted into their Golden Bandstand in 2003. Stevens also made six appearances at the internationally famous annual Glenn Miller Festival in Clarinda, IA, the town in which Miller was born in 1904, and sang at a June 2001 Miller Festival in Fort Morgan, CO, the town in which Miller graduated from high school in 1921. His autobiography, *Band Singer*, that covers his colorful career was published in 2006. Combine all that with the satisfaction he derives mentoring the Benecia High School jazz ensemble and singing with Virl Swan, let there be no doubt that Garry Stevens is enjoying a golden retirement after over seventy years in big band music.

MARTHA TILTON
AND THE ANGEL SANG

In a 1986 Public Television documentary on Benny Goodman, Rosemary Clooney paid tribute to three great female vocalists who gained their initial fame singing with Goodman's band during the Big Band Era. They were, in order of appearance on the swing scene, Helen Ward, Martha Tilton, and Peggy Lee. Of this elite group, the most prolific was pert and buoyant 'Liltin' Martha Tilton, who made fifty-eight recordings with Goodman, including the classic "And the Angels Sing." With her innately wholesome charm and pleasing vocal style she played an important part in the band's huge success in the late 1930s. Here is her story.

Martha Tilton was born into a musically talented family in Corpus Christi, TX, on November 14, 1915. Her mother played piano and her father was gifted with a magnificent singing voice. Tilton's younger sister Liz went on to a brief but successful career as a big band vocalist singing with Ken Baker, Bob Crosby, Jan Garber, and Ray Noble. She also entertained troops during the war before retiring to raise a family. The sisters remained close, frequently vacationing together in Palm Springs until Liz passed away on March 14, 2003.

When she was three months old Tilton's parents relocated to Edna, KS, a small farming community near the junction of the Oklahoma and Missouri borders. Her father was a banker, her mother a housewife. The family's final move came in 1922 when they relocated to Laurel Avenue in Los Angeles's Fairfax District. Laurel Avenue had just been developed and was considered out in the country, separated from Beverly Hills by wheat fields and oil wells.

It was while attending newly built Fairfax High School that Tilton was discovered. Here is her account of the serendipitous occurrence told during a conversation at her Brentwood, CA, home: "I was at my girlfriend's house. Her older sister had a boyfriend who was working his way through the University of Southern California (USC) playing trumpet in a little band he ran. He was over that day and we were playing the piano and singing. He told me that I have a good voice and asked me to come down and sing on his radio show. The next day my girlfriends and I took the bus to downtown Los Angeles to radio station KELW which was located in the basement of the old Federal Outfitting Company on Broadway. I sang a few songs on the show and was thrilled to death just to be on the radio even though I wasn't paid. That's how I got my start."

After a few months on KELW an agent heard Tilton and landed her a job on a major Los Angeles radio station located on the prestigious Wilshire Boulevard Miracle Mile. The show she appeared on was sponsored by the Packard automobile company and featured trumpeter Bobby Sherwood's family band. The Fairfax High student finally received her first paycheck.

Several months later the same agent secured an audition for Tilton at the storied Cocoanut Grove in the Ambassador Hotel with Sid Lippman, who followed Phil Harris as the Grove's house band. She impressed Lippman and landed her first professional singing job before a live audience at Los Angeles's most prominent nightclub. Four weeks later she accepted an offer from Hal Grayson.

"Hal Grayson heard me sing at the Cocoanut Grove," Tilton said. "He had a band while he was at USC and kept on with it after he graduated. It was very popular on the West Coast. That was my first real experience as a big band singer. We played all up and down the coast and spent a lot of time in San Francisco. I recall that we were a particularly big hit at the Club Victor in Seattle that was owned by the Lieutenant Governor of Washington. Bing Crosby's brother, Larry, and his wife used to drive all the way from Spokane to see us play. We became lifelong friends."

After close to three years with Grayson, Tilton joined the Three Hits and a Miss, a vocal quartet formed by Bill Sekler, Grayson's guitarist who also had a good voice, and free-lance vocalist Vincent Degan. The group was unique for its day as it was one of the first to sing four-part harmony. It was extremely popular and did a lot of radio work for the year or so they were together. Then came 1937, Martha Tilton's breakthrough year.

Tilton's career hit stride that year. Her reputation as a big band singer grew when she sang with Jimmy Dorsey for a few months early in the year at Sebastian's Cotton Club in Culver City. Dorsey was in Hollywood playing on Bing Crosby's radio show that was sponsored by Lady Esther, a women's cosmetic. She made her first movie appearance with the Three Hits and a Miss in *Topper* that starred Cary Grant and Constance Bennett. Most important, Benny Goodman discovered her.

Struck with a severe strep throat, Helen Ward decided to retire as Goodman's vocalist in late 1936 to marry wealthy jazz enthusiast Albert Marx. Goodman unsuccessfully tried four female vocalists to replace her. They were Francis Hunt, Peg LaCentra, Margaret McCrae, and Betty Van. The King of Swing even did a recording session with Ella Fitzgerald on loan from Chick Webb. By August 1937 Goodman was still in the market for a female vocalist. Opportunity presented itself and in stepped Martha Tilton.

"Jeff Alexander had a swing chorus that did a couple of numbers on Benny's *Camel Caravan* radio show while he was in town making *Hollywood Hotel* for Warner Brothers," Tilton explained. "The Three Hits and a Miss were part of the chorus along with Jo Stafford. Jeff usually gave me a four-bar solo on each song. Benny's manager, Willard Alexander, was at one of the shows and heard me sing. He recommended me for an audition on the spot."

Tilton continued: "I stayed after the show and sang several songs with Teddy Wilson playing the piano. While I was in the middle of singing my last song Benny got up and walked out the door without saying a word. I thought that he didn't like what he heard and I drove home in tears. I was telling my mother what happened when Willard called and asked where I went. He said, 'Benny had to go to an important meeting at the studio and told me he liked you and that I should hire you. Can you leave to go east as soon as Benny finishes *Hollywood Hotel*?' I said, 'You Bet!', and didn't get home again for two years."

So started a storied two-year career with Goodman that included top billing as his female vocalist at live performances, thirteen top ten recording hits, two of which reached number one, and national exposure as a regular feature on the highly rated weekly *Camel Caravan* show. The band was at its peak of popularity and Martha Tilton was now a household name.

Her most famous record and arguably Goodman's biggest hit ever was "And the Angels Sing." It was originally a Hebrew folk song bought to Goodman by his brilliant trumpeter, Ziggy Elman. Tilton reminisced about the recording session during a 1983 interview on Chuck Cecil's popular *Swingin' Years* radio show: "Benny asked Johnny Mercer to write the lyrics for the song. When we got to the studio in New York, probably in January of 1939, I remember that it was bitter cold and freezing outside. Surprisingly, Johnny hadn't finished the lyrics. He'd write a line and we'd do a take. Then he changed something and we'd do another take. He literally wrote the lyrics to the song while we recorded it."

A highlight of Tilton's career with Goodman was her appearance with the band at its historic January 16, 1938, concert at Carnegie Hall. It was the first concert ever by a jazz band at the hallowed hall of classical music. Tilton wore a tulle pink and white gown she bought at Lord & Taylor for the much-anticipated and controversial occasion. Her renditions of *Loch Lomond* and *Bei Mir Bist Du Schoen* brought down the house and helped ensure the concert's smashing success.

Martha Tilton has fond memories of her days with Goodman: "Benny was always good to me personally and gave me tremendous solo exposure. But I must admit there were a few occasions when I was on the receiving end of his famous Ray. It was a friendly band. We were all very young, got along well, and everyone was a tremendous musician. Jess Stacy, along with Benny, was one of the older guys in the band. He was a great help to me in learning my songs, had a talented sense of humor, and kept the band loose. I saw him often until he passed away a few years ago."

In the spring of 1939 Benny Goodman's band experienced a tremendous turnover in personnel. After nearly two years with virtually no time off, an exhausted Martha Tilton felt the time was right to take a break and leave Goodman to return home to strike out on her own. Goodman immediately replaced her with Louise Tobin, who was then married to Harry James.

Little did Tilton know that her respite would not last long. As soon as she arrived in Los Angeles she signed a contract with NBC as a staff vocalist, setting in motion a high profile career in radio. In addition to numerous guest appearances on individual shows, she was a regular on five shows during the 1940s. They included *The Campana Serenade*, *The Dick Haymes Show*, *Fibber McGee and Molly*, *The Philco Radio Hall of Fame*, and the ever-popular *Your Hit Parade*. She relocated to New York for a few years mid-decade to sing with Paul Whiteman's band on the *The Philco Radio Hall of Fame*. It was the last time she would move from Los Angeles.

 To compliment her radio career during the 40s, Tilton made masses of transcriptions when ASCAP went on strike in 1942. These recordings for radio, made with the backing of the Don Allen Orchestra, which was comprised of Hollywood's top studio musicians, displayed the wide breadth of her vocal skill ranging from ballads to blues to novelties.

Tilton was also active in entertaining troops during the war. She toured twice with Jack Benny, for three months in the South Pacific in 1943 and for three months in Europe in 1944. Thanks to touring together they became good friends. She also launched a new recording career.

Johnny Mercer founded Capitol Records in Hollywood in 1942. Based on his longtime association with Tilton, one of his first moves was to sign her to an exclusive recording contract as their first female solo vocalist: "Johnny came over to our family home on Highland Avenue. He said he, Buddy DeSylva, and Glenn Wallichs were forming a new record label and would like me to go with them. I told John I'd be thrilled to death. Jo Stafford, Ella Mae Morse, Andy Russell and I were with him from the start. We had a lot of fun working together"

Her first song with the new label was the romantic "I'll Remember April," her all-time favorite recording. Tilton had nine hits with Capitol, the biggest of which was the wartime classic "I'll Walk Alone." It was on the charts for twenty-four consecutive weeks in 1944.

During the 1940s, Tilton also appeared in six movies, starring in two, *Swing Hostess* and *Crime Incorporated*. She also did considerable film overdubbing, most notably for Barbara Stanwyck in *Ball of Fire* that also featured Gene Krupa. It was indeed a busy decade for Martha Tilton.

Tilton continued doing radio work during the 1950s spending eight years on the daily Los Angeles *Curt Massey Show* that uniquely appeared simultaneously on ABC, CBS, and NBC. The show moved over to television in the 60s for another eight-year run. In 1955 she appeared in the *Benny Goodman Story* reprising her Carnegie Hall appearance dressed in the same gown she wore seventeen years earlier. She also sang with Goodman at the 1958 Newport Jazz Festival. With her friendship with Jack Benny still strong, she made frequent guest appearances on his radio show throughout the 50s and 60s.

In 1975 Tilton returned to public attention appearing in the made-for-TV film *Queen of the Stardust Ballroom* singing with Orrin Tucker's band. Three years later she sang "Loch Lomond" yet again in Carneige Hall at the 40th anniversary of the 1938 concert. She talked about her experience on the Cecil show: "It was very nostalgic and a lot of fun to do. When Benny introduced me and I came out I got a standing ovation, which was a big thrill to me. I never expected it. I couldn't start singing for almost five minutes. I looked at Benny and Benny looked at me. The clapping just kept going on."

Since the 1978 Carnegie Hall concert, Tilton devoted considerable time to charity work, appeared in several PBS big band specials, and participated in big band tours overseas and in the United States. Her last concert tour was in Australia and the U.S. in 1990 with singer John Gary and bandleader Horace Heidt Jr. She was enshrined in the Big Band Academy of America's Golden Bandstand along with Helen Forrest and Peggy Lee at the Academy's annual reunion in Studio City, CA, on March 3, 1997.

Martha Tilton's music has stood the test of time; her songs are just as appealing to today's public as they were during the Big Band Era. While watching the credits for the popular film *The Life and Times of Hank Greenberg* about the hall of fame baseball slugger at a theater in Los Angeles in 2000, a young couple was overheard asking each other "What is that terrific song on the sound track?" It was Tilton's recording of *Bei Mir Bist Du Schoen* sung with Benny Goodman.

What was Martha Tilton up to in her golden years until she passed away on December 8, 2006? As she told it: "I married James Brooks in 1952. He was a World War II ace and engineering test pilot, and retired as an executive director of North American Aviation. We have had a wonderful marriage for over fifty years and now I'm relaxing and enjoying my five grandchildren. As for my career, I am truly thankful for being fortunate enough to love my work all those years and make a contribution to the big bands. The many friendships I made singing with Benny Goodman are a special memory."

BEA WAIN
A LIFE IN MUSIC

Nineteen thirty-eight was a year of significant historical impact. In world affairs, the stage was set for World War II with Hitler invading Austria and duping British Prime Minister Neville Chamberlain into surrendering the Sudetenland to falsely achieve "peace in our time." In sports, Joe Louis destroyed Max Schmelling in one round in their much-anticipated heavyweight boxing championship rematch. In the movies, Bob Hope made his film debut in *Big Broadcast of 1938* singing "Thanks for the Memories" with Shirley Ross. In radio, Orson Wells shocked the nation with his *War of the Worlds* broadcast. And in music, it was in 1938, with the Big Band Era in full force, that Bea Wain exploded to nationwide fame singing a string of top ten hits with Larry Clinton's orchestra.

Musical attention came to Beatrice Wain at a very early age. Born in The Bronx in 1917, she became an immediate neighborhood celebrity when she actually carried a tune and sang in her baby carriage. By six, she was a regular on *The Children's Hour* radio show earning $2 a week, and started singing club dates at Masonic Lodges and private affairs.

Although Wain's family moved to Manhattan when she completed grammar school, she commuted daily back to the Bronx to attend Theodore Roosevelt High School on Fordham Road. It was during her tenure at Theodore Roosevelt that the irony of life manifested itself to the fullest. Try as she might, Wain could not make the school glee club nor could famed classically trained jazz pianist Johnny Guarnieri, who gained distinction playing the harpsichord in Artie Shaw's Gramercy Five and piano in Benny Goodman's band, make the school orchestra.

Wain went to Theodore Roosevelt High for a specific reason. It was her intent to take their then well known commercial course in office management as an occupational back up if needed. She had no intention of going on to college. Her goal was a career as a singer, and to better prepare her to achieve that goal she also took piano lessons to learn how to read music.

Commenting on her involvement with the piano at her home in Beverly Hills, Wain said: "I studied piano not to become a great pianist, but to learn how to read music so I could teach myself a song. Many singers don't know how to read music, they do it all by ear. Kate Smith, whom I admired very much, was a good example. She was a remarkable singer but could not read a note of music."

After graduation from high school in 1934, Wain started singing on radio with several vocal groups and Gene Kardos's Orchestra at Delmonico's, a Manhattan nightclub. She was part of the Kay Thompson Chorus on *The Chesterfield Show* that featured Andre Kostelanetz, the Fred Waring Chorus on *The Fred Waring Show*, and the Kate Smith Chorus on *The Kate Smith Hour*. By now her reputation around New York as a quality, dependable vocalist was firmly established.

As told by Wain, the Kate Smith Chorus provides an interesting story: "Standing next to me in the Chorus was a soprano by the name of Dorothy Kirsten. She sang high, and I sang low. It was a great experience. All the choristers could read music and each had a wonderful voice. They were also sharp, quick studies because we didn't have much time to rehearse."

It was on both *The Fred Waring Show* and *The Kate Smith Hour* that Wain met star radio announcer Andre Baruch, who at the time shared an apartment in Manhattan with future New York Yankee radio announcer Mel Allen and Ralph Edwards, and who would go on to create and host the famed *This Is Your Life* television show. No account of her career would be complete without mention of Baruch, one of the most famous announcers in radio history, and a truly remarkable individual.

Born in Paris in 1908, Baruch moved with his parents to Brooklyn in 1921 and studied painting at Columbia University and the Pratt Institute. The consummate renaissance man, he was an accomplished pianist, artist, and sculptor. A fine athlete, Baruch achieved a six-handicap level in golf and competed in swimming and track at Columbia.

The story of Baruch's entry into the world of broadcasting gives hope to those who believe in the old adage that a major key to success is being in the right place at the right time. In the early 1930s, he heard that there was an audition for a staff pianist at CBS. Baruch immediately took the subway from Brooklyn to the CBS studios on Madison Avenue in Manhattan for an audition.

When he arrived at the studio there were two lines, one long and one short. He quickly took the short line and was soon asked to read a difficult script containing the names of famous foreign musical composers and conductors. Baruch breezed through the tryout error free because he learned to speak five languages growing up in Paris.

Two days later he received a call from CBS telling him he got the job. He asked if he should bring his music with him. They told him it was not necessary since he won a position as a staff announcer. It turned out that the short line was for the announcing competition, the long line for the piano competition.

As described by Wain, on October 11, 1937, the suave Baruch and Wain had their first date at Benny Goodman's opening at the Hotel Pennsylvania's Madhattan Room: "At that time there were always repeat radio shows, the first for the East Coast, and the second for the West Coast, with a three-hour break in between. The entire Kate Smith show was invited to attend Benny's opening during our break. Andre asked me to go and I was delighted because I had had eyes for him for sometime. Henny Youngman was the emcee that night and introduced us as Andre Baruch and his lovely wife Bea Wain. Andre was embarrassed and quite upset with Henny. It all worked out well. We became close fiends with Henny and used to joke with him about that night at the Madhattan Room."

While Wain was starting to date Andre Baruch, a development was taking place in the world of the big bands that would serve to shape the direction of her career in music. Larry Clinton was a superb arranger and composer with an outstanding reputation in the big band business. He gained that reputation writing for Isham Jones, Tommy Dorsey, and the Casa Loma Orchestra. In late 1937 he decided to start his own band with encouragement from RCA Victor recording chief Eli Oberstein and financial backing from Dorsey. He needed a female vocalist, and focused on Bea Wain as his choice.

"One Thursday evening broadcast, I had a rare four-bar solo on the Kate Smith Chorus," Wain said. "After the show I got a phone call from a man named Larry Clinton. He said he was starting an orchestra and next Tuesday he was scheduled to make his first record for RCA and would like me to be his vocalist. I couldn't believe our conversation. He had never seen me and only heard my short solo on the Kate Smith show. He was going just on that and my reputation. After much deliberation, I agreed and on Tuesday sang "True Confession" that became a top ten hit. That was how I started with Larry Clinton."

May of 1938 was quite a month for Wain. On the first, she married Baruch and on the sixteenth Clinton opened for the summer season at the Glen Island Casino in New Rochelle, NY, playing from 7:00 p.m. to 2:00 a.m., seven nights a week. With the prime air time provided the venue, Clinton became a hot, hit band specializing in adapting the classics to swing. As for Wain, she had three number one hits in 1938, including the year's second biggest hit, "My Reverie," an adaptation of a Debussy piano solo. She was paid $30 each. Bea Wain was now a household name.

After the Glen Island Casino engagement, Clinton took to the road on a demanding and difficult travel schedule, playing the East Coast college and theater circuit. Wain's most consistently requested song at college functions was her 1938 top ten hit "Martha," based on an aria from Friedrich von Flotow's 1847 German opera *Martha*. However, the demands of the road, along with her absence from Baruch and a constant stream of offers from agents, drove her to strike out on her own in mid-1939, when her recording with Clinton of the Mitchell Parish-Peter DeRose collaboration "Deep Purple" reached number one on the charts for nine consecutive weeks. It was the year's biggest hit.

Voted the top female band vocalist in the 1939 *Billboard* college poll, Wain had just started her solo act when she was informed by her manager while playing at the Hippodrome Theater in Baltimore that she had an offer to star on the renowned *Your Hit Parade* radio show. She eagerly accepted the opportunity to move back to New York, remaining with the program until 1944 and recording commercially with RCA Victor through 1941.

Your Hit Parade provided Wain the opportunity to work with a very young Frank Sinatra. Said Wain: "We did the show before a live audience in what is now the Letterman Theater. Frank was always very kind and protective toward me. The one thing I really remember was that he was always surrounded by an entourage, even then."

Wain also had input as to Sinatra's career direction: "I was playing a theater in Passaic, NJ, when Frank stopped by to ask me if I thought he should leave Tommy Dorsey and go out on his own because his wife Nancy just had their first baby. He felt a responsibility to his family to improve his earning power. I told him it had worked out well for me and he should seriously consider it. He must have remembered our conversation, because whenever we ran into each other through the years he would go out of his way to come over and say hello. I have only fond memories of Frank Sinatra."

During the early 1940s, Wain was actually appearing on two *Hit Parade* radio shows. It is a little known fact that while she was a featured vocalist on *Your Hit Parade*, she was also starring on its companion show, *The All Time Hit Parade*, that featured classic American songs from all eras. *Your Hit Parade* aired on Saturday nights, *The All Time Hit Parade*, with backing from Mark Warnow's fifty-piece orchestra, on Wednesdays from Carnegie Hall. The program was billed as "The best tunes of all come from Carnegie Hall." It was the epitome of status and prestige at that time for a radio show to broadcast from Carnegie Hall.

In 1944 Wain's contract with *Your Hit Parade* was up. After one of her last shows at the CBS Playhouse Theater she was approached by Glenn Miller who asked her to join his Army Air Force Band. She declined his offer, and spent the remaining war years—while Baruch was participating in the invasion of North Africa and helping found the Armed Forces Radio Service— entertaining troops at military bases and hospitals and recording V-Discs. She still thinks of that time as one of her most rewarding experiences.

After the war, Baruch and Wain developed their own radio show as much out of serendipity as by design. Wain explains how their good fortune came about: "In 1946, as a pure lark, we answered an ad in Variety by WMCA in Manhattan for a disc jockey." They contacted us and we came up with *The Mr. and Mrs. Music Show*. We were on the air daily with morning and afternoon segments playing records. I also got to sing live and had a superb pianist who frequently worked with Ella Fitzgerald, Ellis Larkins, as an accompanist. After three years we moved over to WABC for two more years doing the same show. I was so fortunate musically. There my accompanist was Mel Powell."

In the early 1950s, the Baruchs moved to Westchester County with Wain comfortably settling into semi-retirement raising her two children, Wayne and Bonnie. By this time Baruch was still at the top in radio, and in the mid 50s he added to his broadcasting and US Steel spokesperson responsibilities by becoming an announcer for his beloved Brooklyn Dodgers, working with the legendary Vince Scully.

Commenting on her Dodger days, Wain said: "I became a great baseball fan, attended all the games at Ebbets Field, and even went to spring training with Andre. Tommy Lasorda and I used to sing on the bus driving to games in Florida. Andre and I developed a strong friendship with Jackie and Rachel Robinson. Rachel and I are still close friends today. The Dodgers wanted Andre to come to Los Angeles with them in 1958. We often wondered what our life would have been like if we came west with Walter O'Malley, who was a marvelous person."

During the 1960s, Wain played occasional club dates but primarily focused on rearing her children, seeing both of them through the University of Pennsylvania, while Baruch carried on in broadcasting concentrating on doing commercials for major corporations. Then in 1971 yet another career opportunity presented itself.

Wain tells the story: "In 1971 Andre made a business trip for an advertising firm to visit a radio station on the beach in Palm Beach, FL. The station manager surprisingly invited Andre and I to do a radio show. We accepted his offer and moved to Palm Beach from Scarsdale and did a daily, four-hour afternoon top-rated talk show with occasional guests like Art Buchwald and James Michener. It was a great time for us."

Now it was 1980 and the Baruchs moved to Beverly Hills, CA, to be closer to their children who were living in Los Angeles. Shortly after they moved, they embarked on a re-creation of the old *Your Hit Parade* show with Baruch writing the script and both doing commentary. The project took several years to complete, resulting in a popular nostalgia program that has been syndicated nationwide since then.

A principal chapter in Wain's life sadly closed when Andre Baruch, in already failing health, passed away in his sleep on September 15, 1991. Since then she has remained remarkably active in outstanding constitution making exclusive appearances and keeping up with old friends from the Big Band Era like Ella Fitzgerald, whom she helped see through her last days in 1996. Her main involvement now is an active commitment to the Society of Singers, an organization dedicated to providing personal counsel and financial assistance to professional vocalists who are in need of help. It is the organization's goal to build a home for singers in distress similar to the Motion Picture and Television Fund residential services in Woodland Hills, California.

In reflecting on all her experiences, Wain said: "I've had a great life. Fifty-three years of a wonderful marriage to a husband that was my biggest fan, two fine children, an opportunity to personally boost our servicemen's morale during the war, and a successful career in music and entertainment that started in 1923. And I'm still on the go. I have many friends from my years in entertainment that I see socially and enjoy going to music-related events with them around Los Angeles."

MARGARET WHITING
STILL A CLASS ACT

Margaret Whiting was destined from birth for pop vocal greatness. Her father was the famous composer and self-taught pianist Richard Whiting; her mother impresario Eleanore Youngblood Whiting. By age three she memorized the lyrics to over 100 songs and by fifteen her voice was fully mature. She grew up in Beverly Hills surrounded by a host of legendary contributors to the Great American Songbook who kept watch over her musical development that evolved into a career that produced twelve gold records and established her as one of the great pop singers of the 20th century. And today Margaret Whiting is as active as ever performing on the cabaret scene and serving as president of the Johnny Mercer Foundation. She still maintains the intense pace she has kept since she first broke into the charts in 1943 with her hit recording of "That Old Black Magic."

Whiting was born on July 22, 1924, in Detroit where her father worked as a songwriter and office manager for music publisher Joseph H. Remick. By 1924 Richard Whiting had established himself as a successful melodist with a succession of hit songs that included "Till We Meet Again," "Japanese Sandman," "Ain't We Got Fun?" and the stage score to *George White's Scandals*. In February 1929 he moved his family to Hollywood where he had already teamed up with lyricist Leo Robin to work for Paramount Pictures on Maurice Chevalier's American film debut in *Innocents of Paris*. The stage was set for a fairytale world at home that provided the environment for Margaret Whiting to nurture her seven decade career in music.

The Whiting family soon moved from Hollywood to Beverly Hills where their residence became an open house for the Hollywood songwriting community. The likes of Harold Arlen, Sammy Cahn, Buddy DeSylva, George Gershwin, Gus Kahn, Jerome Kern, Frank Loesser, Johnny Mercer, Jule Styne, and Jimmy Van Heusen were among the many that regularly stopped by to visit with Richard Whiting and sample Eleanore's famous chocolate cake. This is the atmosphere Margaret Whiting grew up in, absorbing all she heard and saw. But her father's health was not good. Richard Whiting was an extremely nervous person who suffered from high blood pressure. In the fall of 1937 his physical condition started to deteriorate. He died at age forty six in February 1938.

After her father's passing Eleanore continued to host Hollywood celebrities. A frequent visitor was Johnny Mercer, who loved Eleanore's cooking and played a major role in Margaret Whiting's career development. In 1936 he affectionately started referring to her as the kid. A year later he gave Whiting her first piece of career advice. She explained what happened during a telephone conversation from her home in Manhattan that she moved to from Los Angeles in 1968: "I sang one night at a party at the house because my mother wanted to see if I could sing well enough to start taking lessons. I remember that Johnny, Buddy DeSylva, Ruby Keeler, and several MGM executives were there. When I finished Johnny came over to me and said, 'You know kid, you did pretty good. Now you've just got to grow up and learn what life is all about. I think you're going to be wonderful and I'm going to help you.'"

Skitch Henderson was another individual who mentored Whiting: "Not long after my father died, Skitch came to our house to work with my Aunt Margaret who was a vaudeville singer. That was when he was starting to get well known in Hollywood. I sang for him that day and he spent so much time working with me; he was like a member of the family. During the war my aunt and I did a lot of entertaining at Army camps up and down the West Coast and Skitch frequently accompanied us. We remained very close friends for almost seventy years until he died in 2005."

Our Half Hour was a popular local Los Angeles NBC radio program. Skitch Henderson was the program's bandleader and Johnny Mercer a frequent guest personality. In 1941 they provided Whiting her professional debut when she sang "Too Marvelous for Words" as a duet with Mercer. Bob Hope's agent, Jimmy Saphire, heard her and arranged for a four-week appearance in New York on the *Your Hit Parade* radio show. After the four weeks ended, her contract was not extended because George Washington Hill, head of Lucky Strike Tobacco, the show's sponsor, felt that Whiting did not sing on the beat. The day she returned home from New York with Aunt Margaret and disembarked from the Super Chief in Pasadena, she saw all the newspaper headlines announcing that Pearl Harbor was attacked and World War II declared.

During the war the Hollywood Coordinating Committee put together packages to entertain servicemen who were going to be shipped overseas: "I went wherever they sent us. I still have a picture with Shirley Temple, Pat O'Brien, and Louella Parsons at Edwards Air Force Base seeing off the soldiers. That's also when I started working with Bob Hope. I wound up on his radio show for seven years after Frances Langford left the program and traveled with him on several of his troop tours. We did shows at military bases all over the country and overseas in Greenland and Labrador."

It was during the war that Margaret Whiting became a star, and once again Johnny Mercer was involved. In 1942 Mercer formed Capitol Records with Hollywood music store owner Glenn Wallichs and movie producer and tunesmith Buddy DeSylva. Mercer promised Whiting she would sing on Capitol and he did indeed keep his promise when he recorded her with Freddie Slack and his Orchestra just before the August 1942 American Federation of Musicians recording strike.

Freddie Slack is one of the sadly forgotten contributors to the Big Band Era and Capitol's success. According to most accounts, Slack was born on August 7, 1910, in La Crosse, WI. He grew up in nearby Viroqua playing drums, piano, and xylophone in the high school band. After his father died in 1927, the family moved to Chicago where he studied at the American Conservatory of Music then on to Los Angeles in 1931. Slack joined Ben Pollack's band there around 1934. He first came to public recognition with the Jimmy Dorsey Orchestra in early 1937, and in 1939 went over to the Will Bradley Orchestra where he gained fame as a boogie woogie pianist on the band's smash hit "Beat Me, Daddy, Eight to the Bar." Slack connected with Capitol at its start and recorded their first ever hit, "Cow Cow Boogie," with the vocal by Ella Mae Morse. A somewhat eccentric individual who appeared with his orchestra in several early 1940s films, he was occasionally seen walking a lion cub on a tightly held leash about Hollywood and hunting wild boar with a bow and arrow on Santa Catalina Island. Slack recorded with Capitol until 1952 then played engagements on the West Coast until he was found dead in his Hollywood apartment on August 10, 1967.

Whiting's collaboration with Freddie Slack generated her first hit record, "That Old Black Magic." Immediately after the record charted in early 1943, Whiting toured the West Coast with Slack's Orchestra. Although she gained fame during the Big Band Era, it was the only time she ever sang on the road with a big band: "We appeared at sold-out theaters in Los Angeles, San

Diego, and San Francisco. Freddie was a charming, soft spoken individual who was an excellent arranger and musician. I remember that he was extremely serious in the recording studio, no laughs, and all business."

Billy Butterfield recorded Whiting's next two Capitol hits, the pre-strike "My Ideal" that was released in mid 1943 and the post-strike "Moonlight in Vermont," her first million seller that hit the charts in February 1945. For the "My Ideal" recording Butterfield used the Les Brown Orchestra that was playing nearby at the Hollywood Palladium. Then later in 1945 Whiting started to record regularly for Capitol scoring with another huge hit, "It Might As Well Be Spring." She was now part of Capitol's glittering stable of female vocalists that at the time included Betty Hutton, Peggy Lee, Ella Mae Morse, Jo Stafford, and Martha Tilton. Whiting had the longest career of all of them with Capitol, charting forty-six hits during her seventeen years with the label. Fourteen of those hits cracked the top ten, two made it to number one. During her time with Capitol two interesting recording experiences stand out.

Another American Federation of Musicians strike was called by James Petrillo in 1948. Crafty Capitol A&R man, Jim Conklin, got around the strike by sending Frank DeVol to London to record a song he selected with British musicians and then had Whiting sing over the musical track at the Record Recorders studio in Santa Monica, dubbing in her vocal. The perfectly legal maneuver resulted in another gold record, "A Tree in the Meadow," that was the year's eighth-best seller and number one on the chart for five weeks.

A year later Whiting attended a party held by Capitol press executive Bob Stabler at his San Fernando Valley ranch. Stabler heard her sing "Red River Valley" at the bash and the next day suggested to Capitol brass that she pair up to record with country star Jimmy Wakely. His hunch paid off. The first of their five hits together, "Slippin' Around," quickly hit number one and sold over a million copies. As a result, she was invited to Nashville to appear on the *Grand Ole Opry* and the *Sunday Down South* radio shows. Whiting thoroughly enjoyed her Southern experience and developed a long friendship with Minnie Pearl.

The late 40s were a particularly busy time for Whiting: "I spent a lot of time recording at Capitol and did quite a bit of radio work, *Command Performance*, the *Jack Smith Show, Club 15*, the *Lux Radio Theater*, and the *Eddie Cantor Show*. That was also when I was involved on radio and touring with Bob Hope. In 1950 we recorded "Blind Date" together that turned out to be a hit. It was an exciting time that was filled with nonstop activity."

By the late 1950s rock 'n' roll captured the record-buying public and the recording demand for pop vocalists became virtually nonexistent. The golden age of classic popular music was over. Such was the music climate when Margaret Whiting ended her seventeen-year affiliation with Capitol. By then Johnny Mercer had sold the business to EMI and everyone she knew from her salad days was gone. However, it was far from the conclusion of her recording career.

After she left Capitol Whiting first recorded for Dot Records, then in 1960 did a series of albums for Norman Granz's Verve label with Russ Garcia, for whom she has the highest respect both personally and professionally. Her *Jerome Kern Songbook* album with Garcia was critically acclaimed and her personal favorite. Later in the decade Whiting recorded for London, breaking into the Adult Contemporary *Easy Listening* charts with twelve hits, including "The Wheel of Hurt" that charted at number one in 1966. She closed out her recording career with three albums for Audiophile in the late 70s and early 80s and her *Then and Now* album for DRG in 1990 that was well received by Whiting enthusiasts.

Recording hits has actually been just one facet of Whiting's show business career; after she left Capitol in the late 1950s she went on to nearly fifty more diverse years in entertainment. She has and still continues to perform in cabarets and nightclubs. Through the years Whiting headlined in numerous touring Broadway musicals and played Mama Rose in *Gypsy* over thirty times. Ethel Merman applauded her dramatic portrayal of the mother of stripper Gypsy Rose Lee. There were appearances at the Newport Jazz Festival where she paid tribute to Harold Arlen and in several other George Wein productions. She played all the prestigious venues: Las Vegas; Lake Tahoe; the Cocoanut Grove, Ciro's, and the Mocambo in Los Angeles; the Copacabana, Carnegie Hall, and Radio City Music Hall in New York.

Whiting also appeared in two Broadway-related productions during her career. The first came in 1987 in *Taking My Turn*, a musical review with the theme of aged actors reflecting on their careers and personal lives. It ran from June 1983 through January 1984 at the off-Broadway Entermedia Theater for 345 performances and became a TV special. Next came *Dream*, a musical based on Johnny Mercer's lyrics. It ran on-Broadway at the Royale Theater for 133 performances from April 1997 into July 1997. *Dream* was nominated for the 1997 Tony Award for Best Choreography.

Although the Big Band Era is considered to have ended in 1946, Margaret Whiting finally got her chance to travel on the road in 1972 and 1974 when she toured throughout the United States with the *Cavalcade of Bands* recreating the big band sound. The package included Frankie Carle, Bob Crosby, and Freddie Martin. It was so popular that it culminated in a television special: "We all spent three months on each tour traveling in a Greyhound bus and living out of a suitcase. The tour played at all sorts of locations, theaters, auditoriums, and even gymnasiums. It was reliving the Swing Era all over again."

The next major project for Whiting after the *Cavalcade of the Bands* came to a close was *Four Girls Four*, a sensationally popular song and comedy review that at its start featured Whiting, Rosemary Clooney, Rose Marie, and Helen O'Connell. The show consisted of each of the four women individually singing and bantering with the audience then appearing together onstage for a combined closing number that inevitably brought down the house. *Four Girls Four* ran for over twelve years from the late 70s to the late 80s and Whiting was with the show for its duration. Around half way through Rose Marie was replaced by Kay Starr who quickly became close friends with Whiting. While Whiting was with the act it was often featured on television, a medium with which she was most familiar.

Compilations of Margaret Whiting's career have usually given short shrift to her body of work on television. Whiting's TV career started in the early 1950s when she starred with her sister Barbara on the Desilu Studios series *Those Whiting Girls*. Network appearances included the *Dean Martin*, *Dinah Shore*, and *Ed Sullivan* shows plus *Bob Hope Specials*. Ed Sullivan was a close friend of the Whiting family. Barbara Whiting was his daughter Betty's bridesmaid and Betty frequently visited Barbara in Beverly Hills as a teenager during her summer vacations. Over the years Margaret Whiting appeared on numerous Public Television specials, the last of which was the 1997 *The Songs of Johnny Mercer – Too Marvelous for Words* with Melisa Manchester, Johnny Mathis, and the John Pizzarelli Trio. The 1997 Mercer PBS show was an especially satisfying involvement for Whiting.

Though Johnny Mercer passed away in 1976, he remained an important part of Whiting's professional career. Since his death she has organized and conducted many Mercer tributes across the United States. After his wife Ginger died in 1994 Whiting was named president of the Johnny Mercer Foundation. She was Ginger's personal choice to head the organization whose mission is to preserve the Great American Songbook through its Accentuate the Positive Program for children, Johnny Mercer-related special events, the Sundance Theatre Songbook for emerging composers, and the Mercer archives housed at Georgia State University. The Foundation also sponsors seminars such as an August 2006 class at Northwestern University in Chicago where established songwriters taught aspiring songwriters who were anxious to have their work heard and critiqued. Whiting's work with the Foundation exemplifies her willingness to contribute to worthwhile causes.

Few top-tier entertainers have been committed to community service as Margaret Whiting has. Her list of charitable activities that began during World War II is exhaustive. Whiting has entertained at numerous military installations and veterans hospitals. She has sung for Catholic and Jewish charities, the City of Hope, disease-related fund raisers, Shriners hospitals, and at penal institutions. Her willingness to share her good fortune has earned her the sobriquet the Benefit Queen.

Today Margaret Whiting lives happily in Manhattan with her fourth husband, writer, director, and former adult film star Jack Wrangler. In reflecting on her career experiences, Capitol Records was immediately broached: "It was fascinating to observe the birth and development of Capitol with all the unique personalities that were involved. Buddy DeSylva was an exquisite dresser and drove beautiful cars. He was suave, debonair, and had a terrific sense of humor. The businessman was Glenn Wallichs. He was kind of square but charming with a cute sense of humor. Glenn really knew the record business inside out. I remember frequently going to his Music City store in Hollywood with Mel Tormé to buy records. Capitol's first offices were in his store. Johnny, of course, started it all. What a gifted and fascinating trio."

In addition to often visiting with her daughter Debbie who lives nearby on Long Island, what is Margaret Whiting up to now? "I take great pleasure in working with and mentoring young singers and songwriters. I have them over to the house to listen to and critique their work to help make them better. I'm as busy as ever with the Foundation and am proud of the part it played in bringing *The Light in the Piazza* that won six Tony Awards to Broadway in 2005. I particularly enjoy introducing the Great American Songbook to children and working with young talent at Sundance. As the years go by I appreciate all the more the career and life I've had and at this stage I want to give back by helping promising talent establish themselves and make their mark in music and show business."

The Benefit Queen is still going strong.

75. A very young Bob Eberly with the Jimmy Dorsey Orchestra.

76. The debonair Herb Jeffries.

77. Jack Leonard during his
Tommy Dorsey days.

78. A post Tommy Dorsey
Jack Leonard.

79. Dolores O'Neill singing with the Bob Chester Orchestra.

80. Dolores O'Neill while with the Bob Chester Orchestra.

81, 82, 83. Dolores O'Neill singing
with the Gene Krupa Orchestra.

84. Andy Russell in 1945.

85. Andy Russell
with Capitol Records executive
Vice President Glenn Wallichs.

86. A popular Jo Stafford.

87. Kay Starr singing with Charlie Barnet standing at far right.

88. Kay Starr later in her career.

89. Garry Stevens at the far left with the Paul Kain Orchestra at Santa Catalina Island in 1936.

90. Garry Stevens top middle with the Paul Kain Orchestra at the DeWitt Clinton Hotel in Albany in 1937.

91. Garry Stevens playing trumpet with the Paul Kain Orchestra in 1939.

92. Garry Stevens far right singing with the Stardusters in Charlie Spivak's Orchestra in 1942.

93. Garry Stevens singing with the Tex Beneke Orchestra in 1947.

94. Martha Tilton recording at Capitol Records.

95. Bea Wain at the peak of her popularity.

96. Margaret Whiting
recording with Jerry Gray and
his Orchestra
at Capitol Records.

97. Vocalist Margaret Whiting.

PART FOUR

THE ARRANGERS

FRANK COMSTOCK
LES BROWN'S MAN OF RENOWN

In 1996 Les Brown was memorialized in the Guinness Book of World Records as the leader of the longest-lasting big band in the history of popular music. It is possible that Brown might also hold the record for having the longest-serving arranger with a band as well. That would be Frank Comstock, who was Brown's principal arranger without interruption from September 1943 until Brown passed away in 2001. While with Brown, Comstock developed an enduring camaraderie with band vocalist Doris Day, wrote for the band when it played the Bob Hope Show on radio and television, and achieved success as an independent freelancer in the film, recording, and television industries. He had a seven-decade career as an arranger, composer, and orchestrator that few could match in both accomplishment and longevity. And all the while he stayed true to his philosophy of making sure he enjoyed his work and had fun doing it.

When Frank Comstock was born there on September 20, 1922, San Diego was a city that reached a population of one hundred thousand and was named the home base for the Pacific Fleet by the United States Navy. His father was an architect who designed the Sun Valley Idaho Lodge and his mother a pianist and choir vocalist at the local Presbyterian Church. Comstock first expressed an interest in music at seven years of age when he asked his parents for a trombone. He learned how to play the instrument with the Bonham Brothers Boys Band that was sponsored by a local mortuary. When he was in junior high school he played in the school dance band and was encouraged to experiment with arranging by his teacher and bandleader Russell Warren. He started by listening to all the recordings of the popular bands he could find and copied their arrangements. By twelve he was writing his own arrangements for local dance bands without the benefit of any formal music lessons.

During high school Comstock developed friendships with two students who would go on to distinguished music careers. At San Diego High School he became close friends with pianist Paul Smith. They sat in the same harmony class and wrote together. When his family moved to Los Angeles during his junior year he befriended trumpeter Uan Rasey at Huntington Park High School. The Comstock family relocated back to San Diego where he returned to San Diego High for his senior year, graduating at sixteen in 1939. By the time he graduated Comstock was earning a few precious Depression Era dollars a week playing professionally around San Diego

While in high school, Comstock's favorite bands were Count Basie, Benny Goodman, and Jimmie Lunceford. He integrated their styles into the dance band he formed after graduation that played at the Collegiate Club in Balboa Park for around a year. Then in late 1940 a call came from his friend Uan Rasey asking him if he would be interested in joining the newly formed Sonny Dunham Orchestra.

Rasey described what happened during a telephone conversation from his home in Studio City, CA: "In early 1940 Sonny left the Casa Loma Orchestra and took over the Chuck Cascales band in Los Angeles. Chuck was Johnny Richards's brother. He interviewed for musicians and I tried out and got a job playing lead trumpet. One evening we were on the road playing one of Frank's arrangements and Sonny liked it. At the time Sonny needed a trombone player and arranger. He told me to send Frank a telegram to ask him to get on the next train to Portland, which was our next stop, to hook up with the band."

Comstock talked about his time with Dunham at his comfortable home in Huntington Beach, CA, where he has lived for over forty years: "I took Kai Winding's place and was thrilled to be in a big band. It was a fine band, but nothing that I wrote was ever recorded because of Petrillo's recording strike. I feel Sonny's band could have gone far if it wasn't for the strike. Sonny was a very good musician on both the trumpet and trombone. I remember that he played trumpet in the first Metronome All-Star Band in 1939. He could really hit the high notes. I grew professionally, playing and arranging, for Sonny. He got me started in the big band business."

During 1942 legendary personal manager Carlos Gastel handled both Sonny Dunham and Benny Carter. In the course of a casual conversation he told Comstock that Dunham would soon be breaking up the band and that Benny Carter heard his arrangements and was interested in hiring him. Carter was anxious to employ Comstock because he wanted to concentrate on just playing in his band and hand the arranging duties over to someone else. Comstock eagerly accepted Carter's offer but prior to joining the band in Los Angeles he spent a few weeks back home in San Diego playing with Gus Arnheim's small band that included future jazz greats Joe Mondragon and Art Pepper at a club located on the beach.

In commenting on Carter, Comstock has nothing but good things to say: "I spent almost a year with Benny playing in LA. He was the nicest man I ever met; I loved that man. In fact I had a date to have lunch with him the weekend he died. He was easy to work with and appreciative of everything I did. I even got to play trombone for a few weeks. I was in heaven sitting next to J. J. Johnson and in front of Gerald Wilson and Snooky Young in the trumpet section. They were all terrific guys."

Next came Les Brown and His Band of Renown: "I stopped by the Hollywood Palladium to check out Les Brown's band one evening in September 1943. Linton Montgomery, whom I worked with in Sonny Dunham's band, was playing trumpet for Les. When I walked in he stood right up and said, 'Hey Les, get this guy, don't let him go. He's a great arranger.' A few days later I talked to Les and he was impressed when I told him I was arranging for Benny whom he admired. He asked me to write an arrangement, liked it, and offered me a job. I immediately told Benny about it. Benny said, 'Take it and run because I'm breaking up the band in a few weeks.' I started out making fifty bucks an arrangement for Les which was big money back then and I didn't have to copy them myself. I also played trombone for my first few years in the band."

Brown and Comstock had an uncommonly close working relationship; they collaborated together for over fifty years. Comstock found Brown easy to work for. Other than occassional spirited discussions regarding tempo, Brown never told Comstock how to write a song. He would write whatever came to mind and Brown was always satisfied with the arrrangement. His first assignment from Brown was to write an improved arrangement of the band's theme song, "Leap Frog." It's still the arrangement Les Brown Jr. uses today with the current Band of Renown that is regularly performing in Branson, MO.

Les Brown Jr. talked about Comstock from his home in Branson: "My father and Frank got along very well working together for almost sixty years. Frank was always fun to be around and kept the band loose with his wry sense of humor. He was an important contributor to the band's success and we still use his arrangements today."

A highlight of Comstock's career with Brown was the development of a professional association and personal friendship with Doris Day, who started her famous career in show business as a big band singer in her hometown of Cincinnati. There were two catalysts that precipitated the bond between Comstock and Day. The first involved her son Terry. Doris Day's mother Alma traveled with the band to help Day keep an eye on Terry. When Alma slipped on an icy Manhattan sidewalk in front of the Hotel Pennsylvania and broke her leg, Brown "volunteered" Comstock the task of watching Terry while Day was singing with the band. Comstock was able to do so because by then he was a fulltime arranger and no longer played in the trombone section. The duty lasted several months and they became good friends over the years until Terry died in 2004.

The second catalyst was the result of Brown's assessment of Day's future possibilities. When Brown hired Day he immediately sensed she was destined for greatness. Brown asked Comstock to shadow Day so he could get to know her and fashion arrangements she liked and that suited her vocal style to best utilize her immense talent. As a result of these two endeavors, Comstock and Day became kindred spirits.

Comstock has fond memories of working with Doris Day: "With all her fame from the movies and television Doris has been underrated for her work as a big band vocalist. In my opinion she was the best of all the female big band singers. She was unique. Doris had amazing natural talent with an ability to turn it on as needed then quickly revert back to her regular self. She really is the girl next door with a great sense of humor. There was not one person in the band who disliked her, and that's rare. I have good memories of keeping an eye on Terry during those Les Brown days. Doris is a loyal friend. When my late wife Joanie became seriously ill from emphysema she called nearly every day to check up on her. Joanie and I had some great times visiting Doris at her home in Carmel."

Doris Day still enjoys her relationship with Frank Comstock which she talked about from her home in Carmel, CA: "It's always a great pleasure for me to talk about Frank Comstock. In fact, I could probably write my own book about him. From day one in Les Brown's band Frank became my friend. Not just my friend, but he always carried my luggage which was a bit on the heavy side. He never complained and always did it with a smile. Now to get to the nitty-gritty about his talent. His arrangements were always great and I think what made Les Brown's band so popular had much to do with Frank. I absolutely loved singing with Les's band and I can honestly say that I loved all the guys in it. Everyone was so wonderful to me, took great care of me and I'll never forget them for that. Indeed, Frank was one of them. Not only did he look after me and my luggage, he looked after my little boy, Terry, when he and my mother would come to be with me on the road for a week or two at a time. I remember, too, that on Sundays Frank would always ask if we would like to go to Central Park to see the animals, which we always did. Terry liked him very much and called him "Shrank." The best ever picture of my boy was taken by Frank at the Hotel Pennsylvania and is one I shall treasure forever."

Day added: "Years have passed but Frank and I are always in touch even though he lives in Huntington Beach and I live in Carmel. We talk on the phone and laugh a lot, and more often than not, we wind up talking about the Les Brown days. Lest I forget, we also talk about Joanie, his lovely gracious wife, and one of the funniest ladies I have ever known. She was truly a dear, dear friend and I will always miss her. I genuinely enjoy discussing my dear friend Frank, AKA 'Shrank.'"

Doris Day left Les Brown in 1946 to marry Brown's saxophonist George Weidler, but that did not end her professional relationship with Comstock. In 1947 he wrote for her when she appeared at Billy Reed's Little Club in New York and for two months on the *Your Hit Parade* radio show with Frank Sinatra before Day became an instant international celebrity in 1948 when she made her film debut in Warner Brother's *Romance on the High Seas* singing her million seller, "It's Magic." Comstock continued to provide her arrangements after the film when she did two tours with Bob Hope singing with the Les Brown Orchestra before she appeared in her second film, *It's a Great Feeling*. Comstock was also involved with all of her Warner Brothers motion pictures well into the 1950s. Theirs was a happy and productive professional relationship working together at the studio.

According to Comstock, there were three members of the Les Brown band that played important nonmusical roles: "Don Kramer was the drummer with Les's original Duke Blue Devils band in 1936. When I got there he was the business manager. We always shared an office on the road where he conducted the band's business and I wrote. We had some good times together. Butch Stone was the mother hen who kept the band in order and somehow always got tickets to all the ballgames and shows wherever we played. He was a very good baritone saxophone player and in his nineties still sings "A Good Man is Hard to Find" with the band. Stumpy Brown has always been the band archivist who can answer any question concerning its history. He was also a fine trombonist and an underrated vocalist. Stumpy was a big hit when he and Butch did their dance routine."

What particular era of the Les Brown band does Comstock think stands out? "In my opinion Les's band has not been given proper historical recognition. It was a solid straight-ahead swing band that could play fine dance music. Dancers loved the band. Les always felt that the early 50s band was his best and I tend to agree. It had musicians like Abe Most on clarinet, Dave Pell on tenor, Don Fagerquist on trumpet, and Jack Sperling on drums. Just listen to it roar on the *Live at the Hollywood Palladium* CD from September 1953. After Doris left we had two fine female vocalists in Lucy Ann Polk and Jo Ann Greer who both sang with the band around that time. It was a happy band with a happy, clean sound."

Comstock also commented on his association with Margaret Whiting: "Arranging for Les's band provided me a number of opportunities to work with outstanding female singers, not only Doris, Lucy Ann, and Jo Ann, but also Margaret Whiting who sang with the band on Bob Hope's radio and television shows for several years. I did work for her on the show plus several outside projects. Margaret is a gifted vocalist and a true lady, just a charm to work with."

In turn, Margaret Whiting thinks highly of Frank Comstock. She recently talked about their professional relationship from her home in Manhattan: "Frank is just a great guy and did a lot of wonderful arrangements for me. He was so easy to work with and skilled in writing to complement the style of the vocalist. I remember the great times we had working together on the Bob Hope Show."

Although Comstock was affiliated with Les Brown until the bandleader died, he also freelanced and engaged in myriad projects on his own starting in the 50s. One undertaking involved arguably the most innovative jazz vocal group of all time, the pioneering Hi-Lo's and their founder, master jazz vocal arranger Gene Puerling.

"I was doing some work at Starlite Records in Hollywood in 1954 when the Hi-Lo's came to the label from Trend Records," Comstock said. "Over the next few years I arranged ten of their albums starting with the first, *The Hi-Lo's Listen!* Working with Gene was a creative challenge. He wrote like a musician and was an original vocal arranger, always pushing the envelope. Gene and I had a lot of laughs working together. It showed in our music. There was a lot of tongue-in-cheek humor in our writing. Gene was great to work with. We never had any arguments about what we were going to do. There was great communication and we got along fine. I always felt that the reputation I gained working with the HI-Lo's led to my arranging for the Lennon Sisters vocal act after they left the Lawrence Welk Show in 1968."

After the Hi-Lo's disbanded in 1964, Puerling became involved in the formation of The Singers Unlimited in 1967. In addition to singing with the group, as its chief arranger and musical director he incorporated the use of sophisticated over-dubbing techniques that produced a richer sound on their fourteen well-received albums. He reminisced about working with Comstock by telephone from his home in San Anselmo, CA: "As an arranger Frank was a joy and fun to create music with, so much so that I always looked forward to our recording sessions. I actually did not formally study music and Frank was always very patient in working with me. He had my complete trust during the five or so years we spent collaborating together. We still remain friends today."

Comstock also had a twenty-five-year professional involvement with his good friend, Jack Webb. He composed and conducted for several of Webb's Mark VII production company films and TV series, starting with *Dragnet*. His longest stint with Webb was for seven years on *Adam-12*. The two never signed a contract; they operated with only a handshake. It was the same arrangement Comstock had through all his years with Les Brown.

Other activities included arranging for vocal acts, phonograph recordings, motion pictures, television shows, and the Disneyland All-American Band. Comstock's considerable TV work included *Happy Days*, *Laverne and Shirley*, *McHale's Navy*, and the *Bob Hope Show*. Among his many films he arranged "I Want to Be Loved by You" sung by Marilyn Monroe in *Some Like It Hot*, the themes for several Dimitri Tiomkin composed films, and songs for *Finian's Rainbow*, *Hello Dolly*, and *The Music Man*. In 1962 he became an icon to exotica music fans for his *Project Comstock: Music from Outer Space*, a space music album that incorporated the use of the theremin, electric violin, and novachord. Former Glenn Miller trombonist Paul Tanner played the theremin on the recording. All the while Comstock was an avid model railroad devotee, a hobby he frequently shared with fellow enthusiast, Billy May.

By the early 1990s Comstock decided the time had come to slow down and unhurriedly enjoy life. Although he kept active working on special projects of his choosing and a few record dates with Les Brown, he devoted increasing time to his current hobby of painting. Although he favors lighthouses and seascapes he has done over 300 paintings of assorted subjects. Several of his artistic works hang in his Huntington Beach home, impressively complementing the décor. He first started to sketch and paint when he was five years old and continued to dabble in the art forms during slack periods between jobs.

Comstock also enjoys the time he spends with his close-knit family that includes son Bob, daughter Julie, and four grandchildren. They all live just five miles away in Newport Beach and frequently visit him at his Huntington Beach home. The many Comstock family gatherings are a jewel of an activity for him during his retirement years.

A late 1990s high spot was the unexpected development of a friendship with the great Canadian born composer of light orchestral music, Robert Farnon: "I first heard of Bob Farnon while I was working with Gene Puerling, but I never spoke with him. Then one day around nine or ten years ago he called me out of the blue from England, where he had lived since the war, and told me he closely followed my career over the years. He asked me why I wasn't a member of his Society and when I told him I wasn't aware of it he gave me a complimentary lifetime membership. We talked several times a week on the phone until he died in 2005. Although we never met we got along famously."

Frank Comstock has had a very successful seven-decade career in the music business, much of which he attributes to good fortune: "I've been very lucky; everything always seemed to fall into place. For example, when Doris did her screen test at Warner Brothers she used one of my arrangements. Ray Heindorf, who was head of the studio's music department, liked it and I wound up writing vocal and dance scores for her pictures. One of Ray's best friends was Jack Webb, whom I got to know and did work for on a number of his shows for many years. That's how it always seemed to go."

Comstock concluded: "Every project I engaged in was because it was a challenge and I enjoyed doing it. As a result, I had fun and it showed. I was always prepared in great detail for every job I took and made sure that I did what was necessary so that my boss was happy with both my work and working with me. Maybe that's why I was always able to keep busy over the years without much planning and worrying on my part."

FLETCHER HENDERSON, DON REDMAN, AND SY OLIVER
THE INVISIBLE CONTRIBUTORS TO THE BIG BAND ERA

Big band enthusiasts well know the works of Benny Goodman, Jimmy Dorsey, and Tommy Dorsey. Most, however, do not know that the great African American arrangers Fletcher Henderson, Don Redman, and Sy Oliver played an important part in their success. Before we examine the little-known and under-appreciated contributions of African American arrangers to the Big Band Era, let us look at the craft of arranging itself.

Certainly the most important person in a swing band was the leader who put the band together, ran the organization, and gave the band its image through an extension of his personality. But approaching the leader in importance was the arranger who gave the band its unique musical tone and style, and frequently was responsible for its success or failure.

All the big bandleaders hired an arranger. A few, Glenn Miller being the prime example, did much of their own arranging. In fact, Miller developed the clarinet lead over four saxophones that generated the unique sweet band sound that helped to make him famous.

The tasks confronting an arranger were indeed multi-faceted. In addition to the knowledge of music and a sense of creative imagination necessary to write a score with an appealing effect, leadership talent was a requirement. Specifically, after completing a work, the arranger would rehearse the piece with the band instructing the musicians as to how he wanted it played with the leader standing by carefully listening and ready to comment.

Within this highly structured milieu there were several skilled African American musicians who arranged for popular white bands. One was Don Redman who at one time or another wrote for Bobby Byrne, Jimmy Dorsey, Harry James, Ben Pollack, and Paul Whiteman.

The diminutive Donald Matthew Redman was born in Piedmont, WV, in 1900. His parents were music teachers. A child prodigy, he was skilled at the trumpet at three, played in a band at six, and went on to become accomplished at the saxophone, coronet, piano, trombone, and violin as a youth.

After attending Storer College in Harpers Ferry, WV, and musical conservatories in Boston and Detroit, he joined Fletcher Henderson's band in New York in 1923 and wrote many of the arrangements that gave the band its innovative swing style in addition to playing alto saxophone next to the great Coleman Hawkins.

In 1927 Redman left Henderson to assume the musical directorship of McKinney's Cotton Pickers and in 1931 he took over the band formed by Fletcher Henderson's brother Horace. Redman's reputation was such that he was commissioned to write arrangements for other orchestras while leading his own band.

Redman gave up his band in 1940. He went on to work as a free-lance arranger, conducted a big band tour of Europe in 1947, and became Pearl Bailey's musical director in 1951. Don Redman passed away in New York in 1964, a pioneer jazz arranger.

As a commissioned arranger, Redman had particular influence on Jimmy Dorsey's band. Although commercially successful, prior to 1939 Dorsey's band lacked consistency in its arrangements. With the addition of Redman early that year as an arranger, it developed a distinct style for both swing and sweet music to become a truly superb dance orchestra and a jukebox favorite. His arrangement of "Deep Purple" sung by Bob Eberly was one of 1939's top hits.

Jimmy Dorsey's brother Tommy is considered by many to have had the best all-around band of the Era. One of the main reasons for Dorsey's success was his choice of top arrangers, one of which was Sy Oliver.

Trumpeter, vocalist, composer, arranger, and bandleader Melvin Jackson Oliver was born in 1910 in Battle Creek, MI, and grew up in Zanesville, Ohio. He acquired the nickname "Sy," short for psychiatrist, due to his impressive vocabulary acquired from a lifetime of extensive reading.

Oliver was raised in a musical family. His mother was an accomplished pianist and his father was a respected music teacher. Eschewing the piano, he settled on the trumpet. When his father suffered a stroke, he started playing trumpet in numerous bands to earn money to help support the family, joining Zack White's band full time after graduating from high school.

Jimmy Lunceford discovered Oliver in Cincinnati in 1933 and asked him to join his band as a trumpeter and arranger. It is acknowledged that Oliver's arrangements using an easy two-beat style that produced a buoyant, bouncy feeling were instrumental in making the band successful. He was also part of the vocal chorus that was included in his many hit scores.

Tired of traveling with the band, Oliver left Lunceford in 1939. He was immediately offered a substantial pay increase by Tommy Dorsey and decided to join his band, remaining with Dorsey until the late 1940s.

Oliver was able to quickly provide a new direction to Tommy Dorsey's orchestra. Prior to Oliver's arrival, Axel Stordahl and Paul Weston were the mainstay Dorsey arrangers providing highly successful, commercially oriented charts. Oliver proceeded to infuse a new musical style with jazz-oriented arrangements that resulted in blockbuster hits such as "On the Sunny Side of the Street," "Yes Indeed," and "Opus One."

It is also significant to note that the only reason Tommy Dorsey was able to persuade drummer Buddy Rich to join his band in 1939 was the presence of Oliver as an arranger. The highly mercurial Rich would not accept direction from anyone in the band except Oliver, for whom he had the highest professional and personal respect. It was the propelling drive of Rich that helped to make Tommy Dorsey's arguably the best dance band of the early 1940s.

After leaving Dorsey, Oliver spent most of the 1950s as a musical director for Decca records. In the 1960s he did free-lance arranging for Frank Sinatra, Sammy Davis Jr., Ella Fitzgerald, Peggy Lee, Jo Stafford, and the Mills Brothers. Throughout the 1970s Oliver led a band for special occasions including two lengthy engagements at New York's Rainbow Room, retiring in the mid-1980s.

A wryly humorous individual, Oliver died in New York's Mt. Sinai Hospital of lung cancer in 1988, a self-taught arranger.

From the perspective of historical impact, the African American arranger that played an immeasurably important role in Benny Goodman formally kicking off the Big Band Era on August 21, 1935, at the Palomar Ballroom in Los Angeles was Fletcher Henderson, pianist, arranger, and big band organizer and leader.

James Fletcher Henderson was born in Cuthbert, GA, in 1897. He came from a well-to-do family. His father was a high school principal and his mother a music teacher who introduced Henderson to the piano at six years of age.

An outstanding student, Henderson graduated from Atlanta University in 1920 with a degree in chemistry and moved to New York to enroll in Columbia University to pursue a master's degree. However, a part-time job as a song demonstrator with the African American music publishing company of Pace and Handy was to change the course of his professional life.

Totally enthralled with the music business, Henderson abandoned his studies toward a master's degree in chemistry and in 1921 went with Henry Pace to found Black Swan records serving as the musical director of the new firm. At Black Swan, he met and developed a lifelong association with singer Ethel Watters whom he accompanied on a tour of the United States as her bandleader.

By early 1924, Henderson had become well connected to the Harlem jazz scene and was asked to put together a band to play at the Club Alabam. That orchestra is considered to be the first big band to play jazz. That same year Henderson moved on to the Roseland Ballroom off Times Square where he stayed for five years with a band comprised of the top black jazz musicians of the day, including Louis Armstrong who remained with Henderson through 1925.

During the early 1930s the band had drifted down to playing tours and one-nighters on the road with Henderson doing more and more of the arranging. Despite his musical genius and high level of intelligence, Henderson was a poor businessman, unagressive by nature, and had no stomach for discipline. As a result, Henderson was unable to achieve commercial success and disbanded in 1934, setting the stage for his under recognized participation in music history.

In 1934 Benny Goodman put together his first band and was in dire need of arrangements. At the recommendation of jazz critic and promoter John Hammond, Goodman hired the unemployed Henderson to write for his band. It was a wise decision as Henderson's hard driving arrangements gave Goodman's band its distinctive, swinging identity.

Henderson's role in music history was tied to the fate of Goodman who was seriously considering giving up his band during a disastrous nationwide tour during the summer of 1935. August 21 found Goodman opening at the Palomar Ballroom in Los Angeles on the last stop of that tour.

Goodman started out playing standard pop tunes and was met with a lukewarm response. Electing to go for broke, he called for Henderson's energetic "King Porter Stomp" and continued to play primarily Henderson arrangements for the balance of the evening. The audience mobbed the bandstand and Goodman's engagement became a complete sellout making national headlines. Historians consider that Goodman's Palomar engagement marked the official start of the Big Band Era.

There was no doubt that Henderson's arrangements played a major part in Goodman's artistic and commercial success, and Goodman was always willing to publicly acknowledge Henderson's contributions. As a final gesture of appreciation, Goodman dedicated to the memory of Fletcher Henderson a PBS special highlighting his career; it was aired shortly before his death in 1986.

It should also be noted that Fletcher Henderson was not the only African American arranger to write for Benny Goodman. Specifically, Horace Henderson, Jimmy Mundy, and Edgar Sampson contributed arrangements to Goodman with Sampson providing "Don't Be that Way" and "Stomping at the Savoy," two of Goodman's biggest hits.

In 1936 Henderson left Goodman to form a new band that met with but modest success, returning to Goodman as a fulltime arranger from 1939 to 1941. He formed yet another band in 1941 playing engagements at the Roseland and clubs in the Chicago area in the mid-1940s.

Nineteen forty-seven found Henderson once again arranging for Goodman. He came full circle to his roots, conducting tours for his old friend Ethel Watters in 1948 and 1949. Back in New York in 1950, he led a sextet and wrote the score for the show *Jazz Train* that played at Bop City.

Late in 1950 the genteel Henderson suffered a stroke that left him permanently bed ridden. He passed away from a heart attack in 1952 in a Harlem hospital, an arranger whose style became the framework for the Big Band Era.

Don Redman, Sy Oliver, and Fletcher Henderson had much in common. They were born into families with professional parents, raised in a musical environment, well educated for their day, masters of musical notation, and highly skilled in playing their respective instruments. Unfortunately, they were also little recognized for their work with big name white bands. They were the true invisible contributors to the Big Band Era.

JOHNNY MANDEL
FROM THE BIG BAND ERA
TO OSCAR AND GRAMMY AWARDS

Herbert Hoover was elected the thirty-first President of the United States in 1928, the same year a precocious three year old Johnny Mandel gave a piano recital at the Roosevelt Hotel in New York City. His first public appearance marked the start of one of the great careers in American music that includes storied achievement as a big band and jazz musician, arranger, and composer, as an Oscar wining songwriter, and as a Grammy winning arranger and producer. Mandel's accomplishment in just one of those categories would certainly qualify him for entry into any music hall of fame. His career has spanned seven decades and blessed with an amazingly strong constitution he is still in top form and has no intention of segueing into retirement.

John Alfred Mandel was born on November 23, 1925, in Manhattan's Upper West Side. His mother Hannah trained for the opera but never performed, thanks to her parent's stern Victorian values. His father Al, a clothing manufacturer and lover of jazz, died of a heart attack when Mandel was eleven. Johnny Mandel was the product of a strong musical lineage and a home environment that exposed him to both classical music and jazz on records and radio programs.

When he was twelve Mandel became seriously interested in music and started taking trumpet lessons with music publisher and teacher Charles Colin, who passed away in 2000. He talked about his formal musical beginnings during a telephone interview from his home in Malibu: "I started with Charlie Colin in a studio on the 100 block of 48th Street where all the music stores were. Al Porcino, Shorty Rogers, and Bernie Glow were also studying with him. That's when Al discovered he could hit altissimo C. Manny Albam brought his alto sax and hung out there. He'd bring in music from the Savoy Sultans and those kinds of swing bands for us to play. We were all just kids who showed up wanting to learn about music."

The next step in Mandel's musical development involved taking music lessons with Van Alexander when he was fourteen. Alexander was then a well-known arranger and bandleader who scored the 1938 smash hit "A-Tisket, A-Tasket" for Chick Webb and Ella Fitzgerald: "In my first lesson Van went to his closet and from a big stack of manuscripts pulled out a chart of a song Harry Warren wrote in 1937 that he arranged called "Hooray for Spinach." He told me the key is relating what the music looks like on paper to what it sounds like on a record. Then he played a Bluebird recording his band made of the song to demonstrate. Van also said that you always should get your music played no matter who plays it or how it sounds. Otherwise you'll never know what you wrote sounds like. That was all in the first lesson and its still the most valuable advice I ever got."

After a summer of playing in the Catskills in 1942, Mandel continued his music education at the New York Military Academy at Cornwall-on-Hudson. He spent his junior and senior years there on a music scholarship associated with the school's renowned marching band. Mandel became good friends with Stumpy Brown who followed his brothers Les and Warren to the Academy. Brown graduated a year ahead of Mandel and bequeathed him his dance band when he left. Mandel enjoyed his two year stay at the Academy: "It was great. I had my own dance band. I lived in the barracks with all the players. I'd write something and we'd get together in the hall and play it; I had a good band there I could arrange for."

Mandel's professional career began when he played with jazz violinist Joe Venuti's band during the summer of 1943, between his junior and senior years at the Academy. After graduation in 1944 he embarked on a two-and-a-half-year odyssey with a succession of great big bands. The first was former Woody Herman female trumpeter Billie Rogers's band. Next came Henry Jerome. It was with Jerome that he switched to trombone, an instrument he doubled on in school, and met and developed a friendship with vocalist David Allyn. Federal Reserve Board Chairman Alan Greenspan was in Jerome's band at the time playing saxophone and handling the band's payroll as was attorney and Richard Nixon's presidential counselor Leonard Garment who also played saxophone.

Jerome was followed by Boyd Raeburn, who according to Mandel had one of the most exciting bands he ever played with, and then Jimmy Dorsey, with whom he played first trombone taking Buddy Morrow's place. Next in order came Buddy Rich's first band that was backed by Frank Sinatra, Georgie Auld's bop-tinged band, and finally Alvino Rey's huge ten-brass jazz-oriented band. By now it was the end of 1946 and with the Big Band Era coming to a close Mandel was ready to expand his musical horizons.

"There was so much I felt I needed to know musically that I decided to get off the road and fill in the gaps, so I spent most of 1947 attending the Manhattan School of Music along with a summer session at Julliard," Mandel said. "I also hung out a lot at Gil Evans's apartment on 55th Street with Miles Davis and Gerry Mulligan and that group. I lived across the street on 55th and was introduced to Gil by his friend Blossom Dearie who was also a regular. His apartment was dangerously close to 52nd Street when it was really swinging, so all the best young jazz musicians in New York were always coming and going. There were constant discussions going on; it was like a non-stop seminar. What I learned there was priceless; it couldn't have been acquired anywhere else."

In the fall of 1947 Mandel had the urge to return to play with a big band and reunited with Buddy Rich. He spent close to a year with Rich before he left the band in San Francisco to go to Los Angeles to spend the six-month residency required to obtain his union card from Los Angeles Local #47. Unbeknownst to him at the time, his year's sojourn from New York was at a professional cost: "Years later Gerry Mulligan told me that had I stayed in New York I would have been on Miles Davis's *Birth of the Cool* album playing bass trumpet and arranging. They got Kai Winding to play instead."

While he was in Los Angeles Mandel arranged for Woody Herman's Second Herd and wrote "Not Really the Blues," the first chart that the band selected to play whenever Herman left to go home early during the last set. To this day Mandel feels that the Second Herd was one of the great big bands in jazz history. He also was introduced to the world of Latin jazz.

During the last three months of his six month union application Mandel was able to play local LA club dates. Thanks to an introduction from his roommate, percussionist Jackie Mills, he frequently played bass trumpet with popular Cuban bandleader Rene Touzet's ensemble that included Mills, Pete Candoli, Art Pepper, and Herbie Steward. He also arranged the mambo-blues "Barbados" that was first written and recorded by Charlie Parker. Mandel became a Latin jazz enthusiast and throughout his career frequently wove Latin rhythms into his compositions and arrangements.

When he obtained his union card in the spring of 1949 Mandel returned to New York and a whirlwind of musical activity. He played with Chubby Jackson's big band and also wrote for Artie Shaw's superb but not-sufficiently-recognized 1949 big band. In a telephone conversation from his home in Newbury Park, CA, Shaw had good things to say about his experiences with Mandel: "Johnny Mandel is very intelligent, articulate, and highly talented. He made a significant contribution to my 1949 band. Johnny is one of the finest musicians and persons I know."

Mandel also kept active in the New York Latin jazz scene. He played with the popular Luis del Campo and various conjuntos at the many Latin clubs that were then located in the Yorkville section of Manhattan's East Side. The debonair del Campo, who was brought to America from Cuba by Xavier Cougat, is remembered by tropical music fans for succumbing to a heart attack on the dance floor while mamboing with an attractive blonde danseur.

At the end of 1949 Mandel joined the WMGM radio staff orchestra where he was introduced to writing for drama shows. A year later he moved on to television writing visual music for the equivalent of a new Broadway show each week with the ninety minute TV classic *Your Show of Shows* that starred Sid Caesar, Imogene Coca, and Carl Reiner. Those two assignments laid the musical foundation for his soon-to-come career in arranging and composing for the movies.

During his work in radio and television Mandel also kept active in the jazz world performing with and writing for Stan Getz. In August 1950 he played bass trumpet at the Apollo Theater in Getz's short lived but powerhouse big band that included Roy Haynes, Gerry Mulligan, Billy Taylor and Zoot Sims. Charlie Parker, Dizzy Gillespie and Sarah Vaughn were on the bill as well. Mandel also wrote three songs, "Hershey Bar," "Pernod," and "Pot Luck" that Getz recorded with his quintet on Roost Records in 1951.

Come the spring of 1952 Mandel developed an urge to rejoin the big band scene and became a trombonist and one of three principal arrangers, along with his old friends tenor saxophonist Al Cohn and drummer Tiny Kahn, with Elliott Lawrence's big band. Mandel enjoyed his time with Lawrence: "Elliott was a beautiful guy to work for. He would let you do what you wanted and was an excellent conductor. That was his forte. He later recorded an album of my and Tiny Kahn's arrangements on Fantasy. It was a great experience and Elliott loved what we were doing."

After a year with Elliott Lawrence, Mandel got a call to join the trombone section of the Count Basie orchestra. He spent six months with the band and Basie recorded two of his compositions, "Low Life" and "Straight Life." To this day Mandel looks back to his Basie days as a career highlight: "All of us could never wait to get to work at night. Basie was the most marvelous human being I think I may have ever met, and I think anybody, Buddy Rich included, would tell you that. He was one of the greatest persons I ever worked with yet he controlled that band with his little finger."

Since his 1948-49 stay in Los Angeles, Mandel's ultimate goal was to live in Southern California. He achieved his objective in late 1953 when he left Count Basie's band and settled in Los Angeles to give up playing the trombone and concentrate on freelance writing. His activities over the next several years included a professional association with Dick Bock that led to work for Bock's Pacific Jazz Records, arranging for Chet Baker, the Dave Pell Octet, and collaboration on albums with David Allyn, Hoagy Carmichael, and Dick Haymes, for whom Mandel had the highest respect as a vocalist. He also did considerable arranging for Las Vegas productions. Then came 1958 and his breakthrough into the movie business.

The 1958 motion picture *I Want to Live* is considered a film classic. It earned six Academy Award nominations with Susan Hayward winning Best Actress for her gripping portrayal of party girl, consummate Gerry Mulligan fan, and convicted murderess Barbara Graham, who in 1955 was the first woman executed in the State of California in the San Quentin gas chamber.

Johnny Mandel wrote the compelling and exotic music that was considered by the late Leonard Feather to be the first film to have strictly an all jazz score.

Even though Mandel's work for *I Want to Live* was well received by the movie industry, it was not until 1964 that he would write another film score. In the intervening years he did work for several television shows such as *The Andy Williams Show, Ben Casey, Chrysler Theater*, and *Bob Hope Presents the General Electric Theater*. In 1960 Mandel also arranged Frank Sinatra's *Ring-A-Ding Ding* and Jo Stafford's *Jo + Jazz* albums. Stafford enthusiastically commented on her association with Mandel from her home in Los Angeles: "When I think of Johnny Mandel I think of identity. You can always pick out a Johnny Mandel arrangement. It's easy to recognize a voice, but sometimes it's difficult to determine the arranger. Johnny's work is so distinctive that it's easily identifiable. Not every musician can write for vocalists, and Johnny certainly can. It was a pleasure to work with him, he is a true professional."

Nineteen sixty-four marked the year Johnny Mandel officially became a melodist when he wrote the song "Emily" that became the underlying theme for the film *The Americanization of Emily* starring Julie Andrews and James Garner. Johnny Mercer added the lyrics. A year later he penned "The Shadow of Your Smile" for the *Sandpiper* that featured Elizabeth Taylor and Richard Burton. With lyrics by Paul Francis Webster, it became an American standard and huge hit for Tony Bennett, winning Mandel an Academy Award and his first Emmy. Starting with *I Want to Live* in 1958 Mandel has been nominated for an incredible seventeen Grammies, winning five times.

Johnny Mandel would go on to carve out an honored career in the movies that ran through 1987 writing the music and songs for over thirty films and collaborating with lyricists Morgan Ames, Alan and Marilyn Bergman, Dave Frishberg, Paul Williams, and a world-class popular singer. The lyric for "The Shining Sea" from the 1966 film *The Russians Are Coming, the Russians Are Coming* was written by his good friend Peggy Lee: "I called Peggy to see if she would like to write a lyric for a song I wrote. She had no idea what it was for. I sent it over to her and she wrote words that totally depicted what was happening on the screen. When I told her about the movie and what the song was for she said 'How did I do that?'"

Although "The Shadow of Your Smile" is Mandel's best known song, his most financially successful is "Suicide is Painless" from the 1970 film M.A.S.H. It was featured in the movie and became the theme song for the immensely popular M.A.S.H television series that ran from 1972 to 1983 and is still being rerun today. The lyric was written by Director Robert Altman's then fourteen-year-old son Michael before Mandel composed the melody on the night before it was due.

During the late 1980s Mandel transitioned from film writing to concentrate on arranging albums for vocal artists like Natalie Cole, Michael Feinstein, Shirley Horn, Michael Jackson, Diana Krall, Diane Schuur, and Barbara Streisand. He won his fourth and fifth Grammys for his work on Cole's 1991 *Unforgettable* and Horn's 1992 *Here's To Life* albums. His work on Cole's award-winning album included overseeing the technically complex over-dubbing of her vocal with Nat Cole's vocal on his 1951 hit "Unforgettable" to produce the title track.

There was, however, one project that sadly eluded Mandel: "Miles and I were planning to do an album just before he died. It was my project and Quincy Jones was putting us together. Miles liked what I wrote and inquired about my body of work. That's how it got started. It would have made up for my missing being part of the *Birth of the Cool* album forty years earlier."

Having achieved a storied sixty-plus-year career in the music business, Johnny Mandel looks far younger than his true age and is as active as ever. He is working on a series of articles with jazz writer Gene Lees, writing a new edition of his *Johnny Mandel Songbook*, collaborating on projects with Michael Feinstein, and regularly traveling to New York on American Society of Composers Authors and Publishers (ASCAP) business. An ASCAP member since 1956, he has served on their Board of Directors since 1989 and was presented their coveted The Henry Mancini Award in 1997.

The Henry Mancini Award was a fitting tribute to an accomplished big-band musician and arranger, film composer, songwriter, and record producer who got his start in the Catskills during the peak of the Big Band Era. In an interview on National Public Radio's *Jazz Profiles* program Mandel reflected on his many-sided career: "I'm a very lucky person. To be able to spend your life doing something you love for your work is more than anyone can hope for. And you know what? It ain't over yet.

98. Left to right: Les Brown and Frank Comstock July 1998.

99. Left to right: Billy May and Frank Comstock July 1998.

100. Fletcher Henderson at the piano.

101. Louis Armstrong was an important member of
Fletcher Henderson's early band.

102. Sy Oliver and his Glee Club.

103. Don Redman in Times Square in the late 1930s.

104. Johnny Mandel in the middle of Boyd Raeburn's trombone section at the Palace Hotel in San Francisco in 1945.

105. Johnny Mandel in 1953 designated by the arrow in the Count Basie Orchestra at the Riviera Club in St. Louis.

PART FIVE

THE CONTRIBUTORS

CHUCK CECIL
KEEPS THE BIG BAND ERA ALIVE

Music experts consider the Big Band Era to have run from 1935 through 1946. However, thanks to Chuck Cecil and his *Swingin' Years* radio show, the Big Band Era in a sense has never ended.

In 2006 Cecil celebrated the 50th anniversary of his nationally syndicated *Swingin' Years* show that features the music and history of the Big Band Era. But before we talk about the *Swingin' Years*, let's take a look at Chuck Cecil, a man who has led an uncommonly exciting and colorful life.

Chuck Cecil was born on an Oklahoma ranch in 1922. The ranch prospered until struck by a severe draught in 1935 that devastated Oklahoma and the Texas Panhandle. With the entire ranch's water holes bleached dry, the Cecil family auctioned off their livestock and property and moved to California to an apartment in Hollywood, permanently settling in Van Nuys in 1936 in a house Cecil's father built on the banks of the Los Angeles River.

The late 1930s and early 1940s were a heady time at Van Nuys High School. Movie star Jane Russell, football great Bob Waterfield, and an attractive teenager named Norma Jeane Baker, later known as Marilyn Monroe, were among the student body. Cecil knew them all.

After graduating from Van Nuys High in 1941, Cecil attended Los Angeles City College by day and worked the graveyard shift by night as an expediter at the Lockheed plant in Burbank. While at Lockheed, Cecil car pooled to work and became good friends with fellow Van Nuys High alumnus Jim Doughety, who was engaged to Norma Jeane Baker.

Doughety invited Cecil to attend his wedding that took place in June 1942 in a well-to-do home in the Hollywood Hills. After the ceremony the wedding party went to the then-popular Florentine Gardens in Hollywood for dinner and dancing.

"Norma Jeane was quite self-confident and mature for her age," Cecil explained at his Woodland Hills, CA, home. "She was not the least bit shy. However, she gave no indication that she would become as famous as she did."

The summer of 1942 found Cecil landing his first job in radio at KVEC in San Luis Obispo, CA, where he spent four months before being called to active duty by the Navy in December.

"I actually enlisted in the Navy right after the battle of Midway in June of 1942 in a rush of Patriotism," Cecil said. "It was our first clear victory in the Pacific and it motivated me to make my contribution."

It was Cecil's goal to become a fighter pilot. He enrolled in and qualified for the Navy's V-5 pilot training program flying Grumman Wildcats and Chance-Vaught Corsairs, both single-pilot fighter aircraft. When the war ended, he was serving in a replacement squad waiting for his first combat assignment.

In 1946 Cecil found work at radio station KFLW in Klamath Falls, OR. It was there that he met an attractive teenager, Edna Brown, who was the vocalist for Baldy's Band, a popular territory band in Southern Oregon. They married in 1947 and have a close-knit family of four children, sixteen grandchildren, and seven great grandchildren.

Cecil left Klamath Falls in 1947 and after stops in KXOB in Stockton, CA, and KARM in Fresno, CA, he landed at 50,000 watt KFI in Los Angeles.

"Those were the learning years," commented Cecil. "I did everything at those stations from reading news and announcing sports, to spinning records and selling advertising. It was total on-the-job training."

It was at KFI where Cecil created the *Swingin' Years* in 1956: "KFI had openings for news shows. But I noticed that many record companies were reissuing the old big band hits, so I sold the station on giving the *Swingin Years* a try. It clicked right from the start."

After twenty-two years with the station, Cecil left KFI in 1974 to move over to KGIL in San Fernando, CA. Ten years later he went to KPRZ in Los Angeles, then on to National Public Radio station KPCC, in Pasadena, CA, in 1987. In 2000 KPCC experienced a change in programming format and Cecil immediately found spots at KKJZ in Long Beach and KCSN at California State University Northridge. He is featured on weekends at both stations.

Chuck Cecil's *Swingin' Years* is the evolution of a lifetime of love with swing music: "I grew up at the peak of the Big Band Era and saw many of the greats, Stan Kenton at his historic summer of 1941 engagement at the Rendezvous Ballroom in Balboa, CA; Jimmie Lunceford at the Trianon Ballroom in South Gate, CA; and Tommy Dorsey with Frank Sinatra, Connie Haines, Jo Stafford, and the Pied Pipers at the Hollywood Palladium. Claude Thornhill played our high school senior prom at the Hollywood Palladium."

In its current format the *Swingin' Years* consists of standard segments of programming adapted to station needs. In addition to playing songs from the Big Band Era citing all soloists and recording dates, Cecil has created several regular weekly features. His Vintage Years is a twelve-minute segment that combines historical notes with the top hits of a given year. The Hall of Fame consists of a fifteen minute interview with a big band personality.

Turning Time Around compares a contemporary version of a big band classic with the original recording. Big Band Countdown spotlights the top ten hits for a specific week of a Swing Era year interspersed with historical information while Bandstand Jamboree features actual remote broadcasts of live big band performances from venues such as Frank Dailey's Meadowbrook or the Glen Island Casino.

In addition to his weekly show, Cecil has also put together numerous special shows, the jewel of which is his twelve-hour documentary on the career of Glenn Miller. A World War II buff, he has also done features on Pearl Harbor and V-J Day.

To support several hundred hours of programming a year and his many specials, Cecil maintains an extensive music library in his Woodland Hills home, where he tapes the show in his own studio. His library includes 30,000 tracks on 4,000 LPs, 10,000 tracks on 5,000 78s, and 355 taped interviews with the greats of the Big Band Era.

Cecil has had many interesting experiences taping those 355 interviews all the way from drawing out the reticent Count Basie, on one end of the spectrum, through effortlessly chatting with the genteel and gracious Duke Ellington, on the other.

According to Cecil, each interview was unique: "No two musicians were alike. Lionel Hampton, Stan Kenton, and Billy May exuded charisma. Charlie Barnet was a true gentleman, Louis Armstrong a man of great inner strength. Tony Bennett was caring and considerate."

Cecil added: "I must say that all the girl singers, Helen Forrest, Kitty Kallen, Helen O'Connell, and Martha Tilton were outgoing and cooperative. Ella Mae Morse was the most gregarious and truly a marvelous story teller. Dinah Shore was a perfect lady."

Over the last fifty years Cecil has evolved definite thoughts about the best place to conduct an interview: "I always sought unique locations because there seemed to be dryness in studio interviews. For instance, I had a great interview with Doris Day in the foyer of the Hollywood Palladium between acts. I recorded Artie Shaw in an automobile and Tony Martin in a park in Beverly Hills. I did a lot of interviews in my own home, Les Brown, Frankie Carle, Helen Forrest, Jack Leonard, and Art Lund among many others."

Each interview was frequently a surprise in itself: "When I contacted Woody Herman he invited me to his home, Humphrey Bogart and Lauren Bacall's old house in the Hollywood Hills, for the interview. He was exceptionally accommodating but spent a good part of the time while I was there walking around noodling his clarinet. Buddy Rich was another surprise. I vividly recall being apprehensive about meeting with him because he had a well-known reputation for being volatile and difficult to work with. He turned out to be just a gentle pussy cat, a most cooperative person."

Cecil concluded: "I am also fortunate to have had many fine relationships grow over the years. Harry James would not even speak to me when I was starting out in Oregon. I eventually got to know him better at each interview and we wound up having a close and warm business friendship."

On the eve of the 50th anniversary of the *Swingin' Years* a prestigious honor was bestowed on Cecil by the jazz community when on November 6, 2005, the Los Angeles Jazz Society presented him their Jazz Communicator Award at their 20th Anniversary Jazz Tribute Awards Dinner and Concert held at the Millennium Biltmore Hotel in downtown Los Angeles. He was recognized for his myriad contributions to the cause of big band music and his longtime association with Pacific Pioneer Broadcasters that included serving as their past president.

Chuck Cecil looked back on his remarkable career with the big bands with considerable satisfaction: "I've had several famous musicians such as Henry Mancini and Nelson Riddle tell me they were creatively stimulated listening to the *Swingin' Years*. However, my greatest satisfaction has come from simply serving as a vehicle to provide today's listening public an opportunity to hear big band music and read the forty or so letters I receive each week from listeners thanking me for doing my part to keep the Era alive."

HENRY HOLLOWAY
SOUTH AFRICA'S BIG BAND LEGEND

South Africa does not normally come to mind when one surveys international concentrations of Big Band Era music. However, thanks to the dedicated efforts of Henry Holloway, Swing Era music is an important part of South African radio programming. Since 1974 Holloway has broadcast on the South African Broadcasting Corporation (SABC) and Fine Music Radio. In addition to his regular big band programs Holloway has aired nearly thirty long-running special series on the Era and the Great American Songbook. Among those individuals featured were Les Brown, Sammy Cahn, Nat Cole, Jerome Kern, Glenn Miller, Cole Porter, and Frank Sinatra. He also founded the still-active Big Band Society of South Africa and the Glenn Miller Appreciation Society of South Africa with its popular *In the Mood* newsletter. Henry Holloway truly deserves the sobriquet South Africa's Big Band Legend.

Henry Holloway was born on July 15, 1934, in Zebediela, a small town in the northeastern area of the province of Transvaal. When he was ten years old the Holloway family moved to Vereeniging, one of the important industrial centers of South Africa. His family spoke Afrikaans, but he started to learn English soon after the move by reading American comic books that he was able to buy for the first time. During the war years comic books were not available in Zebediela.

It was during his high school years that Holloway came in contact with American big band music: "Most afternoons I used to go to the Phillips Café in Vereeniging to have a milkshake and listen to the jukebox. I soon became an enthusiastic Glenn Miller fan and particularly enjoyed his recording of "Sweet Eloise" sung by Ray Eberle and The Modernaires. I asked the café owner to sell it to me. He said he would have to wait until his record distributor came by to change records and that happened only every six months. Several weeks later he unexpectedly gave it to me for nothing and at sixteen I owned my first Glenn Miller record."

"A strong influence at that time came from listening to *The Voice of America* and the BBC on shortwave radio," Holloway said. "Willis Conover on *The Voice of America* was a great favorite. His style molded me and to this day I believe that much of what I accomplished on radio was thanks to him. He was a definite inspiration and role model."

Stimulated by his interest in Perry Como, Bing Crosby, and Frank Sinatra, in the late 1940s Holloway started singing part-time as a hobby with local bands. In 1961 a South African Chevrolet dealership held a Hunt for Talent competition throughout the country. Backed by the Vic Bryans band in Vereeniging, Holloway auditioned and was asked by event organizer Pete Collins, a cousin of actress Joan Collins, to sing in the finals in Johannesburg. Unfortunately, Bryans could not come with him and he was left to perform with only a local pianist who was far from a world-class accompanist. That disappointing appearance in the contest brought his singing career to a close.

Through the 1960s, as Holloway's record collection grew, his friends kept suggesting that he open a jazz club presenting live performers. He took the entrepreneurial plunge and founded his first club in Vereeniging in 1967. One of the club's regulars was a young attorney, F. W. deKlerk, who would one day become the president of South Africa. Holloway and deKlerk remain close friends and still regularly golf and email each other. After Holloway moved to Johannesburg in 1969 he opened new jazz clubs through 1987 when he relocated to Cape Town. All were commercially successful.

Then came 1974, the year that Holloway serendipitously launched his career in radio: "I approached the SABC and asked if they would be interested in doing a feature on the 30th anniversary of Glenn Miller's death. They asked if I could send them an audition script and after reviewing it inquired if I would be interested in doing a program. I ended up airing a twenty-one part series called *Miller Magic* and at the same time formed the Glenn Miller Appreciation Society of South Africa. To my surprise, I was now a South African radio personality."

Over the next five years Holloway broadcast several big band special features on the SABC and founded the Big Band Society of South Africa in 1977. His programming was so popular that in 1979 the SABC asked him to give up his business career and join the organization on a fulltime basis. It was a difficult decision as Holloway achieved success in journalism as a newspaper editor and in film distribution as a public relations executive. After much deliberation he left the world of commerce and joined the SABC on September 1. It was a decision he never regretted.

Since 1979 Henry Holloway has been a fixture on South African radio playing big band music along with providing historical comments on his song selections. Through the years numerous Big Band Era personalities visited South Africa and appeared on his shows, including Al Cohn, Buddy de Franco, Terry Gibbs, Peanuts Hucko, Paul Tanner, and movie star George Montgomery. Holloway's specials on the big bands, their vocalists, composers, and lyricists that contributed to the Great American Songbook won several broadcasting awards. His work on Glenn Miller is particularly impressive. In 1984 he followed his original twenty-one part series on Miller with another fifty-one part series. Hollway resumed the Miller project in 2004 and broadcast an additional forty-three shows, bringing the 115 chapters of half hour programs to a close in August 2006.

One of his 1984 Miller features was heard by Fred Shaw who was a navigator on a Lancaster bomber that jettisoned its 4,000 pound bomb in the English Channel after an aborted bombing mission to Germany on December 15, 1944. Shaw, who was living in South Africa, contacted Holloway and said he saw a single-engine Norseman aircraft, the type of plane Glenn Miller was flying in that day, crash into the Channel when the Lancaster squadron dumped their bombs in the jettison zone. Fred Shaw told his story to the public for the first time at an April 29 Glenn Miller Appreciation Society meeting in Johannesburg, introducing a stunning, new theory on Miller's disappearance. It quickly received international news coverage and brought the Society to worldwide attention.

Over the last twenty-five years Holloway has made nine trips to the United States forging friendships with many entertainment luminaries. An American travel highlight occurred in 1983 when he was asked by a leading South African travel company to organize a big band tour of the USA. Holloway said yes and put a tour package together. In Southern California he and the twelve tour members personally met with Louis Bellson, Tex Beneke, Johnny Best, Sammy Cahn, Paula Kelly, Billy May, and Paul Tanner. Tanner officially greeted them upon their arrival at Los Angeles International Airport. From there the group saw the Glenn Miller Orchestra led by Larry O'Brien perform in Las Vegas and were provided a tour of famous Big Band Era sites in Manhattan by big band authority George T. Simon. Their final stop was at Rockefeller Center's Rainbow Room where they danced to the Sy Oliver Orchestra. Holloway also spent an afternoon with Sammy Kaye at his swank Park Avenue apartment.

"I enjoyed working with Henry," Paul Tanner said by telephone from his home in Carlsbad, CA: "I introduced the tour to the Glenn Miller alumni that lived in Southern California and personally escorted them to everyone's home for a visit. They were a fine group and appreciated meeting the Miller people. Henry and I have remained good friends since then."

The early 1990s provided Holloway a memorable experience when he developed an association with United States Ambassador to South Africa William Lacy Swing. With the surname Swing and their mutual interest in big band music it was only natural that the Ambassador and Holloway develop a friendship and they did. Swing officially presided over a June 1992 ceremony dedicating Holloway's home music studio he called Swingdom that included a dance floor and meeting facilities.

Holloway's expertise on Glenn Miller was recognized by academia when the University of Cape Town called on him in 1994: "I was asked by the University to do a program on Glenn Miller and organized a five-part lecture that included videos, films, and recordings from my private collection. It was well received; the university's 500 seat auditorium was packed for each day's lecture. In 2004 I returned to do another series on Miller that again drew a capacity attendance. The most popular part of both lectures was my discussion of the theories surrounding Glenn's disappearance over the English Channel. The success of these lectures documents the continuing popularity of Glenn Miller in South Africa."

After twenty-one years with the SABC Holloway changed broadcasting affiliations in 1995 when he was invited by Cape Town-based Fine Music Radio to help launch a new station that features jazz and classical music programming. Of the original twelve broadcasting personalities, Holloway is the only one remaining on the station's staff. His Saturday show *Swing, Sing and All That Jazz* that he brought over from the SABC quickly developed a committed following and played an important part in the new station achieving high listener ratings.

Yet another new opportunity came Holloway's way in 2004 when he was asked by two cruise line companies to lecture on their ships. In April he sailed from Puerto Rico to Scandinavia and the Baltic's on the *Constellation* that *Condé Nast* travel magazine rated as one of the world's leading cruise liners and in November traveled through the Caribbean on the *Saga Rose*. Holloway presented several lectures on the big bands including a four part series on the ever popular Glenn Miller on each ship.

Although Holloway has received many South African broadcasting awards and has been the subject of three SABC television documentaries, recognition in America finally came his way in September 1999 when the National Academy of Recording Arts and Sciences invited him to attend a gala tribute to Les Brown at the Beverly Wilshire Hotel in Beverly Hills. He sat next to Jack Jones at Master of Ceremonies Steve Allen's table and was cited by Allen from the dais. While in Los Angeles Holloway stayed with Academy Award-winning songwriter Ray Evans at his Beverly Hills home and visited with Milt Bernhart, Pat Longo, Artie Malvin, Abe Most, and Artie Shaw, with whom he had corresponded since 1990.

On the way home from the Les Brown event Holloway stopped in London to recount his experiences on the BBC; it was the fifth of his six BBC radio appearances. After Brown passed away in 2001 Holloway did a sixty-part series on the bandleader who the Guinness Book of Records recognizes as the leader of the longest-lasting musical organization in the history of popular music. The odds are high that the sixty continuous hour-long programs on Brown constitute the longest uninterrupted series ever done on a Swing Era bandleader.

A second American tribute occurred in March 2003 when the Big Band Academy of America inducted Holloway into its Golden Bandstand at their annual reunion at the Sportsman's Lodge in Studio City, CA. The late Academy president Milt Bernhart presented Holloway his Golden

Bandstand Award before a capacity crowd of 700 in the Lodge's Empire Ballroom. When he returned home to his ranch near Cape Town, where he also ran a four star guesthouse, he found congratulatory letters from Archbishop Desmond Tutu and South African golfing legend Gary Player.

Big band radio personality Chuck Cecil commented on Holloway's award recognition: "I enjoyed meeting Henry at the Academy's Reunion. His reputation preceded him. He is highly respected in the American broadcasting community and is an important contributor to the cause of big band music. Henry certainly deserves his Golden Bandstand Award for all he has achieved in South Africa where he is so far removed from the jazz mainstream."

From 1976 to 1985 Holloway was married to legendary South African pop vocalist Eve Boswell who sang at royal Command Performances at Buckingham Palace and on the Ed Sullivan and Nat "King" Cole television shows in the United States. They made many trips to the U.K. together where she regularly performed at the London Palladium and had her own TV show. In 1986 he remarried to Marilyn Verster who is known as the "golden voiced lady" of Radio South Africa. For 14 years she was the editor and presenter of their popular *Woman's World* show followed by four years as the program's manager. During the 1970s Verster was also a competitive go-cart racer who was sponsored by Mazda. The Holloway's recently relocated about an hour away from the Cape Town area to Caledon, where he houses one of the world's largest record collections and a home studio in which he records his programs on CD and then couriers them to Cape Town for broadcast on Fine Music Radio.

Reflecting on his 32 year career as a big band radio personality from his Caledon home Henry Holloway said: "I've been most fortunate to have exciting and rewarding careers in both business and radio. Through my radio work I have had the privilege to travel the world and develop friendships with the celebrated personalities of big band music, the music I love. I had great fun organizing and promoting small jazz concerts and black-tie dinner dances that featured big band music at South Africa's finest hotels. But most important, I have the personal satisfaction of knowing that I have kept classic big band music alive and on the air in South Africa."

TOM SHEILS
GLENN MILLER'S RIGHT-HAND MAN

There were many contributors to the success of the Glenn Miller Orchestra: Tex Beneke, Ray Eberle, Marion Hutton, The Modernaires, and Tom Sheils. Yes, the late Tom Sheils, who died in Laguna Beach, CA, after a brief illness on June 24, 2003. Even among Big Band Era enthusiasts, few are aware that without Sheils's efforts there might never have been a Glenn Miller legacy, as we know it today.

Thomas Patrick Sheils was born in Mount Vernon, NY, on April 25, 1916, as the fifth of nine children. His father, a successful trial attorney and personal friend of 1928 presidential candidate Alfred E. Smith, was active in Democratic Party politics and appointed to the New York State Supreme Court by Governor Herbert Lehman.

Sheils grew up in neighboring New Rochelle where he attended Iona Preparatory High School. During his senior year he served as prom chairman and put on a blockbuster dance that featured the then-popular Don Bestor Orchestra and the theater act of Rubinoff and His Violin. The event was so successful that it became part of Iona lore and would change the course of Sheils's life four years later.

After graduating in 1934 Sheils followed his two older brothers to the University of Notre Dame, receiving a bachelor's degree in business administration in 1938. While at Notre Dame he put together a band called the Notre Dame Modernaires and was quickly sent a cease and desist order by the original The Modernaires vocal group's attorney regarding the use of its name. Ironically, The Modernaires would later play an important part in his business career. He also wrote a music column in the school paper reviewing big band releases he was sent by record companies. Included in those releases were recordings by a then little-known bandleader named Glenn Miller. Sheils exhibited an entrepreneurial bent by keeping the up-tempo records of Count Basie, Duke Ellington, and Benny Goodman, and selling the sweet band records at a discount to fellow students.

With the Great Depression at its peak, Sheils moved back home in June of 1938 and took a job selling classified ads on the telephone for the Hearst-owned *New York Journal American* newspaper for $15 a week. When his friends from Iona prep heard he was back in New York they immediately contacted him and asked if he could help organize the school's winter prom. His legendary 1934 work was not forgotten. The first of a chain of events that would involve Sheils playing a significant role in making Glenn Miller the most famous bandleader in the world just a year later were now set in motion.

Glenn Miller formed his first band in 1937. He was unsuccessful, disbanding in January 1938. Miller tried again, starting up in March of 1938 and in June landed an engagement at the Paradise Restaurant at 49th Street and Broadway in Manhattan playing second billing to Freddie Fisher and his Schnickelfritzers, a six-piece novelty band that was a forerunner of the Spike Jones-type of orchestra. Glenn Miller was still struggling.

Still a strong supporter of Iona Prep, Sheils agreed to help out with the school's prom. His first move was to go to Boston-based Charlie Shribman's New York booking office located across the street from the Paradise Restaurant and talk to Shribman's representative, Bob Bundy, about securing a band for the event. Sheils tells what transpired in a telephone interview from his home in Laguna Woods, CA: "I told Bundy I was looking for a band for the prom. He asked how much money I had to spend. I told him $500. Then Bundy said 'I have a band, Glenn Miller, that's playing across the street at the Paradise Restaurant and is available on December 26.' I remember reviewing Miller's records at Notre Dame and liked his sound. We worked out a deal and he split half of his ten per cent commission with me—$25 dollars."

On the evening of December 26, 1938, the fourteen-piece Glenn Miller Orchestra plus vocalists Ray Eberle and Marion Hutton arrived at the Iona gymnasium on a bitter cold evening. They started playing promptly at 8:00 p.m. and took a half-hour break at 10:00 p.m. As soon as the break began Miller walked up to Sheils and introduced himself and said: "I'm Glenn Miller and I understand that you had a lot to do with getting me this job. I want to express my thanks because without this date I couldn't make my payroll this week."

Notwithstanding Miller's expression of appreciation, Sheils truly liked the band and after the prom he decided to help promote it. He lived within walking distance of the Glen Island Casino in New Rochelle where a coveted summer-season engagement with its considerable airtime would bring invaluable exposure to a band. Ozzie Nelson, the Casa Loma Orchestra, the Dorsey Brothers, and Larry Clinton gained their fame there. Sheils frequented the Casino every summer and got to know the management, owner Mike DeZutter and manager Lockwood Conkling. He persuaded them to go the Paradise Restaurant and hear Miller who was back playing there during December and early January. The end result was that they signed Miller for the 1939 summer season. It would turn out to be the break he sorely needed.

The Glen Island Casino engagement did indeed serve Miller well. With nightly national radio broadcasts complemented by a string of hit records, his popularity exploded beyond his wildest expectations. Glenn Miller now had the hottest big band in the country, thanks in part to the assistance of Tom Sheils.

Paul Tanner, Miller's trombonist, saw it all happen and acknowledges Sheils's contributions from his home in Carlsbad, CA: "There is no doubt that Tom Sheils played an important part in helping us land the Glen Island Casino engagement for the summer of 1939. By the time we closed in August you couldn't even find a parking spot. Playing there put us over the top. By that alone Tom deserves a solid place in Glenn Miller history."

During the summer of 1939 Sheils stopped by the Casino practically every evening: "I would get home from work in Manhattan on the subway and grab a bite to eat and go over to Glen Island and hang out with the musicians. My parents were away for the summer, so after the band finished playing for the night I would invite them all to come over to my house and we would play records and chat. Some of them would even jam a little. My girlfriend even got involved. I was dating Helen Burke, a singer whom I met at a big band rehearsal in White Plains, NY. We got married in 1942. She became good friends with Marion Hutton; they went to the beach together almost every afternoon. Out of all the guys in Glenn's band I developed particularly close friendships with Chummy MacGregor and Hal McIntyre."

Thanks to that summer's adventures, Sheils decided he wanted to break into the music business and work for Miller. However, there was a problem. Miller thought Sheils was a frivolous "crepe-soled Westchester County chooch," then common vernacular for what today would be considered a groupie from a well-to-do family. Enter pianist MacGregor and saxophonist McIntyre who interceded on Sheils's behalf with Miller.

In January of 1940 Glenn Miller began a three-month engagement at the Café Rouge of the Hotel Pennsylvania in Manhattan where he played to a packed house and broadcast his popular *Moonlight Serenade* radio show sponsored by Chesterfield cigarettes from a nearby CBS studio. Thanks to the machinations of MacGregor and McIntyre, Sheils took a taxi ride with Miller from the CBS studio to the Victoria Barber Shop on 52nd Street where Miller was scheduled to get a haircut between his late afternoon rehearsal and the dance set at the Café Rouge. Sheils pleaded his case with Miller at the Victoria to convince him of his seriousness in pursuing a career in the music business. Miller liked what he heard and hired Sheils at $50 a week while he was reclining in the barber chair getting a shave.

A master at public relations, Miller assigned Sheils to visit major cities throughout the East to promote his records. But just as Sheils was about to embark in the new Oldsmobile station wagon Miller bought from a dealership in Atchison, KS, owned by the father of The Modernaires Ralph Brewster his duties suddenly changed from record promotion to radio production.

The NBC-Blue network offered Miller the one-hour *Sunset Serenade* sustaining radio show that debuted August 30, 1941, at the Steel Pier in Atlantic City, NJ. On each program five military camps would submit a song they selected that was played by the Miller Orchestra. Listeners would vote for their favorite by mailing in a penny postcard. The camp that won would then receive a combination radio-phonograph and fifty records. Sheils was, in effect, assigned to produce the program, a responsibility he held until it went off the air, as part of the *Moonlight Serenade* show in September 1942. It was a demanding job given the fact that the coordination of five new military organizations were involved for each broadcast. When the show ended, the stage was set for Tom Sheils to assume a new assignment from Miller that would establish him in the personal management business.

The ever commercially shrewd Miller had personal management contracts with all the people who worked for him to represent them if they ever went out on their own. The contracts stipulated a ten per cent management fee that Miller never bothered to collect as a gesture to help them get started. Just before he broke up his band on September 27, 1942, at the Central Theater in Passaic, NJ, to join the Army as a captain, Miller designated Sheils to act on his behalf and handle all the contracts.

Also before disbanding, Sheils helped Miller put together the Glenn Miller Singers that included Beneke, Hutton, and The Modernaires. Immediately after Miller's last performance at the Central Theater the Glenn Miller Singers took a train to Worcester, MA, where they performed in a theater the next day for the first time. Soon after their Worcester debut the group opened as the headline act at the Roxy Theater in New York with Chico Marx leading the stage band. Marx's boy singer was Mel Tormé, with whom Sheils developed an instant friendship. After nearly six months of playing the top theaters in the East and Midwest, Uncle Sam stepped in. Beneke joined the Navy and Hutton soon ventured out on her own. Sheils replaced her with Paula Kelly and continued to represent the reconstituted The Modernaires for the next forty years. However, little did Sheils foresee in late 1944 that his time with Glenn Miller was about to sadly come to a close.

The plane that Glenn Miller was flying on from England to Paris to make arrangements for his band's first European appearance went down over the English Channel on December 15, 1944. Tom Sheils was with Miller's wife Helen on December 23 when she received official notice that her husband was missing in flight: "I was working in a small office Miller kept on 57th Street with his secretary Polly Haynes while he was overseas. Glenn gave me full power of attorney to sign checks. As a matter of fact, I gave Helen an allowance of $100 a week to spend on clothing and hats, she loved hats. Helen and my wife would shop together and became very good friends."

Sheils continued: "Helen called me at the office to ask if I would drive Glenn's Cadillac for a few days to keep the engine in shape. Since I was driving a $20 used Essex, I jumped at the chance and took the bus over to their home in Tenafly, NJ, to get the car and drive around New Rochelle to impress my friends. When I returned the car late that afternoon I found Helen in tears sitting on her bed in a bathrobe holding the telegram from the War Department that informed her that Glenn was lost in flight. I was the first person to talk with her after she found out what happened. I was dumbfounded and for a long time felt that Glenn would be found and come home."

What would Sheils's business future have been like had Miller lived? Here are his thoughts: "Just about a week before Glenn was lost he sent me a V-mail on microfilm from England outlining his plans for when he would return. I'm aggravated because I can't find the letter; I'm sure it would be quite valuable today. He had financially backed Hal McIntyre, Charlie Spivak, and Claude Thornhill and we were going to have our own booking agency with his band heading it up. Using his band's influence he was planning on securing top bookings around the country. Glenn also talked in the letter about expanding his publishing company, Mutual Music that Leo Talent was running, and his plans to have me continue to represent everyone he had under personal management contracts. He also mentioned that he planned to move to the West Coast and had a standing offer from Coca-Cola to do a one-hour radio show as soon as he returned from the war."

Looking back, Sheils commented on his six-year business association with Miller: "I truly enjoyed working for Glenn because in addition to his musical talents he was a very astute businessman. I really learned a lot working for him. But he also had a human side. Before he went overseas he came to New York every Saturday from where he was stationed at Yale University to do his *I Sustain the Wings* radio show. We would meet at the Hotel Astor where he kept a room to change to a fresh uniform then have lunch at Lindy's before the show so I could update him on what was going on with his business affairs. On one occasion he told me to look in the trunk of his Cadillac where he had something for my son Tommy. It was set of leather blocks that Glenn purchased in New Haven. He was so proud that they didn't have sharp edges like the more common wooden blocks. I'm still amazed that a man as busy as he was took the time to browse through a toy store and do that."

After the war, Sheils continued to live in New Rochelle and grow his personal management business. In addition to The Modernaires with Paula Kelly, he represented Evelyn Knight, who had a string of hits in the later 1940s that included two number-one songs—"A Little Bird Told Me" and "Powder Your Face with Sunshine"—and who performed as a chanteuse at smart supper clubs. Then came an opportunity to move to California.

In 1947 Bob Crosby's *Club 15* music program that originated in Hollywood went on the air. Sheils landed The Modernaires with Paula Kelly and a feature spot on the nightly fifteen-minute radio show and followed them west. He moved his entire business operation to Hollywood and settled in the San Fernando Valley. Two years later he added to his stable of talent: "In 1949 I was in Saint Louis handling The Modernaires opening at a theater when I met Peter Marshall who was appearing on the same bill as a comedy team with Tommy Noonan. We struck up a friendship and I wound up representing him for thirty-five years. I immediately recognized that Peter was a fine singer and got him to pursue that talent."

Commenting at his home in Encino, CA, about his relationship with Sheils, Marshall had nothing but good things to say: "I was proud to have a man like Tom Sheils represent me. He was a Notre Dame grad who had the highest ethics and morals of any agent I ever came in contact with. I knew I was being represented by a true gentleman."

During the 1950s Sheils continued to prosper signing New York Metropolitan Opera Wagnerian soprano Helen Traubel, Carmel Quinn who gained fame singing with Arthur Godfrey, the popular DeCastro Sisters close-harmony vocal trio that had a gold record with "Teach Me Tonight," and a promising young comedian named Johnny Carson: "Johnny and I met at a party in Hollywood. We got together and I was instrumental in helping him land the *Who Do You Trust?* television game show. At first he was reluctant to take the *Tonight Show* in 1962 because he felt that after five years he was set on daytime TV. Fortunately, I and a few others convinced him to give it a try."

After Sheils signed Carson at his Hollywood office, he entered into a partnership with lifelong friend Al Bruno creating the partnership of Sheils and Bruno Associates. Bruno headed up operations in New York and Sheils in Beverly Hills. Together they added country star Jimmy Dean, television personality Mike Douglas, singers Clark Dennis and Carol Richards, radio personality Geoff Edwards, and comedians Kay Stevens and Woody Woodbury. In the early 1970s Gloria Burke, Helen's sister-in-law, joined the firm as Sheils's executive secretary. She still represents Peter Marshall and the current The Modernaires with Paula Kelly Jr.

Sheils's legendary career as a personal manager hit its peak in the early to mid 1960s. At one point he had four of his clients simultaneously appearing in Las Vegas. Johnny Carson was at the Sahara, Jimmy Dean at the Flamingo, and the DeCastro sisters at the Stardust. To top it off, his old friend Tex Beneke and his Orchestra was playing in the Sahara Lounge with The Modernaires with Paula Kelly.

Throughout his business life Sheils maintained a close watch on the Glenn Miller legacy. He put together numerous Miller reunion packages and was involved with the immensely popular 1980 *One More Time* salute at the Hollywood Palladium. It was produced and hosted by Peter Marshall and included the Tex Beneke Orchestra, Bob Eberly, Helen O'Connell, and The Modernaires with Paula Kelly Jr. He has also been interviewed about Miller on numerous radio and television shows. His most recent TV appearance was on E! Entertainment Television's popular *Mysteries and Scandals* show that investigated Miller's disappearance.

Sheils also kept in solid contact with the old Miller gang, particularly Beneke, Johnny Desmond, and big band historian George T. Simon, who wrote the definitive book on Glenn Miller. He was also close to Billy May and Paul Tanner. In fact, Sheils frequently chatted by telephone with Tanner and often got together with May who lived nearby. In 2002 Sheils and May drove to La Jolla, CA, to visit the now-late Miller trumpeter Johnny Best who suffered an accident in a fall some years ago.

The late Billy May enthusiastically talked about his sixty-three year friendship with Sheils from his home in San Juan Capistrano: "I met Tom when I joined Miller's band the night FDR was reelected in 1940. When everyone discusses Glenn they always talk about his hit records and musicians, but no one ever mentions the guys behind the scene that made his organization run. Tom was one of those guys. He was very valuable to Glenn on the business side."

After forty-one years in the personal management profession, Tom Sheils retired to his vacation home in the San Gabriel Mountain resort community of Wrightwood, CA, in 1983 where he lived until he relocated to Laguna Woods, CA, in 1990 after Helen passed away. Even in retirement he still worked on keeping the memory of Glenn Miller alive. In March 2002 he hosted a tribute to Miller at The Renaissance at the Wellington Retirement Community in Laguna Hills, CA. His longtime friend Dr. Alan Cass, curator of the Glenn Miller Archives at the University of Colorado, narrated a presentation on Miller. Jonnie Dee Miller, Glenn Miller's daughter, Bobby Byrne, Jimmy Dorsey's trombonist, Billy May, and Paul Tanner were among the participants.

Shortly before passing away Sheils talked about his forty-five-year business career. His comments were not at all surprising: "I had both an exciting and rewarding run. I managed a lot of famous entertainers, each with their unique personalities, and experienced the entire Big Band Era as an actual participant. But the accomplishment I'm most proud of is the fact that I had a hand in helping Glenn Miller become successful his second time around. Working with him was a stroke of good fortune that I'll ever be thankful for."

GEORGE T. SIMON GROWS UP

When studying the history of the Big Band Era, one quickly realizes that the work of one historian stands tall above all others. That historian is the late George T. Simon who passed away in New York on February 13, 2001. Simon is by far the most well-known chronicler of the Era. He was a writer for and editor of *Metronome* for twenty years, and authored nine best-selling books on the subject. A friend and confidant of virtually every major Era personality, he saw them all perform at the most famous ballrooms throughout the United States. To this day quotes from his books widely appear in print publications. George T. Simon is still recognized as the most famous scribe of that musical period dominated by powerful fifteen-piece bands that literally had everyone dancing in the aisles.

George Thomas Simon was born on May 9, 1912, to an upper-middle-class New York family that lived in a brownstone house on West 89th Street off Central Park. Simon's was a family of considerable accomplishment. His brother Henry became a professor of English at Columbia University. Brother Alfred became musical director of New York radio station WQXR, and brother Richard was both the co-founder of the publishing firm of Simon and Schuster and the father of pop singer and songwriter Carly Simon.

Simon started to play the drums when he was twelve years old. Although the five-story Simon house had an entire floor devoted to the family's interest in classical music and show tunes and was stocked with two pianos and two organs, he set up shop in the basement with his drum set, phonograph, and collection of jazz records. Little did George Simon realize that he was on his way to a lifelong, professional career in music.

Carrying on his family's tradition of commitment to higher education, Simon attended Harvard University, graduating with a bachelor's degree in economics in 1934. While at Harvard, he formed his own jazz band, George Simon and His Confederates, that concentrated on playing swing music. He called his band the Confederates because they did not belong to the musician's union.

After graduation from Harvard, Simon put his economics degree to practical use at the peak of the Great Depression selling men's slippers at Macy's and kewpie dolls store-to-store in Manhattan for a friend of his father. He also formed a new band playing sporadic gigs in the New York area, again calling it the Confederates so he could continue to use the band's banner he had made in Boston. Then came 1935 and a job that would change the course of his entire life.

Founded in 1883, *Metronome* magazine historically concentrated its monthly coverage on classical and popular music. In an attempt to add swing coverage to its format, editor Doran K. Antrim hired Simon for $25 a month because Simon suggested to Antrim that *Metronome* run regular dance band reviews, which had never been done by a music magazine before. Simon came aboard in early 1935 and was so successful that Antrim offered him the publication's editorship in 1939.

Simon talked about his unique approach to writing in his early days at *Metronome* during a telephone conversation from his West Side Manhattan home: "I wrote under four or five different names because we had no one else covering swing music on staff. I started arguments with myself. I would change my identity to Joe Hanscom and Peter Embry and would have them fighting among themselves through letters to the editor I wrote and would then answer under my name."

In addition to writing under pseudonyms, Simon also regularly graded bands from A to D, sparing no one from his biting criticism. In fact, he was responsible for creating the famous Big Band Era term Mickey-Mouse Bands in satirical reference to sweet bands that used certain gimmicks to distinguish themselves, such as Shep Fields and His Rippling Rhythm characterized by Fields blowing bubbles through a straw in a glass of water, and Gray Gordon and his Tic-Toc Rhythm with sidemen beating two temple blocks together during every number they played. Simon definitely preferred rhythmic swing bands with powerful percussion over sweet society bands.

Soon after Simon joined *Metronome*, he developed a strong association with a young trombonist and arranger named Glenn Miller:"After I joined *Metronome*, I started following Ray Noble's band while he was playing at the Rainbow Room on the top floor of the RCA Building in Radio City. Glenn was arranging for Ray and that's where I met him. I invited him over for dinner one night and to my delight he charmed my parents who were suspect of jazz musicians. We became close friends. I helped him form his first band in 1937 and played some drums. One night we were driving under the Third Avenue el in mid-town Manhattan and he confronted me and said that I should make a decision between a career as a drummer or writer. Realizing I was no Gene Krupa, I opted for journalism."

Simon commented on his war years with Miller: "Our association continued through World War II while we were in the service together. He asked me to assist him in locating personnel for his truly great Army Air Force Band based at Yale, and I actually made a bit of a comeback and did some drumming in the band. After he went overseas I stayed in New Haven and managed his band unit that remained in the States."

Simon joined the Army in 1942. In addition to working with Miller, he produced V-discs for military distribution and continued to write for *Metronome*, starting his personal editorial column Simon Says in 1943. While he was in uniform, Barry Ulanov took over as the magazine's editor.

After the war, Simon returned to *Metronome* as a writer and co-editor with Ulanov until 1955 when he left to branch out into independent record and television production, and eventually work for the Grammy Awards in various musical and promotional capacities for twenty-seven years. Moreover, he had no idea that when he left *Metronome* that in 1967 he would publish a landmark book and embark on a whole new career as a prolific author of nine publications on the Big Band Era that would mark him as the genre's leading authority.

Four of Simon's nine books have become big band classics that are acknowledged industry standards. The first of the four, his 1967 *The Big Bands*, now in its fourth edition and twenty-fourth printing, is the most comprehensive historical chronicle of the Era extant. The physically huge *Simon Says: the Sights and Sounds of the Swing Era*, is a compilation of his *Metronome* articles that magically transports the reader back to that point in time. *Glenn Miller and His Orchestra* is the definitive work on the Era's most famous personality. *The Big Bands Songbook* covers the history of seventy-two of the top hit songs of the Big Band Era.

Simon published his last book, *The Big Bands Trivia Quiz Book*, in 1985. It's an engaging series of one hundred challenging quiz questions covering the scope of the entire Era. Not content to rest on his laurels, he was frequently interviewed on public television big band specials and big band radio programs.

Reflecting on the Era, Simon offered some very interesting personal opinions. As for the best all around band, his choice is clear: "I think the best all around band, both swing and sweet, was Tommy Dorsey's band. He could do everything and had those great singers like Frank Sinatra and Jo Stafford, and excellent musicians like Bunny Berigan, Bud Freeman, and Buddy Rich."

It's a three-way tie for the most underrated band: "Claude Thornhill had a magnificent band, but he came along a little late. Woody Herman never achieved the fame he should have. Then there's always Red Norvo. His taste was impeccable. Everything he played was soft and subtle, and really swung."

The nod for creativity goes to Duke Ellington: "Duke Ellington stands at the top in creativity and in many ways above everyone else, even though his band was sometimes inconsistent in live performances. I fondly remember him as a witty, warm, and urbane gentleman. He was truly a class act."

Simon even had a unique slant on the famous "Goodman Ray" that struck fear into the hearts of his musicians: "Benny and I had an extensive discussion about the "Ray." He told me that very often he would be staring at somebody on the bandstand while he was actually thinking of something else. Naturally, the musician would think Benny was directing his anger at him when in fact it was the case of a genius at work lost in concentration and totally oblivious to his surroundings."

And finally, who was the best businessman of all the Era's bandleaders? "More than any leader I knew, Glenn Miller knew exactly what he wanted and how to go about getting it. He knew he had to have a style of his own when his first band collapsed and he developed one with his famous clarinet lead. He organized his second band hiring the right musicians that would play his musical style, and he made all the right business decisions. His ability to navigate the world of commerce is not sufficiently recognized."

In looking back on his long and multifaceted career in the music business, Simon offered an interesting perspective on himself: "When I started out with *Metronome*, I was enthusiastically naïve and wanted to be accepted by the bandleaders and vocalists. In contemporary vernacular, I was a bit of a groupie. As a result, some of my early articles smack of hero worship. As time went on, I matured and became a more objective writer. Now I'm finally to the point where I can proudly say that I've finally grown up professionally."

106. Chuck Cecil around 1980.

107. Chuck Cecil in 2007.

108. Left to right: Artie Shaw and Henry Holloway in 1999.

109. Left to right: Steve Allen and Henry Holloway in 1999.

110. Left to right: Neal Hefti and Henry Holloway in 1999.

111. Henry Holloway with his 2003 Golden Bandstand Award.

112. Tom Sheils seated rear center conducting Glenn Miller's business affairs October-November 1941.

113. February 1945 ceremony posthumously awarding Glenn Miller the Bronze Star. Tom Sheils center, Helen Miller holding the Bronze Star to his left, Sergeant George T. Simon far right.

114. George T. Simon left,
Herman "Trigger" Alpert right,
New Haven, CT,
circa April 1943.

PHOTO CREDITS

1-4, Courtesy Van Alexander
5, 12, 15-17, 19, 22, 23, 26, 27, 29, 66, 72, 75-78, 84, 85, 87, 94-96, 100-102, Courtesy Wayne Knight Collection
6-11, Courtesy Horace Heidt, Jr.
13, 14, 53, 54, Courtesy Roc Hillman
18, Courtesy CTSIMAGES
20, 21, Courtesy Marilyn King
24, 25, 28, Courtesy Curtis International Associates
30, Courtesy Orrin Tucker
31-34, 52, 103, Courtesy Duncan Schiedt
35, 37, 38, Courtesy David Bernhart
36, Courtesy ©Ray Avery/CTSIMAGES
39-41, Courtesy Buddy Childers
42, Courtesy Jack Costanzo
43-45, 67, 68, Courtesy Lionel Sesma
46-49, Courtesy Rosalind Cron
50, 51, Courtesy Henry Jerome Music, Inc.
55-59, Courtesy Barbara Knowles Pinches
60, 62, Courtesy Virginia LaPorta
61, Courtesy Woody Herman Society
63, Courtesy John LaPorta
64, 65, Courtesy Peggy Clark
69-71, Courtesy Butch Stone
73, Courtesy Paul Tanner
74, Courtesy Zeke Zarchy
79-83, Courtesy Dolores O'Neill
86, Courtesy Joe Stafford
88, Courtesy Kay Starr
89-93, Courtesy Garry Stevens
97, Courtesy Margaret Whiting
98, 99, Courtesy Frank Comstock
104, 105, Courtesy Johnny Mandel
106, 107, Courtesy Chuck Cecil
108-111, Courtesy Henry Holloway
112, 114, Courtesy Edward F. Polic Collection
113, Courtesy Tom Sheils

PHOTO CREDITS

1-4, Courtesy Van Alexander

5, 12, 15-17, 19, 22-23, 26, 27, 29, 66, 72, 75-78, 84, 85, 87, 95-97, 101-103, Courtesy Wayne Knight Collection

6-11, Courtesy Horace Heidt, Jr.

13-14, 53, 54, Courtesy Roc Hillman

18, CTSIMAGES

20-21, Courtesy Marilyn King

24, 25, 28, Courtesy Curtis International Associates

30, Courtesy Orrin Tucker

31-34, 52, 104, Courtesy Duncan Schiedt

35, 37, 38, Courtesy David Bernhart

36, Courtesy Ray Avery/CTSIMAGES

39-41, Courtesy Buddy Childers

42, Courtesy Jack Costanzo

43-45, 67, 68, Courtesy Lionel Sesma

46-49, Courtesy Rosalind Cron

50, 51, Courtesy Henry Jerome Music, Inc.

55-59, Courtesy Barbara Knowles Pinches

60, 62, Courtesy Virginia LaPorta

61, Courtesy Woody Herman Society

63, Courtesy John LaPorta

64, 65, Courtesy Peggy Clark

69-71, Courtesy Butch Stone

73, Courtesy Paul Tanner

74, Courtesy Zeke Zarchy

79-83, Courtesy Dolores O'Neill

86, Courtesy Joe Stafford

88, Courtesy Kay Starr

89-94, Courtesy Garry Stevens

98, Courtesy Margaret Whiting

99-100, Courtesy Frank Comstock

105-106, Courtesy Johnny Mandel

107-108, Courtesy Chuck Cecil

109-112, Courtesy Henry Holloway

113, 114, Courtesy Tom Sheils/Tom Sheils Collection

115, Courtesy from the Edward F. Polic Collection

INDEX